MEMOIRS OF A VERY CIVIL SERVANT

Mackenzie King to Pierre Trudeau

MEMOIRS OF A VERY CIVIL SERVANT

Mackenzie King to Pierre Trudeau

Gordon Robertson

UNIVERSITY OF TORONTO PRESS
Toronto Buffalo London

© University of Toronto Press Incorporated 2000
Toronto Buffalo London

Printed in Canada

ISBN 0-8020-4445-X

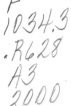

∞

Printed on acid-free paper

Canadian Cataloguing in Publication Data

Robertson, Gordon, 1917–
    Memoirs of a very civil servant : Mackenzie King to Pierre Trudeau

    Includes bibliographical references and index.
    ISBN 0-8020-4445-X

    1. Robertson, Gordon, 1917– . 2. Canada – Politics and
    government – 1935– . 3. Civil service – Canada – Biography.
    I. Title.

    FC601.R63A3 2000   971.06′092   C00-930862-8
    F1034.3.R625A3 2000

All photographs are from the author's collection. Maps by William
Constable.

University of Toronto Press acknowledges the financial assistance to its
publishing program of the Canada Council for the Arts and the Ontario
Arts Council.

University of Toronto Press acknowledges the financial support for its
publishing activities of the Government of Canada through the Book
Publishing Industry Development Program (BPIDP).

Preface

Early in 1997 *Maclean's* magazine asked twenty-five specialists in Canadian political history to rank the prime ministers of Canada since Confederation on a scale from zero to ten. The top six in their collective rating were: Mackenzie King, Sir John A. Macdonald, Sir Wilfrid Laurier, Louis St Laurent, Pierre Trudeau, and Lester Pearson. About a year earlier, in working on this book, I had done a rating of my own and had selected the same six. It was my good fortune during thirty-eight years in the public service to work closely with four of those top leaders of our country. They presided over and guided the conduct and policies of our governments for fifty of the eighty years since the First World War. They all had an outstanding influence on the kind of Canada we have today. I worked with one or another of them from 1945 to 1953 and from 1963 to 1979 – twenty-four years in all.

One of the national contributions Mr St Laurent made was to decide in 1953 that the time had come to end the state of 'absence of mind' in which Canada had treated the 40 per cent of our country that lies north of the provinces: the Yukon and Northwest Territories and, especially, the true Arctic – the great area beyond the tree line then and still inhabited almost entirely by Inuit. Another decision he took was to put a new team in charge of the new policy. Jean Lesage, later to become premier of Quebec, was to be the minister, and I, at the ripe age of thirty-six, was to be his deputy minister and also commissioner of the Northwest Territories.

As commissioner I was to combine the roles of a provincial premier and of speaker of a provincial legislature. That legislature – the Council of the Northwest Territories – was in part elected by the voters of the western, subarctic part of the Territories and in part appointed by federal order-in-council. There was no cabinet: the commissioner alone was the government. From that lonely post I was to be responsible for handling virtually the full range of problems and services in the Territories that are 'provincial' in the rest of Canada. The area involved was enormous – just over one-third of the country.

It was surely the most challenging and fascinating job a Canadian could have. In association with Lesage, and with a small but dedicated team of young officers, I was able to make my own contribution to a Canada in which the North and its Aboriginal people would become active participants.

The process is still unfolding. The Council recommended to the Diefenbaker government in 1961 that the Territories should be divided to bring government closer to the people of both parts. The plan became a victim of the change of government in Ottawa in 1963 and did not resurface for twenty years. However, by 1966, there were elected members on the Council from all parts of the Territories, and in 1975, for the first time in Canadian history, a legislative body had a majority of Aboriginal members. The Council received a new name: it became the Legislative Assembly of the Northwest Territories and was given authority to name two members to the executive committee that shared the powers of government with the commissioner. On 1 April 1999, after years of preparation, the division recommended in 1961 at last took place: the new territory of Nunavut was created with a population 80 per cent Inuit. The problems are and will be enormous, but having the responsibility for government firmly in the hands of the people of each area is the most hopeful course.

This book is about my combination of experiences – with four outstanding prime ministers and with the revolution of the last forty years in the north. It is also, at the end, about national unity – the one problem that can blight our high hopes about the Canadian future.

In 1963 the Royal Commission on Bilingualism and Biculturalism reported that 'Canada, without being fully conscious of the fact, is passing through the greatest crisis in its history.' In December 1967, as one of his last acts before announcing his decision to retire, Pearson called a federal-provincial conference to begin a process of constitutional reform in the hope of solving the problem of growing separatism in Quebec. Thirty years later the problem still is unresolved. Four prime ministers have tried their hand: Pearson, Trudeau, Mulroney, and Chrétien. From 1963 to 1979, as secretary to the cabinet, I was the senior adviser to Pearson and Trudeau. Since retiring from the public service I have written, spoken, and worked on the same problem. It must be dealt with: it will not simply go away, however weary of it the country may be.

It is not easy for Canadians who did not live through the pre-war years, or whose lives have been engrossed with the normal activities of education, work, and family, to realize how much we have changed as a country and as a society since the last war. When I began collecting stamps, my father gave me the small collection he had made when he was a boy in the 1890s. One of the Canadian issues was to honour the Diamond Jubilee of Queen Victoria in 1897. It was a large stamp with a map of the world on it. Britain, Canada, and the British Empire were bright red; all the rest of the world was sombre grey-green. The theme on the stamp was: 'We hold a vaster Empire than has been.' The implication of the boast on a Canadian stamp was clear. Canada was not held within the Empire: it was part owner. Our share in the management was not apparent, but that was a problem for another day. Canada was proud to be a 'Dominion' within the Empire – an undefined something more than a colony, self-governing internally but with a British governor general and with only the most limited start at sharing with imperial Britain its control of our foreign relations. The demonstration of our absence of international status came in 1914: when Britain declared war on Germany, Canada was at war. No consultation and no action or consent by our Parliament or government were required.

That status was not enough for countries that shed so much blood in the war. Our prime minister during the war, Sir Robert Borden, insisted on Canadian participation in the peace conference and on Canadian signature to the treaty that emerged. Later, Canada and South Africa led in the development of 'Dominion status,' with legal definition of it in the Statute of Westminster in 1931. The statute put into law the declaration of the Imperial Conference of 1926 that the dominions were in no way subordinate to Britain. 'They are autonomous communities within the British Empire, equal in status, in no way subordinate one to another in any aspect of their domestic or external affairs, though united by a common allegiance to the Crown, and freely associated as members of the British Commonwealth.'[1] But even that status was uncertain enough that it was not clear whether the declaration of war by Britain on 3 September 1939 included the dominions too. The other dominions did not argue the point, but King decided that Parliament had to be consulted before Canada would take its position. He knew what Parliament's answer would be, but the fact of a separate Canadian decision was important politically and constitutionally.

These questions of status and of the less-than-sovereign nature of Canada did not concern me before university. However, the facts of family and home environment predisposed me towards Canadian nationhood. My mother was a Norwegian American whose family immigrated to Canada in 1908 after a generation in the United States. For them, Britain was the remote and tyrannical power rejected by the American Revolution. My father's enthusiasm for empire was, I think, always diluted by two stronger attachments: to Scotland and to Nova Scotia. His family had come from Scotland in 1784. My sister and I were brought up on the battles of the clans, the perfidy of the English, and the fact that Scotland was never conquered. As a good Scot, he was always ambiguous in his regard for England and the English.

My prairie environment thrust Canadian history at me from early years. Regina, where we lived from 1919, had been the capital of the old North-West Territories before Saskatchewan and Alberta became provinces in 1905. The rough stone buildings of that period of territorial glory still stood on the north side of Dewdney Avenue. Farther west was the headquarters of the RCMP, Regina's pride and a fascinating place for childhood visits. At the gable on the second floor of one building in the barracks compound was the door out of which Louis Riel had stepped to the scaffold on which he was hanged in 1885. My childhood impression was that he was a 'bad thing' but that the Indians and Metis he led had genuine grievances – not unlike the Highlanders of Scotland following the suppression of the Jacobites after the 'rising' in 1745. Today Riel is becoming a 'good thing,' possibly a father of Confederation. My father would be disgusted.

With such a background I was ripe for two stimulating years at the University of Saskatchewan under Professor R. MacGregor Dawson. A Nova Scotian, a Scot, and an enthusiastic Canadian, he was one of what has been called the 'Political Nationhood School' of Canadian historians and constitutionalists after the First World War. Canada became my 'thing' – its government, its shedding of the remnants of colonialism, its development of Canadian symbols and sources of pride, its achievement of complete national status. There was nothing remarkable in that: many young Canadians of the 1930s shared those views. My special luck was that, by a series of accidents, I came into positions in the public service of

Canada and associations with four prime ministers where I could do something about it.

This book is an attempt to throw some light on the qualities of the leaders with whom I worked, on the fascinating north that has changed so much so fast, and on our problem of national unity that has changed so little – all as seen from a place near the top of government in Canada.

R.G.R.
Ottawa, February 2000

Acknowledgments

I owe a debt of gratitude to a number of people whose comments and advice have helped me in writing a book that turned out to be a much more difficult challenge than I had expected. In part that was because the problem of our national unity, in which I was directly involved as a public servant from the 1960s onward, continued to take new twists and turns. It seemed a mistake not to continue the account of my activity, outside government after 1979, in what will be seen as one of the most critical periods in our entire history. With the opinion of the Supreme Court in 1998 on the right of secession for Quebec, and the assessment by both the federal government and that of Quebec of its implications, we appear to have reached a pause. It also comes at a point where my own part has ceased to be active.

At the University of Toronto Press, I particularly thank Gerry Hallowell, senior editor, Canadian history, for his counsel and advice from beginning to end. He has encouraged, but with wise criticism and suggestion. Peter Russell, Professor of Political Science at the University of Toronto and author of *Constitutional Odyssey*, the most authoritative book on the long agony with which I deal from a different viewpoint and less comprehensively, lent his wisdom to the report of the Manuscript Review Committee. His suggestions for revision have greatly improved my book. I am deeply grateful to him. Finally, I am indebted to 'Reader B,' whose identity I do not know but whose comments, while blunt, were most helpful.

I wish also to thank my editor, Curtis Fahey, whose meticulous questions and comments have required an improved expression of many parts of my text. It is comforting to think that few errors can have escaped his eagle eye.

Acknowledgments

Friends and former colleagues in Northern Affairs – Graham Rowley, Bob Phillips, and Arthur Kroeger – have helped with recollections of people and events in the Northwest Territories during that time when we implemented Prime Minister St Laurent's mandate of 1953 to produce an active program for the North.

Members of my family, and especially my dear wife, have given encouragement, comment, and advice during several years when it seemed not at all clear if so seeming endless a project would at last work out. Pauline Sabourin, who wrestled with my crabbed writing – nearly as bad as Mackenzie King's even without his stubby pencil – had unending patience with repeated drafts and revisions. I am very grateful to her.

And finally I am more grateful than I can adequately say to Basil Robinson, a former colleague in the Department of External Affairs and later deputy minister of the Department of Indian and Northern Affairs and then of External Affairs. Apart from his knowledge of the public service, people, and governments during the time with which this book deals, he brought his experience in writing an excellent book on John Diefenbaker, the fifth and most puzzling of our prime ministers from Mackenzie King to Pierre Trudeau. Basil read, commented on, and criticized with constructive suggestions every chapter and page. His advice has been invaluable. Without it this book would have much less grace and many more deficiencies and shortcomings than it has – for all of which I am responsible.

PART ONE

From the Prairies to Ottawa, 1917–1941

chapter one

From the Prairies to Oxford, 1917–1938

The battle of Vimy Ridge in April 1917 made a great fighting reputation for the Canadian Corps. The corps took the commanding ridge after both French and British attempts to do so had failed. There were more than ten thousand casualties in the five-day assault; and one of them was my father, a lieutenant in the 195th Battalion. The rank of lieutenant in the infantry was, I have been told, the most dangerous in the Canadian army since the lieutenants were expected to be first out of the trenches and to lead from the front. My observation in my later life was that my father did not understand fear: it was not part of his make-up. He would almost certainly have been one of the very first out into the deadly open. He was badly wounded and not expected to live, and so, when I appeared on the scene a month later, I was given his name: Gordon.

I was born in the home of my mother's parents in Davidson, Saskatchewan, then a town of about three hundred on the baldest of prairie. Both my grandparents, Amund and Lena Paulsen, were Norwegian Americans who had arrived in Canada only a few years before. Norwegian was the language of the home. My mother, Lydie Adelia, was the only daughter and I was the only grandson. No circumstances could have been better designed to ensure that I would be showered with the love and attention of three adoring 'parents.'

My grandfather, in spite of the handicap of losing an arm in an accident while in the United States, had done well in Canada. He even had a car – a Tudhope, with enormous wheels, rock hard tires, and a top held down by great leather straps that ran to a bar at the front on which the headlights were perched. The steering wheel was on the right side. The gear shift and emergency brake were outside the car, so a door on that side was impossible. One climbed in from the left, where there was a fair amount of room in front of the bucket seat. That seat was where I had my afternoon naps in warm weather. I slept better as the car lurched and bumped over the roads in the deep gumbo around the town than in a quiet but lonely bedroom. Nothing was too good for the only grandson whose father might not come back.

Meeting My Father

If I was not completely spoiled it was because my father did come back. He was a strong, determined man who had decided, against medical advice, that he could both retain his shattered leg and survive. What my father decided to do he did, and so, I soon learned, did the rest of us.

I crashed into this immovable object when I was about eighteen months old. My mother took me from my warm and sheltered nest, and from 'Poppa' and Grandma, to meet that total stranger in Montreal when he came back from England. We then caught 'the Ocean Limited' late in the day and left, in one compartment, for Nova Scotia. Things became more strained as both my father and I grew more tired. The night, my mother told me later, was a horror for all concerned.

My father had spent nearly two years in hospitals in France and England, with four operations and much of the time in great pain. His nerves were not yet fully repaired and it was his first night with the bride he had left more than two years before. I resented this foreign presence: I had been used to no competition for my mother's attention and my roars of outrage were not to be quieted. My father must have been equally furious and frustrated. Even with nerves in order, he did not take kindly to obstreperous children. I do not think that the relations between my father and me ever quite recovered.

We did manage to survive to reach the farm of my father's parents in Churchville, Nova Scotia, a settlement so completely Scottish that the one non-Scot had the high hill on which he lived named for him – Irish Mountain. My great, great, great grandparents had been the first settlers there in 1784. The family tradition, probably true, was that the pioneer and his two sons, after choosing their land, spent the first weeks under the shelter of an elm tree a few yards from a brook that passed near the barnyard. The tree, by the 1900s, was gigantic. (It died of Dutch elm disease in 1989.) They built their first cabin on a rise a hundred yards away, and the hollow from the excavation they made underneath it was still there in my boyhood. The cabin sheltered the family for fifty years until the house was built in 1834.

Our stay in Nova Scotia was brief: about a year in Halifax, where my father became soldier-settlement commissioner, responsible for helping returning veterans to find a place in peace-time Nova Scotia. The real opportunities for him were in the west, and in 1919 he was appointed livestock commissioner for Saskatchewan. My father, after graduating in agriculture in 1912 from MacDonald College, the agriculture faculty of McGill University, had obeyed the injunction of Horace Greeley to young men and gone west. Before he enlisted in 1916, he had risen to be manager of an enormous American-owned farm not far from Davidson.

My sister Lucille was born, like me, in our grandparents' house in Davidson in October 1920. In Regina, we lived first in a small cottage and soon in a larger house on Smith Street, named after Donald Smith, Lord Strathcona, who drove the last spike in the Canadian Pacific Railway. Without the CPR, Regina would not have existed, and without the attempt of a group of land developers to extort a great profit from the sale of land at the intended location for the town, Regina would not have been where it was. The site had nothing to distinguish or to recommend it. A dam on Wascana Creek, to make an artificial lake, created the only amenity to relieve the baldness of the prairie.

My father was in the style of the Victorian husband, father, and head of the family. My mother, fortunately, was not of a combative nature, nor did she have any ideas of gender equality. If she had been other than she was, the family would have been torn by stress. My father could not be changed by argument or confrontation – only by careful handling and by time. As the only son, until my brother Ronald arrived in 1930, I was the raw material to be moulded by my father's views about masculine courage, vigour, and strength of character. My perceptive sister later said that we three children lived with three different fathers. Mine was the young, strong, unreformed male, recently back from a military life he enjoyed and determined to produce a boy who measured up to his high manly standards. Her father was quite different, mainly because she was female, but also because she responded to the romantic, Celtic side of my father's character. My brother, when he came thirteen years after me, was the comfort of my parents' later years. His father was the product of the softening that time could produce even on the military character that I had encountered in 1918.

My school years in Regina were unremarkable. I never quite measured up to my father's expectations in manly sports, although I was a participant, albeit an undistinguished one, in most of them. However, I stood straight, kept my hands out of my pockets, never chewed gum, and learned to ride a horse.

The manner of the latter was of the 'be a man' approach. I had no desire for a horse, but my father announced one day in late November that he had bought one for me: a cross between a Welsh pony and an Arabian. It was larger than a pony, but smaller than a horse and, as I discovered, full of spirit. I was about eleven or twelve years old. The horse was, my father said, in a barn at the Regina Exhibition grounds; here was a bridle; it would be up to me to care for the horse, to learn to ride it, and to keep it exercised. No saddle, no riding lessons, no instructions – just me and the horse. There was a man at the grounds to give it hay and oats since the barn was some miles from our house.

I think I was thrown off about a dozen times, with Chief, as I named him, taking off across the prairie to nibble the grass sticking up through the hard snow. He was a devil at appearing not to see me stealing up on the reins where they lay on the snow as he chewed the grass – until I got within a foot or two of them. Then he was off for another quarter of a mile. It was a trying way to learn to ride. The saddle came for my birthday in May, along with a converted garage on our lot in town to keep Chief in. Riding then began to be fun.

The Distaff Side

My father was a great joiner of men's organizations: the Royal Canadian Legion, the Masons, and the Regina Rifle Regiment, in which he rose to be lieutenant-colonel. He was secretary of many livestock associations in the province, the organizer of the Pure Bred Sire Area program to improve livestock in Saskatchewan, and the driving force behind virtually everything he was in. The result was almost constant absence from home in the evenings and a reliable presence only on Sundays. Virtually the entire task of running the house and tending the family fell on Mother.

Our house in Regina had been built some time before the First World War. It survived the 'Regina cyclone' of 1912 – a tornado that destroyed nearly all the houses on the other side of Smith Street. I used to play in and around the foundations of the houses that had been demolished in the storm and not rebuilt. Houses of the vintage of ours were of frame construction with no insulation – siding on the outside of two-by-four studs and plaster walls inside. Heating was by coal-fired furnaces, with hot air circulating through large ducts by convection. When it was twenty-five to forty degrees below zero Fahrenheit, as it frequently was in a prairie winter, running the furnace was a vital and tiring task. Until I became old enough to help, my mother did virtually all of it: removing the ashes and shovelling in coal early in the morning; stoking periodically during the day; removing the ashes and banking the fire solidly last thing at night. Clinkers were her constant dread: hard hunks of congealed waste within the coal that jammed the grates so the ashes could not be shaken out. The fire had to be worked aside so the clinker could be levered out – then the fire rebuilt. That happened many a night.

It was so cold in the morning in the bedroom that my sister and I shared that mother collected our clothes and herded us down to the kitchen to dress in front of the coal-oil stove, from which four burners cast enough heat to make a bearable circle in the frigid gloom.

On Monday mornings mother was up before five to light the jacket heater in the basement to heat a boiler of water for the washing. She had laid the fire and filled the boiler on Sunday – a breach of the sabbath that she thought the Lord would understand. Apart from electric energy to turn the dolly in the washing machine and the wringer, there was nothing automatic about the task. And at the end, the half-wet wash had to be hung with bare hands, in temperatures thirty to forty degrees below zero on the lines outside: freeze-drying, my mother thought, made it whiter. It was like so many boards to be brought in, frozen solid, a few hours later.

Mother was the yielding, comforting, encouraging factor that was vital in my younger years. As I grew older I became less frightened of my father and more able to cope with his strong views. There was nothing of hostility in them. They emanated from an unshakeable sense of the responsibility of the paterfamilias to direct, form, and discipline his son to meet and discharge the responsibilities of manhood. His decisions could be forestalled or avoided with skill, or occasionally evaded by delay and non-performance. They could, however, not be debated. 'Don't argue' was a not infrequent command.

As I look back on my boyhood, it is clear to me that my experiences with my father were a demonstration of the truth of Professor Charles Taylor's thesis that a 'crucial feature of human life is its fundamentally dialogical character.' His statement that we 'define our identity always in dialogue with, sometimes in struggle against, the things our significant others want to see in us'[1] was profoundly true for me. My 'dialogue' was both with and against my father. There was bound to be resistance to so great a force and it led me to be less sympathetic than I should have been to the romantic qualities that Lucille understood. On the other hand, I responded to the high standards he set in industry and application – and in results – from the moment I entered school. His interest there was constant and stimulating. My dialogue with my mother was totally positive. Indeed, I think we had an unstated mutual-defence pact simply to cope with that strong personality that bore on us both – my first acquaintance with collective security.

My Father and the Clan

For a romantic Scot like my father, the 'Clan' was central. The fact that it was the mark of a primitive tribal society in the Highlands of Scotland was a proposition he did not entertain. Within the clan, the genealogy of a family is important and my father had preserved ours with zest, and sometimes with imagination.

With a pretty high degree of certainty, he managed to trace the family back to 1690 to one Robert Robertson who was the factor, or manager, of a part of the estates of Lady Lovat. His grandson, John, was a tenant farmer and emigrated in 1784 with a wife and six children – two sons and four daughters in their teens and early twenties. The six children married and produced sixty grandchildren, most of whom settled in Pictou County. Our family came from the younger son, William. In a manner not uncommon in Nova Scotia and Quebec, the younger son was the old-age security of his parents. William inherited the largest part of the original land, the cabin, and the farm buildings.

My father's zeal for family led him, in the 1920s, to conceive the idea of a great family reunion in 1934 – the 150th anniversary of the 'arrival' and of the founding of the village of Churchville. He appointed himself 'secretary and manager' of the reunion, and it would certainly not have happened without his genealogical passion and knowledge or without his energy and organizing ablity. It took five or six years to follow up the six family lines, to get the names and addresses of hundreds of descendants in North America, Australia, and elsewhere, to write letters, raise funds, and make all the plans. In July 1934 several hundred descendants converged on the ancestral farm for four days of commemoration, athletic events, dancing, feasting, and religious service. For each of the six original families there was registration and issuance of a ribbon of different colour. It was probably the first time that most of them had known who their remote ancestors were and whom they were related to. The high point of the celebration was the unveiling of a bronze plaque on a great rough-stone cairn about a hundred yards from the farmhouse, very close to where the original cabin had been.

My father's zeal for family did not diminish with age. In a printed pamphlet of 'Family Records' he put out in January 1970, the final line

pointedly said, 'The Two Hundredth Anniversary will be held in 1984.'
He did not expect to see it, but the message to my sister, my brother, and
me was clear. It was up to us to deliver. My father died in 1978 but the
anniversary indeed was marked. The diminished size of the celebration
from the one of 1934 exposed the weakening of moral fibre that had
worried my father all along. He would, however, have approved of the
second bronze plaque we put on the cairn.

Drought and the Depression, 1930 to 1938

The 1930s were a heart-breaking time to live in Saskatchewan. To the
worldwide depression was added the worst drought the prairies had ever
experienced, and Saskatchewan had much the worst of it – especially in
the southern half of the province. James Gray, who lived in Winnipeg,
travelled by car across the prairies in July 1936, and what he saw was not
at all unusual for anyone living in Saskatchewan at that time.

> In less than half a day, I had had my fill of black blizzards. There was escape
> occasionally from the dust as the nature of the terrain changed, but there
> was no escape from the heat and no escape either from the desolation
> around us. Even the Russian thistle, which covered the abandoned fields
> like a worn-out carpet, was stunted and brown with dust. Here and there,
> half-starved horses and cattle hung over fences, or huddled in the shade of
> barns and sheds trying to escape from the flies that tormented them. We
> drove through village after village without a sign of life, past empty farm
> after empty farm. The fences along the road were drifted high with the
> blowing dust and the weeds of seven years' drouth. This year's crop of
> Russian thistle would not go tumbling before the wind for another six
> weeks, but traces of the weed from the year before still protruded through
> the drifted silt at the fence-posts. Here and there, the fence was completely
> covered, indicating drifted soil at least three feet deep.[2]

The people who had lived on the farms Gray saw would have abandoned them only after several years of heartbreaking crop failure and
increasing destitution. There was no safety net in those days and no
organized system for disaster assistance. In August 1931 the Canadian
Red Cross sent out a nation-wide appeal for help for 125,000 destitute
farm people in Saskatchewan. Volunteer agencies organized the Saskatchewan Voluntary Rural Relief Committee. In some areas virtually
every family had to go 'on relief,' both in the country and in the towns.
My uncle, my mother's younger brother, who had operated the Saskatch-

9

ewan Wheat Pool elevator in Davidson for many years, was first moved to an area where there was some grain when there was none around Davidson, and then, when that failed too, was let go. With no grain, virtually all elevators ceased to operate. And, without the elevators, many towns could not survive. Unemployment became the normal condition.

My grandfather, who had succeeded so well in twenty-five years, was wiped out. There was no protection for small businessmen or for farmers. His several sections of land produced nothing, year after year, and were seized for unpaid taxes. When my grandmother died in October 1930, our only comfort was that she did not live to see the full disaster of their old age.

Much of the provincial public service was laid off – with no unemployment insurance, only whatever savings people might have and then relief. My father's excellent record, and perhaps his status as a wounded veteran, stood between us and the relief line. He, like the other lucky ones, suffered a severe cut in salary but remained livestock commissioner.

Saskatchewan and the prairies generally were not alone in the disaster; they simply suffered the most. The Depression was across Canada and around the world. Much of the relief in the west was organized on a municipal basis, with minimum and uncertain financial assistance from the nearly bankrupt provincial governments. There was no system of federal-provincial transfers, and 'equalization' for governments was as unheard of as social security for individuals. The demonstration of the inadequacy of the national financial system to cope with economic depression was the main factor that led to the establishment of the Royal Commission on Dominion-Provincial Relations in 1937.

For the 1930s it was a matter of hesitant and makeshift response as the collapse spread. There were relatively few women in paid employment then, so unemployment was largely a male problem. The cities took care of their own unemployed. Single men became transients in search of work and 'riding the rods' on the trains became the means of moving about. Work camps, under the Department of National Defence, were organized in bush areas to provide useful-seeming tasks and also housing for young men. They were paid twenty cents a day plus a tobacco allowance.

In 1935 an 'On-to-Ottawa Trek' was organized to bring complaints from the west to the attention of the government of Prime Minister R.B. Bennett. The government used the RCMP to stop the trek in Regina, and in June a strikers' delegation met Bennett and some of his cabinet in Ottawa. The meeting was an angry failure, and the strikers in Regina decided to resume the trek to Ottawa. By accident I found myself in the middle of the next phase.

On Sunday, 30 June 1935, the trekkers gathered at the Regina Market Square, ready to move on. That evening, knowing nothing of the meeting, I walked down Scarth Street to the post office on the corner of Eleventh Avenue to mail a letter. As I dropped the letter in, I heard some noise on Eleventh and walked around the corner of the building to see what it was. I found myself facing a mass of running men who soon engulfed me. It was the retreat from the Market Square, a few blocks to the east, after the RCMP and the city police had broken up the meeting. In a matter of minutes, the men had passed and it was the police, some on horseback, who were coming at me. I decided that it was no place for a young male who might easily be taken for a trekker and beat a hasty retreat up Scarth Street.

One city detective was killed, several policemen were wounded by rocks, a number of civilians were shot – none fatally – and many were injured by police clubs. The leaders were arrested and the trek was over.

Learning about Labour
One thing I did that met my father's high standards was to succeed in school. He was proud of my various awards, with a suitably engraved gold watch to mark the governor general's medal at the end of high school. Even without that, there would have been no doubt about my going to university: somehow it would have happened. However, I was as anxious as my father was to find a way to help with the cost. There were no scholarships and no student loans. My father got me a job in 1935 as a labourer on the Experimental Farm at Indian Head, a small town about fifty miles east of Regina. The superintendent had been in his class of 1912 at MacDonald College.

I have always suspected my father of another motive than just the money I would earn. I wanted to take political science and economics for an honours BA at Saskatoon. My father did not oppose, but he made clear his disdain for a degree that would not equip me with a profession – agriculture, engineering, law, medicine, accounting. What would I do with political science and economics? It would do me no harm to see how hard life could be if I did not acquire a profession.

The 'rough gang,' as my labourer colleagues and I were called at the farm, went into the fields at 7:00 A.M. sharp, which meant being at the work-assignment office in one of the barns at 6:45. The hours were 7:00 to 6:00, five days a week, with an hour off at noon for 'dinner' in the boarding house. There was early closing on Saturday, when we worked only 7:00 to 5:00, again with a one-hour lunch break. A fifty-nine-hour week at twenty-one cents an hour, or $12.39 a week. My room, with three meals, was one dollar a day so the fifty-nine hours of work netted me $5.39 a week.

Some days the work was exhausting, some days just hard, and other days relatively easy. However, even easy work, like thinning hundred-yard rows of carrot seedlings down to one seedling every three inches, and getting every weed out of pure-seed plots that spread over acres of land that had to be meticulously cultivated by hand, left fingers, knees, and back sore and aching. If my father had intended to make a point about the wisdom of being equipped for a career, he succeeded. I thought I would die the first week at the farm and the second was only slightly better. However, by the end of the summer I was all bone and muscle and not a little pleased with myself. It was also an excellent experience to get to know and usually to like the men I worked with. The only important adjustment I had to make, apart from toughening up, was to drop the genteel practice of washing my hands before sitting down to dinner at noon. I found the first day that that was a sure route to starvation. There was little left but bread and butter when I got to the table: all the meat had gone.

The next two summers I got a job at the Purity Dairy in Regina, still as a labourer but with better pay. I think it was thirty cents an hour with a nine-hour day: only a fifty-four-hour week. As I could live at home, I netted $16.20 a week – a veritable fortune.

I was one of the few workmen who could multiply, add, and subtract with reasonable accuracy, so the third summer I was stationed partly in the office and partly on the shipping deck. I recorded the weight of the cans of milk and cream, took down the grade that the 'grader' shouted at me after he tasted each can, and then figured out what the farmer was owed after deducting the freight charge from his shipping point in the province. They paid a bit more for that level of skill, but not much. There were plenty of people available.

I often wondered about the relationship between the wages I received and what I hear university students getting for summer jobs now – if they can find them. My late brother-in-law, Bill Lawson, then senior deputy governor of the Bank of Canada, looked into the matter for me. Using the 'cost-price index' standard for the value of money, it appeared that, with the 1935–9 average as 100, the index for 1993 was 1134. In other words the value of $1.00 in 1935–9 was the same as that of $11.34 in 1993.

On that basis, my twenty-one cents became $2.38 an hour in 1993 money – far below the minimum wage and about a fifth of probable pay for summer work. The ferocity of the Depression plus the drought of the 1930s, and the absence of any minimum-wage legislation, were undoubtedly the main factors that drove wages to the low levels of the 1930s. However, a substantial amount of the difference must represent the increase in standards and expectations between the wealthy Canada of today and the relatively poor country it was sixty years ago.

The University of Saskatchewan

My transition to university was made through a year at Regina College. It had originally been run by the Methodist Church, but, like so much else in the Depression, it went bankrupt. In 1934 it was taken over by the University of Saskatchewan to provide the first two years of arts and science. The change was just in time for me to move into the second year, which could be done from Grade 12 in the high school system.

The greatest advantages of Regina College were its small size and the young faculty, provided by juniors in the faculty of the University in Saskatoon who either were prepared to move to Regina or could be directed to do so. Their youth and the small size of classes – from ten or twelve to thirty or forty in the largest – made for close personal contact. One of the young lecturers was Hilda Neatby, who thirteen years later, in 1947, became a member of the Royal Commission on National Development in the Arts, Letters, and Sciences, and one of the most respected academics in Canada.

In the 1930s it was next to impossible for a woman, however well qualified, to find an academic position in Saskatchewan or elsewhere in western Canada. It was the unattractiveness of the new college to the history faculty in Saskatoon that led President Walter Murray to offer Neatby $900 and room and board for nine months' teaching at Regina College.[3] As she told me many years later, she leaped at it – for there was nothing else but high school teaching, if that could be got, even though she had a PhD from the University of Minnesota.

Neatby was a brilliant teacher, and I benefited greatly from her relentless insistence on the need for clear thinking, effective organization, and concise expression. My earliest essays for Professor Neatby's course in nineteenth-century European history got a C and a D. The shock was devastating: I had scarcely ever got a rating less than A or some equivalent in my entire high school career. I sought an interview and was told in no uncertain terms all the things that were wrong with the ill-thought, shallow, puerile effort I had handed in. She made it clear that my sin was the greater because she was convinced that I could have done much better if I had not felt I could get away with intellectual laziness and sloppy writing. It was the best single thing that happened to me at Regina College. When I got over the shock and realized how right Neatby was, I was, as the evangelists say, 'reborn.' Hilda and I were to become warm friends in later years. Both her character and her courage were shown in her scathing attack on some of the developments in educational philosophy after the war. Her book *So Little for the Mind*, published in 1953, brought her under furious attack from the education establishment, but much comment today – over forty years later – on the state of the educational system confirms many of the criticisms she made.

While the University of Saskatchewan in 1935 was a great deal bigger and more complex than Regina College, it was small among Canadian universities and very small indeed by today's standards. For undergraduates, I think that is an advantage, provided the faculty are of good quality. That was, in general, the case at the University of Saskatchewan.

It was Professor MacGregor Dawson, the head and sole member of the department of political science, who was the most stimulating person in my years in Saskatoon. The first year there I took the foundation course in political science – a general course on the principles of parliamentary government and the structure of the federal system and the government of Canada. I think that Dawson, with his zest for life, his joyous sense of humour, and his enthusiasm for his subject, could have made almost anything interesting. However, all those qualities found unlimited scope in his analyses of politics and politicians, the struggles for power, the triumphs and disasters, and all that is involved in the political process.

No one emerged from the Dawson's course without an interest in politics and government in Canada. For me, it was conclusive: that was the subject I wanted to pursue. Just how, or in what role, was still unclear.

The following year, Dawson had a seminar on the development of dominion status. At that time he was writing a book on the subject. There were just three of us in the seminar, all friends from Regina and all sharing a large room in the men's residence, Qu'Appelle Hall. Bill Lederman, later dean of law at Dalhousie University, founder and first dean of law at Queen's University, and one of the most distinguished constitutionalists Canada has produced, was one. The other was Courtney McEwen, who planned to go into law but was diverted into business. The seminar was every second week for three hours, with a major essay for each one.

The essays produced a frenzy of activity the day or two before the seminar as each of us strove to get his opus into shape. Usually the final writing went on far into the night. Bill was very solid, workmanlike, and serious, and usually had the best essay. Courtney was normally in the worst state, but one night he finished first. He lit his pipe in triumph and relief – and his eye lit on Bill, hard at work. In a moment of mischief, he leaned over with the match and put it to Bill's last page. Bill, in a frenzy, banged the fire out with his bare hands before it went beyond that page, and he delivered a diatribe made the hotter by his burnt fingers and hands. The essay, less one page, was saved, but the same could not be said for civil relations. By the next year, when we roomed together again, the episode was forgotten – but not the peaceful Lederman's capacity for righteous wrath.

Bill and I remained close friends and in frequent contact until his death in 1992. We were awarded the Rhodes scholarship for Saskatchewan in succeeding years: I for 1938 and Bill for 1939. He was an outstanding Canadian and widely recognized in the legal and academic professions, and also among practitioners in politics and government, as having developed some of the most important and most lasting insights into the nature and operation of our constitution. He was made an officer of the Order of Canada in 1981.

The Rhodes Scholarship
Under the Saskatchewan system of that day, a candidate for an honours BA first wrote examinations, after the third university year, for a pass BA. All three of us were, therefore, writing for that degree in 1937: Courtney as possibly the end of the line or to go on in law; Bill to move to the Faculty of Law; and I to go on to the honours BA. Bill and I had both decided to become candidates for the Rhodes Scholarship. We had remarkably similar records: pretty much the same courses with much the same results; much the same participation in 'manly sports,' although Bill was better in water polo than I was in anything I took on. On the other hand, I had been more active in student politics. I was president of the College of Arts and Science one year and was narrowly defeated in the election for president of the Students' Representative Council the next. There were several other candidates for the scholarship, but we thought that we had a pretty fair chance. Or rather one of us did!

We were both finalists and invited (separately) to the ultimate test: breakfast with the Rhodes selection committee for the province. So far as we could tell after the ordeals, neither of us had used the wrong fork, had been trapped into some inane comment or argument, or had insulted any of the committee. It is impossible to know in such a process on what a decision turns. In the end, the result was as mentioned above: I got the Rhodes for 1938 and Bill had to make another run for 1939.

The one year of difference in selection had an unforeseen result. I was in the last group of scholars to go to Oxford in the normal way before the war. Like most of those selected for 1939, Bill's scholarship was postponed until after the war. He finally went up to Oxford in 1946 after serving in the Canadian army.

My start on the journey to Oxford on 19 September 1938 was in a manner entirely fitting for the still-depressed condition of Saskatchewan. Every farmer shipping a carload of livestock to 'the east' was entitled to have a 'hand' accompany them to see that they were properly fed and watered, or to do the task himself if the shipper so wished. My father knew nearly every livestock shipper in the province, so he arranged for two contracts – one for me and one for a friend, Al Traynor, who wanted to go to Toronto to move from pre-medicine at Saskatchewan to the medical school at the University of Toronto. The University of Saskatchewan did not have a complete medical school. The contracts would be from Winnipeg, the gateway to or from the west. We went from Regina to Winnipeg by day coach.

When Al and I found the Winnipeg stockyards, our starting point, we also found a problem. His contract was on the CPR and mine on the CNR and both had us going to Toronto, while I had hoped to get a train to Montreal. For a couple of dollars I bought a contract held by a chap named A. Perron on the CPR, so Traynor and I could travel together.

A caboose attached to a locomotive took Traynor and me about five miles to the freight yards, which in Winnipeg were then gigantic. We were led on foot across innumerable tracks, in the dark, lit only by rare floodlights, to the 'colonist car' that would be part of the freight train in which our cattle were. It was only after we settled down on the wooden seats, in great relief, that we realized we had both left our brand new overcoats in the stockyards – five miles away. That was no joke in 1938.

We had to strike out in the semi-darkness to find the freight office, well concealed among hundreds of freight cars. A phone call to the stockyard found that, by some miracle, the coats had not been picked up by any of the dozen men we had seen there. The coats were sent by taxi to the freight office, and the task then was to find our colonist car again. It had been moved in making up the freight train – but moved where?

One of us recalled that there had been a wood stove in the car with a fire burning in it. Where there was fire there might be smoke, and if there was, we might be able to see it across the tops of the freight cars. With joy and amazement, we spotted a wisp of smoke rising up a hundred yards or so away. The next task was to get there.

It is not easy to hold a direction in a dark freight yard where you have to go over or under or between freight cars but never in a straight line. Nor is it soothing to the nerves not to know which cars will stay in place and which may move as the shunting proceeds. Even without the thin mattress we had been issued we would have slept well on the wooden berths that night.

Travelling by colonist car attached to a freight train was, we found, quite an agreeable way to travel, provided one was not in a hurry. It took four nights and three days from Winnipeg to Toronto. The stops to feed and water the cattle provided an opportunity for pleasant walks along the right of way. The company was varied and interesting since transients, or hoboes as some unkindly called them, were riding the tops of the freight cars, where it got desperately cold in the September nights. There were eight or ten of us in the colonist car and, while we could not let the transients in by day, we took a chance on doing it at night. When any of the train crew came along from the caboose, the nocturnal passengers hid under the seats or in closed upper berths. The crew were happy enough not to look too thoroughly for unauthorized visitors as long as they were out of sight. There was no point in borrowing trouble. As for our guests, either they were honest or gratitude overcame temptation. No one in the car lost anything.

Being an accessory to a carload of cattle and mixing with the homeless unemployed epitomized precisely the condition of Saskatchewan in the 1930s. It was a different way of life to which I was moving.

chapter two

From Oxford to Ottawa, 1938–1941

The sailing dinner on 23 September for the new crop of Rhodes Scholars was on a different level than the colonist car. It was in the elegance of the Windsor Hotel in Montreal: 'black tie,' appropriate wines, talk about Oxford, and the port at the end moving the right way – to the left. It was my first chance to meet two men who were to become lifetime friends and colleagues: Bill Lawson from Manitoba, later my brother-in-law, and Ed Ritchie from New Brunswick, later Canadian ambassador to the United States and under-secretary of state for external affairs.

The following day, as we boarded the *Empress of Britain* at Quebec City, the papers were screaming the news of the mobilization of Czechoslovakia in the face of threats from Nazi Germany. Our first year at Oxford was to be one of apprehension of war, the second was to be the 'phoney war' until the lightning conquest of Europe by Hitler in June 1940, and the third Oxford year was not to be ours at all.

Bill Lawson and I shared a cabin in third class. On 26 September, as we emerged from the Strait of Belle Isle, we learned why the CPR lured passengers with the slogan '40 per cent less ocean to Britain' – meaning 40 per cent less than a crossing from New York. The sea was high, the ship heaved drunkenly, and we were both wildly sick: any ocean was too much. But we survived, and the fifth day from Quebec we were thrilled to see the coast of England through the mist as the ship sailed on to Cherbourg. The harbour there was protected by three lines of anti-submarine nets. Eight submarines like enormous green fish swam out as we moved in. Several cruisers and destroyers were moored some distance away. After the passengers for France and elsewhere in Europe had landed, it was out again and across the channel to Southampton. We sailed in by night, following a narrow, winding route marked by the flickering lights of buoys.

Labarge, later deputy minister of customs and excise in Ottawa, had not been warned by his tutor that he would certainly fail his law exams in June 1939 if he went on the tour. What he needed was four weeks of solid work, not four weeks of high life in Switzerland. Ray's replacement was Don Duffie from New Brunswick, later the Reverend Monsignor Duffie, president of St Thomas University in Fredericton. Ed Ritchie and I on the defence were quite inadequate to provide the kind of protection Don needed to keep any close shot out of the goal. There was some dispute whether the Czechs beat us 24–0 or 23–1. The scorekeeper appeared to be confused by the unprecedented mathematics involved. Not all results were that humiliating, but we won only one game in the series. It was the last time the Swiss hoteliers had any illusion that Oxford was in a class to play in the European championships for the Spengler Cup or the Aspang Cup.

The next holiday trip to Europe, in the Easter vacation of 1939, was different. Ross Anderson and I set off for the south of France and Italy, with a return through Germany, well loaded with law books and a determination to learn something about the glories of ancient Rome and also about fascist Italy and Nazi Germany. While we were in Italy the Germans moved into Czechoslovakia in defiance of the Munich agreement of September 1938.

We were in Rome for the celebration by the Fascist Party of the twentieth anniversary of its founding. The Young Fascists, boys from six up, paraded with black shirts, cocked hats, and small guns. Older boys had grey-green uniforms with full-size guns. The girls' units were in black, without guns but very well drilled.

On 28 March we attended a ceremony in the Piazza Venezia, the great forum in the centre of Rome, where the dictator, Benito Mussolini, presented medals and took the salute from 18,000 troops. He was a stiff, stout, pompous little figure, but it was hard to be amused. Even more disturbing was the exuberance of an enormous crowd of people that night when Mussolini, in response to half an hour of deafening shouts, appeared on the balcony of the nearby Palazzo Venezia. It would require a stout heart for a Roman in the crowd not to believe in the popularity of 'The Leader' and the loyalty of his followers. Mussolini had to return to the balcony five times before the cheers would die.

In Munich, the birth place of Nazism, one got an impression of a harder, more relentless discipline among the 'black shirts' we saw. On 20 April we were in Cologne for Hitler's birthday, marked by a tremendous display of mechanized might: motorcycle troops, motorized anti-aircraft and machine-gun batteries, artillery, pontoon divisions, and an unending stream of personnel carriers, loaded with troops. The speed of the German conquest of Czechoslovakia was easy to understand.

On 22 May 1939 an Italo-German pact was signed providing for automatic and complete collaboration between the two countries in any case where either party was drawn into a war against 'its wishes.' Any separate peace in such a war was excluded.

Oxford Notwithstanding

For three terms of eight weeks each from September 1938 to the end of June 1939, the work, the life, and the sports at Oxford continued for the last year of 'peace.' In February, Cambridge added the final blow to a humiliating Oxford hockey year by beating us 2–0.

The same month brought me some comfort in another form of competition – a 'moot' or mock trial, presided over by Dr Goodhart, the university professor of jurisprudence. It was the first time I had tried my legal legs in anything but essays for my tutor. Ross Anderson was my associate and we won our case. However, the real triumph was relayed to me two days later by Dr Cheshire: 'Dr Goodhart says your argument was the best he ever listened to in "a moot case."' Perhaps that comment made me over-confident, for two weeks later I came down from my cloud.

The essay that week was on defamation, and specifically on 'qualified privilege' as a defence: that the person charged with having slandered another person had been in a special situation when he made the comment and therefore it was privileged. While I was writing my essay Mundell and Anderson dropped in as they often did. Was I going to refer to the case of Langley versus Davies in my essay? I had not heard of it, so they gave me the facts. It was too late to read the judgment in the law reports but the case was clearly important, so I put it in my essay with some discussion of the implications. Cheshire was very interested, as he had missed the case. I enlarged on it to him.

A couple of hours after the tutorial Mundell and Anderson dropped by again. Mundell enquired in a friendly way about my tutorial. I said it had gone very well, partly because Cheshire had been so interested in Langley versus Davies. He had missed the report of it and agreed that it filled a real gap in the law. Then Mundell confessed all. He had had his tutorial next after mine and had told Cheshire there was no such case – except in the fertile minds of Mundell and Anderson. Cheshire's only comment had been: 'My, wasn't it a good thing I said I didn't know the case!' Mundell held the door of my room open for a hasty retreat as fury and finally laughter followed shocked horror at the trap I had fallen into. Cheshire never mentioned the case and I saw no need to try to explain: nothing would help but time – and future care.

Around the Baltic Sea

Having got the flavour of southern Europe, I wanted to use the summer vacation to see something of the north. It might also be the last chance. Tensions were growing with the British guarantee of the Polish borders and the steady increase of demands by Germany on Poland for the Free City of Danzig and the Polish corridor to the Baltic Sea. Ross Anderson and Ed Ritchie were also interested. A trip around the Baltic was far too long to do by bicycle, and we were much too poor for a car – any car – so a motorcycle with a sidecar seemed the solution. We bought one – a single cylinder B.S.A. – for £37. We learned a few facts of life when we sought insurance. Our being students added 25 per cent to the premium. None of us had experience driving a motorcycle and we wanted continental coverage with multiple drivers. The only thing we could change, if we were to go at all, was the number of drivers: each one covered increased the price. So it was decided: I would be the driver, since my Saskatchewan licence included motorcycles even though I had never driven one.

None of us gave any thought to the factor Winston Churchill spoke about later that summer when he objected to a two-month adjournment of the House of Commons. He referred to August and September as 'the danger months in Europe, when the harvests have been gathered, and when the powers of evil are at their strongest.'[1] We added a pillion seat over the rear wheel for Ed Ritchie. Ross, the smallest, fitted in the sidecar with luggage packed all around him. We left Oxford on 2 July with no fixed schedule but the probability of six weeks or more travelling, part by sea but most by road.

Our plan was to go from Harwich to Esbjerg in Denmark by boat, then across the straits to Sweden and on to Norway. We would arrive in Stockholm for our one fixed engagement: to help celebrate the wedding of Fred McLean, the Saskatchewan Rhodes Scholar for 1935, to Kathe Ollert, a Swedish girl, on 16 July. The visit to Norway was for me one of the objects of the trip: the chance to visit the 'roots' of my mother's family. Sadly, it was the only part of the trip that had to be cancelled: my unskilful driving in Denmark ended in a crash from which we emerged with, miraculously, no injuries apart from a few bruises. The damage to the motorcycle was substantial. I was never entirely able to persuade Ed and Ross that it was pure luck that the accident occurred at Vedbaek, a resort town north of Copenhagen, and the home of the only girl I knew in Denmark, Beulah Nielsen. I had visited her there two days before; we were just a half a mile from her house.

Beulah's father, Olaf Nielsen, took everything in hand. A garage picked up the machine and assessed the damage while we settled our nerves with whisky and cigars on the Nielsens' back porch. They insisted on buying our tickets (return) back to Copenhagen, where Mrs Nielsen had telephoned to get rooms for us. Mr Nielsen would phone us when the motorcycle was repaired. Three days later we were invited to the Nielsens' for lunch and then taken to the garage. Mr Nielsen, a banker, pointed out the unwisdom of our paying the substantial repair bill so early in our trip: we might be in trouble later if we did. He would send us the bill in Oxford. Six weeks later, after visiting twelve countries, we ended up in Oxford with ten pence among us. We added Nielsen's sound financial advice to the long list of reasons for our gratitude. Not long before war broke out on 3 September, I received a letter from Beulah Nielsen conveying a request from her father not to pay him for the repairs in Denmark because he wanted it to be a gift to us! So ended that warm display of Danish hospitality.

We found Sweden remarkably like parts of Canada, but nothing had prepared us for the charm and beauty of Stockholm. We were, however, prepared for Swedish formality: we had been told that the dress for the official party in Fred's wedding would be white tie and tails and white gloves! Getting into those on a hot July afternoon in the YMCA dormitory caused a sensation – but rather less than when we boarded a tram to head for our destination. We could not afford a taxi and it seemed unwise to ride a motorcycle with tails flapping against the motor and the rear wheel. The groom was handsome, the bride was beautiful, the toasts at the dinner were unending, and custom required the schnapps to be completely drained each time. Dancing followed until a sumptuous buffet supper at two o'clock in the morning – at which time, at that latitude, it was quite light.

The trip by ship out of Stockholm harbour on a fine summer evening must be the most beautiful exit from any city on earth. As we left, three days after the wedding, the ship glided through calm water, past rocky spruce-covered islands, then out into the Gulf of Bothnia and across to the Aaland Islands, which we reached at about midnight. A large party in the twilight sang a farewell to a girl leaving for Finland. By that time the dawn was breaking and there seemed no point in going to bed.

Finland was even more like Canada than Sweden and the roads were so bad I might well have been back in Saskatchewan. Little did I know that there was worse to come in Estonia. The cobbled streets of Talinn threatened to shake both the machine and us to pieces. We hoped for bad gravel roads like those in Finland when we got out of the city: nothing could be worse than the cobbles. But worse it was. The road was made of large stones so rough and uneven that it was all I could do to keep hold of the handlebars. The rattling and banging were so great, and the holding on so desperate, that neither Ross nor I noticed, some miles out of Talinn, that Ed Ritchie was no longer with us. Wild gesticulation by some peasants making hay led me to stop. Ed was a dim figure several hundred yards back, running desperately on the rough stones. We slept that night in a hay field sheltered by new hay put to dry on sloping wooden racks: unthatched roofs. We washed next morning by a swim in the sea and were delighted to find the roads in Latvia much better.

Riga had many attractions – parks with an outdoor symphony concert every summer evening, beautiful beaches not far away and, not least, a B.S.A. motorcycle dealer. By that time a great many things required attention. Only when they were done did we learn that it was all a gift. 'English' people were so rare, and Britain so important a friend to those lonely Latvians, that we were the beneficiaries of their hopes and fears.

The roads in Lithuania were almost as bad as in Estonia, so much so that we broke a bar holding the sidecar onto its supporting spring. On 28 July we crossed into East Prussia, then a detached part of Germany, cut off from the rest by the Polish corridor. Even the ordinary German roads were beautifully paved; the 'autobahns' or trunk highways were superb, of concrete, built for heavy vehicles of the kind an army needs. Most of the traffic we met or passed was military – truckloads of troops, guns, motorcycles. It was not commerce or industry the autobahns were for: they were military roads, with location dictated by the tactics of expected war. Troops could be moved with great speed in case of need and clearly the armament was enormous.

From East Prussia we crossed the Nogat River into the 'Free City of Danzig' and into a seething cauldron of hatreds. The Vistula River also flows into the Baltic at Danzig. Some bridges were under Polish control, others were under Danzig control, but in the latter cases the uniforms on the customs officers were identical with German uniforms. Anti-tank barriers at the access to the bridges were formidable.

We had planned to stay at the German students' house at the University of Danzig but, when we got there, we found it had been taken over by the Nazi Party, with storm troopers, black shirts, soldiers everywhere. Presumably they were – or purported to be – residents and citizens of the Free City, which was supposed to be demilitarized and neutral. We ended up staying at the Polish students' house.

The friendship of the Polish students spoke eloquently of their isolation and loneliness. Nazis dominated the city administration, the Gestapo (the German secret police) appeared to have free rein, and the animosities were intense and freely expressed on the streets and in the stores. The hospitality the Polish students extended to the three ambassadors of 'England,' on which all their hopes rested, was without limit. It went on after dinner each night with toasts, speeches, and celebration far longer and later than any other circumstances would excuse.

The young Poles we met had a remarkable and totally unjustified confidence in the capacity of Poland to meet a German attack. They did not expect any direct help from England and France so it was not at all clear how they thought the dreadful Nazi power could be resisted. They lived in Danzig under constant bullying, permitted or aided by the administration in defiance of international guarantees of neutrality. Most of the Polish students had left the university before the end of the last term under threat of violence and warnings that they could not pass their examinations in any case. I suspect that the few who stayed had been recruited by the Polish government specifically to preserve a Polish presence at the university and to provide information. In any event, the Polish students' house refused payment for our stay. We never, afterward, heard what was the fate of the courageous young men we met and grew to like.

Magdeburg in Germany, a hundred miles beyond Berlin, provided an interesting contrast. A German air-force officer approached us as we were talking after dinner in our hotel and asked, in good English, if he could talk with us. He was direct: 'Why does England not want Germany to have Danzig?' It had been wrongfully taken from Germany after the war and must be returned. Germany would take it – not this year, but in 1940 when the strain of armament and mobilization had become too great for Poland. There would be no war, because the Poles would be unable to resist and England would not help them. His belief in Adolf Hitler and the justice of the German cause was total. Germany had moved into Czechoslovakia because the Czechs had called Germany in to restore order: 'The Leader has said it, and it is so.' The Leader had not promised at Munich that the Sudeten areas of Czechoslovakia were 'his last territorial demand in Europe,' as we alleged. He had promised to consult England whenever England was interested but 'in the rest of Europe it was none of England's business.'

It should not have been the jolt it was to encounter so total an acceptance by an educated and intelligent man of the position portrayed in the controlled press and Nazi propaganda. The officer believed it completely. He was equally convinced of the malice and provocation of the countries – especially England – that were trying to block the just demands of Germany.

Perhaps it was a new realization of how serious things were becoming that caused us to travel the longest day of our trip – 240 miles from Magdeburg to Enschede in Holland. The autobahns made it easy and the attraction of getting out of Germany and into Holland was great. The frontier barricades, tank traps, and fortified bridges made it clear that the Dutch were not putting much trust in German respect for their neutrality. When we reached the Dutch-Belgian frontier four days later it was quite different: no barricades, no tank traps, no fortifications around bridges. The basis of planning appeared to be that what happened to one would happen to both – as turned out to be the case when Germany attacked six months later.

Our crossing from Ostende to Dover was mercifully calm. We got to England about 9:15 at night. Since we had enough money to have dinner in Dover, or to pass a night in a hotel, but not for both, we ate and drove through a cold night and arrived in Oxford at 4:00 in the morning. The coffee stall at the railway station opened at 5:30: never was coffee and a warm room more needed. The 'wind-chill' of the speeding motorcycle, cutting through our inadequate clothes, had left us stiff with cold. It was 14 August and we had driven 2,855 miles in thirteen countries, counting Danzig.

Scotland and War

Both Ed Ritchie and I had 'roots' in Scotland and a return to Canada without having been there would be unthinkable. Using the motorcycle while opportunity offered seemed the only solution, so on 21 August we set out, with the same three of us in the same places. My diary of the trip is eloquent about the beauties of the Lake District and the Highlands, but the real goal was ancestors. We did not do very well: deaths and departures left places that were important in our family histories but few people.

My paternal ancestors, before leaving Scotland, had lived on a farm in Kilmorack, not far from Beauly about twelve miles west of Inverness, often called the capital of the Highlands. The closest I came to a possible ancestor was an eighteenth-century gravestone: 'In memory of Isabel Robertson, only lawful child of Duncan Robertson.' The statement sounds . proud and not at all critical of Duncan. It seems rather to be directed at a person or persons now long forgotten who had been parading a spurious legitimacy that Isabel resented.

I did learn that the estates of Lord Lovat had been forfeited to the crown because Lovat had taken the wrong side, that of Bonnie Prince Charlie, in 1745. Things moved slowly in those days, and it was in 1777 that my ancestor's brother William had had to get a new lease from the crown for the land he farmed. It is possible that John, my triple-great grandfather, did not succeed in renewing his own lease. If so, that would explain emigration to Nova Scotia in 1784, by a man of fifty-nine and his entire family. Action against Jacobites or suspected Jacobites in the years after the 1745 rising was purposefully harsh and prolonged.

We managed to visit the battle field of Culloden where the Highlanders were crushed by the superior royalist forces. A cairn stands in memory of 'the gallant Highlanders who fell fighting for Scotland and Prince Charles.' Our spirits were restored later that day going through the pass of Killiecrankie. There in 1689 the Scots under Viscount Dundee had equally decisively defeated the English. Such were the glories and the tragedies on which I had been brought up, always with a romantic Scottish bias.

Edinburgh was the only city we saw to rival Stockholm in beauty. The castle by night is worth a long trip, as is the cathedral in Durham. We were in Durham on 1 September when we learned that German troops had attacked across the Polish frontiers we had left only a month before.

As we approached Leicester in the near darkness that night we were stopped by the police. We could proceed only if we covered our one inadequate light, or put it out altogether. We taped on several thicknesses of paper, put the light on dim, and were allowed to grope along as best we could. All was black: our first taste of a blackout. It was a slow trip to fumble our way through a strange, darkened city to the youth hostel on the other side of town.

We got to Oxford the next day and on 3 September heard Prime Minister Chamberlain announce on the radio that Great Britain was at war with Germany.

Finishing at Oxford
Dr Johnson said that 'when a man knows he is to be hanged in a fortnight, it concentrates his mind wonderfully.' I had done little think-

ing as we went around Europe about my course of action if war broke out. Now the question could not be avoided. After some uncertainty, it was decided that Oxford would carry on for one more academic year so people could complete their degrees. I had no confidence in the Chamberlain government and believed that it and the Daladier government in France through their blunders had got the world into war, in large part because they hoped Hitler, if given enough concessions by 'the West,' could be led to make war on Soviet Russia and destroy the communism they so feared. If I were to become a soldier, it would be in the Canadian forces, not the British. So I decided to complete my degree, then return to Canada.

In the course of the autumn I saw an advertisement at Rhodes House that the Canadian Department of External Affairs was holding a competition for the starting level in its diplomatic ranks – at that time third secretary. I decided I might as well apply, as did a good many hundred other young Canadian males: the competition, in accordance with the gender roles of that day, was for men only. After some months I was advised I had survived the first screening of basic qualifications. I was summoned to the Canadian High Commission at Canada House in London for written examinations: two papers, three hours each, on 9 January 1940. The next step, an oral examination, had a distinguished trio of examiners: the Canadian high commissioner in London, Vincent Massey, a future ambassador to the United States, Hume Wrong, and, the most junior of the three, Lester B. Pearson. I learned many years later that, while the recommendation of that trinity was favourable for me, Massey had, in forwarding their report to Ottawa, expressed the view that 'while Robertson had been at Oxford, it had not taken.' Whether that failure to 'take' was disclosed by my Saskatchewan accent, coarseness of manners, or some inadequacy in witty, Oxford-style repartee, I never discovered.

The winter of 1939–40 at Oxford was the coldest since 1929. The good part was the skating on the Cherwell and on Christ Church meadow. The bad part was the water trickling down my bedroom walls (there was no heat there) and the ice on the water jug for washing in the morning. There was no running water – apart from the walls. The best way to get both clean and warm was a bath, but that required a trip across two quadrangles to the basement of a sixteenth-century building, with the snow whisking up under the bathrobe as one walked.

The winter and the early spring of 1940 were the 'phoney war' when little happened in western Europe or Britain. The blackout was complete, and I spent one or two nights per week as an air-raid warden, but Oxford had only one real warning and no actual raid. With 'Schools' – the examinations – looming in June, the university took on a more serious hue than the usual casual Oxford style.

The Oxford examination system was a high-risk, high-pressure operation. In the normal case the work of three years – in our case the work of two but the content of three – and success or failure for a degree hinged entirely on nine examinations of three hours each, written in five days. The only concession to nerves and fatigue was that the five days were usually balanced around a Sunday with three before and two after, or the reverse. Papers were graded in the Greek alphabet – alpha, beta, gamma, with pluses or minuses. Normally an oral examination was added on to the papers. In 1940, because of the pressures to clean things up as fast as possible, orals were held in cases mainly of uncertainty about the level for a candidate. The total result for each person came out in a 'First,' 'Second,' 'Third,' – or Failed.

On 8 April the phoney war ended with the attack on Norway and Denmark. Both countries were quickly overrun and on 10 May the full force of German power was turned on Holland, Belgium, and France. By that same night Chamberlain was out as prime minister of Great Britain and Churchill took over. The German blitzkrieg crashed through the allied forces and by 3 June the British army was evacuated from Dunkirk – alive, but weaponless. On 16 June the Pétain government took office in France and sought an armistice with Hitler. On 18 June Mr Churchill warned that 'the battle of Britain is about to begin.' It was in these circumstances that 'Schools' began on Thursday, 6 June: two papers a day for three days; Sunday to prepare for the next attack; two papers on Monday and one on Tuesday morning.

I confided to my diary on Sunday that I had no hope of a First: 'Far too much to remember – I just can't hold onto it all.' I gave myself two alphas and four betas on the six papers that far. On Tuesday, after the next three papers, I gave myself one alpha and two betas. A good solid Second. No disgrace but no distinction.

On 17 June the French army ceased fighting. In five weeks the Maginot Line had been turned or broken through and what had been thought to be the finest army in the world was smashed. Hitler had been three days out in his schedule: he had called for France to be crushed by 14 June.

On 27 June we sold our motorcycle for £12: it was a buyer's market! On 28 June the Schools results were posted. I was so confident of a Second that I started searching in that list and my heart sank: my name was not there. It was Ross Anderson who had enough hope to look higher up the list and there we were: not only Firsts, but the only Firsts in the entire jurisprudence 'school.' Cheshire was told by the chairman of the examiners that Ross and I had got virtually identical marks. He was also told that our exclusive hold on the First Class might not last. Two other candidates, Neuman and Falck, were to be 'vivaed' for possible Firsts: they were both Germans and were then in British internment camps. They had been allowed to stay out of internment until their Schools were over. However, Ross and I got our Firsts with no vivas – and we never did find out what happened to Neuman and Falck.

RMS *Antonia*

On 8 July a half-dozen Canadian Rhodes Scholars joined about a hundred and fifty children and some mothers from London who were being sent to Canada for the duration of the war. The air raids were making life in London a horror and it was certain to get worse. We boarded the RMS *Antonia* and in the evening of 10 July we moved down the Mersey to its mouth and anchored overnight. On 11 July we moved out with a destroyer escort. That evening two heavy bumps against the hull were not explained. The best uninformed guess was that a mine had broken loose and, happily, failed to explode. On 12 July, well north of Ireland and out into the Atlantic, our destroyer escort turned back: we were on our own. A speed of fifteen knots and a far northerly course were to be our protection against the U-boats.

Most of the children – and most of us – were seasick for the first couple of days. The children were remarkably good and those whose mothers were not there (the large majority) were brave, although courage failed at times. We were more use for diverting, amusing, and comforting than in any nursing or mothering role; the eight or ten mothers did that. Birds, icebergs, games, and sing-songs helped get the children through. On 19 July we docked at Quebec. The journey to Montreal was overnight in colonist cars – the kind I had gotten to know two years before. Canada must have seemed very primitive to our English guests.

The *Antonia* was torpedoed and sunk on a later trip – as was the *Empress of Britain* on which we had gone to Britain two years before.

From Toronto to Ottawa

While in Regina during the summer I had a medical examination. My eyesight did not meet the standards in place at that early stage in the war so I reverted to my pre-war intention of going to the University of

Toronto to work for an MA under MacGregor Dawson. He had moved there from the University of Saskatchewan. My father delivered the opinion that I might as well be playing golf: an MA was a waste of time. That was all I needed to decide that I would somehow handle everything on my own skimpy resources. I had a small scholarship and would be paid $350 for the academic year, to be assistant to the editor of the *Canadian Journal of Economics and Political Science*. I found that, with ingenuity, lunch could be had for fifteen cents a day. An old Saskatchewan friend, Rusty Macdonald, and I shared a room and a double bed in a boarding house.

At the university I joined the Canadian Officers Training Corps (COTC) in the artillery unit. Connie Smythe, the owner of the Toronto Maple Leafs and of much else besides, was my commanding officer.

In passing through Ottawa en route home in July 1940 I had had interviews with all the top people in External Affairs: the under-secretary, O.D. Skelton, the assistant under-secretary, Laurent Beaudry, the legal adviser, J.E. Read, Norman Robertson, and Hugh Keenleyside. In October I was advised that I had made the eligible list in the third-secretary competition – number twelve out of fifteen. Six had already been appointed and more would be called in shortly.

My two options for future action came together a few weeks after the COTC field training at Niagara-on-the-Lake in May 1941. I received a telephone call from Ottawa: I was to report for a position in the Legal Division by the end of June. A few days later came a call from Connie Smythe who was prepared to recommend me for a commission in the artillery – bad eyes and all. If the sequence had been the reverse my next few years would have been different.

Funds were running low. I decided to send my trunk and a large suitcase to Ottawa by express and to hitch-hike with the other small one. It was not then the easiest way to travel: gasoline was rationed and cars on the road were few. However, it had for me the greatest of virtues: it was cheap. My last ride was on a Coca-Cola truck from which I descended at the corner of Somerset and Preston streets in Ottawa. A streetcar got me to the centre of the city and a room in the YMCA. I turned up in the East Block the following morning to report to the Department of External Affairs.

PART TWO

External Affairs and
Mackenzie King,
1941–1948

chapter three

The Department of External Affairs, 1941–1945

The East Block, built before Confederation when Queen Victoria settled on the 'lumber village' that had been Bytown to become the capital of Canada, had no difficulty containing the whole Department of External Affairs – and also the Prime Minister's Office, the Privy Council Office, the Cabinet Chamber, and the Department of Finance. Government was small and departments were tiny, especially External Affairs. In 1937 there were eleven officers in Ottawa. As war approached, one former officer returned to help with the increase in work, but even after the outbreak of war in 1939 and a host of new responsibilities, no new officers were added until 1940–1 when those who had succeeded in my competition came in. The support staff numbered forty-three. The total staff in Ottawa at that time was only fifty-five.

O.D. Skelton, who had become under-secretary of state for external affairs in 1925, had been determined to create a first-class foreign service. His success in doing so was his great contribution to Canada's capacity to cope with the problems of the war and plans for a better post-war world. When he died of a heart attack, undoubtedly brought on by stress and overwork, on 28 January 1941, at the age of sixty-two, Mackenzie King's problem was not to find a competent successor but to choose among four men already in the department, all of whom could have discharged the position with distinction: Hume Wrong, Lester Pearson, H.L. Keenleyside, and Norman Robertson. A bit junior to these were others whose subsequent careers reflected the same high quality, notably J.W. Pickersgill, Escott Reid, and Charles Ritchie. When, in 1945, consideration was being given at a meeting of Great Power representatives to the naming of the first secretary-general of the United Nations, Edward Stettinius, the American secretary of state, said that Lester Pearson and

Norman Robertson were at the top of the American list of five preferred candidates for the post. In the event, no North American was acceptable to the Soviet Union.[1]

The Legal Division and Marriage

It was my good fortune, because of my law degree, to join what had been the only clearly defined division in the department of that day – the Legal Division, under John Read. He had been dean of law at Dalhousie University and was appointed legal adviser in 1929. In keeping with the frugal style of the department, the division consisted of just two officers: the legal adviser and Max Wershof, who had been appointed in 1937. There was no training program in the department for new recruits and some of my colleagues in the 1940–1 crop suffered from the lack. I did not. John Read had been a professor and he took the job of teaching me very seriously. Max took everything seriously. He was meticulously accurate, a first-class lawyer, and he regarded my training as a personal responsibility. We sat face to face in an office in the attic of the East Block and Max was an endless source of information, admonition, and advice. There could not have been a better model or mentor at the outset of my career.

Canada had limited experience before 1939 of the legal issues created by war. In the First World War most of these had been handled by the British government since Canada, at that time, had no international status of its own. By 1939 many of the problems had been foreseen and planned for: declarations of war, treatment of enemy aliens in Canada, problems of protection of enemy property and of Canadian property in enemy countries, trading with enemy companies or persons, and others. However, many had not been foreseen and became highly complex.

The measure of the need and of the growing problems of 'manpower' was that the Department of External Affairs abandoned its policy of looking only to men for staffing to do officers' tasks. Recruitment began of university-educated women – but not with the status or the pay of the men doing the same job. The female recruits came in as Clerks Grade 4, with a starting salary of $1,620 and no officer status: third secretaries were officers and started at $2,280. While the circumstances of war muted criticism about the discrimination, it is a measure of the changes in attitude in the post-war period that what would be illegal now seemed not only acceptable but normal then. It did, however, cause resentment as work got heavier and it became obvious that the women carried as great a load as the men.

The Legal Division got a prize from the process in Kathleen Bingay, who led her class in law at the University of Alberta. Her qualities as a lawyer, her high intelligence, and her scorn for anything trite or pedantic made her a formidable colleague and a fascinating friend. It was a challenging and endlessly interesting two years of introduction to External Affairs and the legal problems of war to work with John Read, Max Wershof, and 'Doff' Bingay. Read's standing as an international lawyer was demonstrated by his election at the first Assembly of the United Nations in 1946 as a judge on the new International Court of Justice.

While the pace in the wartime department was intense, it did not utterly exclude personal life. The friendship with Bill Lawson that began on the *Empress of Britain* took on a new dimension when I married his twin sister, Bea, in August 1943. It was the happiest decision of my life and enriched it in many dimensions. I was absurdly unmusical, as my mother had found after pushing me through several years of sullen and unproductive piano lessons, and my appreciation of art was on the same low level. Bea had genuine talent in both fields, although I never could persuade her to have the showings of her paintings that they deserved. The violin was her other joy. She played in quartets and in other groups of talented friends. It still is a joy to her and to me in our eighth decade.

The marriage brought two children: a son, John, and a daughter, Karen, and now six grandchildren of whom at least one, Ian, displays the musical talent that did not come from my side of the family. The larger family provided not only close friendships but built-in discussion in fields of public policy of which I knew little: with Bill, who became senior deputy governor of the Bank of Canada, on economic and monetary policy; and with Douglas Fraser, who married Bea's sister Margaret and became deputy chairman of the National Energy Board, on energy policy. It was a happy, intelligent group that made for lively conversation, the more so after Bill married Katharine Macdonnell, daughter of J.M. Macdonnell, later a minister in the Diefenbaker government.

Apart from the larger joys, marriage meant that Bea and I had our housing problems solved for us when the other three in my four-man bachelor establishment, of which Bill was one, went off to the Canadian forces. I remained in External Affairs since service there was ruled to be the equivalent of service in the armed forces for purposes of National Selective Service. Our only problem was whether we could afford what we thought was the high rent of $60 a month, when wartime taxes and compulsory war loans were taken off our salaries. Bea was by then working in the Department of National Defence.

Assistant to the Under-secretary

In November 1943 I succeeded Saul Rae, another of the 1940–1 recruits who was being posted abroad, as assistant to the under-secretary, Norman Robertson. That move involved a change in responsibilities and a much more hectic working life. It was not the best accompaniment to a new marriage but it made possible one of the most stimulating experiences of my life: that of working for the man who, in the words of John Holmes, later director of the Canadian Institute of International Affairs, was 'the greatest mandarin of them all.'[2]

Under Skelton, with no formal organization in the department, everything of any consequence came to the under-secretary for approval or signature. In the summer of 1941, Norman Robertson, no organizer but urged on by Hume Wrong and Hugh Keenleyside, approved a four-part structure for the department – Diplomatic and Economic; Commonwealth and European; American and Far Eastern; Legal – in which each division was to have a clearly designated chief. That helped, but the problem of centralization remained, partly because the prime minister was our minister and King would deal with only one official: the under-secretary. Another problem was Treasury Board regulations about signing authority for actions involving even trifling amounts of money. They required ministerial signature, which brought the prime minister, and therefore the under-secretary, into the act. As Pearson said in exasperation in a memorandum to Robertson in October 1941, four months after the new organization came into effect: 'Personally, I don't see how you are going to show the prime minister how to win the war and make the peace if you have to spend two hours each day talking about the cost of Désy's table linen or the salary of the newest stenographer.'[3]

Apart from departmental problems was the fact that Norman Robertson had increasingly become what Skelton had been, the prime minister's adviser and consultant on a great many questions of war and of wartime economic policy that were far outside the responsibilities of External Affairs. Robertson was the only official other than the secretary to the cabinet, Arnold Heeney, who regularly attended meetings of the war committee of the cabinet along with the chiefs of staff of the armed forces. King turned to him for anything and everything that came up there, which covered all the major policies of running Canada's part in the war.

The final part of the problem was that NAR, as we often called him, was anything but systematic. His desk was constantly deep in papers, piles where only he and Marjory McKenzie, who had been Skelton's secretary at Queen's University, could locate – and dared try to locate – certain items that had been set aside because they raised serious problems on which he had not had time to think through fully all the implications. McKenzie was the keeper of the under-secretary's confidential papers, and the authorized or unauthorized commentator on anything she thought more than usually absurd or ill-expressed. She had both an MA and a clear, firm mind of her own. She was the only one I ever heard comment to NAR about his 'alleged memory.' His recall was almost total on virtually everything he had read, heard, or seen but every now and then some detail would slip – for him, but not for Marjory.

When I succeeded Saul in 1943 it quickly became apparent that, because NAR was so swamped with papers and problems, almost everything not of top priority was delayed. Frustrated officers of any rank under assistant under-secretary expected me to get signature or action somehow on everything before it was too late. This meant knowing what was in the 'in basket,' which overflowed, and being able to tell the under-secretary in thirty seconds, seized between meetings, what a paper involved, whether there was a problem, and what best to do. Too much caution just added to delay; too much rashness brought its risks; it called for a degree of perception that grew more sure as I came to know both the job and the under-secretary.

A hazardous area was checking the votes and proceedings and also the *Hansards* of the House of Commons for questions on which the prime minister would have to answer as secretary of state for external affairs or on which, because they involved major issues of policy, he might look to NAR for an answer. On such things, coordination with the Prime Minister's Office was critical, which meant with Jack Pickersgill.

Pickersgill, I soon learned, was a man of extraordinary capacity and versatility. He had come into the Department of External Affairs by winning a national competition in 1937 and was assigned almost immediately – and without choice by him – to the Prime Minister's Office. Assignments there were often brief for King was notoriously difficult to serve and virtually impossible to satisfy. Pickersgill was the outstanding exception. He gradually developed an unequalled ability to know how his unpredictable chief would react to almost any question that arose about any matter, political, personal, or policy. Over the years, 'Clear it with Jack' became the safest advice for anyone, politician or official, handling anything about which the prime minister might be concerned. I turned to Jack from my beginning in the under-secretary's office: he was just down the hall about fifty feet away. He was always there and invariably helpful. He became a close friend and I a great admirer.

The Problem of the Japanese

A problem of great difficulty and political sensitivity that the under-secretary considered he could not leave to be handled at a lower level arose with the attack by Japan on Pearl Harbor on 7 December 1941. There were some 22,000 ethnic Japanese living in British Columbia, many of them on the coast in the fishing industry with thousands of boats. Some were Canadian British subjects by birth or naturalization (the status of Canadian citizen did not exist); others were Japanese nationals in Canada as landed immigrants. For some time, there had been hostility towards the Japanese by people in British Columbia, partly because they were so industrious and competitive. To this hostility was then, in 1941, added a sense of fear, made the greater by what was considered to be the treachery of the Japanese attack when the United States and they were still at peace.

On 10 December came the news of the sinking in Asian waters by Japanese aircraft of the British battleships *Prince of Wales* and *Repulse* with six hundred officers and men. On 25 December Hong Kong surrendered to the Japanese, with its British and Canadian garrison. The sense in British Columbia was of Japanese naval domination of the Pacific, of being totally unprotected, and of great concern about possible Japanese agents and sympathizers on the Canadian coast. Such worries seemed credible since Nazi Germany had found agents and sympathizers among the Sudeten Germans in Czechoslovakia and among the Quisling supporters in Norway.

The apprehension in British Columbia was strongly pressed on the government by Members of Parliament from the province, with vigorous support from Hon. Ian Mackenzie, the British Columbia minister. They argued for confiscation of Japanese property, forced relocation away from the coast, and no distinction in treatment between British subjects of Japanese origin, whether naturalized or native-born, and citizens of Japan. On 8–9 January 1942 federal representatives met with representatives of the government of British Columbia and provincial organizations. The federal group argued for a moderate policy that would have permitted enlistment of Japanese Canadians in the armed forces and no removal of Japanese nationals or Japanese British subjects from the coast except where there was specific cause to believe that an individual's loyalty was doubtful. The British Columbia representatives rejected the proposals. They were united in pressing for complete evacuation from the coast and confiscation of property. On 24 February 1942 the government largely accepted the British Columbia arguments. All Japanese, whether British subjects or not, were to be removed from the coast. The policy that had been adopted in the United States was less sweeping in terms of the area from which Japanese persons were removed but just as inclusive of all categories of Japanese, whether American or not.

With the policy settled for the duration of the war, it was clear that the next issue, which might be equally difficult, would be what was to happen to the Japanese after the war. Robertson thought that it would be best to defer any consideration by the government until public emotions could subside.[4]

I had not been involved in any part of the argument about wartime policy but I had to learn as much of it as I could when, in August 1943, while still in the Legal Division, I was directed to prepare a memorandum to the prime minister on policy for the post-war period. The undersecretary was well aware of the injustices that had been caused by the wartime measures and he was determined to get as fair and reasonable a post-war policy as possible. It had, however, to be acceptable to the government and to the Canadian public. A Gallup Poll in early 1944 indicated that 83 per cent of the people interviewed were in favour of deporting all Japanese nationals after the war. Only 59 per cent were in favour of allowing even Japanese Canadians to remain in Canada. Robertson hoped that, if the hard core of disloyal persons could be segregated and deported after the war, it might be possible to permit the remainder to stay in Canada and, if they wished, to return to British Columbia. A commission would be appointed to review the cases of the Japanese whose loyalty was doubtful.

The post-war policy memorandum I prepared under NAR's direction in March 1944 was based on those principles of differentiation and adjudication and on his hope that, at that stage, when victory was in sight and emotions had cooled, a moderate policy might prevail. The memorandum, after consideration by an interdepartmental committee and then by the war committee of the cabinet, was finally approved. The policy was announced in the House of Commons on 4 August 1944, by the prime minister.

Approval of the post-war arrangement had been by no means certain. The cruel treatment of Canadian prisoners of war in Japanese hands in Hong Kong during four years of war had created animosities that did not die easily; there were still strong passions in many places – including the breast of Ian Mackenzie. My colleague, 'Doff' Bingay, and I had such a sense of relief and triumph when King finally read the announcement we had prepared that it took some effort not to cheer – and probably be ejected from the gallery of the House of Commons by the protective staff.

Out of an ethnic Japanese population of some 23,500 by 1945, about 3,900 went to Japan. Some were Japanese nationals who went voluntarily along with their families, others were deportees, again along with their families. The property loss and financial injury to a great many of the Japanese who remained in Canada had been great. Compensation was dreadfully slow in coming and was only a fraction of the value of the losses, partly because it was for years difficult for many Canadians to separate the injustice to many ethnic Japanese in Canada from their anger about the treatment of Canadian prisoners in Hong Kong.

Norman Robertson has, in my judgment, been unfairly criticized for his role in our wartime Japanese policy. He abhorred the racism that underlay the near panic in British Columbia. However, he would have lost credibility as the prime minister's adviser in this critical area and would have increased the risk of even more drastic policies if he had pressed the prime minister to adopt positions that would not have been acceptable when emotions were as strong as they were after the Japanese aggression at Pearl Harbor and in Southeast Asia and particularly after the fall of Hong Kong. King and the government faced a national crisis over manpower policy leading to the highly divisive referendum on conscription in 1942. That problem grew in intensity and nearly destroyed the government in the final conscription crisis of 1944. It is unrealistic to believe that the prime minister could have accepted a policy that would have provoked another crisis on top of those national problems at a critical stage in the war. While wartime Japanese policy in the United States was somewhat more generous than in Canada, there too President Roosevelt, as late as June 1944, felt that he had to exercise great care about 'ending the orders excluding Japanese-Americans from the West Coast.'[5]

Hugh Keenleyside, like Robertson a British Columbian, records in his memoirs his surprise at learning after King's death that the prime minister's displeasure at his advice during the 1942 crisis – that relocation of the Japanese away from the coast as a wartime measure was both unnecessary and unjust – might have been a factor in his 'promotion' to be ambassador to Mexico. On 7 February 1942 King had been, as he says in his diary, 'revising a statement of policy regarding Japanese in B.C., something prepared by Keenleyside.' He recorded: 'I do not think much of his judgment and have been disappointed in his abilities.'[6]

It was not unusual to suffer King's displeasure: virtually everyone who worked with him fell into disgrace from time to time. However, an adviser on matters as politically explosive as was the problem of the Japanese in 1942 could not properly indulge the luxury of pressing a harassed prime minister to adopt a policy that he considered unwise and unacceptable. Norman Robertson understood that; Hugh Keenleyside apparently did not. That difference in sensitivity, which King would sense, is undoubtedly one reason why he chose NAR to be undersecretary in 1941. Policy advice, like politics, is the art of the possible in a democracy.

The San Francisco Conference
With the successful landing in Normandy in June 1944, and the progress of United States, British, and Canadian forces in France and the Low Countries, post-war planning took on a new urgency. During that summer representatives of the four great powers (the United States, the United Kingdom, the Soviet Union, and China) met at Dumbarton Oaks in Washington to draft a proposed United Nations charter for an organization to replace the League of Nations and, it was hoped, preserve peace in the world after the war. The founding conference was planned for San Francisco in the spring of 1945.

The importance the Canadian government attached to the conference was reflected in the delegation, much the largest and most prestigious Canada had sent to any conference. The prime minister was to head it with St Laurent as his deputy. The rest of the accredited representatives were parliamentarians: the government leader in the Senate, Senator J.H. King, and a Conservative, Senator Lucien Noraud; Gordon Graydon, acting as leader of the opposition in the House of Commons for John Bracken, who had not yet been elected to Parliament; M.J. Coldwell, the leader of the Co-operative Commonwealth Federation (CCF); and Cora Casselman, Liberal MP for Edmonton East. The advisers were equally impressive: thirteen in all, including Norman Robertson, Hume Wrong, and Lester Pearson.

Preparations for the conference, to open on 25 April, received a shock on 12 April with the death of President Roosevelt. From the time the United States came into the war on 7 December 1941, Roosevelt, Churchill, and Stalin had been the great leaders on the allied side. Although the end of the war was in sight, Roosevelt's leadership was thought essential to ensure United States participation in the post-war world. Memories of the American failure to accept the League of Nations after the First World War, when President Wilson's illness took him out of action, became haunting fears. With Roosevelt's death, could that happen to the United Nations? Vice-President Harry Truman was an untried and virtually unknown figure outside the United States.

I had been told in February that I was to be secretary of the Canadian delegation. I was to be responsible for all staff and administrative arrangements to ensure the smooth working of the delegation. I took the responsibility seriously and worked out all the requirements for staff, accommodation, offices, equipment, and supplies down to the last typewriter and paper clip. An office for conference planning and preparation had been set up in Washington with Alger Hiss, the conference's secretary general, in charge. All countries attending the conference were advised where and how to register their requirements. Escott Reid, then at the embassy in Washington, told me when he had sent in our requirements that Canada was the first country to complete this administrative task.

I decided to arrive in San Francisco two days ahead of the rest of the delegation to be sure that everything was in order. Davidson Dunton, then head of the Wartime Information Board, decided to do the same to check on the press and media arrangements. We went out together by train: there was no civilian air travel at that stage of the war. My only mistake was in not going out a week ahead.

As soon as I registered at the St Francis Hotel, where our delegation had been allotted space, I went around with the assistant manager, he with his list and I with mine, to check it all. The prime minister's suite and those of the accredited delegates were excellent, as were all the rooms for the rest of the delegation. I then asked to see the offices. Offices? None had been asked for!

It was one of the worst moments of my life. In two days the delegation, headed by an ever-critical prime minister, would be there. It was my first really big independent assignment for the department – and the absolutely vital offices did not exist, nor did any of the equipment and supplies I had ordered. I was aghast.

Whatever may have been Alger Hiss's guilt or innocence in the later charges that he was a Soviet agent, he could not have taken hold of the problem better when I got to see him an hour or so afterwards. I had a copy of the list we had submitted of our administrative requirements and Hiss made no effort to suggest that the lapse had not been somewhere in his large secretariat as it wrestled with its gigantic problems, made worse by wartime stringencies. There was no unallocated hotel space anywhere in San Francisco, and I never learned what unfortunate people were removed from twenty-some rooms in the less elegant Flanagan Hotel across the street, but we moved enough staff there to free up the necessary rooms for offices in the St Francis. Equipment and supplies were found – not all we had asked for, but enough to operate. By the time I met the delegation at the station in Oakland, most of the damage had been repaired. I aged a year or two in those forty-eight hours.

The prime minister stayed at the conference until 14 May, when he went back to Canada to campaign in the general election coming on 11 June. In the less than three weeks that he was at the conference, King's mind was only marginally on it. The election was too close and too precarious. At the first of our daily delegation meetings it was no surprise to be told that Canada would keep a low profile. Obviously, nothing was wanted that might become a matter of controversy or dispute back home. However, with the host of committees on different aspects of the conference from morning to late at night, there was more than enough to do within the prime minister's injunction.

King returned to San Francisco on 23 June, the Liberal Party having won the election with a reduced majority. However, the prime minister had lost his own seat in Prince Albert, Saskatchewan. He had obtained a small majority among the voters living in the constituency, but he had lost the vote of the men and women in the armed forces by a larger amount, not to the Progressive Conservatives as he had expected but to the CCF.

The Canadian delegation at San Francisco was one of the most effective at the conference, largely owing to the planning and preparation on policy issues and also to the exhausting effort of our senior advisers. It was a strenuous two months but there is no doubt that the Canadian representatives made a significant contribution to the shape of the new international organization.

A Prime Minister Has Priority
It had been widely expected in Canada that the Liberals would lose the 1945 election. They had been in power for ten years and bore all the scars of the war, the greatest of which had been the manpower policy and conscription crisis of 1944. King was personally intensely unpopular with the armed forces and had been loudly booed on one official visit to an army unit in Britain. Perhaps he himself expected to lose, for, before the election, he appointed two of the three senior members of his staff to governor-in-council positions in the public service. Only Jack Pickersgill among the most senior, and James Gibson, both External Affairs officers

on assignment, remained by 11 June. Clearly some reinforcement was needed.

Jack took the matter up with King soon after the prime minister's return to San Francisco on 23 June and told me the result: King wished me to move to his office. My great liking and admiration for Jack Pickersgill were the only redeeming features in an otherwise obnoxious prospect. I wanted nothing less than to leave External Affairs, although I would be on loan and would remain on its officer list. The thought of leaving Norman Robertson after less than two years was a great sorrow: my admiration for him had grown with every day of association. And to add to it all, I had been in the East Block long enough to learn what a difficult boss King was.

It was a Sunday morning when I was advised that the prime minister wished to see me. He left no doubt that he was not putting a choice before me. He launched immediately into an eloquent exposition of the burdens that he, as head of government, had to bear, of the load that he would now have to resume at his advanced age because of the confidence the people of Canada had in him as reflected in the election, and of the privilege that was to be mine now that he had chosen me to help him carry a small part of that great task. I am not sure that my response conveyed fully the heartfelt gratitude that King undoubtedly thought appropriate. I am not a good actor. However, there was no doubt where I would work when I got back to Ottawa. The conference ended the next day.

chapter four

Working for Mackenzie King, 1945–1948

The Prime Minister's Office of fifty years ago was tiny. In August 1945, when I became a member, Jack Pickersgill was not only the head of the office but one of only two officers left in the East Block. Two others were at Laurier House: Edouard Handy and James A. Gibson. The two officers who had been technically senior to Jack, but much subordinate in importance and in influence with King, had been appointed to positions in the public service: Walter Turnbull, the principal secretary, to be deputy postmaster general, and H.R.L. Henry, King's private secretary, to be registrar of the Exchequer Court. Jack's title, at his insistence, was not to be principal secretary but special assistant to the prime minister. He was there to advise on domestic problems, to draft speeches, not to arrange appointments with the prime minister and do administrative tasks. The only other thing entirely clear was that he had complete authority for the office: it was for him to decide how it was to be organized and manned – subject to the approval of the prime minister.

My own role, when I came in, had little more definition. My title was secretary of the Prime Minister's Office: a new style that conveyed nothing and could mean anything. I was to be second in command, to handle anything that Jack wanted me to take on, and to act for him whenever he was away.

The structure met no standards of clarity or precision but proved thoroughly satisfactory. For King, the essential thing was that Pickersgill should be available for whatever was of highest priority in his eyes at any particular time. With a session of Parliament approaching, this would be the speech from the throne, consultations with ministers, and helping the mover and the seconder of the motion in reply to the speech from the throne with their addresses in the House of Commons. During the session, it would be close attendance on the debates in the House of Commons, questions on the order paper, and replies for the prime minister – or sometimes other ministers – to give. At any time of the year it could be any matter of policy, or any question that King chose, in response to his intuition or for more specific reasons, to regard as important. And all the time my job was to ensure that the office dealt with correspondence, prepared material for the prime minister, and adjusted to the prime ministerial demands of the moment. Flexibility, versatility, energy, and a capacity to interpret – and to anticipate – King's often obscure and Byzantine reactions were the essential qualifications. Jack had them to a degree not approached by anyone else.

In all his years as prime minister, King, the most difficult of men to satisfy, probably had no one who came as close as Jack to the perfection that he thought was the least he, as prime minister, had a right to expect. As Jack said: 'Mackenzie King never admitted he was adequately served, but he no longer searched for a superman to head the office. Once or twice he even expressed satisfaction with my work, though complaints were more frequent. I was anxious to give him no legitimate ground for dissatisfaction, no easy feat. There was no way to get firm direction from Mackenzie King or to be sure he would not change direction unpredictably at any moment.'[1]

Far from being bothered by the undefined and constantly changing nature of my job – to fall in with whatever Jack did not have time to do – I enjoyed it immensely. It provided a totally new range of activities and an association with one of the most stimulating, engaging, and warm-hearted people I have known. King was a constant problem: Jack never was. We worked together for three and a half years with no moment of strain or misunderstanding. Our friendship, and that of our two families, was the greatest of the rewards for King's change of my career in 1945.

Gideon Matte, who had managed King's election campaign in Prince Albert, Saskatchewan, joined the office in the autumn of 1945 as private secretary and receptionist. He was not, I think, happy in the job. The other 'officer' was Evelyn Horne who, like Doff Bingay and other women in External Affairs, suffered the discrimination of the day. She was in charge of correspondence and did the job well. All she needed to be an 'officer' was a gender change. The PMO was soon strengthened by the addition of Ross Martin and Michel Gauvin, both back from active service during the war. Ross, like Jack, became a close friend. He later ran afoul of the prime minister for a mix-up about not being at the station for King's departure for Europe – something anyone less engrossed with his own ego than King would at least have enquired about before condemning. But King had no doubts: Martin was to be fired. Jack Pickersgill has described[2] how he made it clear to the prime minister, if he pushed the case, it would be Pickersgill who would go. King let it drop, but Ross never returned to favour. By this time his disgrace was probably even deeper: he had been the cause of King appearing to be unjust – an idea impossible for King to accept.

King had his seventieth birthday in November 1944. The war, with its crises, had worn down even his enormous energy and the election in June 1945 was exhausting for a man of his age. Added to it was the humiliation of personal defeat in Prince Albert and the need to find a new constituency. That was arranged and on 6 August 1945 King easily won a by-election in Glengarry, Ontario. On 6 September the new Parliament opened. The prime minister was clearly tired. He spent as much time as he could at Laurier House, where there were offices and King's study on the third floor. James Gibson, Ed Handy, and a loyal, long-suffering staff bore the greatest burden of satisfying a weary man.

Getting to Know the Prime Minister

The routine of the office was to have an officer on duty every day, including the weekend, until 11:00 at night. It was King's custom to listen to the CBC news on the radio (there was no television for another ten years) and then to call the office before retiring. On my first night on duty, in my first week in the office, it was no surprise to have the phone ring shortly after 10:00. King was to be involved the following day in some minor ceremonial of which I was aware and where there appeared to be no conceivable problem. But King raised the question whether, when X happened, Y would follow: an issue about which there was, I thought, no possible doubt. I began to explain my clear understanding of the arrangements with an unfortunate choice of words: 'Well I assume, Mr King, ...' I got no farther. 'Robertson, as long as you are in this office you will *never* "assume" *anything*.' I was soon to know that that was almost literally true. The sequence of Tuesday, 20 August, *might* be 'assumed' to follow after Monday, 19 August, but that was about the limit. The related aphorism, issued many times before Murphy discovered his law, was 'Robertson, you *can't* be too careful.' There was no excuse for anything whatever going wrong even if an undesirable result was produced by the most improbable circumstance and every reasonable precaution had been taken. Perfection was a bare pass in working for King, but only he knew from day to day what it was, especially for any course of action involving him personally, or for a reply to a letter from someone who might have some remote background of which we were dimly aware without being sure how much favour or suspicion would be attached to whatever his letter said. The prime minister's revisions, written with a blunt stub of a pencil (he hated sharp pencils), could go around all the margins of our proposed reply. Miss Zavitske, a veteran in the staff at Laurier House, was often our interpreter as to what some squiggle or blur was meant to say – and even she could get it wrong at times.

Miss Zavitske was such an institution that I never, while I worked for King, got to know her first name – Lucy. She was simply an unseen presence, high on the third floor of Laurier House, which had been left to King in Lady Laurier's will as his personal residence. She could be resorted to like an oracle in times of need. She and King's valet, John Nicol – also known only by his surname – were old retainers: Nicol with King at least from 1921, she from some date earlier than 1938. It would not have suited King's self-image – or his concern about giving a weapon to political enemies – to admit that he had a valet at public expense. He was carried on our 'establishment' list as 'confidential messenger.'

I got to know another side of King when on 30 September 1945 I was directed to travel in his private railway car – Car 101 – to meet him in Washington, where he was flown a day earlier to inform President Harry Truman about the Soviet espionage system that had just been revealed in Ottawa by Igor Gouzenko. We were then to take the train to New York, from where King would depart for England on the *Queen Mary*, with Norman Robertson, to meet Prime Minister Clement Attlee to discuss with him the same sensational development as well as other matters.

It is a fascinating reflection of the change in means of communication, and of the concept of 'time,' in the last fifty years that King did not consider in 1945 that he could safely communicate with the president of the United States or the prime minister of Britain except by going personally, with a delay of a week or more, in order to speak face to face with the other leaders. Nor did it appear to him that speed of warning about this ominous action by the Soviet Union justified the risk of something quicker than a personal visit.

In New York, King stayed at the Harvard Club as he liked to do. He had been at Harvard for post-graduate work and enjoyed the association. It was also cheaper than a hotel. He had arranged to meet Jacques Gréber, who had come over from France on the *Queen Mary*, and was en route to Ottawa to resume his work on the planning of the national capital, which had been interrupted in 1939 by the outbreak of the war. Emmet P. Murphy, the deputy minister of public works, had come to New York from Ottawa to meet Gréber and to learn of the plans and to help with whatever arrangements might emerge from the discussion with King.

The meeting took place at about eight o'clock in the evening in the lounge of the Harvard Club and was almost entirely a discussion between the prime minister and Gréber about concepts Gréber had developed for the capital before the war, the nature of the studies that would have to be undertaken, the degree to which time and the growth of Ottawa during the war would alter plans, and other related matters. King was interested in seeing a capital emerge worthy of the country that Canada had become by reason of its part in the war, its increased status in the world, and the development of its industries and economy. He was the member of the Harvard Club and the host, but his hospitality did not extend to any refreshment despite the clinking of glasses in the adjacent bar and at tables around us.

After an hour or so, King, who was weary from his discussions in Washington, and the trip to New York suggested that we adjourn to the bar before retiring. The faces of Gréber and Murphy lit up – as, I am sure, did mine. At the bar, King drummed with his pudgy fingers on the wooden surface, a gesture that, I learned, often occurred when he was not entirely comfortable in some situation. He looked at his guests, bar-order form in hand, and said: 'Well gentlemen, will we all have lemon-ade?' No one had the courage to suggest a preference for anything else. We solemnly drained the sour juice from the elegant glasses with as much show of satisfaction as we could muster. King went off to his bed in the club, and we to ours.

I soon learned that it was not just King's wartime teetotalism that dictated his choice of drinks that night: it was also his parsimony. He was a shameless miser and would resort to almost any device to avoid any charge, however minor, to his expense account or, worst of all, to him personally. On the trip back to Ottawa on Car 101, I was to be the prime minister's host and to look after the needs and comfort of his French guest. The trip started in the late afternoon and I confirmed that dinner would be quite satisfactory. But wine? Not a bottle. There were a few soft things that could hardly be worse to prepare Gréber's palate for dinner, but no spirits. Any stock I had with King would have plunged if he had known that the first item I ever packed for any trip was a bottle of scotch. Gréber's approval of my addition to the prime minister's hospitality was clear. We became good friends. Bea regarded him as a special challenge for dinner to talk about the capital plans.

On later trips to Commonwealth conferences and United Nations and other meetings in Europe, I was King's 'banker.' I soon learned that if I did not have his signature for any money I gave him or any account I paid for him, at the moment of the transaction, there was little prospect of having the charge accepted later as something that should go on his expense account. After a few costly mistakes, I had slips prepared, small enough to carry in my pocketbook, with space for a date and reading, 'Received from R.G. Robertson the sum of ...,' and a line below for the prime minister's signature. King intensely disliked this application of his admonition, 'Robertson, you *can't* be too careful,' but he never quite declined to sign if the slip was on top of the £10 or £20 – or however many French francs or U.S. dollars – I gave him or paid at his request.

Another of King's idiosyncracies was the significance he saw in numbers, dates, the alignment of the hands of the clock as the moment for decision, and, especially, the length of his service as prime minister. The last became a matter of great moment during the conference of Commonwealth prime ministers in London in May–June 1946.

In the Prime Minister's Office we had determined with meticulous care the years and days of service of the prime ministers of Britain, Canada, and other Commonwealth countries. The champion by a long way was Sir Robert Walpole, from 3 April 1721 to 11 February 1742: 7,619 days. The runner-up was Sir John A. Macdonald, whose terms from 1867 to 1873 and 1878 to 1891 added up to 6,937 days. The magic moment of equalling Sir John would be reached on 7 June 1946. Those of us who were in London with King knew that the great event would have to be appropriately marked – but how?

Norman Robertson, an omnivorous reader, had seen in a bookstore on Charing Cross Road a three-volume presentation set of F.S. Oliver's biography of Walpole entitled *The Endless Adventure*. What about that? There was some concern about it. Could it be misinterpreted – presenting, on a day of victory, a reminder that there was still an undefeated champion? However, there was no better idea. The set was bought and inscribed by Norman Robertson, Jack Pickersgill, James Gibson, Edouard Handy, and me. Our concern was, for once, unnecessary. King recorded in his diary: '... a memorable day ... I felt deeply touched by this exceptionally appropriate gift in its association with the day.'

King's satisfaction was only momentarily upset when, on turning over the leaves of one volume while expressing his appreciation, he came upon a passage where Oliver was considering what qualities prime ministers of long and successful record, such as Walpole, William Pitt, and W.E. Gladstone, might have in common. This was too fascinating and King read it out aloud to us before knowing where the analysis might lead – for once he forgot about 'not assuming anything.' Oliver concluded that he could find no common factor among the long-surviving political leaders except an inordinate desire for power. The reading ended there. But on so important a day, the prime minister was not without his own comforting interpretation.

King tried to ensure that no day ended without dictating to Ed Handy for the diary what the main events had been, what discussions of importance he had had, and, above all, his own version of what he and others had said. No one but Handy received these meditations and he was as secretive as a clam about them. But it seemed harmless to tell me the day after our presentation that King had referred to Oliver's conclusion and considered whether the assessment applied to him. He had found that, in the place of the inordinate desire for power Oliver had detected in the prime ministers he considered, he himself had an unending desire to serve. Bruce Hutchison was not aware of this distinction about motives when, in 1964, he referred to King's 'ceaseless itch for power, an egotism unique and ruthless because he conceived himself as God's chosen instrument.'[3] Hutchison had it right.

An aspect of King's 'egotism' that emerged not infrequently was his desire to use his power, whether as prime minister or simply as employer, to dominate and to humiliate people who could not defend themselves. I was an embarrassed witness to such an occasion in the corridor of the Dorchester Hotel as I waited with King and Vincent Massey, then high commissioner in London, for the elevator during the visit in 1946. I did not know what had happened in King's suite, but he was in no mood to curb his wrath to save Massey's feelings with someone else present. He gave him quite a dressing down. I later learned that relations were strained because King George VI wished to confer the Companion of Honour, an award strictly in the gift of the sovereign, on Massey before he left the office of high commissioner, which he was on the point of doing.

King frequently resented what he thought were efforts by Massey at 'self-aggrandizement' and, while Massey is tactful in his memoirs,[4] it is clear from Claude Bissell's biography that King deliberately withheld the approval that only he and the cabinet in Ottawa could give for Massey to accept the honour until the very day King George proposed to award it. Then, with a telephone call to St Laurent in Ottawa, all was cleared in the nick of time. Bissell comments: 'The episode showed King enjoying sadistically the exercise of power, first humiliating a dependent, then restoring him with protestations of affection and high regard.'[5] There was another unpleasant incident on the *Queen Mary* on which both the prime minister and the Masseys were sailing to Canada.

During the stay in London I had an indirect contact with one of King's idiosyncracies that has received too much attention and misinterpretation: his belief in the possibility of having contact with loved ones or friends who had 'departed this life.' It came when, on the last day, the prime minister gave me an envelope with instruction to deliver it to the person at the address written on it in his own hand. It turned out to be in a drab part of east-end London with row houses jammed end to end. The woman who answered the door was bedraggled in hair, face, and dress. She said she was indeed the person named. After some hesitation I turned the envelope over to her and returned to the Dorchester Hotel, wondering if I should have demanded proof of her identity: 'Robertson, never assume anything!' Yet if I had dared poke into King's personal affairs, that would be an even greater crime.

For my own comfort, I decided to ask Ed Handy who, for the daily diary, knew everything. With a caution about the utter privacy of the information, Ed told me that it had been payment by King for the services of a medium with whom the prime minister sometimes had seances when in London. It must have been the only payment in some two weeks that he did not ask me to make out of my own pocket in the hope that it would end up on my expense account.

More than twenty years later I got a second contact with King's spiritualism. After the death of Norman Robertson, I was asked if I would take his place as one of the literary executors established in King's will. Their main responsibility, as distinct from that of the executors for the financial and other parts of the will, was to decide what parts of his diary and other record were to be published and to make appropriate arrangements accordingly. Jack Pickersgill told me that the general instruction in the will was that the diary was to be destroyed, with the exception of those parts that King would direct were to be preserved. The problem for the literary executors was that no such direction had been made before death overtook King in 1950.

It was clear from the will that King intended that at least part of his voluminous record was to be published. For everyone who knew him, it was also certain that he would want a large part published in order to give his own account of the great events in the history of Canada, in the development of labour relations and social policy, in the winning of the war, and in a host of other matters in which he had been, not only involved, but in very many cases the most important actor. The decision of the literary executors had been, Jack told me, that, in the absence of any specific direction to destroy, they should preserve and make available for research and publication all of the diary and record except parts that were purely personal. It was too valuable a record to do anything else.

The only part of the record that had not been examined under this rule when I became an executor in 1968 was a number of 'scribblers' – soft-covered, ruled books all Canadian schoolchildren used from Grade 1 up. The 'scribblers' were the right instrument for their purpose: a place for the mediums to record their communications with the spirits King had sought to contact in 'the other world.' Jack Pickersgill, Guy Roberge, and I were asked to examine that record and to decide whether there was any part that should be preserved as not being purely personal.

No school child could get out of Grade 1 with the writing or the confusion in the scribblers. Presumably allowance has to be made for the likelihood that the writing was done by the medium in a darkened room on her lap (it seemed always to be a 'her') or on a shaking table. The incoherent scribbles were obviously what the medium thought she heard in response to questions to spirits vaguely identified with members of King's family, Sir Wilfrid Laurier, and others to whom King had been particularly close. Most of it, to any reader in broad daylight, was meaningless gibberish.

Two things became clear. There was nothing and could be nothing with enough coherence to constitute any 'direction' or 'comment' on policy – the kind of thing that has been imagined by critics all-too-ready to believe that King had a streak of madness in him. The other thing was that there was nothing of any value or relevance for the public record. King would never have directed that any part be preserved. Jack and I burned the scribblers, page by page, in the Pickersgills' fireplace.

The Canadian Citizenship Act

At the end of the war in 1945, after the enormous military and economic effort that Canada had put forth, we found ourselves still with many remnants of our pre-war semi-colonial status. Full equality with Britain had been legally asserted in the Statute of Westminster in 1931 but that did not establish a means of amending our constitution by ourselves, nor give us a flag other than the British merchant-marine flag with our coat of arms on the fly, nor did it alter the anomalous situation in which the significant legal status of Canadians was *not* that of 'Canadian' but that of 'British subject.'

There did exist a status of 'Canadian citizen,' but it was a working definition in the Immigration Act of 1910. It was solely to determine whether a person did or did not have the legal right to enter Canada. It served no other purpose. There was also a technical status of 'Canadian national,' defined by the Canadian Nationals Act of 1931. But that status was only for League of Nations purposes, so a 'Canadian national' had legal existence and could be appointed to the International Court of Justice and other League organizations. There was also a Naturalization Act, passed in 1914. But a naturalized person under that act became a British subject, not a Canadian citizen or a 'Canadian' anything.

When Paul Martin became a minister in April 1945, the portfolio King assigned to him was that of secretary of state. Within his department was a Naturalization Branch and Martin, who had become aware of the lack of any real status of 'Canadian,' asked his deputy minister, E.H. Coleman, to give him a memorandum about what 'naturalization' did for the status of any alien resident in Canada who wanted to become a 'Canadian.' A memorandum from the branch of 23 April 1945 set it out: 'Under the Act in force since January, 1915, the Secretary of State may grant a certificate of naturalization commonly called "Imperial," as it is recognized by British authorities the world over, whereas under previous legislation, courts issued certificates effective within Canada only.' The memorandum later set forth the naturalization procedure for 'ordinary aliens.' It said: 'Since the 1st January, 1943, no alien may apply for naturalization unless he has in his possession an official receipt from the Secretary of State of Canada of his Declaration of Intention to become a British subject, filed one year previously with the Clerk of the Court of the district in which he resides. The regulations require that the Declaration of Intention be made "in duplicate, under oath, before, and only in the office of the Clerk of the Court of the judicial district in which the applicant resides and during office hours."' As to married women, their status for the most part depended on that of their husbands: 'A woman who marries a British subject is deemed to be a British subject; she will need, however, in order to establish her status, to produce her marriage certificate and her husband's title to British nationality.' In the entire ten-page memorandum, the word 'Canadian' did not occur once. There was no reason why it should. Canadian anything was not part of the process or the status. 'British subject' was the magic formula, granted under a common code that had been accepted by all parts of the British Empire at imperial conferences up to that of 1930.

Martin had first become interested in the status of Canadians when visiting a military cemetery at Dieppe. He spoke to King about it after becoming a minister in 1945. He writes: 'Mackenzie King had demonstrated considerable enthusiasm for a citizenship act when I first mentioned it to him during the election campaign. I could see that I had struck a sympathetic chord, as I talked to him about my experiences at Dieppe and my conviction that it was essential to incorporate into law a definition of what constituted a Canadian. In my own mind, and I am certain in the prime minister's, this piece of legislation fitted in with Laurier's vision of a separate Canadian nation.'[6]

Well before that conversation, Martin had become aware that it would be impossible for him to produce the legislation he had in mind if he had to rely on his department. 'The drafting of that bill,' he says, 'made me aware for the first time as a minister of the need to establish my independence from bureaucratic advisors. My deputy, Dr E.H. Coleman, belonged to the old school of empire and was opposed in principle to the enactment of such a measure. Although he helped me as best he could, I went elsewhere to find the support and knowledge I needed to draw up the legislation.'[7]

It was apparently Arnold Heeney, then clerk of the Privy Council, who suggested to Martin that I could help him if he could get the prime minister to surrender some part of my time. Martin says:

In spite of King's offer to help me, he replied to my request for Robertson's services by expostulating, 'Robertson! He won't be able to help you.' This, I knew was a device to discourage my temporary use of one of the most intelligent men on King's staff. In the end, however, the prime minister consented and Gordon was grudgingly lent to me. Thus it was that Robertson and David Mundell of the department of justice, as well as representatives from external affairs, the department of immigration and the privy council, set up a committee to study the question of citizenship throughout the summer of 1945.[8]

David Mundell was the same man who had conjured up the fictitious case of Langley versus Davies for my embarrassment in my tutorial at Exeter College. He had a first-rate mind, a superb knowledge of a broad range of law, and all the ingenuity that he had demonstrated at my expense. At Oxford we had formed the habit of discussing legal cases and problems as we roamed the historic city and the English country-side. Now we did it about the concepts and principles that should be embodied in a new Canadian citizenship act, while walking around Parliament Hill and along the Rideau Canal. Mundell had a great talent for comprehending the legal implications of a concept and then, as we walked, beginning to shape a statutory provision that would make it law, while taking into account exceptions or qualifications that would be needed. Without Mundell, the ground-breaking act would have been much more difficult to produce. The single reference to him in Paul Martin's memoirs does not do justice to his role in developing the act. It was very much the product of close and frequent discussions between the two of us, with final decision by Martin.

The Canadian Citizenship Bill had to be dropped from the parliamentary program in 1945 and it was reintroduced in 1946. It was received in the House of Commons with almost universal approval in principle, modified in a few details and debated with the length and care it deserved. The only questions on which there was any significant difference of view involved the treatment of the status of British subjects. There were two aspects.

One was the position of non-Canadian British subjects who, on passage of the act, had resided in Canada for five years or more – five years' residence being the prescribed period of residence for naturalization of non-British immigrants to Canada. Hitherto the fact of residence was all that was required: they were British subjects to start with and acquired rights in Canada automatically. Should such British subjects also automatically become Canadian citizens (as the bill provided), or should they be required to go through a 'naturalization' process as other people not born in Canada or to Canadian parents had to do? Should a term less than the standard five years be provided for them? There were insistent and worried questions by many MPs about hypothetical situations and possible problems for various categories of British subjects. It led to my first contact with the minister of justice, St Laurent. Martin undertook, after a certain adjournment, to get St Laurent's interpretation of one troublesome possibility in order to reassure some opposition members.

The two of us went into St Laurent's office. He had not been in the House and had not been following the debate. Martin set out the problem: the provisions of the bill, the hypothetical facts, and the questions at issue. St Laurent listened carefully, saying nothing until Martin had completed his exposition. He then asked two or three questions, on the most critical and doubtful points. After Martin gave his answers, St Laurent got up and went to his bookshelves. The office was lined with volumes of statutes, law reports, and legal tomes of various kinds. He pulled one out, found what he wanted, and read for two or three minutes. He then located another volume and did the same. With no further question or comment he then delivered an opinion that was crystal clear. I have long forgotten what the problem was but not the meticulous way it was analysed and the precision of the language in which judgment was delivered. After hearing St Laurent's analysis, it seemed all too obvious: one wondered why there had been doubt. Martin accepted St Laurent's opinion without question, as did the members of the House who had raised the issue. It was an impressive performance by a man who became still more impressive as I came to know him later on.

The other 'British subject issue' was whether the act should provide, as the bill then did, that 'a Canadian citizen is a British subject,' or whether our citizenship should stand alone without involving the old, traditional imperial status. The cabinet well knew that the political difficulties would be great in many parts of Canada if the British status was not retained, and so it was. There was some opposition, but only enough for Martin to demonstrate that the bill's provisions were a 'middle ground,' a reasonable compromise on a delicate issue.

The British government was by no means happy about the innovative course that Canada was adopting. The status of British subject had for centuries been the bedrock on which the rights and status of subjects of His Majesty (or Her Majesty) rested, wherever those subjects might be born, travel, or reside. Under the accepted code, all Commonwealth countries had common definitions of the British subjects for whom they respectively took responsibility. They might then, as Canada had done, have their own provisions for immigration, or residence, or issuance of passports, or other things but all, at the base, provided the same fundamental status which all recognized and which was accepted by all foreign countries – that of British subject.

To the British government and its officers, the status of 'British subject' was, like that of Roman citizen in the ancient world, the highest privilege to which any person could aspire. The idea of anyone not cherishing it was to them unthinkable. Canadians were now thinking it. The accepted imperial approach was being turned on its head. Canada was departing from the 'common code' system and preferring a local status which would be prior in importance.

The representations by the British government were made with the greatest civility in exchanges of telegrams between Ottawa and London. The other Commonwealth countries were informed of our plan but only the British had objections. In direct discussion, especially among officials, the cool courtesy of the diplomatic exchanges occasionally cracked. Arguments against the Canadian plan ranged from the practical to the metaphysical. One of the more passionate pleas took on almost religious overtones, like a debate about the divisibility of the Trinity. It was not possible to divide the crown, and therefore it was not possible to divide the status of subjects of the crown in the way Canada was proposing to do. However, reason did in the end prevail, especially when it turned out that some of the other Commonwealth countries such as Australia and South Africa would almost certainly follow Canada's lead. A memorandum for the prime minister in April 1946 advised him of proposals for a Commonwealth meeting on nationality.

The conference in February 1947 had representatives from ten Commonwealth countries – all but India. There was agreement to adopt the Canadian plan. The advantages were well set out in the explanatory notes to a new British Nationality Bill when it was introduced in February, 1948. Paragraph 7 read:

> A scheme of legislation which combines provisions defining the persons who are citizens of the several parts of the Commonwealth with provisions for maintaining the common status of British subjects throughout the Commonwealth has the advantage of giving a clear recognition to the separate identity of particular countries of the Commonwealth, of clarifying the position with regard to diplomatic protection and of enabling a Government when making treaties with other countries to define with precision who are the persons belonging to its country and on whose behalf it is negotiating.

It was a graceful acceptance of the Canadian heresy which became the new orthodoxy. Paul Martin, Dave Mundell, and I had the satisfaction of knowing we had done something that would increase the sense of Canadian nationhood and add to Canada's status in the eyes of the world, while doing no injury whatever to the Commonwealth association.

In Canada the Canadian Citizenship Act was proclaimed, effective 1 January 1947. However, that is not the only thing for which I remember the day. It was also probably the only day when King may have thought that I had some degree of the perception he deserved but so rarely found in a member of his staff.

The prime minister always 'received' at Laurier House on New Year's morning after returning from the governor general's levee. He expected his senior staff to be there – to greet him with wishes for the year and to make conversation with his visitors. I had celebrated rather too well the night before and had walked the two miles to Laurier House in the hope that the cold air would clear my head. It did.

As I greeted King I asked him if he realized how significant a day it was. 'No Robertson, I don't. Why is it significant?'

'This is the first day since the year you were born [1874] when the numbers 4 and 7 have occurred in designation of a year.'

For the first and only time, King put his left hand over mine as I clasped his right. He looked at me closely for a moment. 'Is that right Robertson?'

'Yes, Mr King, it is.'

'Isn't that significant Robertson!' He held my hand a moment longer and then let it go with an abstracted look.

I never again reached that high point in his regard but it was a good start for the year.

The first ceremony for the conferring of certificates of Canadian citizenship under the new act took place before the judges of the Supreme Court of Canada on 3 January. The prime minister received certificate number one. In his diary for that day he recorded that he found the whole ceremony 'deeply moving.' He added:

Later, when giving the address of the evening, I was given a wonderful reception, both at the beginning and at the close. I was quite surprised how quickly the audience applauded, when I began by saying 'I speak as a citizen of Canada.' There was an instantaneous applause and I had to wait before getting on to the next sentence. I noticed too quite a response when I referred to Canada being founded on the fusion of two proud races. One could have heard a pin drop, excepting when the movie machines were continually at work. The applause at the end was so long that I had to rise and acknowledge it with a bow to the audience and the Chief Justice.[9]

The diary goes on about the joy and the sense of honour he had: 'To be the first citizen of Canada in the two senses of the word: 1) in the position I enjoy and 2) in the certificate of the fuller citizenship which has come about as a result of legislation enacted by [the] administration of which I am the head makes me very happy indeed.'[10]

I had written the notes that King used for his remarks. As always, the final text was very much his own but it incorporated most of the ideas I had suggested. Did the success of the whole operation, the year of intensive work in addition to my normal duties in the prime minister's office, and the joy of the final ceremony lead to any commendation or even recognition by King? Not a word. I was not surprised. I had learned that, with King, the best one could hope for was a grudging, grumpy silence. Approval was impossible; praise was out of the question. He was a rotten boss to work for in spite of everything he preached about labour relations in his book *Industry and Humanity*.

With Paul Martin it was quite different. It was a joy to work with him and we became the warmest of friends. He was intelligent, perceptive, appreciative, and all association with him was leavened by his delightful sense of humour. Many of his best jokes were on himself. There was no pretension or pomposity about him. He was to go on to great success in Parliament and government but the prize he most sought escaped him: the leadership of the Liberal Party and the prime ministership of Canada. He did, however, deservedly draw great satisfaction from being responsible, as minister of national health and welfare from 1946 to 1957, for much of the social security and health programs that still relieve the hazards of life for the people of Canada. He was a delightful man and a great Canadian citizen.

It became increasingly apparent in 1947 that King's energies were diminishing. His interest in both the House of Commons and the cabinet flagged. More than once he left his ministers arguing over some point in a cabinet meeting while he went around the corner to his office in the East Block to have tea. Both he and his colleagues knew that they could reach no conclusion without him – and they equally knew they could not smoke. I suspect that King found satisfaction in both these certainties: he occasionally became unusually relaxed and talkative. He once spoke to me of his wish that he could, before he retired, name a Canadian as governor general – but there was no one suitable. Youthful rashness led me to suggest that surely Vincent Massey would be appropriate. His reaction was immediate. 'Robertson, I will not have this country run by Alice Massey!' The Masseys had been friends of his for thirty years, but clearly there were wounds, still raw.

King never addressed any of the staff by anything other than their surname – until one day when Frank Salisbury, the British portrait artist, and his wife came to Ottawa. King had chosen him to do his official portrait to hang in the Parliament Building. He brought the Salisburys in one afternoon to see his office; mine was immediately outside and, as usual, I closed the communicating door when I heard them arrive. The

will not object if I smoke when we are together?' King in the best of health would have objected. No minister dared to smoke anything, even a cigarette, in a cabinet meeting whether King was present or not. Clearly this could not happen and the surest way was to invoke what seemed a possible medical ruling: 'I am afraid, Mr Churchill, that Mr King's doctors have said smoke might have an injurious effect on his heart condition.'

Churchill grunted, glared at me, and puffed a bit harder, both in the elevator and in King's living room while I went into the bedroom with the information that Churchill had arrived. When I went out to invite Churchill to go in, he gave a final puff on the cigar and put it, still impressively large, on an ash tray on the mantel. With a final glare at me he pointed to it and instructed his bodyguard: 'Watch it.'

It was there when he emerged after his meeting with King and he was still puffing it comfortably as he got into his limousine. The King, Churchill, and the others who came knew that it was likely to be their final meeting with a figure who had succeeded remarkably in the difficult task of political leadership.

On 31 October, the prime minister and our small group sailed on the *Queen Elizabeth* from Southampton. The voyage was a trial from beginning to end. King was obviously feeling depressed both by his health and by his impending resignation as prime minister and he sought reasons to feel neglected and hurt.

King directed that Ed Handy and I should turn up at his stateroom at nine o'clock each morning to report to him anything that had come in the ship's news and to learn his wishes for the day. The most interesting event to report was the astonishing re-election of Harry Truman over Thomas Dewey as president of the United States. The Chicago *Tribune* had been sufficiently sure of Dewey's election that it headlined it as a fact before all the western results were in. King had been hoping for a Truman victory and he had even ventured to say, as he went to bed on the American election day: 'A lot of people may be surprised by this election.' His intuition must have been working even in mid-Atlantic.

However, that was the only bright spot in a miserable trip. The lowest point was reached one morning when Handy and I rapped on the stateroom door at the appointed hour and then tried the latch in our usual way. It was always unlocked and King always ready. That morning the door was locked and there was no answer. We rapped again: no answer. We did it a third time: still locked and no response. We withdrew down the corridor just a few feet to discuss what might have happened and what we should do. As we were thinking of the possibilities we heard the door being unlocked. We waited a bit then returned, rapped, and opened the door in the usual way. King was ready, in his bed. He wondered why we were late. We told him we had been there on time but the door had been locked. King looked accusingly at us: 'It was open now, wasn't it?' He did not go so far as to accuse us of fabricating an excuse for our sloth and our neglect of him but his manner made it clear. When the *Queen Elizabeth* had to heave to and remain motionless in impenetrable fog for nearly twenty-four hours, the question was whether anyone's patience could endure that extra day a short distance from New York.

We reached Ottawa on 7 November. King's record for that day reads: 'Delighted to reach Ottawa with the sun shining brightly as we came into the city. The hands of the clock were in a straight line a little after half past twelve when I took a last look at them. I looked at Mother's picture and then came into the sitting room and looked at further park improvements and also got glimpses of the Parliament Buildings.'[12]

King's Greatest Contribution

King, still prime minister, attended his last meeting of the cabinet five days later on 12 November 1948. Reporting on his trip to Paris and London, he talked about his illness and weariness and the fact that he had deferred his retirement too long. It was indicative of his interest in the national capital that the only piece of business he wanted to bring forward was a slate of new appointments to the Federal District Commission. After saying goodbye and leaving the cabinet chamber, King met the press. The most interesting item was about his greatest contributions to Canada during his many years in office. He recorded in his diary: 'Bird [John Bird, then a correspondent for the Southam Press] asked what I regarded as the most memorable moment in my political life. I replied that I did not think of any moment in particular, but I would say that certainly I regarded having helped to keep Canada united throughout the war as the main contribution I had made. That I thought our policies in that regard had been fully vindicated and the war effort and other efforts depended upon the unity of the country.'[13]

Pickersgill, in *Seeing Canada Whole*, sets forth the skill that King brought to bear on the problem of conscription throughout the war and the way he handled the ultimate crisis, which could have destroyed his government in 1944 when victory was almost won. I think it is certainly no exaggeration to say that no one but King, not even Sir John A. Macdonald, could have emerged from that dangerous welter of contending views with the loss of only two ministers and with his government intact. It is a case study, not only of political skill and leadership, but also of the capacity of King to outmanoeuvre opponents whether in cabinet or in Parliament.

The minister of national defence, J.L. Ralston, who was convinced that conscription had become necessary in 1944 and who thought he had King's word that it would be invoked when it was 'necessary,' resigned after a meeting of the cabinet in which King revealed that General A.G.L. McNaughton, formerly commander of the Canadian army in Britain, was prepared to take over as minister and to try to find reinforcements without conscription. When that effort failed, King reversed policy and accepted a program of limited conscription. That led to the most ardent opponent of conscription, the minister of national defence for air, 'Chubby' Power, resigning. With conscription now government policy, the opposition in the House of Commons was deprived of its principal issue. The government survived.

It was a superb display of the resources King could deploy when his and his government's survival were involved. Pickersgill says of the final vote on 7 December 1944: 'The parliamentary crisis was over without disaster. Surviving the conscription crisis of 1944 was the most dramatic achievement in Mackenzie King's career. It meant that he would turn out to be the only head of government of a free country to last through the Second World War – the greatest of his many records of durability.'[14]

But the political and parliamentary skills were simply an essential part of achieving what was clearly the primary policy objective throughout King's long and successful career – preserving the unity of Canada. King had seen the depth of the divisions created by conscription in 1917 and had been defeated in his own constituency in the elections of that year for standing with Sir Wilfrid Laurier in opposition to it. It is not surprising that national unity became so great and so constant a cause for him.

If King had given the press a fuller analysis of his contributions to national unity, he might well have mentioned the development of 'Dominion status' in his first two administrations in the 1920s. The needs of the First World War had led to the creation of an Imperial War Cabinet in 1917 for making decisions about the conduct of the war and the larger issues of British foreign policy. The prime minister of Britain chaired it. The prime ministers of the dominions were members of the War Cabinet and ministers of all imperial governments attended as needed. After the war the British government and others saw value in carrying the concept of unified imperial government and the 'cabinet' institution into the peace that followed. Australia and New Zealand, in their isolation in the South Pacific, were especially interested in a plan that would maintain close cooperation with Great Britain. In October 1920 the British government summoned a conference of prime ministers for 1921. The invitation read: 'The Dominions are invited to attend the Imperial Conference in June on the lines of the Imperial War Cabinet meetings which took place in 1917 and 1918, to deal with many urgent problems of common interest which call for the co-ordinaton of policy and action by the different Governments of the Empire.'[15]

General Smuts, the prime minister of South Africa, and Arthur Meighen, then prime minister of Canada, had doubts about the 'cabinet' idea and the meeting was instead called a 'Conference of Prime Ministers.' In fact, however, there were 'unmistakable revivals of the meetings of the War Cabinet in the subjects discussed and the decisions taken.'[16] An essential feature of the Imperial Cabinet plan was that there should be a single foreign policy for all. Events in the next two years, and the policies of King's first administration, demonstrated the problems of the plan. At the conference of prime ministers in 1923 King and General Smuts, against strong pressure from Britain, Australia, and New Zealand, strongly opposed the 'cabinet' concept and a unified foreign policy.

Without that firm position in 1923, and again at the conference in 1926, there would have been no Balfour Declaration with its statement of equality of the 'self-governing communities composed of Great Britain and the Dominions' and no Statute of Westminster in 1931 to put the concept of equal status into law. King's policy in the Commonwealth meetings in the 1920s laid the basis for Canada's separate declaration of war in 1939 and for a policy of Canadian independence during the war that was essential to the internal unity he was determined to preserve. Altogether there was a remarkable coherence of policy over a period of twenty years that made possible Mr King's 'main contribution.'

The value of that contribution is more apparent now than fifty years ago when King gave his assessment. As this is written, it is not clear how the issue of 'sovereignty' for Quebec will turn out. If there had been in 1944 the bitter division over conscription that there was in 1917, the problem of today would be even more difficult than it is and the future of Canada much more doubtful.

Yet King's claim to being our greatest prime minister rests on much more than his contribution to our national unity and his longevity in office. His victories in general elections from 1921 to 1945, with the exception of that in 1930, are an accurate reflection of the way he was able to appeal to Canadians across the regional, ethnic, and linguistic divisions of the country. He had a sensitivity and judgment about policies that would unite rather than divide that were equalled only by Sir John A. Macdonald and Sir Wilfrid Laurier, if, indeed, by them.

King did not himself understand Quebec. What he did understand – and what he never forgot – was that Quebec was different and that it was vital, for his government but also for the country, that the concerns of Quebec be carefully considered on any policy or action of possible interest to it. From the beginning of his prime ministership in 1921 to the death in 1941 of Ernest Lapointe, his minister of justice and Quebec lieutenant, it was on Lapointe's judgment above all that King relied in his thinking about Quebec. After that it was increasingly to St Laurent that King turned, although there were others both in the cabinet and outside it whose views he sought. King would have had no difficulty with the concept that Quebec is a 'distinct society.' He knew it, he respected it, and he was constantly alert to avoid giving offence to it even when – or especially when – the chauvinism of English-speaking Canada pressed for policies that were repugnant to French-speaking Canada and Quebec.

More broadly, King's place as the greatest of Canadian prime ministers rests on the success of his policies and decisions at the national level and his equally outstanding success as a political leader. Bruce Hutchison has provided the best analysis of the nature of political leadership in Canada: 'Only two prime ministerial methods are available, the method of the logical mind and the method of the illogical gut, and both have been used by different men with different results. Our three supposedly greatest prime ministers, Macdonald, Laurier and King, always used the gut method. They trusted their hunches more than the advice of experts and usually they were right.'[17] The 'true artist of politics,' Hutchison says, 'can never explain his superior work.' He quotes King as saying, 'Either I see a thing at once or I don't see it at all.' I do not think that King was entirely frank in that statement. He often spent a lot of time and talked to a lot of people before the 'thing' was clear – and especially the timing. Two maxims were constant in his discourse: 'It is not just what you do but when you do it' and 'what you prevent may be more important than what you do.'

Isaiah Berlin devoted an essay to the question 'What is it to have good judgment in politics?' After examining the talents and records of many successful political leaders, he focused on Bismarck as 'perhaps the most effective of all nineteenth century statesmen.' Berlin was firm that there is no 'natural science of politics any more than a natural science of ethics.' His conclusion about Bismarck was that: 'he was successful because he had the particular gift of using his experience and observation to guess successfully how things would turn out.'[18]

King did not start with that capacity: it was built up through his years of total focus on politics, politicians, and, most of all, the attitudes and reactions of the people of Canada. In his most successful period of leadership – during the war – his judgment approached infallibility – or so it must have seemed to some of his despairing political opponents. Would he never make a mistake?

The success of King's policy judgments was, of course, part of his success as a political leader. But he did take 'the party' very seriously. The first obligation of the political leader was, he said, to handle things so that the party would win, for without gaining office nothing could be done. He was proud that it was his party, under him, that introduced old age pensions in 1927, unemployment insurance in 1940, and family allowances in 1944. He had less to do with, but had responsibility for, the successful post-war reconstruction program that took shape before he left office. His final contribution to his party was to leave it strong, and with a strong leader whom he had carefully and sensitively persuaded to remain in office to succeed him.

Much nonsense has been talked and written about King's spiritualism, his diary confessions about falling from grace, and his idiosyncrasies. None was of any serious consequence. King was a lonely man and, throughout his life, intensely self-centred. He also had a firm sense of divine guidance in the work he had undertaken to do, much of it stimulated by his mother to whose memory he remained devoted to the end of his life. I saw him in his last years, when the loneliness, the concentration on self, and the idiosyncrasies were probably more marked than in his younger years. They did not make for an attractive person. There was never any sense that he had the least interest in his ministers, his Members of Parliament, or his staff as people. He was interested in them only in the way they could fit in or contribute to his government, his party, and himself.

The question is how so remote and so calculating a leader could retain the services and the loyalty of strong ministers, for King during the war years had one of the strongest cabinets in our history. During the war commitment to the war effort was a major factor for ministers such as J.L. Ilsley, who disliked King, and J.G. Gardiner, who knew that King disliked him. Party loyalty and political ambition were other factors. But King gave great scope to ministers in whom he had confidence – Louis St Laurent, C.D. Howe, J.L. Ilsley, Brooke Claxton, Douglas Abbott, Paul Martin. And, finally, whether they liked him or not, they had learned that he was usually right. Success is a great glue in holding any organization together but especially one subject to the hazards of parliamentary attack and periodic elections.

The King I saw and worked for had fed on royal jelly too long and demonstrated Lord Acton's dictum that all power corrupts. Without power, and the prime ministerial status that provided it, he had no interest in life. He survived retirement little more than eighteen months. For all his contributions to Canada, he was, unlike Macdonald and Laurier, mourned by very few.

PART THREE

Louis St Laurent and a New North, 1948–1963

chapter five

Working with Louis St Laurent, 1948–1953

Louis St Laurent became prime minister on 15 November 1948. He was the first French-speaking prime minister since Sir Wilfrid Laurier's defeat in the election of 1911 and only the second in our history since Confederation. The Prime Minister's Office reflected that fact and also the very limited place that was then given to the French language in the public service of Canada generally. There was no language problem in either the government or the service: the language was English. Under section 133 of the British North America Act of 1867, French could be used in either House of Parliament and the statutes of Canada had to be published in both languages, but the practice of government had not gone beyond those legal necessities. It was not a conscious decision of policy – the question simply did not occur, as, apparently, it had not occurred at any time since Confederation, with no thought about the unfairness that imposed on French-speaking citizens who might need to deal with the government or on French Canadians who might wish to join the public service. Except in a few special situations, they had to compete – and succeed or fail – in their second language.

As a product of Saskatchewan, I had no French of any use outside a high school classroom. However, it was obvious that the office of a French-speaking prime minister had to have a capacity to think and to write in French and to deal with Quebec and with voters there in their own language. Jack Pickersgill had been particularly aware of this reality and plans had been laid accordingly. I moved to the Privy Council Office, just a hundred feet down the corridor on the second floor of the East Bock, and Jules Léger took my place as 'number two' in the PMO.

In a further shuffle, the clerk of the Privy Council and secretary to the cabinet, Arnold Heeney, moved, early in 1949, to be under-secretary of state for external affairs. He was replaced by my old chief, Norman Robertson. He had been in London as high commissioner for Canada since 1946, recovering his health from five unrelenting years of pressure from the war and the endless demands and frustrations of working as King's principal adviser – the task that had killed O.D. Skelton in 1941.

The Privy Council Office had been a purely clerical office, handling and recording orders-in-council, until the appointment of Arnold Heeney as the first secretary to the cabinet in 1940. His new position was combined with the then-existing one of clerk of the Privy Council. To handle the problems of war Heeney built up a new, small secretariat for the work of the cabinet and cabinet committees, of which I became a member. In 1971, when I was secretary to the cabinet, I described the way Heeney had found cabinet operations in 1940 when he was appointed:

> There was no agenda, no secretariat, no official present at meetings to record what went on, no minute of decisions taken, and no system to communicate the decisions to the departments responsible to implement them. Subjects to be discussed at each meeting were settled by the prime minister with no advance notice to Ministers. As Ministers had no notice of what was going to come up, they were normally quite unprepared for the discussion or for the decisions expected of them. It was obviously a system that could operate only where the pace of events was relatively slow and where the matters requiring decision were not overly intricate or complex. Even so, it was a singularly inefficient and unfair way for a collective executive to reach decisions for which all would share responsibility. After a meeting few knew precisely what had been decided; there could be no confidence that all relevant information had been available or considered; and the accurate transmission of decisions, if it occurred at all, was a happy accident.[1]

Arnold Heeney was an excellent administrator and he established a system that ensured effective operation of government during the fighting of the war. With grudging acceptance from Mackenzie King, Heeney managed to obtain admission of himself, as secretary, as well as recording secretaries into the war committee of the cabinet, which became the real cabinet for war purposes. Not until after the war did he get any official into the cabinet itself. King was well aware of the advantage the prime minister had if there was no agenda and no general notice to ministers in advance of what was going to be considered at a meeting. The war situation had been special but, once it was over, King's preference would have been to get back to the comfort of the pre-war, unorganized situation. It was no small feat for Heeney to persuade him to agree to introducing the war-committee system for the cabinet itself. In 1949 the Privy Council office and the cabinet secretariat within it were tiny, usually no more than nine or ten officers, almost all on loan from other departments.

The secretary to the cabinet was and is the senior deputy minister in the public service: the prime minister's own deputy minister, an important link between an always-busy prime minister and his ministers, and a bridge between the political level of government and the public service. He was also in a position to advise and assist the prime minister on any issue of policy or any problem of government the prime minister chose to discuss or that the secretary to the cabinet thought should be brought to his attention. The intention in the move of Norman Robertson to the job was that he should play the policy role especially – just as he had for King from the position of under-secretary of state for external affairs. Unfortunately, it did not work. As J.L. Granatstein says in his biography of Norman Robertson: 'Robertson was not a self-starter and never had been. He needed someone to get him underway on a problem, someone like Mackenzie King, who telephoned him at any hour with a series of impossible demands to which Robertson responded with superhuman efforts. St Laurent himself responded rather than initiated and did not seem able to operate in a way that meshed with Robertson's. The result was that both men sat in their offices waiting for the other to take the initiative.'[2]

This did not mean that Robertson was not both busy and valuable. He chaired the interdepartmental committee on external trade policy, which coordinated planning on major economic policies extending well beyond foreign trade. The war had forced a total coordination of economic policies and responsibilities that caused formal lines between departments to yield to urgent necessity. The Bank of Canada, where there was so much financial and economic talent, also worked with departments on policies well outside the strict responsibilities of a central bank. As a result of that habit of cooperation, and of the respect that developed among the men (there were no women) who joined together to solve all manner of problems, the wartime practice carried over in the early years of peace. The committee included the governor of the Bank of Canada, Graham Towers, the deputy minister of Finance, Clifford Clark, the deputy ministers of trade and commerce and national revenue, and A.F.W. Plumptre, the assistant under-secretary of state for external affairs responsible for international economic issues. Other deputy ministers attended as required for specific questions. I, with a certain amount of terror as a lawyer and political scientist, became secretary of the committee where almost all discussion was economic and where the conclusions depended on my imperfect understanding of issues and differences of view. Advice went to the cabinet committee on economic policy and recommendations from that to the cabinet. Robertson, with his capacious mind and the ability to relate all aspects of virtually all fields to every kind of problem, was the ideal chairman, respected by all and trusted by all.

Robertson's reputation and standing were not limited to Canada. He had for many years been known and respected in Washington, and in his three years in London he had acquired an extraordinary status with British ministers and officials. As a result, he spent a great deal of time moving between Ottawa, London, and Washington in the summer of 1949 on trade and commercial issues of critical importance. He was accepted in all three capitals as the senior Canadian expert on commercial subjects. Granatstein quotes from a United States Treasury briefing for the American representatives for talks in Washington in August 1949. In these secret notes, Robertson was described as an 'outstanding Canadian economist' and as 'one of the closest advisers of prime minister St Laurent.' Further, 'he is a man of liberal outlook and is said to be devoid of class or racial prejudice. Straightforward and honest, he inspires his associates with confidence in his judgment ... His tact and judgment make him an excellent presiding officer.'[3]

For me, it was a joy to work with Robertson again but a joy that was diminished by the knowledge that he was not happy in his new role. He felt frustrated by his inability to establish the relationship he would have liked with the prime minister. I think, too, that he felt frustrated at not being able to play a role in foreign policy more generally. There was always a friendly awkwardness between him and his former subordinate, Lester Pearson, now secretary of state for external affairs and therefore Norman's superior. Their relations were good but the inversion of roles was not easy.

Granatstein's statement about Norman Robertson and St Laurent not being initiators is overdrawn. An outstanding demonstration of Robertson's ingenuity and initiative came with the discovery of foot-and-mouth disease in Canadian cattle in the west in 1952. Canada could no longer export beef to the United States, by far our biggest market. At the meeting of the interdepartmental committee on external trade policy on

10 March 1952, Robertson suggested a three-way deal among Canada, the United Kingdom, and Australia. Australia normally marketed its beef in the United Kingdom. If it switched its export to the United States to replace Canadian beef there, Canada could supply the British market where restrictions were not as tight as in the United States. The idea was accepted, the other parties agreed, and Canadian farmers escaped a very serious financial blow. Robertson and the minister of agriculture, J.G. Gardiner, often disagreed on export policies but this was one case when Gardiner found himself an enthusiastic supporter. It was a most ingenious plan and Robertson's reputation in both Britain and the United States helped to gain cooperation.

As to St Laurent, he had no hesitation about initiating where and when he thought it wise. One area that St Laurent grasped in 1949 had lain untouched since 1936: the unfinished problem of Canada's constitutional status.

Matching Our Constitution to Our Status

The Statute of Westminster, 1931, which provided for the equal status of the dominions with Great Britain, included, at Canadian request, a clause saying in effect: 'Not quite equal in our case, please.' The provinces had achieved one of their rare cases of unanimity in seeking to ensure that, whatever the British statute did for Canadian status generally, it would not transfer to the Parliament of Canada the power to amend our constitution, which had resided with the Parliament at Westminster since 1867 and, indeed, before that. In moving the resolution in our House of Commons on 30 June 1931 for an address to His Majesty requesting the enactment of the Statute of Westminster, Prime Minister Bennett referred to 'the apprehension of some of the provinces that, under provisions as broad as those to be inserted in the Statute of Westminster, a dominion parliament might encroach upon the jurisdiction of a provincial legislature and exercise powers beyond its competence.' He pointed out that 'lest it be concluded by inference that the rights of the provinces as defined by the British North America Act had been by reason of this Statute curtailed, lessened, modified or repealed,' a section of the Statute of special application to Canada declared, with the unanimous concurrence of the provinces, that such was not the case.[4]

With the worldwide depression that had begun in 1929, there were more urgent things to do than tackling this gap between Canada's formal status of equality and the fact of constitutional inequality. In

January 1935 the House of Commons got around to the matter since the Bennett government had concluded that increased federal powers might help it to deal with 'urgent economic problems which are essentially national in scope.'[5] A House of Commons committee was established to explore the problem. After two sessions, and discovery that the provinces were not prepared to make either written or oral submissions to it, the committee recognized 'the urgent necessity for prompt consideration of amendments to the British North America Act with reference to a redistribution of legislative power and to clarify the field of taxation.' In respect to the provinces, the committee concluded that 'the opinions of the provinces should be obtained' and it recommended that a 'dominion-provincial conference on the question be held as early as possible.'[6]

By the time the Dominion-Provincial Conference convened late in 1935, an election had been held and Bennett was no longer prime minister. The conference agreed, that, 'as in the case of all the other self-governing Dominions, Canada should have the power to amend the Canadian Constitution provided a method of procedure therefor satisfactory to the Dominion Parliament and the provincial legislatures be devised.' To this end, it recommended that the 'Minister of Justice convene at an early date a meeting of appropriate officials of the Dominion and of the provinces to prepare a draft of such method of procedure, to be submitted to a subsequent conference.'[7]

Ernest Lapointe's committee met at length, agreed on a procedure of amendment, and reported to the governments on 2 March 1936. In the depths of the depression an amending procedure for the constitution did not appear to King to be something that should absorb a lot of the time of political leaders. To quote from H.B. Neatby's account: 'The proposed procedures were never adopted. New Brunswick had opposed any change in amendment procedures at the Dominion-Provincial Conference and had not participated in the committee discussions. The federal government refused to take any further steps until New Brunswick relented. But King made no effort to force the issue. He still saw no urgent need for a major constitutional revision and so he gave formal amendment procedures a low priority.'[8] Three years later the war swept the constitution off the agenda.

What was recommended by the Dominion-Provincial Committee in 1936 was remarkably like the arrangements we now have as a result of constitutional provisions enacted in 1949 and 1982. The committee proposed a division of the constitution's provisions into four categories:

matters concerning the federal government only, matters affecting the federal government and one or more but not all the provinces, general matters affecting the federal government and all the provinces and, finally, 'entrenched clauses.' This fourfold division is also set out in the Constitution Act, 1982, and the procedure stipulated there for amending each category is virtually identical to the recommendations of the 1936 committee. It is impossible not to wonder whether we might have avoided all the agony of the attempts at 'patriation' of the constitution – starting in 1968 and continuing through the failure of the Victoria Charter in 1971 and the crisis of the 1981 'agreement without Quebec' which has become such a source of bitterness – if only King's government in 1936 had pursued the agreement then reached by the provincial attorneys general. However, a formal agreement with the provincial governments, followed by approval of their legislatures, was probably beyond reach, for in August 1936 the Liberal government of Adélard Godbout in Quebec was defeated and Maurice Duplessis, an uncompromising foe of the federal government, came to power. It is not likely that his views would have been different in 1936 than they were in 1949–50; when, as we shall see in a moment, he attempted to block constitutional reform.

That said, the failure to try to act in 1936 may in part have reflected a blind spot in King's assessment of constitutional priorities. While he had been the most influential force behind the development of 'Dominion status' in the 1920s, he was not a constitutional lawyer and I at no time detected any interest on his part in the unfinished business of the constitution. It was St Laurent who, after the gap of thirteen years, revived the issue in a national broadcast on 9 May 1949. He declared:

The record of Canadians in two World Wars demonstrated beyond any question our ability and our capacity to bear the responsibilities of full nationhood. But our adult nationhood is not yet fully recognized in our Constitution and our laws ... a method should be worked out to amend our Constitution in Canada ... we do not want the Canadian Constitution to be too rigid, but we do want to make sure it contains the fullest safeguards of provincial rights, of the use of the two official languages, and of those other historic rights which are the sacred trusts of our national partnership.[9]

The election of 27 June 1949 was a triumph for St Laurent. The Liberals won 192 seats out of 262. The Progressive Conservative Party, led by George Drew, dropped from 67 to 41. The way was clear for the prime minister to implement the policies he had advocated in the election.

We in the Privy Council Office had expected him to call for a Dominion-Provincial Conference on the constitution soon after the new Parliament assembled. Jack Pickersgill has described how we were taken by surprise:

> St Laurent himself, without advice from anyone so far as I am aware, made a revolutionary proposal in August 1949: that before a federal-provincial conference was held, Parliament should act to transfer the jurisdiction to make amendments to Canada. His main reason for wanting Parliament to act before a federal-provincial conference was held was to make sure that the provincial governments would be given no excuse to suppose they were entitled to any voice in making amendments to the areas of the Constitution exclusively within the federal jurisdiction.[10]

So much for St Laurent not being an initiator.

The British North America Act 1949 (No. 2)

What St Laurent was proposing was that the Parliament of Canada, without consultation with the provinces, should pass an address to the king seeking an amendment by the British Parliament to put our Parliament in the same position with respect to the parts of the constitution that were purely federal as the legislatures of the provinces had been in since 1867 with respect to parts that were purely provincial. Section 92(1) of the British North America Act provided that the legislature of a province could 'exclusively make laws' in relation to 'the Amendment from Time to Time ... of the Constitution of the Province, except as regards the Office of Lieutenant Governor.' St Laurent would give Parliament a comparable power but exclude 'matters coming within the classes of subjects by this Act assigned exclusively to the Legislatures of the Provinces, or in relation to rights or privileges by this or any other Constitutional Act granted or secured to the Provinces or any one or more of them or in relation to rights or privileges with respect to schools or the use of the English or the French language.'[11]

In the same memorandum, the prime minister suggested that a separate section should give Parliament and the legislatures of the provinces power to amend the constitution in relation to all other matters, 'but that any Act of the Parliament of Canada making or amending such provisions shall not have effect unless and until it is also adopted and enacted as law by the Legislatures of all the Provinces.'[12] Jack Pickersgill persuaded St Laurent that to include this power without consulting the provinces would be unwise and it was dropped. The remainder of St Laurent's draft, with scarcely a word changed, was incorporated in a resolution introduced in the House of Commons on 17 October 1949.

As the only one in either the Privy Council Office or the Prime Minister's Office with a background in constitutional law, it became my responsibility to give the prime minister whatever help he wanted on his constitutional initiative. A major task was to prepare his speech to introduce the resolution. That brought me into my first close contact with St Laurent. No experience could have been happier.

St Laurent's mind was crystal clear: he cut through to the essentials of any problem and gave his decision at once. He knew the general line he wanted for his remarks and it was easy to build his logic into a statement that would enable the House to understand what was involved and why the proposal was important. The inevitable contrast with the agony my colleagues and I had suffered in the Hôtel Crillon with a weary and frustrated King less than a year before was unfair but, had he been young and well, he would still almost certainly have been a problem. They were very different men.

St Laurent did not want a complete text: he wanted notes, which he would then use to develop the argument on his feet, with words and style of his own choosing. At only one point, as I listened from the gallery, did I wish that St Laurent had been just a bit like Mackenzie King and more questioning about the notes I gave him.

In developing the case for action in the constitutional area where Parliament could properly act without consulting the provinces, St Laurent outlined the procedure that had been followed in each of the twelve constitutional amendments there had been up to that time, the uncertainty that resulted from having no clearly defined amending procedure, and the repeated failures there had been from 1927 onward in trying to get agreement with the provinces on one. While preparing the notes, I had come across some satirical verse by the English author A.P. Herbert that struck me as apposite. His verse was about a fictitious 'Royal Commission on Kissing,' established because of medical concern about the dangers to British health of spreading contagious diseases through the unsanitary custom of kissing. The satire was good fun. Herbert's fictitious royal commission, after a very long time, finally reported. 'The necessity for action was clear to everyone, But the view was very general that nothing could be done.' That was exactly, I thought, what had happened for over twenty years about finding a way to amend our constitution.

Forgetting King's admonition that one should never assume anything, I did not warn the prime minister that the lines were pure fun about a 'royal commission' that had never existed. An even worse failure on my part was to forget that A.P. Herbert, in addition to being an author and satirist, was Member of Parliament for Oxford University in the 'Mother of Parliaments' at Westminster.

The prime minister, embellishing my notes in impressive style with the House paying close attention, read the Herbert lines as prose in a context he created on the spot. *Hansard* records what followed:

> MR ST LAURENT: In considering one of these amendments in the British House of Commons A.P. Herbert was reported as follows: 'The necessity for action was clear to everyone. But the view was very general that nothing could be done.' As a matter of fact nothing has been done about that procedure for the eighty-two years which have elapsed since the proclamation of the act on July 1, 1867.
>
> MR DIEFENBAKER: What date was that?
>
> MR ST LAURENT: I have not the exact reference here. I think it was in the discussion on the terms of union.
>
> MR DIEFENBAKER: Redistribution.[13]

Neither lawyer turned a hair as each gave a convincing impression to the House of Commons of knowing some obscure but relevant detail of parliamentary debate in Britain that did not exist. I lived in terror for weeks after. Suppose someone told the prime minister – or worse, told Diefenbaker. And suppose, worst of all, a Member of Parliament rose on a point of order and accused the prime minister of misleading the House!

I had acquired a great admiration for St Laurent's penetrating intelligence and sure judgment. Now I realized that there was another dimension: a debating skill and deftness that even John Diefenbaker could not rattle. The prime minister never asked me about the amendment on which he said A.P. Herbert had spoken in Britain and I saw no need to enlighten him. It was a stupid mistake on my part that even as charitable a man as St Laurent would have found hard to forgive.

When George Drew, the Leader of the opposition, rose to reply to the prime minister's address, he agreed about the importance of the proposal to give the Parliament of Canada, for the first time, power to amend the British North America Act. He did not think that 'there is the slightest difference of opinion anywhere in this House as to the amendment of the constitution being made in Canada.' However, as had been expected, he criticized the failure first to consult the provinces.

This had been the position of Premier Maurice Duplessis of Quebec and Premier Ernest Manning of Alberta when the government's intention was communicated to them, and the other premiers, in letters sent on 14 September. St Laurent had politely but firmly adhered to the position that action to give the Parliament of Canada 'the same power to amend the constitution of Canada which the provincial authorities already enjoy under section 32 of the British North America Act to amend the constitution of the provinces'[14] was not a matter on which it was 'appropriate' to consult the provincial authorities. He was equally firm in the House of Commons and the motion of the Progressive Conservatives, supported by the Social Credit Party, for provincial consultation before Parliament acted was defeated 137 to 38. The amendment was approved in the Parliament at Westminster as the British North America Act, 1949 (No. 2). Amendment No. 1 for 1949 had been the admission of Newfoundland as Canada's tenth province.

The First Constitutional Conference of 1950
After informing the premiers about his intention to have Parliament act on the amendment of the constitution in purely federal matters, St Laurent's letter of 14 September 1949 had turned to the need for a procedure of amendment for 'those provisions of the constitution which concern both federal and provincial authorities.' His letter said: 'The federal government would appreciate the opportunity of consulting with the governments of all the provinces on this matter in the manner most convenient to the provincial governments, at an early date after the conclusion of the session of parliament. Our aim is to reach agreement, as soon as possible, on a method of amendment which will relieve the United Kingdom parliament of an embarrassing obligation, and establish within Canada full and final responsibility for all our national affairs.'[15]

The conference opened in Ottawa on 10 January 1950. I was there throughout as the prime minister's personal adviser and assistant. The minister of justice and lawyers from Justice covered legal aspects. In concluding his opening statement, the prime minister said: 'To sum up, the federal government believes that any satisfactory method of amendment must meet three tests. It must protect minority rights absolutely. It must preserve the federal character of the Canadian nation by preserving the autonomy, within their respective spheres, of the provincial legislatures and of parliament itself. It must have sufficient flexibility to enable our country with all its great human and natural resources to continue to go forward as a dynamic nation.'[16]

Premier Duplessis's opening remarks were notable chiefly for a clear assertion of the compact theory of Confederation: 'When Confederation was discussed and decided upon, it was based on the principle of complete provincial autonomy. And this for excellent reasons, the most important of which is that Confederation is not only from its very beginning an agreement between four pioneer provinces but it is a sacred covenant between two great races whose friendly co-operation is essential to the weal and prosperity of all concerned.'[17] That position about a 'sacred covenant' and the rigidity that flowed from it was to be the major factor in defeating the effort in 1950 to arrive at an amending formula.

After a day of discussion about possible categories of constitutional provisions, with differing requirements for amendment, a committee of attorneys general was set up under the chairmanship of the minister of justice, Stuart Garson. In its report on 12 January, it recommended six categories of constitutional provisions, each to have a different requirement for amendment. The conference agreed to establish a standing committee to receive the views of each government and to 'use its best efforts to harmonize' them, after which the conference would reassemble.

Duplessis and the Quebec Conference, 1950

It was agreed, on the invitation of Premier Duplessis, to hold the second conference in Quebec, opening on 25 September. I was advised that, in order to make arrangements as secretary of the conference, I would have to see the premier himself. Nothing could or would be decided except by him. I arranged an appointment in May or June through his principal secretary, Tourigny.

When I was ushered into a very impressive office, Duplessis's first action was to press four buttons on a board of about twenty on his desk. In a matter of minutes, four men came in, were introduced, and took chairs behind him: all were ministers, and none said a word in the entire interview. They were stage-setting. But it was also a message of power and authority, for them and for me. Duplessis was affable and decisive in dealing with every question I posed and in directing his secretary to arrange for every need I expressed. When I came to accommodation for the federal and provincial delegates, Duplessis asked me how many I thought there would be. I said I thought about seventy-five, not including the Quebec delegation – about a fifth of what a comparable meeting today would require, apart from press, radio, and television. Duplessis, a bachelor who lived in the Château Frontenac, said that that morning he had summoned the manager of the Château, George Jessop, to his suite. He had told him of our meeting and that the question of accommodation would come up – for about seventy-five people.

'I said to him, Robertson, "They will all stay in the Château Frontenac."' Duplessis's face gleamed with amusement.

'Jessop said: "But Prime Minister, the conference is to be in September, at the height of the tourist season! The Château has been fully booked for months. I will personally arrange the very best rooms possible in Quebec for every delegate and some, I hope, can be accommodated in the Château. But all? – It is impossible, Prime Minister."'

Duplessis stopped and looked at me. I waited, and he resumed:

'So I said to him: "Mr Jessop, this is a very simple question. The question is this: Does the Château Frontenac wish to continue to sell alcoholic beverages or does it not?"'

'You can be sure, Mr Robertson, that all the delegates for the conference will stay in the Château Frontenac.' He was right. They all did. The rest of the arrangements were handled with equal confidence and all worked out exactly as Premier Duplessis decided.

The conference sessions were held in the elegant chamber of the Legislative Assembly of Quebec – the green chamber, in contrast with the even more elegant red chamber of the Legislative Council. Quebec was at that time the only province that still had the two houses for its legislature that all the colonies had at Confederation in 1867.

The noon adjournment of the conference on the second day gave me another glimpse of Duplessis's power and the fear it inspired. I was standing inside the main door of the legislative building, a great double door, of which one half was open, talking to a member of the press. We were to one side, facing the door, with a commissionaire idling beside it. Suddenly he was galvanized into action, scrambling to release the bolts at top and bottom that held the closed half of the door. The cause of the feverish effort was soon apparent. From behind us, the premier was approaching the door: precisely on the centre line. He did not slow his pace or deviate in the least. The door would be open or a head would fall. The door was open with inches to spare and the commissionaire at rigid salute. Duplessis took no notice. Expression unchanged, he went through it at centre point and was assisted into his limousine.

In the conference, Garson submitted the report of the committee of attorneys general on the classification of sections of the British North America Act for purposes of amendment. Of the 140 sections in the act, there were 45 on which it had not been possible to get agreement. 'Not surprisingly, these were the most important sections – Provisions which concern parliament and all the provincial legislatures and Provisions concerning fundamental rights and the amendment of the amending procedure.'[18]

The first two days, held in public, made no progress. On the third day the conference went into committee of the whole and sat in camera. The next day, 28 September, the conference approved a press release which, in declaring progress, made clear the fact of failure. The problem of getting agreement was referred back to the committee of attorneys general. They were, after discussion and meeting, to report to a third plenary session of the conference 'to be held immediately after the Federal-Provincial Conference on fiscal and other matters which is to meet in Ottawa on December 4, 1950.'[19]

The third plenary session did not happen because the hoped-for solution by the attorneys general did not emerge. Duplessis's position at the Ottawa conference had been that nothing should be changed in the constitution without the concurrence of the legislatures of all the provinces. However, the attorney general of Quebec had participated in the work of Garson's committee without any indication that Quebec could not agree to more flexible procedures for some of the different types of amendment covered by the committee report. It gradually became clear that the appearance of acceptance had been simply a part of an atmosphere of hospitality for the Quebec conference. Once it had taken place, with the cordiality with which Duplessis surrounded it, his social obligations were discharged and his position re-emerged unchanged and inflexible. The committee was not terminated: there was simply a reluctant recognition that progress would not be achieved as long as the genial host of the Quebec conference remained in power. It was not until 1959 that death did what no election after 1939 was able to do and removed Duplessis's tight grip on Quebec.

The two conferences in 1950, along with the normal work of the Privy Council Office, made a busy year but I was aided by a highly intelligent junior who had joined the staff in the summer of 1949 – Pierre Elliott Trudeau. He had come to us from England by way of Turkey, the Middle East, and China; Quebec under Premier Duplessis was not a congenial place for Trudeau. It was a compliment to one so young that the premier personally intervened to prevent his joining the faculty of the Université de Montréal. Duplessis did not like articulate people of independent mind with the courage to say what they thought of the way Quebec was being governed. In the circumstances, the federal civil service had attractions. 'And why the Privy Council Office?' Trudeau writes in his *Memoirs*. 'Because as the secretariat to the cabinet, it was the key decision-making centre, and because I wanted to observe in practice what I had just finished studying in theory ... I have never had cause to regret this choice. The two years that I spent there were an apprenticeship that was later to prove very useful. But I didn't have the temperament of a bureaucrat and I eventually decided to shift my focus.'[20]

Pierre was clearly right about his temperament. As his subsequent career showed, he wanted full freedom to develop his own conclusions on the issues of the day, to enjoy the cut and thrust of argument, and to follow his own star. Pierre did not talk to me about any unhappiness with his work or his role in the office, nor did he suggest any change that might have been possible. I doubt if there would have been anything that would make the constraints of the public service long acceptable to his free spirit. In any event, I was both surprised and sorry to hear his decision to leave in the autumn of 1951. I admired his intellect, appreciated his help, and enjoyed his company. However, there was no point in trying to persuade him to stay in a role that could not long satisfy him. Our relations were always good and we worked well together. Our two years' association provided a basis of confidence and regard when we came together in a very different relationship when Pierre became prime minister in 1968.

Library of Parliament in Peril

In 1916 a fire had completely destroyed the Centre Block of the Parliament buildings, which had been built before Confederation. Nothing was saved from the flames except the circular Gothic building that was the Library of Parliament. It survived because it was connected to the Centre Block only by a short corridor with fire doors – and they had been closed in time. In 1952 it appeared that another fire – this time in the library – might finish the disaster of 1916. By the time it was extinguished, the damage to the library, both inside and out, as well as to a great many books, was extensive.

The prime minister was away from Ottawa at the time. On 14 August 1952 the deputy minister of public works, Emmet Murphy, reported to the cabinet on the damage. C.D. Howe was acting prime minister. A general reconstruction of the library was estimated to cost $950,000. However, Murphy argued for another solution: demolition of the library and construction on the same site of a new combined parliamentary and national library at an estimated cost of around $6,000,000. The National Library did not exist at that time but it was planned: no site had been decided. Howe expressed himself as being attracted to the idea of a new combined library 'as being the most practical and efficient,' and several other ministers expressed similar views. A minority were dubious.

The record of decision was that the cabinet

(a) deferred decision upon the alternatives put forward by the Minister of Public Works for reconditioning of the Library of Parliament or the construction of a new combined Parliamentary and National Library until such time as the Prime Minister could be present;

(b) agreed that the Prime Minister be informed that the members of the Cabinet present were inclined on balance to favour the removal of the existing structure and the construction on the same site of a new structure which would serve the purpose both of the Library of Parliament and of the National Library.[21]

Howe asked me, as acting secretary to the cabinet, to report the discussion to Pickersgill and to the prime minister on their return.

In a memorandum to the prime minister, after reporting the discussion, I expressed my own 'great misgivings about this whole line of discussion and about the measure of support it appears to be getting.' I went on to say:

The Parliamentary Library has, I think, acquired quite a national significance, partly because of its very unusual architecture on the splendid site above the river, and partly because it is the only portion of the old Parliament Building ante-dating Confederation which survived the fire of 1916. It has appeared on our postage stamps, and it probably has attached to it more emotional significance than any other building in the national capital. Most other countries with more historic buildings and less wealth than Canada think it wise to spend large sums in the preservation of their historic structures, and I think that a great many people would regard it as something approaching a national scandal if we were to destroy the Parliamentary Library.[22]

I found an important ally in the parliamentary librarian, F.A. Hardy. I suspect that it was through him that the Montreal *Gazette* and the Ottawa *Journal* got wind of the 'new library' idea. Both came out strongly against it, as later did the Winnipeg *Free Press*.

A special committee of cabinet looked into the options for the library and came back to the cabinet on 9 October. The cabinet agreed: '(a) there be no attempt to combine the Library of Parliament and the National Library in a single structure on Parliament Hill; (b) an architect be retained by the Department of Public Works to prepare detailed plans for the renovation of the Library of Parliament building which would retain the exterior appearance exactly as at present.'[23]

That was a major success. The exterior would be saved – but what about the interior? It was entirely of wood, with superb carving done by hand nearly a hundred years before, completely in harmony with the spirit of the Gothic architecture as interpreted by the Victorian tastes of the time.

I had St Laurent's direction to keep in touch with the handling of the job by the Department of Public Works and I soon learned that the wood panels were being considered a fire hazard.

On 16 October 1952 I sent a memorandum to Pickersgill 'at the risk of becoming boring.' I had found out that, with chemical treatment, the panels would not be a hazard and went on: 'The only real argument for replacing the panelling is, therefore, one of taste. I think we are much too close to the Victorian era to be able to judge with much confidence or finality about the merits of its work. It is usual for a succeeding generation to decry what has gone before. Our position is not too far removed from that of the restorers of many English and continental buildings who chose to improve on what had been done in the generation before. I do not know of a single case where their efforts have not been regretted and condemned.'[24] Jack sent my memorandum on to the prime minister with the notation: 'I am not convinced, but I am shaken.'

The prime minister lent his support to the cause of preserving the panels. A report by the minister of public works to the cabinet on 18 February 1953 included the recommendation of a 'special committee' of which the prime minister, in a remarkable indication of interest, had found time to be a member. It covered the entire plan, including the treatment of the interior. The 'ornamental woodwork would be treated to make it fire resistant and replaced' – that is, it would be restored to its original position. The cabinet approved the recommendation.

That should have ended the struggle but it didn't. In June 1953, when the prime minister and Pickersgill were in London at the conference of

Commonwealth prime ministers, I learned that the barbarians were once more at the panels. Hardy had been told by Murphy that 'they were not going to be able to save the panelling inside the library.'

On 4 June I sent a note to Pickersgill by 'Air Bag,' knowing that he would put it in front of the prime minister. Referring to what Hardy had told me, I said: 'On learning this I phoned Mr. Murphy to point out to him that the cabinet had decided that the interior appearance as well as the exterior appearance was to be retained as at present, and that the wooden panelling was to be preserved. He said that he had not understood that it was a matter of any importance.'[25]

In my letter to Pickersgill I gave chapter and verse on every conclusion by the special cabinet committee on the library, on the report of the architect who had been retained (and who favoured preserving the panels), on the methods of fireproofing, and on the views of the joint Senate–House of Commons committee on the library which had agreed on 26 February that 'the present interior and exterior appearance, including panelling and stonework, be maintained as much as possible consistent with a high degree of fireproofing.' I ended my letter: 'I have got Mr. Murphy's assurance that on no account will he let the contractor start ripping out the panelling, as he was at one stage prepared to do. The matter will, however, have to be decided definitely almost at once since it affects an early stage of the work.'[26]

St Laurent had become completely convinced: the restoration, inside and out, was to preserve the visual aspects of the original structure. From then on I was confident I knew his mind and could speak for him. What was equally important was that the deputy minister of public works had finally acquired that conviction too.

By August I had achieved the dignity of assistant secretary to the cabinet (there was only one in those days) and decided that I could tell the deputy minister of public works what would be approved and what would not and get the prime minister's approval after the event. Any such confidence would have been impossible with King. It was a great spur to action to be able to close a letter of 26 August 1953 to Murphy with four pages of specifics about what would and what would not do in response to queries he had raised, ending with the words: 'I shall bring your letter and this reply to the attention of the prime minister.' St Laurent approved.

When I went into the library in the winter of 1994–5 for the first time in several years, I had the same reaction that, I gather, many visitors have: that of being moved by its beauty but also of seeing it as a testimonial to the confidence in Canada that inspired the leaders and the people of what was, in 1865, a small, poor colony on an undeveloped subarctic frontier. I have no doubt that the decision to preserve the jewel that is the Library of Parliament was right. I feel almost as confident that the library would not have come through a perilous passage if I had not been as relentlessly persistent forty years ago as I was. Nor would it have survived if St Laurent had not been so patient and reasonable a man. He was open to argument and, once persuaded of a course, he was not to be changed. The library is today, in a very real sense, his monument. In a more historically conscious country like Britain it would have a plaque in his honour.

Canada and the Law of the Sea

The 'fishing war' between Canada and Spain in March 1995 dramatized for Canadians as never before the importance for us of the law of the sea. Then, as now, the limit of fishery control by a state under generally recognized international law was two hundred miles from its coasts. The 'nose' and the 'tail' of the Grand Banks, as the seabed shelves gradually off the Newfoundland coast, were just outside that distance, and it was there that Spanish trawlers were fishing for the dwindling stock of turbot. Canada, under its law, purported to exercise control in the interest of conservation because fish swim and the turbot were 'straddling stocks' that moved from the Canadian zone to the area immediately outside. Spain rejected the Canadian argument. It claimed that our action in boarding the *Estai*, a Spanish trawler lawfully fishing on the high seas, and taking it into St John's was piracy, a flagrant breach of international law. It was for Canadians superb drama, played out in press and television with great skill by the minister of fisheries, Brian Tobin. What was not mentioned in any discussion I saw or heard, however, was that this was simply, in a new and belligerent form, a further part in the role Canada had been playing for nearly forty years in pushing for the development of the law of the sea.

When Newfoundland became part of Canada in 1949, the most generally recognized limit of territorial waters was three miles. There was no concept of a fishing zone beyond those three miles: outside the three miles was the high sea, open to everyone with no control, national or international. Canada was one of the countries that began and has since continually pressed for the much more effective regime we have today. The 1995 'war,' with its shots across the bow and boarding in the open sea, was different in method but not in purpose from the creative policy on the law of the sea that our governments have been following since the first Law of the Sea conference in 1958.

The internationally recognized extent of the territorial sea can be of great importance for a country like Canada. In general, the outer limit of that sea is its territorial boundary. The country has sovereignty over its territorial sea subject only to the right of innocent passage by the ships of other countries. The sovereignty extends vertically as well as horizontally. Canada has the longest coastline in the world. As a result, international law determining the rules for the measurement of territorial waters has more importance for us than for any other country.

A conference at The Hague in 1930 had attempted to bring order out of differences in the laws about territorial waters then applied by various countries but without success. The majority in 1930 favoured three marine miles measured from the low-water line on all coasts except for bays, where the three miles were to be measured from a headland-to-headland 'closing line' that could not be more than ten miles in length. If the bay could not be 'closed' by a line ten miles or less, measurements would have to be taken from the low-water line around the shore of the bay. Those were the rules accepted by the countries of the British Commonwealth, the United States, France, Japan, and many other states.

Before 1930, British policy on territorial waters had been accepted as Canadian policy with no questions asked, subject to specific cases mostly involving our coastal boundaries with the United States. We had no real policy of our own. In 1932 and 1937 a committee of the federal departments concerned looked at some problems about our territorial waters but did not recommend any change in our application of the British doctrine.

After the war, new circumstances led to new policies in several countries. More and more claimed limits beyond three miles. In 1949 an International Law Commission was established to attempt once again to codify the 'regime of the high seas.' In the case of Canada, the entry that same year of Newfoundland into Confederation produced a new situation in the Gulf of St Lawrence. While the Gulf is enormous in size, it was now for the first time almost entirely surrounded by Canadian territory. During the debate on Newfoundland in the House of Commons on 8 February 1949, St Laurent said: 'We intend to contend ... that the waters west of Newfoundland constituting the Gulf of St Lawrence shall become an inland sea.'[27] If it could be established as an inland sea, our territorial waters would then be outside that 'sea,' measured from baselines across the openings between the coast of Newfoundland and the coasts of Labrador on the north and Cape Breton on the south.

Another new factor of importance for Canada was introduced in 1951 when the International Court of Justice ruled in favour of Norway in the Anglo-Norwegian fisheries case. In 1935 Norway had drawn baselines along its coast that did not follow the low-water line as international law in general required. It then measured its terrritorial sea (four miles was their law) out from those lines. The court ruled in Norway's favour. By a majority of ten to two the judges decided that, 'where a coast is deeply indented and cut into' or where a coast 'is bordered by an archipelago,' baselines could be drawn and 'the baseline becomes independent of the low water mark.' Our coastlines in the Pacific and the Arctic are deeply indented. Moreover, in the Arctic we have one of the largest archipelagos in the world. It was possible that it could be completely closed in by straight baselines under the new decision. The waters inside those lines would then become inland waters of Canada, subject to one exception only – a right of innocent passage through any strait used for international navigation.[28]

The cabinet decided that the interdepartmental committee on territorial waters, which had not met since 1937, should be revived. The committee met on 9 November 1949, with the secretary to the cabinet, Norman Robertson, as chairman. I was a member of the committee and Pierre Trudeau, then on our staff in the Privy Council Office, was secretary. Eight interested departments were represented.

The committee became one of the most active and productive there had been to that time. In October 1952 George Curtis, dean of law at the University of British Columbia, was retained to do a full analysis of international law on territorial waters and of the Canadian interests. When Norman Robertson returned to London as high commissioner in May 1952, I succeeded him as chairman of the committee. A cabinet committee on territorial waters was established in 1955 to receive and consider the reports of our committee and to make recommendations to the cabinet. As a result of this start in 1952, Canada was the best prepared of all countries for discussions that began in the United Nations in 1956 and continued at a special Law of the Sea conference in Geneva in 1958.

By the spring of 1956 the government had come to the conclusion, based on our committee reports, that Canada should move to the Norwegian 'straight baseline' system wherever our coasts resembled theirs and should adopt a twelve-mile limit for our territorial sea, rather than the three miles that had been the long-established policy of Canada and the rest of the Commonwealth. The change of policy became public when, on being pressed in the House of Commons on 30 July 1956, the prime minister said: 'I do not think we should venture to claim that the territorial waters extend beyond the twelve-mile limit.'[29]

This was a sharp jolt to the United Kingdom and the United States. In a private meeting at the United Nations in New York, their representatives said that they were 'surprised and dismayed' to learn that Canada intended to support the twelve-mile limit. St Laurent's government did not alter its decision, but the people of Canada altered the government in the election of 10 June 1957. The new Progressive Conservative government, led by Diefenbaker, changed many things and one was the new Canadian position on territorial waters.

George Drew had been named high comissioner to London and one issue raised with him by the British government at an early stage in his new mission was Canada's stated intention to adopt the twelve-mile limit. As before, the British strongly objected.

The most important objective for Canada in adopting a twelve-mile limit was to gain control over the additional nine miles of water in order to exclude foreign fishing. To gain that control, without the Diefenbaker government having to adopt a position that put it in direct conflict with the United Kingdom and the United States, our committee proposed a new idea that was not part of international law to that time: a limit of three miles for the territorial sea plus a 'fishing zone' of nine miles in which the coastal state would have exclusive fishing rights. This became the 'Canadian proposal' at the Geneva Conference in 1958. It attracted much interest and support, especially from the developing countries. It was not, however, enough for some countries that had already established limits of territorial waters wider than three miles.

When it became clear at the conference that the '3 plus 9' formula could not succeed, the government agreed that the Canadian delegation could propose a revised formula – '6 plus 6' – six miles of territorial sea and, outside that, a six-mile exclusive fishing zone. This appealed to many countries, but it also brought Canada back into conflict with Britain and the United States over the width of the territorial sea, which was important to them.

The conflict sharpened as it became clear that the new 'Canadian proposal' was gaining support and as Canada became increasingly identified as the leader of the countries seeking a regime that was more in the interest of newer, less powerful states. If it became the accepted international regime, it would be a major shift from the dominance of the older powers whose interests were in navies, open seas, and high-sea fishing.

Drew was a doughty fighter and it appealed to him to be leading a cause that many delegations praised as a fair and reasonable compromise between the traditional positions of the naval powers and the new, extremely wide claims of some countries with rich offshore fisheries. He developed all the zeal of a convert from his initial belief that the traditional British position should be Canada's position. The head of the British delegation, Sir Reginald Manningham-Buller, was equally if not more strongly attached to 'freedom of the seas' with the three-mile limit as vital for British naval power.

In the interests of peace, but especially in the hope of getting a position on which the three countries could agree, the head of the American delegation at Geneva, Arthur Dean, invited Sir Reginald, Drew, and their senior advisers, of which I was one, to a dinner from which some agreement might, he hoped, somehow emerge. It did not. The dinner became steadily more acrimonious and ended with Drew, after considerable provocation, informing Britain's attorney general that he was 'a pompous ass.'

The following morning the legal adviser to the British delegation, Sir Gerald Fitzmaurice, telephoned Jim Nutt, the senior legal adviser of our delegation, to inform him of the crisis: 'Our heads of delegation almost came to blows.' However, Sir Reginald was prepared to drop the matter if Drew apologized to him. Nutt conveyed the message to me and to our formidable head of delegation. His vocabulary and his wrath had lost none of their heat overnight. His reply, which Jim duly conveyed, left no doubt that there would be no apology – unless Sir Reginald was disposed to make one to Drew.

There was a second conference on the Law of the Sea in 1960 and a third in 1964. Agreement was reached on many issues and the Canadian status gained in 1958 made Canada a leading player. On the breadth of the territorial sea, more and more countries moved to the twelve-mile limit, just as we had argued to the British and Americans they would do if no agreement could be reached on our compromise of '6 plus 6.' It was the destructive opposition by Britain and the United States to the Canadian initiative that made it possible for something worse, from their point of view, to get the two-thirds majority. In 1970 Canada adopted the twelve-mile limit itself. We moved to the generally accepted 200-mile zone of today in 1977. With that we at last had a law and an international regime more in accord with our interests – but still with the problems that the 'fishery war' of 1995 revealed.

A Churchillian Visit, 1952

Churchill's superlative wartime leadership had ended dramatically in 1945. Victory in Europe was achieved on 8 May of that year. On 16 July the three allied leaders – Churchill, Truman, and Stalin – met at Potsdam, the heart of pre-war Prussia, to determine the fate of post-war Germany and to lay plans for a new Europe. On 21 July a victory parade of British troops in Berlin saluted their hero without whose inspiration in the darkest days victory would have been impossible. Five days later, on 26 July 1945, the British voters demonstrated their democratic concern about the future, not their gratitude for the past, and defeated Churchill and his government. It was the new prime minister, Attlee, who went back to conclude the Potsdam Conference for Britain.

Six years later another election on 25 October 1951 brought Churchill back to office and on 4 January 1952 he went to Washington for talks with President Truman. The plan was for Mr and Mrs Churchill to come on to Ottawa for a banquet in his honour. That plan was apparently imperilled by Churchill's hurt at an ill-timed decision in Ottawa that the Royal Canadian Navy would no longer play 'Rule Britannia.' Two exchanges of telegrams between an offended Chuchill and St Laurent had not produced any change. Sir John Colville, private secretary to Churchill for many years, records the crisis and the final decision to come to Canada anyway:

> ... it was an ill-humoured, unco-operative Churchill who eventually boarded a special night sleeper at Washington bound for Ottawa. In the morning St Laurent and his whole cabinet were assembled at the railway station to greet him. Behind them were the massed bands of the Canadian army, navy and air-force. As the old man stepped down on to the platform, the massed bands struck 'Rule Britannia.' He stood there, hat in hand, with tears pouring down his cheeks; and henceforward nobody ever dared to utter even the mildest criticism of Monsieur St Laurent or of Canada.[30]

By accident I became an attendant at the private lunch given by the prime minister for Churchill on the Sunday following his arrival. My wife and I had bought our first house in the summer of 1951, part of a housing project in Manor Park, a new subdivision of Ottawa. There was still much to be done and I had decided to devote a part of the Sunday to painting the basement floor. My mother would not have approved. I was well into the job when a telephone call came from the Prime Minister's Office. Norman Robertson, secretary to the cabinet, had been suddenly taken ill and could not attend the prime minister's lunch. The table was laid, place cards were set, and all was to start in half an hour. Could I come in Norman's place? I gulped and said I could: the chance to see Churchill again was not to be missed.

Clean but smelling of turpentine, I arrived at the gate of 24 Sussex Drive well after the guests had been bidden to be there. I was held up by the RCMP guard. He was not impressed by my light green Chevrolet car: it bore no resemblance to an official limousine. Nor did I look like a minister, a general, or even a 'mandarin': I was much too young. He did find that there was a 'Robertson' on his list but was still uncertain and hesitant when he realized that a car had arrived behind mine with the red plate and gold crown of the governor general on it – and Churchill and Anthony Eden inside. The only solution was to let me pass and to hope I was not some clever journalist in disguise.

All the other guests were in the drawing room and Churchill was ushered in just minutes after I got there. He was visibly older than in 1948 and was guided with care to a chair specially set for him. After introductions, no one spoke to him as he gave full attention to his well-filled glass – presumably of scotch. At the luncheon table he sat in the centre on one side, opposite St Laurent. Conversation went on around him, but he said nothing. It was apparent that his party knew the lunch routine and that the Canadian hosts had been well briefed. It was not until after a good lunch, several glasses of wine, and two of cognac that suddenly a current turned on. Churchill came to life and Anthony Eden became the object of his teasing and raillery. Eden handled the banter in good style, even though a lot of it was about his impatience to see Churchill retire – which he did not admit but did not entirely deny. From then until his departure, one saw the private Churchill for whom one of life's greatest delights was the company of friends and colleagues who could take part in the wit and conversation for which he was famous. My basement floor did not get finished for another week or two.

The Reluctant Prime Minister

St Laurent was probably the only one of our prime ministers who did not want the job. He did not even want to be in politics. He joined King's government in 1941 over the resistance of his wife and family only because he thought it was his duty to do so at a time when young

Canadians were being asked to risk their lives in the war. He saw it as his war service when the death of Ernest Lapointe, King's leader in Quebec, left a gap that he was told he could best fill. He assured his wife that it would be for the duration of the war only and that it might be over in a year or two.

In 1948 St Laurent was reluctant to be a candidate for the leadership of the Liberal Party when King stepped down. King pressed him hard, as did others in the cabinet and the party. He allowed his name to stand but would wage no campaign. The only temptation towards the leadership and the office of prime minister was probably Sir Wilfrid Laurier's expressed view that it was a unique set of circumstances that had made him prime minister in 1896 and probably no French-Canadian Catholic would ever be acceptable to the country again. It would be good for French Canadians and for the country to demonstrate that was not the case.

St Laurent's administrations from 1949 to 1956 probably gave Canada the most consistently good, financially responsible, trouble-free government the country has had in its entire history, before as well as after Confederation. Part of that was owing to the united concentration of Canadians on getting back to the business of peace and economic development after all the disruption of war. But a part of that unanimity was because of good planning, policies, and administration by the governments that St Laurent led.

I saw St Laurent in cabinet over four years. He was a superbly effective chairman. He read every cabinet paper, thought through every proposal and problem, ensured that every essential issue was discussed, and led his colleagues to a consensus with sure judgment. Jack Pickersgill succeeded Norman Robertson as clerk of the Privy Council and secretary to the cabinet on 12 June 1952. While he had worked with St Laurent as prime minister for nearly four years, the new job gave him his first view of him in the handling of his cabinet. His comments fit exactly with my own observations: 'As St Laurent hated to waste time, cabinet meetings were exceedingly business-like ... He was always attentive and rarely impatient. No minister was restrained from presenting his views for fear St Laurent might take offence, but I believe some ministers were restrained by the fear of appearing to be ill-informed or ineffective. More than any prime minister I have known, St Laurent dominated his cabinet, not by imposing his authority, but by his sheer intellect, his wide knowledge, and his unequalled persuasiveness.'[31]

St Laurent's cabinets operated with a business-like efficiency impossible under King's methods, notoriously absent under Diefenbaker, and of uncertain reliability under Pearson. The efficiency showed and could be counted on until St Laurent's last year in office.

Like King, he gave the unity of Canada the first place in his policy objectives – a priority he stated specifically after winning his second election in 1953. Related to that priority was completion of the development of Canada 'from colony to nation,' as Professor A.R.M. Lower termed the process. He saw no conflict between that and active participation in the Commonwealth: quite the reverse. He viewed the Commonwealth as an effective agency in helping countries just emerging from colonial status, like India, Pakistan, and Ceylon, to become completely independent without allowing nationalism to push them into chauvinism and resentful isolation. As the leader of a people who had, like the people of so many new Commonwealth countries, been conquered by Great Britain, St Laurent could speak to their prime ministers and presidents in a way that no other member of the Commonwealth conferences could. He, a French-Canadian prime minister, was a demonstration of what was possible through democracy and tolerance. He had no doubts about the value of a forum for the kind of discussion and cooperation the Commonwealth conferences made possible.

It was because of his unique position that Nehru and other Asian Commonwealth leaders pressed St Laurent to undertake the visit to their countries in 1954. A visit to twelve countries, the Asian ones in intense heat, spread over nearly six weeks was too much for a man of seventy-two. The consequences were almost certainly a factor in St Laurent's inadequate handling of the pipeline crisis in 1956.

St Laurent was a leading architect, along with Lester Pearson, of the North Atlantic Treaty Organization and a strong proponent of Canadian participation in it. So soon after the war, which had been unpopular in Quebec, and during which the divisiveness of conscription had strained Canadian unity, this might have raised political problems without the authority and respect that St Laurent commanded. He firmly supported Canada's active role in the United Nations and the creative initiatives of Pearson as secretary of state for external affairs. None of that international activism would have been possible with King as prime minister.

St Laurent's greatest single contribution to the unity of Canada was probably made before he became prime minister – in the conscription crisis of 1944. When King decided that limited conscription for overseas service had to be resorted to, his 'Record' for 1944–5 makes it clear that the support of St Laurent was critical in the cabinet itself. Following that decision was the parliamentary debate. The importance of St Laurent's address in the House of Commons on 6 December 1944 is reflected in King's entry in his diary for that day: '... the feature of this afternoon's debate was St Laurent's magnificent speech. Magnificent in the sense that it was forthright, honest, sincere, straightforward and true. His decision to stand or fall with me was tremendously applauded in the House ... He is indeed a sterling character. The House gave his utterance a great reception. There was not an interruption while he was speaking.'[32]

King's enthusiasm is understandable: without St Laurent's firm position the support of many Members of Parliament from Quebec would have been uncertain, if not, impossible. It was an eloquent comment on the status St Laurent had acquired, in Quebec especially, that so much depended on a man who had entered Parliament only three years before. He had an important share in King's success in avoiding the kind of crisis that shook the country over the same issue in 1917.

St Laurent did not have King's parliamentary skills. If he had had them, the pipeline crisis would not have happened in 1956. But it is also possible that the TransCanada Pipeline would not have happened either. It was a bold project and boldness was not a merit in King's eyes. He often said, to his staff and to his diary, that the things he prevented were at least as important as the things he did. St Laurent was more prepared to take risks. His leadership was clearer than King's, with none of the tortuous qualities that kept King's opponents – and sometimes his own followers – off balance and uncertain. He was direct, open, and honest in public as in private. Those qualities were an important part of the confidence he inspired until the last unfortunate year.

Jack Pickersgill knew St Laurent better than anyone else. Near the end of his account of his relations with St Laurent, he says: 'My admiration for him increased steadily. What I admired most was not his superb intelligence and his judgment, which rarely failed, but his genuine modesty, his lack of concern for his place in history, and his complete freedom from meanness or malice of any kind. To me, he was the greatest Canadian of our time.'[33]

Pickersgill repeated that judgment to me many times during the more than twenty years he lived after writing it. I at no time heard him make a direct comparison with other prime ministers, although he did believe that one of the reasons others – including King – may have seemed to be more wizardly in solving problems was that they did not have the same capacity to foresee them. St Laurent, he said, foresaw them and acted to avoid them before the public knew they were there. There is probably a lot in that. St Laurent did not have King's aversion to act until it was absolutely essential. However, he did not have as difficult a time to lead the country as King did during the war nor did he leave his party as strong as King left it to him – an important political obligation for a leader. It is not clear how much St Laurent should be blamed for that failure. He did not realize how exhausting the trips of 1954 would be, just as King did not anticipate the effects on his health of his final trip of 1948. The exhaustion of 1954 led to the failure to control the parliamentary process in 1956 which led to defeat in 1957.

When the whole of St Laurent's record of accomplishment is taken into account, there can be no question, in my view, that he is among the half dozen greatest of our prime ministers. He probably ranks very close to Macdonald and Laurier as the one most admired and respected by the Canadian people of his day and by his own colleagues. In modesty and humanity he had no peer.

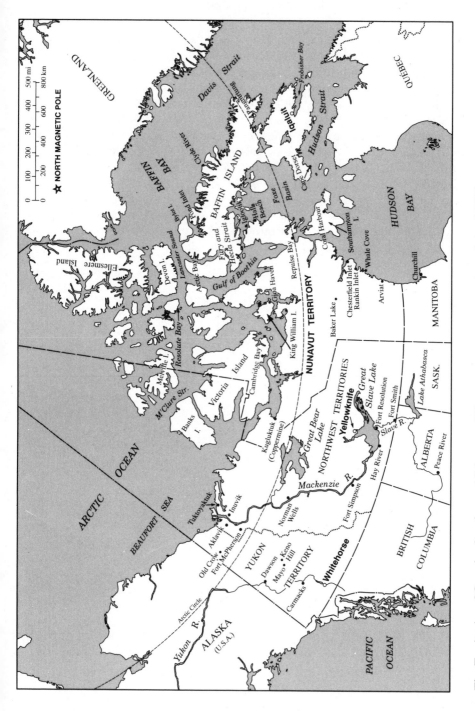

The Territories of Canada after the establishment of Nunavut as a separate territory, 1 April 1999.

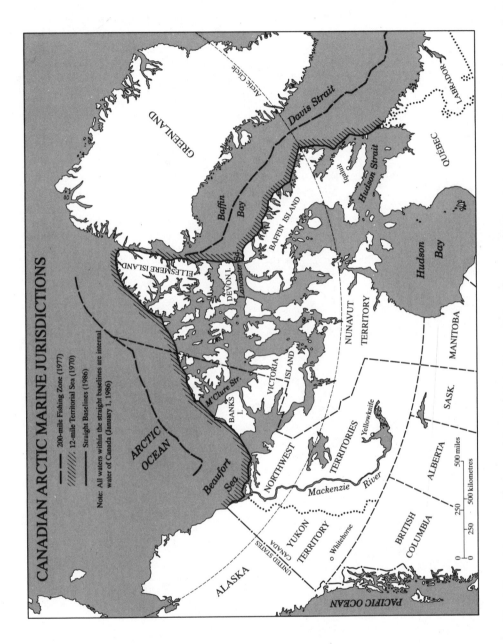

CANADIAN ARCTIC MARINE JURISDICTIONS

—— 200-mile Fishing Zone (1977)
////// 12-mile Territorial Sea (1970)
—— Straight Baselines (1986)

Note: All waters within the straight baselines are internal water of Canada (January 1, 1986)

GREENLAND

Davis Strait

Baffin Bay

Hudson Strait

QUÉBEC

LABRADOR

Iqaluit

ELLESMERE ISLAND

DEVON I.

Lancaster Sd.

BAFFIN ISLAND

Hudson Bay

NUNAVUT TERRITORY

MANITOBA

M'Clure Str.

VICTORIA ISLAND

BANKS I.

ARCTIC OCEAN

Beaufort Sea

NORTHWEST TERRITORIES

Yellowknife

Mackenzie River

SASK.

ALBERTA

YUKON TERRITORY

o Whitehorse

BRITISH COLUMBIA

UNITED STATES
CANADA

ALASKA

PACIFIC OCEAN

Arctic Circle

0   250   500 miles
0   250   500 kilometres

105

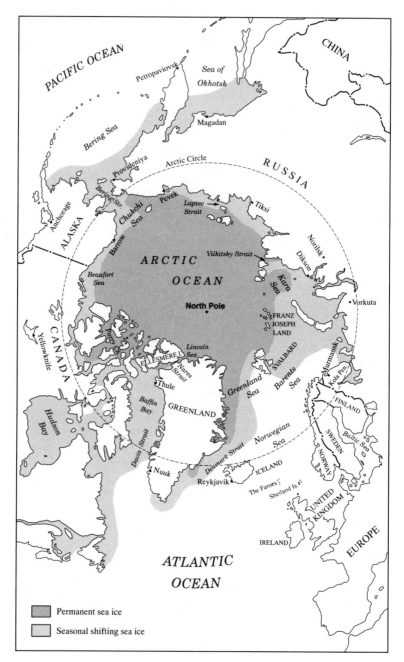

The Circumpolar North.

chapter six

Canada Discovers the North, 1953–1957

The second election in which St Laurent ran as prime minister and leader of the Liberal Party took place on 10 August 1953. Like the first in 1949, it was a resounding victory. The Liberals won 170 seats out of 265. By early September the prime minister was rested and ready to plan his new administration. On 16 September I was told that St Laurent wished to see me. It was not a total surprise. Jack Pickersgill had warned me the day before that the prime minister had decided to offer me the position of deputy minister of resources and development.

That department had a curious array of unconnected responsibilities that only history could explain. Its National Parks Branch administered all the National Parks of Canada, the National Historic Parks, and our National Historic Sites. The Engineering and Water Resources Branch was responsible for federal policy and administration in all the lakes and rivers that came under federal jurisdiction. Its engineering section provided technical advice for the Canadian section of the International Joint Commission in relation to our boundary waters with the United States. The Northern Administration and Lands Branch was what was left of the great Department of the Interior, which had administered all of Canada outside provincial boundaries from Confederation onward, including the enormous federal crown lands on which the settlement of the west occurred. The Forestry Branch was responsible for virtually all Canadian research on trees and forests and for advising provinces and the lumber industry on scientific and technical matters. The Canadian Government Travel Bureau was the national tourist promotion agency of the day. To round things out, the National Museum was a branch of the department. To try to be an umbrella to it all were the Administration Services of the department and a small deputy minister's staff.

I knew virtually nothing about anything the department covered. The only thing I was sure I would be interested in was the 'northern' part. While only northern 'administration' was mentioned in the departmental act, I knew that the department had general responsibility for all things in the Northwest Territories and the Yukon Territory that did not come under any other department. I knew, too, that the deputy minister had a second hat: that of commissioner of the Northwest Territories. In that role he headed the Territorial government.

The really significant thing for me was that, if I became deputy minister of the department, I would sever all connection with the Department of External Affairs – the real focus of my interest in entering the public service in the first place. I was glad to have twenty-four hours to think it over.

In the nearly four years I had been working with St Laurent our relations had become easy and relaxed. When I went into his office, he told me that the government had decided that there must be a more active policy for the Canadian north and an administration that dealt with it really as a part of Canada rather than as something that was thought about only when some problem arose. To develop a new approach, he had decided that there should be a new 'team': a new minister and a new deputy minister. The minister was going to be Jean Lesage, a bright young member from Quebec, who had no ministerial experience but who had been in Parliament for eight years and parliamentary assistant to the secretary of state for external affairs and later to the minister of finance. Lesage's deputy minister should be someone who knew government and who was young and vigorous: me.

I thanked the prime minister for his confidence in me, which I very genuinely appreciated: it was a great compliment. I then went on: 'I think, Mr St Laurent, that, if you had reviewed all the departments of government to find the one of which I know the least, it would be Resources and Development.' The prime minister smiled at me like a benevolent father. 'Well, Gordon, I said that you are young. I suppose it is just possible that you may learn.'

That settled it. The date for Lesage and me to take over was fixed at 15 November. The inscription on St Laurent's photograph, signed for me on that day, was 'To my friend Gordon Robertson with warm regards and best wishes.' I felt I needed them. I was thirty-six – about fifteen years younger than the youngest branch director in the department. I had never administered any staff larger than a dozen or so. My new empire

In planning for my new department, it was an advantage to continue to be in the Privy Council Office for some weeks until I was to take over as deputy minister on 15 November. It gave me a direct access to the prime minister that would otherwise not have been possible. I discussed with Phillips what might best be done to implement the cabinet's wish for early indication of the government's new policy in the north. The most immediate way to draw attention to it lay in the speech from the throne to open the first session of the new Parliament. The speech could announce new legislation that would for the first time establish a department with comprehensive responsibility for the Canadian North. The prime minister liked the idea and proposed a name for the department forthwith: why not 'Northern Territories and National Resources'? Bob Phillips was not happy about the limiting tone of 'Territories': there were people too. There were also problems and there would be policies that would not be limited to the Territorial boundaries. 'Northern Affairs' would have the broader scope that was wanted. He suggested the 'Department of Northern Affairs and Development.'[3]

With Pickersgill's agreement, I sent a memorandum to the prime minister on 7 October. After outlining the arguments in favour of a new act, I said:

In a new Act there should, I think, be much more on the North. It probably should include reference to:

(a) administration of the Yukon and N.W.T.;

(b) coordination of government activities in the Yukon and N.W.T. (which is the responsibility of the Department under the Cabinet decision of February 19, 1953);

(c) measures for the economic and political development of the Yukon and N.W.T.;

(d) protection of the Eskimos and measures to strengthen their economic and social position;

(e) measures for the effective administration and control of the Arctic Archipelago. (This might be done in such a fashion as to give a legislative statement of our sovereignty over the entire Archipelago.)

For the name of the department I adopted Bob's suggestion of 'Affairs' and proposed 'Department of National Resources and Northern Affairs.' Why I put 'Northern Affairs' second in the departmental name I do not know. It did not show much political sense. It was the only thing the prime minister disagreed with: the new department was, he said, to have the name 'Northern Affairs and National Resources' and so it became. It retained that name until a reorganization in 1968 moved the responsibility for Indians and Indian affairs to the department. It then became the Department of Indian Affairs and Northern Development – DIAND in the acronyms of government.

In moving second reading of Bill 6 'respecting the Department of Northern Affairs and National Resources' on 8 December 1953, the prime minister said that the effect of the legislation would be 'to give a new emphasis and scope to work already being done, and to indicate that the government and Parliament wish to see such greater emphasis made a continuing feature of the operation of government.' He added: 'Apparently we have administered these vast territories of the north in an almost continuing state of absence of mind. I think all honourable members now feel that the territories are vastly important to Canada and that it is time that more attention was focussed upon their possibilities and what they will mean to this Canadian nation.'[4] In commenting on the implications of the legislation, St Laurent said:

> This will be the first time that this designation 'northern affairs' will have appeared in the name of a department of the government of Canada. I hope it will be felt, as we felt, that it is desirable that this be done as one of the indications of the growing interest in the importance of these northern territories ... The Minister will have the specific duty to co-ordinate the activities of all government departments in the Northwest Territories and the Yukon. It will also be his responsibility to promote measures for further economic and political development in the Northwest Territories and the Yukon and to develop knowledge of the problems in the north and the means of dealing with them through scientific investigations and technological research.[5]

The prime minister went into the new importance that the Canadian North had acquired because of its strategic location. He said: 'The Canadian northland lies between the two greatest powers in the world ... There will no doubt have to be joint measures taken for the security of the North American continent ... All these joint undertakings are carried out under the principle of full respect for the sovereignty of the country in which they are carried out.'[6] The newly elected president of the United States, Dwight Eisenhower, had addressed the House of Commons only three weeks before and had spoken of the Canadian North in the Cold War world and of this understanding between the two countries. The establishment of a 'Department of Northern Affairs,' would,

St Laurent said, be 'symbolic of the actuality of the exercise of Canadian sovereignty in these northern lands right up to the pole.' Reaching to the North Pole was a bit of hyperbole even though Canada had, since early in the century, been putting 'sector lines' on polar projections of maps of Canada to indicate a claim to all land within the sector. There is a lot of frozen ocean and no land at all between the northern tip of Ellesmere Island and the North Pole, ocean that is the 'open sea' in international law. The sector lines created much confusion. Canada at no time claimed the open sea of the Arctic. It claimed all land within the lines – known or unknown.

Hon. George Drew, leader of the opposition, expressed 'general support for the measure.' The act received third reading two days later, on 10 December 1953.

The non-partisan nature of the support for the new northern policy was made clear later that day when a bill to amend the Northwest Territories Act was introduced. The amendments were to make some changes in procedures for the election of members of the Council of the Northwest Territories. Drew enquired whether it would not be desirable to raise the number of elected members from three to five. Lesage, only three weeks in office, said that he would consult the members of the Council themselves since, by happy accident, the Council was then meeting in Ottawa. After the Christmas recess, on 19 January 1954, he reported that the Council had considered whether it would be desirable to increase its elected membership to five as Drew proposed by creating constituencies in the Arctic, especially in the eastern part of the Territories which was unrepresented in the Council. He said: 'The view of the members of the Council was that the population and state of development in the districts of Keewatin and Franklin is not such at the present time that it would be desirable or even feasible to have an elected member from a constituency that covered those areas.'[7]

The members of the Council were, however, in favour of an increase in elected representation and recommended that a fourth constituency be established in the western region – the District of Mackenzie – before the election of 1954. Representation for the eastern Arctic should be considered at a later date. Drew expressed full agreement and provision for a fourth elected member was made.

Policy Priorities for the North
The staff available in my department to plan and to carry out the undefined policies that the prime minister, and now the Parliament of

Canada, said they wanted in the Canadian North was not impressive. Bob Phillips later put the situation tersely:

> When the Department of Northern Affairs and National Resources was formed in 1953, the total staff of its Northern Administration and Lands Branch was 376. Of these people, 150 were in Ottawa, the rest thinly scattered in the larger settlements of the Yukon and the Mackenzie. There were only twenty-six teachers. Game and forestry and the administration of Wood Buffalo National Park were the main concerns of the field staff. There were four administative officers in all the Northwest Territories, all junior, not one of them beyond the tree-line, not one in Arctic Quebec. The Commissioner of the Yukon had one junior administrator to assist him. There was one junior engineer in all the north. Not a single social worker concerned with the north was employed in the north or in Ottawa. The entire northern budget for capital and operating expenses in that first year of the new department was four million dollars.[8]

The department of which I became deputy minister, before its renaming, was Resources and Development. General Hugh Young, who was my predecessor, had done a lot to improve administration but he had got little support from his minister or the government, which had taken no interest in the north before Pearson's worries in January 1953. This alerted Bob Phillips and me to the importance of developing public interest in the north, for without such interest and the political support it would generate the north might yield to other priorities and pressures.

I found that there were several good administrators in the department: the assistant deputy minister, C.W. Jackson, whose interests and experience did not, however, relate to the North, and the director of the Northern Administration and Lands Branch, F.J.G. Cunningham. But only three individuals who seemed likely to be of much help with new policy: C.H. Herbert, a one-man economic division, who was killed in a car accident two years later; and two quite recent arrivals in the department, Graham W. Rowley, who was an encyclopedia of knowledge of the Arctic and was secretary of the advisory committee on northern development, and Bent Gestur Sivertz, who had entered the public service, like me, in the Department of External Affairs. I quickly arranged to get Bob Phillips to join the department and it was on Herbert, until his death, and these three, together with some excellent people who joined us later, that I relied for ideas and judgment to ensure that I, the least knowledgeable of all at the outset, would be able in turn to advise our new minister, Jean Lesage. It was he who would be responsible before the prime minister and the country for whatever we did or failed to do.

St Laurent had chosen the right man to be minister. Lesage was completely bilingual, with a well-developed and quick intelligence, interested in new ideas, and able to probe them with a lawyer's skill and a politician's awareness of what would be publicly acceptable and what would not. His subsequent career as premier of Quebec from 1960 to 1966 and as the 'Father of the Quiet Revolution' in that province revealed the same ability and energy that he brought to the department in the three and a half years he was our minister. As premier, Lesage would be accused by some of having a Gaullist sense of grandeur that contributed to his defeat in the Quebec election of 1966. There was no sign of that during my happy relationship with him, both when he was my minister and when, after he became premier of Quebec, I was frequently a channel of communication between Ottawa and Quebec – in both directions. We became good friends. I admired Jean's capacity to be at the same time an enthusiastic Canadian and a strong champion of Quebec. My confidence that he was both made it easier to help build some bridges during tense times in 1964 and 1965.

As we worked together, minister and officials, in the winter of 1953–4, it became clear that a major human problem had been developing in the North for several years and that, unless effective measures were taken, the next generation of Aboriginal people would be trapped in lives of increasing hardship and worsening health with no means of escape. One aspect of the problem lay in the philosophy about education – or non-education – that had prevailed with relatively little change from the earliest arrival of Europeans in the North: a philosophy that assumed that the native people would continue indefinitely to pursue a traditional, subsistence lifestyle. For that, no formal education was necessary; indeed it might be positively harmful. The essence of this attitude was summed up in October 1934 at the end of a report to the Council of the Northwest Territories by Dr J.A. Urquhart, a departmental medical officer stationed in Aklavik: 'These children, whether boys or girls, are going to live out their lives in the country. It is, therefore, necessary that everything possible should be done to avoid having the boys over-educated in a scholastic way, particularly if this is to be at the expense of their ability to make a living off hunting, trapping and fishing.'[9]

The philosophy and the reasoning had changed very little in the twenty years from Urquhart's comments. They were defensible as long as conditions were such that a successful, independent life could be supported 'on the land' in the traditional way by all Aboriginals. Yet even then it was open to question if the 'successful independent life' meant enduring a level of hardship, damage to health, and premature death that was considered unacceptable for other Canadian citizens. In any event, it soon became clear that an independent traditional life could no longer be supported by all the Aboriginal people in the North. Moreover, the situation had been worsening with no prospect of change. Diamond Jenness, one of the most knowledgeable people about the Canadian Inuit, had this to say in a report in 1962:

Each year it was becoming more and more impossible for the Eskimos to gain even a bare subsistence, because, quite apart from the fluctuations in the supply of fish and game, their incomes, which hinged directly in the prices of furs, were diminishing rather than increasing, while their needs – or what they had come to consider their needs – were growing both in price and in number. Unless then they could find some source or sources of income additional to the trap-line, or in place of it, they would continue to lean on the government more and more heavily until they became permanent dependants on a dole, victims of all the evils such dependence brings.[10]

Notwithstanding the facts of increasing welfare needs especially in the Arctic areas in the early 1950s, and of falling fur prices, the committee on Eskimo affairs, involving government departments, police, the churches, and the HBC, which met in Ottawa on 19 and 20 May 1952, affirmed 'that Eskimos should be encouraged and helped to live off the land and to follow their traditional way of life.' The affirmation about encouragement may have stemmed more from the lack of any apparent alternative to the 'traditional way of life' than from conviction that trapping and hunting could be sufficient for the future. The committee did agree to establish a subcommittee 'to deal exclusively with education.'[11] However, there was nothing in the report to impart a sense of urgency to the limited program that had begun in 1947.

The philosophy of leaving the Inuit way of life substantially untouched by formal education had also applied for the most part to the Indians of the Northwest Territories, except for the intervention of the Roman Catholic and Anglican churches, with some financial support from the government, in the establishment of residential schools in three or four settlements along the Mackenzie River. In 1947, under the leadership of H.L. Keenleyside, then deputy minister and commissioner of the Northwest Territories, the government began a program of building schools for both Indian and non-Indian children and for some Inuit children at a few settlements. This did not get very far. In 1950 only 117 Inuit children were getting full-time schooling. There was no vocational training. That same year, in all the schools in the Northwest Territories, the total number enrolled in all grades, white and Aboriginal, was only 651 in a total population of 16,000. Of those, only 111 had gone beyond Grade 4. Seven were in high school.

As a matter of principle, and in recognition of the fact that Aboriginal children were Canadian and had the same rights as other Canadian children to education and to some choice about their way of life that only education could make possible, it was clear that a major change had to be made. But what made it urgent was the way the game resources were declining as the human population was increasing. The reasons for that decline were complicated – and will be discussed later – but it was clear that, in the future, the Aboriginal population would not be able to survive on the resources that had made their Native way of life possible in the past.

But that was not the whole human problem. The infant mortality rate for Inuit and northern Indian babies was six times the national average; the death rate for children between one and four was thirteen times the average. Tuberculosis was widespread among both Indians and Inuit. In 1956, 1,578 Inuit – one-seventh of the total population – were in sanatoria. The Department of National Health and Welfare had taken over care for the health of both Indians and Inuit in the Northwest Territories in 1948. Its advice to us was that a major factor in the high rate of tuberculosis and of infant and child mortality was bad housing, especially for the Inuit.

The snow house, generally used by Inuit at that time, is a miracle of human ingenuity but it had some problems. One was that there was no hard-packed snow suitable for building a snow house until well into the Arctic winter, so a large proportion of the Inuit had to survive a part of it in cold, drafty tents made of seal or caribou hides laid over poles, sometimes on top of walls of turf or stone. We were told that such shelters were a major factor in the high level of pulmonary diseases among babies and young children. The other problem came later in the season. Unless effectively lined with skins or canvas, snow houses dripped if they got too warm inside the dome of the roof. The dampness and the possibility of chilling, especially for the young, made the houses a source of every kind of pulmonary ailment. Unless we were to ignore this medical advice, we had to do something about housing.

Jean Lesage announced the policy that was to be the future basis of government action on behalf of the native people of the north:

> The objective of government policy is relatively easy to define. It is to give the Eskimos the same rights, privileges, opportunities, and responsibilities as all other Canadians; in short, to enable them to share fully the national life of Canada.
>
> The broader needs – and they are immediate needs – are health, education and a sound economy. They are not separate problems, each is related to the other. It is not enough to cure disease, the cause of disease must be removed and this is largely a matter of education and improvement of economic conditions. Education must be provided, but this depends on good health and the needs of the economy. A sound economy means a diversified economy not based on the white fox alone; but for new occupations, both health and education are required. In providing health, education and the broad economy the complications are infinite.[12]

The complications were indeed infinite. The fundamental problem in the enormous expanse of the Northwest Territories was to make reasonably effective provision for health services, and to make education possible for Aboriginal children, while still having their parents rely on the only economy that was generally available: the traditional life using the resources of land and sea. That had to be relied on less in the future, but it would still be the main support for many years to come.

Not surprisingly, many Aboriginal people preferred the security of living near a settlement or a nursing station to the risks of total dependence on the game that might come – or might not. Over the years there was a gradual drift to places where schools and nursing stations were established. That reduced the pressure on the traditional resources but did not provide alternative sources of income except for a few. Family allowances and welfare became increasingly important.

The policy was, I think, right. The old neglect could not continue. But the problems of transition are with us still. The 'sound economy' is the most difficult of all.

To Resolute Bay and the North Pole

The months after I took up the job of deputy minister of Northern Affairs and National Resources were the most intensive learning period of my life. All the functions of the department were new to me, as were virtually all the people I was working with. There were six branches,

120

almost totally unrelated to one another, and the director of each was anxious to persuade the new deputy minister of the importance, the mysteries, and especially the needs of his branch.

While the northern problem was the one with which I had been especially charged by the prime minister, both morale and the needs of preparing the financial estimates for financing the next fiscal year meant that I had to spend a lot of time with every branch – national parks, forestry, water resources, national museums, travel bureau – to form a judgment about priorities for money and learn enough of it all that I could provide informed advice to my new minister. To get an increase in funds for the department to begin to implement the new policies, the officials and the ministers of the Treasury Board had to be convinced: no easy task in those days of frugal administration and responsible budgets. It was a frantic, fascinating winter.

One of the things I learned about was a move of a number of Inuit from Port Harrison, now called Inukjuak, in Arctic Quebec, to establish two new settlements in the Arctic Islands – at Resolute Bay and Grise Fiord. The move had taken place in late August and early September of 1953, about three months before I became deputy minister. The reason for it, I was told, was the serious decline in caribou and game generally in the area inland from the east coast of Hudson Bay – the 'hungry coast,' as it was known in the north. I had no reason to find that explanation improbable: it was precisely what I was hearing about game and resources in far too many parts of the north. I was told that the relocation had gone well, with an RCMP detachment assigned in each case to stay nearby at the two new locations to keep an eye on things – to help but not to interfere with the establishment of a traditional, self-supporting way of life. The point was to move the Inuit from a depleted area to good ones in the hope that they would not have to rely on the welfare that was, in several areas, undermining the independence of a remarkable people.

In March 1954 I learned that the minister of national defence, Brooke Claxton, was going to the Arctic to inspect the defence bases at Churchill and Resolute Bay, with a side trip to the American base at Thule in Greenland. Claxton knew me from my Privy Council Office days and he invited me to join the trip. He had two other guests: General A.G.L. McNaughton, senior Canadian officer in the United Kingdom during the war, then minister of national defence, and in 1954 chairman of the Canadian section of the Permanent Joint Board on Defence of North America; and Leonard Brockington, a Calgary lawyer and broadcaster, who had retired in Ottawa after an unhappy period trying to put Mackenzie King's speeches into elegant and inspiring English early in the war. King wanted, Brockington thought, to inspire the people of Canada the way Winston Churchill did the people of Britain with rousing words and ringing phrases. But he also wanted to be sure that every possible qualification was inserted in every sentence and paragraph. Brockington had finally resigned in despair.

The stop at Churchill was notable chiefly for the ferocious cold – more than forty degrees below zero Fahrenheit with strong winds producing a wind-chill that froze flesh in seconds. I learned then that it is one of the coldest places in the Arctic; even the High Arctic Islands are warmer because there low temperatures are accompanied by calm. Because of these brutal facts it was ideal for training in Arctic warfare. The other notable thing was that Brooke never seemed to sleep. He was awake at 2:00 A.M. when I left whatever group he was talking to at the base and he was equally wide awake, dressed, and breakfasted at 6:30 when I got up. He was a vigorous, active, intelligent man and one of the best ministers Canada has had.

At Resolute Bay my interest was not in the defence base but in seeing the new Inuit settlement, located about three or four miles from the base. It was the last week of March. The sun was high and bright but the air was bitterly cold, about thirty degrees below zero. As we approached the settlement, there seemed to be nothing there, until one realized that all the snow houses had snow drifted against and over them until they were simply undulations in the landscape.

Whatever the problems of the snow house for the health of babies, it is a triumph of human invention. The floor of the approach tunnel through which one crawls to the door is about twelve inches lower than the floor of the house. The colder air of the tunnel, being heavier, does not flow into the house. The top of the door is low – about eighteen to twenty-four inches above the floor. The warm air, being light, is at the top of the house and so does not flow out the low door. Inside, sleeping, eating, sitting, and talking take place on a platform of snow covered by furs that is almost two feet above the floor of the house – again applied physics: the cold air stays down. Light came from a square block of clear ice in the dome of the house and from the soapstone seal-oil lamp which was also the source of heat for people and for cooking. The families all had good fur clothing and there were ample furs around for beds at night. The people were smiling as only Inuit can smile.

In each snow house a non-Inuit resource had been applied to an Inuit problem: the dripping from the roof. Some inventive person had found

to Greenwich was ninety-six degrees, so Keith simply found and followed that. But how did he know which was the Greenwich meridian? It was a fascinating, baffling, and most impressive seminar in the sky of which I grasped little except the difficulty of the problem. I understood why the United States Air Force borrowed Greenaway as a life-insurance policy for polar flying, which it did from time to time.

After we got beyond the northern edge of the Arctic archipelago, the ocean below was cut in all directions by great pressure ridges – jagged piles of ice forced up when ice pans crashed and pressed against one another. It was easy to make out the ridges and to get some idea of their height because the sun was low in March at those polar latitudes and the shadows of the ridges were long. Occasionally there were stretches of open water where the ice pans had been pulled apart by the winds or ocean currents. Our North Star aircraft, with flames belching out of the exhaust stacks on the sides of the engines and a noise that was deafening, roared over the frozen desert for hours. It was about a thousand miles each way. Nothing distinguished the Pole except Greenaway's assurance that we were there. We flew around the world three times in about twenty minutes and then headed for home – ninety-six degrees from Greenwich, clearly and accurately determined by our youthful navigator with his pie plates, star sightings, and grid. Greenaway was much more interesting and impressive than the North Pole. We got to Resolute on time.

Canada's Presence in the North
One of the things that particularly bothered the prime minister was the apparent incapacity of the government to act effectively as the 'Canadian owner' of our northern territory. The area is enormous and our resources then were very limited but they were not, he thought, being used as well as they could be. This was in spite of the fact that an advisory committee on northern development (ACND) had been set up in January 1948. Its purpose was 'to advise the government on questions of policy relating to civilian and military undertakings in northern Canada and to provide for the effective coordination of all government activities in the area.' The chairman in 1948 had been Hugh Keenleyside, deputy minister of mines and resources, an enormous department which left the deputy minister with little time for northern questions. After him the chairman was General Hugh Young, deputy minister of a portion of the reorganized department then called Resources and Development. I succeeded to the chairmanship when I took on Young's job, which became deputy minister of northern affairs.

I learned from Graham Rowley that, while the committee had had several meetings in 1948, it had not been very effective and meetings had ceased in 1949. Hugh Young had wanted to reactivate it but had not got ministerial support until Pearson had expressed his concerns in the cabinet in January 1953. Graham had become secretary of the committee on 1 August of that year. From that point, the ACND was the most important single instrument in achieving the prime minister's objective of making government more effective in the north. Graham, as its secretary, was an invaluable combination of Arctic lore, administrative vigilance, and good advice.

The ACND recommended, and the cabinet agreed, that Canada should undertake the annual resupply of the Joint Arctic Weather Stations, with a cargo vessel and a tanker to be chartered for the purpose. That helped to reduce United States activity in our Arctic and Canadians no longer had to rely on American resources for transportation in their own country.

In October 1953 the ACND had begun discussion of a question that was to loom large: the unsatisfactory situation that was emerging at Aklavik, the largest settlement in the western Arctic and the administrative centre for that region. A report from Rowley said: 'The shortcomings of the site of the town were becoming apparent as it grew. Land suitable for buildings was very limited and what there was was being eroded by the river, the whole town was subject to flooding, water supply and sewage disposal were very difficult because the site was in the middle of the delta, there was no source of gravel, and no area that could be developed into a year-round airfield.' The committee instructed the secretariat to prepare a paper setting out the problem in detail.

When the ACND secretariat assembled the plans of all departments for their requirements at Aklavik, it became apparent they could not be accommodated on the small delta island. A new site would have to be found and the increased government activities based there. The first meeting I attended as chairman was on 23 November 1953. At the second meeting, on 21 December, I reported that Parliament had passed the Department of Northern Affairs and National Resources Act. The legislation at once had more than symbolic value since coordination of government activities in the north had been specifically made the responsibility of my department.

To strengthen the department for its expanded role, Jean Lesage and I had got the approval of the Treasury Board for a few more senior staff. In addition to Ben Sivertz, now promoted to a new position as chief of the Arctic Division, and Bob Phillips as executive officer in my office, we got approval for a second assistant deputy minister. For our success in getting Maurice Lamontagne to fill that position we had Premier Duplessis to thank.

Lamontagne was an outstanding economist and political scientist among, at that time, a very few francophones so qualified in Quebec. He was at l'Université Laval and should have been kept in Quebec as a rare and precious asset. However, he was a product of Father Georges-Henri Lévesque's faculty of social sciences, which was notoriously advanced in its thinking about the social problems of Quebec. That was bad enough, but he was also too intelligent and outspoken for Duplessis's taste. It was made clear to the university that there would be a price for it to pay if the premier's wishes were not obeyed – and his wish was to see no more of Lamontagne at Laval. So Maurice joined our department as assistant deputy minister. He was so great a success that before many months had passed we lost him to the Prime Minister's Office. His place was then taken by Ernest Côté, another capable officer we got from External Affairs.

Lesage had decided that as soon as Parliament adjourned he and I would begin our education about the department, and especially about the problems of the north, on the ground. We would visit all the National Parks and Historic Parks in the west, and then go north to the Yukon and Northwest Territories. Lamontagne would join us for the northern part, as would Gordon Stead, the Treasury Board officer who handled financial questions relating to the north.

The Yukon Territory
No part of Canada has the aura of romance of the Yukon. The gold rush would have done it alone, but Robert Service's 'Songs of a Sourdough,' 'The Cremation of Sam McGee,' and other poems brought the places and the myths of the territory to all Canadians. One of my early and fond memories is of my father reciting the poem about 'Sam McGee,' who had come from the deep American south to join the gold rush. My child's imagination could see McGee, as he was being cremated in the 'heat of the furnace roar,' telling his friend to 'please close that door, for it's warm in here. Since I left Plum Tree down in Tennessee it's the first time I've been warm!'

The romance started right on the Alaskan coast at Skagway, where 'Soapy Smith' and his gang had ruled in the 1890s and had robbed the 'stampeders' of as much of their money as possible before they tackled the hideous climb up the Chilkoot or the White Pass to the rugged and barren plateau above. From there they had to make their way to Lake Labarge and the headwaters of the Yukon River which would take them, if they were lucky, to Dawson City, Bonanza Creek, and gold. Few got much gold and fewer still came out with any, but the stories were superb.

The White Pass and Yukon Railway really did go up the White Pass – a narrow gauge line because there would not have been room, except at staggering cost, for a standard gauge with greater width of rails, larger locomotives, and heavier cars. No one could go up that line without excitement. Looking down sheer cliffs as the train clung to absurdly narrow shelves, chopped and blasted out of the rock, one could still see in places the trail far below, worn by hundreds of weary feet many decades before. The top of the climb is a land as stark and barren as the moon. Many a heart must have quailed on seeing it.

Whitehorse was the starting point for river navigation for the stern-wheel vessels that carried freight and passengers to Dawson. It had been just a shipping point during the gold rush but it had become the capital of the Yukon Territory in 1951. The former capital, Dawson, had shrunk as the gold ran out. The fatal blow was the location of the Alaska Highway. Whitehorse was on it: Dawson was not.

From Whitehorse, Lesage and I were taken in a small cavalcade of cars by Aubrey Simmons, the Member of Parliament for the Yukon, to the lead-zinc-silver mine at Mayo and the hospitality of its guest house where the appalling dust of the road could be removed by showers and soothing drinks. The next day was on to Dawson, where the Yukon Order of Pioneers – YOOP to everyone in the Territory – ensured that we saw all that was still visible of what had been, in its day, the most populous centre in Canada west of Winnipeg. It was a living museum: utterly fascinating.

While a few hardy prospectors were still panning for gold the way it had been done in the gold-rush days, in the 1950s placer mining really paid only if done on a large scale by companies that could afford the costs of giant dredges, with endless chains of buckets digging gravel many cubic yards at a time and washing it down with water delivered in a steady flow by hydraulic pumps. The dredges left behind them on the upstream end the most remarkable topography of ordered rows of clean, washed gravel, stretching as far back as the eye could see. The water and the fine sand went to the downstream end of the dredge where the heavy gold was caught, as it settled, in mats of rubber or coconut fibre. In 1953 there were two placer-gold mining companies operating dredges and 1,358 placer claims were in good standing. Gold produced in 1953 had been worth $2,400,000.

Mining was and is the mainstay of the Yukon. By 1953 silver was the most important metal, worth $5,245,000, with lead and zinc together, as they so often occur, worth $6,120,000

Government of the Yukon Territory was by a commissioner, appointed by order-in-council, from among the officers of the Department of Northern Affairs and National Resources. An elected Council of five members had legislative powers similar to those of a provincial legislature except for natural resources, which were under federal control. While Indians and Metis constituted about half of the population of the Yukon, they did not, at that time, take any active part in Territorial politics. They had their own tribal or social structures. Nearly all lived by trapping and hunting.

From Whitehorse, Lesage and I flew south to Edmonton to turn around and go north again to the Northwest Territories. The mountains were a wall between the two territories with no communication between them at that time by water, land, or air.

The Northwest Territories
In 1954 the Northwest Territories was the only part of Canada for which the original routes of transportation – by water – still retained their historic dominance. In the whole vast area there was only one short length of gravelled highway, from the Alberta boundary to Hay River on the south shore of Great Slave Lake. The settlements, apart from Yellowknife, were very much where the logic of river transportation determined. For the District of Mackenzie – virtually all of the wooded part of the Territories which made up the subarctic, in contrast with the true Arctic beyond the tree line – the great route of discovery and later of freight and human movement was the Slave-Mackenzie river System.

Air transport had developed after the war from bush flying to air lines as far as Yellowknife, but that was the end of the line. Beyond Yellowknife in the west, and everywhere in the Arctic east, the only means of transport other than the canoe in summer or dog sled in winter was still the bush plane, usually flown by an enterprising pilot who had gone heavily into debt at the bank to buy a small Norseman or Beaver. Ben Sivertz, who taught navigation in the navy during the war, said:

In those days problems of travel were incredible. Single-engine planes on floats in summer and skis in winter had neither radar nor gyro compasses ... Few people realize how difficult it is to navigate with a magnetic compass in a bumpy and swinging cockpit of a small plane near the North Magnetic

Pole which makes astonishing angles of variation. Such planes are on visual flight rules which means the pilot must be able to see the ground, and as soon as he is away from lakes and rivers a map is essential for safe flying over the million-and-a-quarter square miles.[13]

The Peace River and the Athabaska River come together west of Lake Athabasca to form the Slave River. The rivers are navigable for shallow tugs and barges until the Slave approaches sixty degrees north – the southern boundary of the NWT. A string of rapids there imposed a portage of several miles in fur-trading days and led to the growth of a small post – Fort Fitzgerald. Where the portage ended and the Slave was again navigable a second post grew up – Fort Smith. It is just inside the NWT and in 1954 it was the headquarters of administration for the entire Mackenzie District, including the western Arctic and the western Arctic islands. The district administrator was an Englishman, L.A.C.O. Hunt, known to everyone in the District as 'Laco.'

In true English fashion, Laco's parents had sent him to a boarding school, but with a difference. The last few years were in a school in southern France. One result was that Laco could talk to Bishop Trocellier, the Roman Catholic bishop of the Mackenzie, whose seat was in Fort Smith, in the French of Provence that the bishop spoke. The other result of the French influence was to give a special quality to Laco's natural capacity to enjoy life. He did enjoy it and people enjoyed him. He was also a good administrator.

Laco had given due consideration to hospitality for the new minister and his group. He, of course, had a party for us to meet all the staff and the RCMP officers, whose headquarters for the western Arctic were also at Fort Smith. The minute scale of northern activity was reflected in a group that could easily be accommodated in the Hunts' small living room. But something special was needed: something that could be done nowhere else.

Wood Buffalo National Park, a little smaller than the province of Nova Scotia, is bounded on the east by the Athabaska and Slave rivers and stretches for more than two hundred miles through northern Alberta into the NWT. It was established in 1922 as a protected habitat for wildlife. Its most noted residents are the world's last whooping cranes and, at the time of our visit, there were about 12,000 wood buffalo. The operating headquarters were on the bank of the Slave River a bit south of Fort Fitzgerald, just above the first rapids. Laco decided that the unique experience for Lesage would be a lunch with a menu of buffalo steaks and wild rice in the middle of the river – the only place where one would not be prey to the swarms of mosquitoes that are a plague in northern summers. A large barge, used as a floating dock and for the movement of heavy machinery and supplies for park operation, could be moored to a buoy anchored in the river; cooking could be in the cookhouse on shore; movement from one to the other and for the guests could be in the park work boat. The river is wide, there was a good breeze, and Laco's calculation was right: there were no mosquitoes or flies.

The geography and the August day were equal to the grandeur of the conception. The air was crystal clear, the temperature just right, the great river poured ahead to the roaring rapids, and the tall spruce and pines stretched on either side to infinity. The barge was simply a floating floor, with no sides whatever. So we had a sense of the miraculous: epicurean dining on an untamed river in a northern wilderness. True to his French education, Laco's wines were excellent. He assuaged all doubts about eating the protected buffalo. They were increasing so fast that they had to be culled annually and excess young bulls were both a nuisance and a menace.

Fort Smith itself was a delightful town, built on sandy soil on the west bank of the Slave, with pines, birch, and poplars to give a park-like atmosphere and to break the winter winds. The HBC had established a trading post there in 1870 and its hotel, inside a generous compound in the old company style, provided cottage-like comfort. The Catholic Church had arrived not long after the HBC – 'here before Christ,' in northern lore – and had an array of white-painted wooden buildings: a church, a residence for the bishop and for priests and brothers, a residence for Indian children, and a school. The RCMP compound was a meticulous park with the tree-lined river on one side. The small town was well laid out. There was no place in the Territories that could rival Fort Smith in the sense of order and history it provided.

Our next stop, Hay River, was the only place in the NWT of that day that was important because of a road: the Mackenzie Highway which connected with the Alberta highway system at Grimshaw. The highway, built in 1948, made Hay River the staging point for shipping freight north down the Mackenzie and also across Great Slave Lake to Yellowknife, thus avoiding the portage around the rapids on the Slave. It was also the base for the commercial fishery on Great Slave Lake, with refrigerated trucks hauling the catch of whitefish to southern markets, mostly in the United States. Hay River was to pay the price of being located on the delta of the river when a serious flood in 1963 inundated nearly the entire town. As commissioner of the Northwest Territories, I called a special session of the Council of the Northwest Territories to meet immediately that spring in an unflooded school hall. The Territorial government provided compensation for the worst of the flood losses and decided to rebuild most of the town on higher ground along the river.

At Hay River in 1954 we divided our group for one day. Lesage stayed there for meetings with business and Liberal Party groups. I went with the rest of our party to Pine Point, over a hundred miles away and a few miles in from the south shore of Great Slave Lake, where a hopeful lead-zinc deposit was being investigated. If it was to be economic it would be only with the reduced costs a railway could provide to haul concentrates south. With that possibility we glimpsed, for the first time, the chance of getting a railway into the territory. If that happened, we hoped it might do something to bring down the high transportation costs that were, and still remain, one of the greatest problems for economic development in the north.

An attractive feature of the day's trip for me was that the man in charge of the work for Pine Point Mines was Don Douglas, my brother-in-law. He, along with my sister Lucille, and their daughter Jill, then nine years old, formed one of only three families at the work site. It was not too lonely in the summer months when a work crew was present, but in winter the sense of being the only people within a radius of about one hundred miles, in temperatures forty or fifty degrees below zero, must have been daunting, even for people brought up in Saskatchewan as both the Douglases were. However, they stayed through two winters, the mine did come into production, and the railway was built. Pine Point was a thriving, modern town when next I visited it in 1974. Unfortunately, costs stayed high, especially because of increasing flows of water as work followed the ore body to lower levels, and the mine gradualy became uneconomic. It ceased operation in 1987. Without the freight for the mine, the railway was not economic so the hoped-for improvement in general freight costs did not emerge.

At Yellowknife in 1954 our party was lucky in the bush pilot we got: a promising young operator who had just added a de Havilland Otter to the Beaver that had been his 'fleet' to that time. The young man was Max Ward, whose enterprise and courage were to carry him to the creation of Wardair, for many years one of the worldwide charter airlines. Max was the embodiment of what was needed to develop the north. Along with enterprise, youth, and courage, he combined imagination and solid reliability. No one, however nervous, could feel that his fate could be in better hands than Max's. Jean Lesage was such a flier. Our trip would have been no joy for him with any other pilot in the Territories of that day.

Max flew us the length of the Mackenzie River to the Beaufort Sea, with side trips up the Liard and, farther north, across Great Bear Lake to Port Radium and then to Coppermine on the Arctic coast. From Coppermine the return was across the great barren interior to Yellowknife. We visited twelve settlements in both the Arctic and subarctic regions, talked to Indians, Metis, Inuit, and whites, and ended up with as concentrated a knowledge of the north of that time as was possible in a few weeks – a coverage that would have taken months or years but for people like Max Ward who could find their way anywhere – provided they could see the ground.

A New Arctic Town

Aklavik was both fascinating and depressing. The fascination was in the cultural mix. It was the only settlement of that time in which Indians, Metis, Inuit, and whites lived together and where all the agencies active in the north – governmental, religious, and private – provided their services or traded their goods to a confusing mix of humanity in transition. The Inuit put on a drum dance in honour of the minister in the school hall. It went on until morning, but there was no night there in early August – just a bit of greyness at the time the clocks asserted it to be midnight. The Inuit and Indian children, regardless of age, were still around at two o'clock – or three, or four. It was not clear when they slept, or if they did. Their parents did not seem to be concerned.

The depressing part was confirmation of the utter unsuitability of Aklavik as the location for administration and services for the western Arctic. Geographically it was right: at the end of river transportation and the beginning of coastal shipping for the settlements on the coast and in the Arctic islands of the west. Somewhere in that area there was need for a good airport, an administrative base for federal and territorial purposes, and for the education, health, and economic-development services that were our first priorities. Aklavik itself was right for the trappers and traders: close to game and traplines and easy to supply by river. But the alluvial island flooded every spring. A new hospital, a new school with residences for children, a safe source of water, sewage disposal, and an airfield – none would be possible there.

The single major decision Lesage had to take in the course of the trip was whether development could or could not go ahead at Aklavik. There was no doubt about the answer. The next decision was what site should be chosen for a new town that could be the centre for all the activities that would be involved for the development of the western Arctic and the lower Mackenzie basin.

After the cabinet had approved the recommendation of the advisory committee on northern development to explore possible sites for a new town, a scientific team had been set up headed by Curtis Merrill, an engineer and geologist in the Defence Research Board. Other members were drawn from the departments of Mines and Technical Surveys, Public Works, and Transport, the Division of Building Research of the National Research Council, and other agencies. The interested departments and the team established a list of 'factors' to be sought in a site for a new town. Five of them were 'essential': economic and social suitability for the Aboriginal people; good ground for utilities, foundations, and roads; and an access to a navigable river channel; a site for an airfield; and an adequate and safe water supply. Three factors were 'highly desirable': adequate sewage disposal; availability of sand and gravel; the possibility of development as a trans-shipment point from river to coastal transport. There were also three 'desirable' factors relating to sources of fuel and power – wood supply, coal supply, and hydro-electric development. No possible site had any of these three 'desirable' qualities, so they disappeared from the objectives.

The team was set up in December 1953 and did its assessment from March 1954 to our arrival in August. Initially, on the basis of maps and local knowledge, the team had focused on seven sites: four on the west side of the Mackenzie delta and three on the east. They advised Lesage that no site on the west side met most of the 'essential' or 'highly desirable' needs. Of the three on the east side, two were 'reasonably suitable.' Only one site – 'East 3,' or 'E-3' – met every 'essential' and 'highly desirable' factor.

The report was unwelcome. The hope had been to find a site on the west since most of the native people and their traplines were on that side of the delta and the best solution would have them moving from Aklavik to the new town while still being close to their economic base. It would be best for social, educational, and health purposes and also for the gradual introduction of the local people into the new employment opportunities that we hoped would come. Lesage required convincing that no west site would do. We flew to the four and had the defects of each site demonstrated. In the end he was satisfied and attention focused on E-3. It was on the east channel of the Mackenzie River, which has several channels and an infinity of loops and twists as it winds its way through the delta. The location was about sixty miles south of the Beaufort Sea at sixty-nine degrees north. It was surprisingly well wooded, especially with birch trees which were attractive and afforded some shelter from Arctic winds and also indicated good gravelly soil under the surface. The site was underlain by permafrost – permanently frozen ground which, there, extended downward for over three hundred feet. That was the condition everywhere in that region and it was the greatest single problem to be taken into account in planning the first modern, large-scale town in the Canadian Arctic.

On our return to Ottawa I reported to the ACND on the recommended site. The committee recommended it to the cabinet, which approved. We were then off on a great venture. The Foundation Engineering Company of Canada was retained for devising the engineering aspects of the operation, for developing a town plan, and for providing the new town's water supply and services. An interdepartmental committee was set up to coordinate the various needs and to deal with all the problems that were sure to emerge as the work went on. The Department of Public Works was to handle the contracting. The Department of Northern Affairs and National Resources was to have overall responsibility. Lesage and I thought that we and our department had a pretty substantial challenge before us after our first twelve months on the job.

As the town at 'E-3' developed, the question of a name arose. 'New Aklavik' had little to commend it, especially as Aklavik means 'place of a black bear' in the Inuit language. There were no bears of any colour at E-3. Moreover, the purpose of the town was far removed from the trapping and trading that supported Aklavik. The name Inuvik was the result of rumination by Graham Rowley before his shaving mirror.

Graham came to me one morning with his idea for a name and, in reply to my query, explained that it meant 'place of man.' It seemed right both in sound and in meaning, but it would never be accepted locally if it was suggested by 'Ottawa.' Fortunately, the constituency of Mackenzie Delta was represented on the Council of the Northwest Territories by a Danish trapper and trader, Knut Lang, who had settled south of Aklavik some twenty years before. He was highly regarded by the people of the delta, regardless of race. Graham wrote to Knut on 16 April 1956 with his suggestion for a name: 'It is Inuvik. It is a short simple name, easy to pronounce and spell, and sufficiently different from Aklavik to ensure that there would be no confusion. It is easy to remember and it is not duplicated anywhere in Canada. If my memory of Eskimo is correct it means "place of man," which would seem suitable for a townsite chosen by man (and not by brown bears).'

Knut liked the idea. When he proposed the name, at the next session of the Council, he was wise enough to say that it had been suggested to him in Aklavik without any laboured precision as to just who had done the suggesting. The Council liked 'Inuvik,' the people of the constituency liked it, and the Canadian Board on Geographical Names preferred it to 'Arctic City' and 'Nanuk,' which had been proposed from other sources. The name and the town became accepted symbols of social, political, and economic change in the north.

The Hazards of Arctic Flying, 1954

From Aklavik we flew north to Tuktoyaktuk on the Beaufort Sea, a site from which the Inuit had traditionally taken the beluga, the white whales that congregate offshore there in the summer breeding season. Their inner skin, muktuk, is considered a delicacy – an opinion I have not been able to share after several encounters in the warm hospitality of Inuit hunting groups.

Whether Lesage dared me, or I him, I do not know but somehow a challenge emerged to take a swim in the Beaufort Sea. It was a clear day, with not much wind and somewhere we got towels. The shore shelved gradually so it was not possible to pop in and pop out – but we popped as quickly as we could. It is not to be recommended, even in August.

When we turned south in our trip it was to visit Port Radium on the east shore of Great Bear Lake and from there to turn northeast to Coppermine, the largest Inuit settlement in the western Arctic.

Port Radium was the source of much of the uranium that went into the development of the atomic bomb. We went there unannounced and found, to our surprise, that Bill Bennett, the president of crown-owned Eldorado Mining and Refining which operated the mine, was there. His headquarters was in Ottawa. He was happy to put us up overnight but his hospitality could not extend further. It turned out that, unknown to us, the Duke of Edinburgh was at Coppermine and was arriving at Port Radium about noon the next day. To extend appropriate hospitality, Bill's wife, Betty, and a small party were arriving from Ottawa via Yellowknife. Clearly an uninvited ministerial party was not needed or wanted. We left for Coppermine early the next morning.

Coppermine is a pleasant settlement on a clear and sunny summer morning. Most Inuit settlements at that time were uniformly either Anglican or Catholic in religious adherence. Coppermine was solidly

Anglican. While the Catholic Church had divided the Arctic into two sees, the West based in Fort Smith and the East based in Churchill, the Anglican Church had a single see and the bishop's seat was Aklavik. The bishop, Donald Marsh, rejoiced in what must have been one of the most stirring titles in the church: 'Donald the Arctic.' The bishop and Mrs Marsh were at Coppermine for the Duke's visit. The Duke had left shortly before we arrived, which was exactly what we had hoped would happen. He was on an unofficial visit and there was no place for the minister or the commissioner to complicate things.

Bishop Marsh was not at all in accord with our proposition that the Inuit children should be given a full education to equip them, if they wanted, for ways of life other than their traditional one. He did not really debate the troublesome facts about the increasing human population and the diminishing wildlife resoures. It was simply that he was philosophically attached to an idealized, unspoiled Inuit lifestyle of self reliance and family-centred culture which he wanted to see continue as long and as unchanged as possible. His idea of appropriate education was embodied in the tent hostel that the Anglican Church operated at Coppermine in the spring and early summer months each year. The children, brought in from the surrounding area, got a few weeks of school but spent the rest of the year 'on the land.' None got beyond the most elementary grades. The bishop gradually conceded the substance of our argument for better education to face a future that was bound to change, but it was always grudging – and with the question 'What are you educating them for?' Admittedly, not an easy question to answer. It was all too easy, however, to see what the result would be if there were no choice and the traditional way of life collapsed. I was more than once tempted to respond with a question of my own: 'What would you be keeping them uneducated for?' I never asked it. I decided it was better to do what we had to do for the future we foresaw and hope for the bishop's reluctant cooperation. On the whole we got it, but not easily.

From the first weeks of our northern appointments, Lesage and I had had several discussions with bishops Trocellier and Marsh about education for Indian and Inuit children in the Northwest Territories and what to do about the residential schools that both churches had there. Neither church had the means, either financial or human, for full educational programs. I did more of the discussing with Bishop Marsh than Lesage did. Donald the Arctic, like many of the clergy on both denominational sides in the north, found his Christian charity sometimes unequal to the still intense missionary rivalry between the two churches. He saw 'Rome' as a threat to be distrusted and resisted and at times he tested Lesage's forgiveness. Our conversation in the house of the Anglican missionary at Coppermine was cordial, but it stayed away from education.

Our flight from Coppermine to Yellowknife was to be straight across the desolate and unpopulated interior: above the Arctic tundra and small lakes most of the way, changing to small trees and bushes, with water reflecting the sun from the enormous areas of muskeg, as we approached Great Slave Lake.

Lesage usually occupied the co-pilot's seat beside Max Ward, but we left Coppermine after lunch and Jean liked a siesta when it was possible. He could go to sleep in seconds in a bouncing car or a roaring bush plane – nervous flyer and all – and wake up refreshed, however brief the nap. Mackenzie King had that knack too. Jean left his post for a more comfortable place in the passenger area and I became co-pilot. I soon noticed Ward listening intently to something coming through his headset so I put mine on.

Max was listening to a conversation between the pilot of a plane and the Department of Transport weather station at Coppermine. The pilot was taking Mrs Bennett and her party from Yellowknife to the Eldorado landing strip to welcome the Duke of Edinburgh. The pilot and the plane were lost. He said that he was over a coast: he thought it was the south coast of Great Bear Lake. Max could talk to Coppermine but not to the pilot, nor could the pilot talk to Max: all had to go through the weather station which had no aids to navigation and no knowledge of northern geography. Max asked Coppermine radio to get the pilot to describe the terrain over which he was flying and he soon became convinced that the lost plane was not over Great Bear Lake at all. It was flying along the Arctic coast – far north of where the pilot thought he was. The plane had wheels, not floats like ours, so it could not land on water – only on smooth ground – and the fuel was low. It took both exact knowledge and cool confidence for Max to ask Coppermine to tell the pilot where he almost certainly was, that there was a sandbar at Coppermine which must be straight ahead of him, and to counsel him to try to reach it and to land there with his wheels up. The pilot did as he was told except getting his wheels up. The plane did not, however, flip over as Max had feared if the wheels dug into the sand. The party miraculously emerged frightened and jolted but unhurt. If it had not been for Max Ward, the likelihood of any safe outcome for Mrs Bennett and her group would have been slim. There were few places on the Arctic coast where a plane without floats could land and survive. Max was one of the very few who knew where one such place was. It was sheer luck that there was enough fuel to reach it.

There were, I think, only three airfields in the whole of the Territories at that time with any means of guiding or aiding pilots in trouble: Yellowknife, Resolute Bay, and Frobisher Bay (now Iqaluit), and both their range and the knowledge of their radio operators were limited. I was more than glad after that experience that our long journey to isolated places had been in the hands of Max Ward.

Public Support for Northern Policy

Early efforts to get financial support for an active northern policy made it clear that the department would have great difficulty in the face of all the interests there were competing for government funds unless we could increase public knowledge and stir public imagination. The 'absence of mind' about the North to which St Laurent referred had prevailed because there was no consciousness of the North, little interest in it, and no sense that it was a potentially significant part of Canda. Most maps of Canada, even to the end of the war, did not bother to include the empty unknown that lay north of the provinces. The North in Mercator's projection was simply an array of parallel vertical lines that went off the top of the page. Polar projections, giving some idea of the shape of the North, were rare in schools or in general use. It was Bob Phillips more than anyone else who realized how important a public-information program was if we were to have any chance to attract the kind of staff and to get the financial support we needed.

It was not simply that Bob understood the need. He had great imagination about ways to stimulate interest and he wrote in an easy, readable style that was attractive to a wide audience. He realized that some of the best stories about the North were right in departmental files. They were made accessible. As we built up a junior northern staff they were encouraged to talk to journalists, who did not include them in their scepticism about 'bureaucrats.'

Bob was both the creator and the principal author for a departmental publication – 'North' – that became sufficiently interesting and known to support itself by subscriptions. Our booklet 'This is the Arctic' became the third bestseller in the history of Canadian government publishing. Demand grew for talks to the Association of Canadian Clubs and these events attracted good audiences.

The ultimate tribute to the success of our public-information campaign came in 1958 when Diefenbaker, stimulated by our then minister,

Alvin Hamilton, made his 'Vision of the North' a central part of his successful campaign for a majority government. Most of the vision came out of our departmental files, with additions and emphasis by Alvin and bright colour lavishly spread by the prime minister.

Implementing the New Policy

Jean Lesage's comment that 'in providing health, education and a sound economy the complications are infinite' did not apply only to the policy implications or the impact on the people of the Territories. It was equally true of the implementation of the programs.

In part the difficulties were geographical and physical: the climate in the Canadian Arctic is one of the most hostile on earth, apart from the uninhabited Antarctic. That complicated every aspect of construction of schools, of houses for teachers, of heating, of water supply, and of sewage. The distances from sources of supply in the South are enormous and the staggering costs required that all movement be by water in the short summer season, or by tractor trains over frozen winter roads since there were then no properly built roads outside the settlements around Great Slave Lake. The combination of problems imposed a minimum of a three-year cycle for any program that involved construction: a year to plan and to prepare, a year to assemble supplies and to ship, a year to build. And at that time all the people with skills to build and to provide the trades had to come from the south: there were none resident in the small posts in the Territories. Every piece of lumber, bag of cement, and bat of insulation, every nail, pane of glass, tap, and pipe had to be shipped thousands of miles. There were no hardware stores for anything that might be forgotten. Only after all the planning, buying, shipping, and building had been done could the intended purpose of educating or of health treatment begin – provided we had the teachers and nurses to do it, and had built the houses for them to live in. Administration had not been important in my working life in External Affairs, the Prime Minister's Office, or the Privy Council Office, but I had a crash course in my northern roles, both as deputy minister and as commissioner.

There had been a start on school construction by the department and the Council of the Northwest Territories in 1947. In 1953 there were six small schools for Inuit children, four in the Northwest Territories and two in Arctic Quebec, financed by the federal government, and four schools for 'non-Indian' children in the Mackenzie District financed by the Territorial government. There were also seven schools for Indian children built between 1948 and 1953 by the Indian Affairs Branch of the Department of Citizenship and Immigration. For Northern Affairs schools, the Alberta school curriculum was used. It is revealing of the limited scope of the program to that point that its administration was under the Education and Welfare Section of the Territorial Division of the Northern Administration and Lands Branch: not even a separate education section, no matter how far down, with which to develop a more comprehensive program.

It was clear that the attack on the complications had to begin in Ottawa. Ben Sivertz, chief of the new 'Arctic Division,' was an ingenious administrator who could tackle any problem and also motivate people far beyond what duty required. There was ample scope for those talents in building and directing a new division focused entirely on the Arctic.

The Department of National Health and Welfare was responsible for the health of Aboriginal people in the North. Much of its attention had been directed to the tuberculosis epidemic. It had two main treatment hospitals for tuberculosis, one in Quebec City and one in Edmonton. In 1954 a new division of Northern Health Services was established 'to concentrate on the coordination of existing health services and to plan for future requirements.' Its scope was to include 'all residents of the North,' with no race lines drawn.

A unit in Northern Affairs was needed to focus entirely on education but it could not be established until a suitable education specialist could be found to head it. In 1955 the Education Division was set up with J.V. (Joe) Jacobson to build a staff suitable for the unique problems of educating Aboriginal children and also with capacity to develop a curriculum that would suit them. The division had to recruit teachers who would fit into small native communities and whose nervous systems could cope with the cold, long winter darkness and isolation and also with the difficulties of language and cultural sensitivities. It was a heavy task that Joe took on, especially with the differences of opinion that surrounded almost every aspect of policy, curriculum, and teaching.

Our programs from 1955 onward included Indian children in the Northwest Territories because of an agreement between me, as commissioner of the Northwest Territories, and my old boss Jack Pickersgill as minister of Citizenship and Immigration. The department's annual report recorded that 'effective April 1, 1955, the Department of Northern Affairs and National Resources assumed responsibility for the education of Indians in the Northwest Territories. The result was that all schools operated formerly by the Indian Affairs Branch in the Mackenzie District were taken over by the Department.'

Deciding that education had to be made available for all children of school age in the Northwest Territories was not too difficult; how to do it was another matter. Both the Indians in the Mackenzie District and the Inuit in the Arctic lived almost entirely by hunting and trapping. That meant that few lived in settlements, visiting them only briefly to sell pelts at the trading posts and to buy essential supplies. It was because of those facts that the churches had established residential schools for Indian children: only by providing housing for them could the children be available to be taught. There were a few settlements where one-room or two-room schools did or could operate, but if most children were to have the chance to be educated there would have to be residences with more accommodation than the residential Indian schools could provide.

A further consideration was that, with the sparse, scattered population of the Territories, it would be enormously costly if schools were to be segregated on ethnic or religious lines. In other words, schools had to be simply schools, with education for all children. Where housing was necessary, that too would have to be without ethnic division. We realized that we would probably meet great resistance if we tried to do away with denominational differences for the residences since they would be 'home' for the children living in them. The churches might consider that religious instruction in the residence would be a vital part of the children's upbringing.

Lesage and I began discussions with Bishop Trocellier and Bishop Marsh in the early months of 1954. The department's proposal was to build hostels for the accommodation of school-age children in the settlements where the churches then had residential Indian schools. The schools were all firetraps – old, costly to heat, and in need of replacement. In recent years charges have emerged about abuse of Aboriginal children in some northern residential schools. We heard nothing of that at any stage in our negotiations. It was not a factor in the change to government-financed residences. They were a part of the new policy largely because the churches could not finance the necessary facilities for the expanded program.

Under our plan, the department would enter into contracts with the churches for the operation of each hostel, in which the children would be either Catholic or Protestant depending on the residential school that had previously existed. The school to be established by the department would be non-denominational and with no ethnic lines. In other words, in addition to the children living in the hostel, other children in the community, or who could come to the community to live with relatives or friends, would attend the same school.

It was a fairly large pill we were asking the churches to swallow, since the formula meant an end to their previous autonomy in education. The attraction for them was relief from costs that were increasingly heavy, provision of better facilities, and the knowledge that a better education would be available for more Aboriginal children.

Lesage and I were not surprised when Bishop Trocellier took the firm position that, while the schools could be for any and all denominations, it would be essential to have denominational classrooms for the elementary grades. Jean handled that sensitive negotiation, with intervals between discussions so the bishop could consult his priests and brothers at Fort Smith. The bishop was a shrewd negotiator. We wanted to keep the denominational division of schoolrooms as 'elementary' as possible since there would be very few children for several years who would be beyond Grades 3 or 4. In the end, if I remember rightly, separation to Grade 6 was agreed on.

The department realized that the 'hostel plus school' arrangement would almost certainly be temporary. The need for hostels would diminish to the extent that changes in the native economies, with diminishing capacity to live on the land and increasing alternative employments, led to more and larger settlements. Greater reliance on family allowances and welfare, if employment was inadequate, would also lead more people to the security of settlements. There was no program to encourage settlements as such, but the growing Aboriginal population as health services improved, and the diminishing capacity of wildlife resources to support it, led to a more rapid growth of fixed communities than we had expected in 1954 and 1955.

Hostels and schools were built under this arrangement at Inuvik, Fort McPherson, and Fort Simpson. Small schools were built in settlements as more and more had enough residents to make them feasible. By 1957 the program had developed to the point where the department's annual report was able to be specific as to objective and progress: 'The ultimate aim of the Department in the field of education is the provision of basic elementary education for all children in the Northwest Territories, and advanced academic or vocational education for students and adults with special aptitudes. This program is being developed by the construction of additional federal day schools and hostels, by providing an increased number of bursaries and other aids for students, and by the development of special curricula for northern schools.'[14]

In 1957 the department had twenty-nine schools of its own in operation with seventy-nine teachers. It assisted four residential schools still operating at that time and six hospital schools. There were 3,100 pupils in the schools and another 500 in part-time schools. Some 1,500 Inuit children were receiving education on either a full-time or part-time basis.

Teaching had to be in English, not by design but by necessity. There were eight native languages in the NWT – seven among the Indian people of the Mackenzie District and Inuktitut for the Inuit of the entire Territory. There were then no qualified teachers in any of those languages. In later years it became possible to have locally engaged teaching assistants so that the native languages could be used to some degree, especially in the elementary grades.

The importance of education became more apparent each year, especially for the Inuit, as the decline in the number of caribou accelerated. The report for 1957–8 said:

It becomes increasingly evident that Arctic lands will no longer support the traditional hunting and trapping economy of the Eskimos; even less will they support the rapidly growing Eskimo population. Consequently, new outlets must be found to preserve the Eskimos' economic independence and to permit them to share in the rising living standards of the country.

One of the principal new opportunities for the Eskimos is wage employment in mining, transportation, administration, and defence installations. About 10 to 15 per cent of the population is now in wage employment, and although the number is growing, it is unlikely to exceed 50 per cent of the population in the next generation.[15]

The problems of the Inuit varied greatly, depending on the region. In some, 'resources of the land,' which included the sea, were reasonably good, in others disastrously bad. The possibilities of new resource use also varied from place to place, as did the possibilities of employment. To help with the complex of problems, and to assist the Inuit to adapt, a new category of resident officers was established. The 1957–8 report stated: 'Northern Service Officers [NSOs] have been established at Frobisher Bay, Cape Dorset, Fort Chimo, Great Whale River, Churchill, Rankin Inlet, Baker Lake, Tuktoyaktuk, and Cambridge Bay, and a new post was opened at Sugluk, early in 1958. The work of the Northern Service Officers is as varied as the country in which they live. A few are concerned with the problems of people in remote areas relatively unaffected by inroads from the south, while others work almost entirely with Eskimos in wage employment in mining, on the DEW Line, and elsewhere.'[16]

The End of the Lesage Regime

It is difficult to convey to Canadians now used to changes in government in Ottawa any idea of the shock produced by the defeat of the St Laurent government in the election of 10 June 1957. The Liberals had won every national election from 1935 onward – twenty-two continuous years in office. They appeared to be the normal, almost inevitable, governing party. The Progressive Conservatives, moreover, seemed to be in a weakened condition after the retirement of George Drew for reasons of health and the choice of a new leader, John Diefenbaker, only six months before, in December 1956. As Jack Pickersgill says:

> When the election of 1957 was announced on 25 April, members of Parliament and the public felt that the St Laurent government had recovered from the low point of midsummer 1956 and expected the prime minister to march forward to his third victory. Mackenzie King had won two landslide victories and had won by a narrow majority in the postwar election of 1945. St Laurent had won two landslide victories, and the general expectation was that he should do at least as well as Mackenzie King by winning a third election. On the night of 10 June government and country were shocked to discover how wrong they had been, and no one was more shocked than I.[17]

St Laurent resigned as prime minister on 21 June and with him went the government and our minister, Jean Lesage.

I was enormously saddened to have to say goodbye to a man who had been an excellent minister and who had become a close friend. In August 1957 Bea and I drove to Nova Scotia with our two children to visit my parents who had retired to our ancestral farm just two years before. En route we stopped at the Lesages' summer cottage on the south shore of the St Lawrence near Montmagny. Jean was deeply depressed. His brilliant and promising career had collapsed. He was still a Member of Parliament, but the status, prestige, and perquisites – as well as the income – of a minister had vanished. There was nothing Bea or I could say that was of much comfort to Jean or Corinne. It would have been too improbable to imagine that in only three years Premier Duplessis and his successor, Paul Sauvé, would both be dead and Jean, having led the Liberal Party of Quebec to victory in the provincial election of 1960, would be premier of Quebec. The next phase of Jean's career was to be more fascinating and more glorious than it could possibly have been if St Laurent's government had not gone down to defeat.

chapter seven

Governing the Northwest Territories, 1953–1957

The Northwest Territories Act provided that 'the Commissioner in council may, subject to the Act and any other Act of the Parliament of Canada, make ordinances for the government of the Territories' in relation to classes of subjects that were listed. The ordinances were laws with the same legal effect in the Territories as enactments of provincial legislatures in the provinces. The 'subjects' were the same, with a few exceptions, as those with which a provincial legislature can deal. The most important exception was public lands and non-renewable resources, such as minerals, oil, and gas. Control of these was federal, just as it had been in the prairie provinces until 1930. The administration of justice and labour relations were also federal responsibilities. Finally, the Territories could not, as provinces can, borrow money except from the federal government. This was not, in reality, a restriction: Territorial credit for borrowing would have been dubious and expensive. Instead of borrowing, both the Yukon and the Northwest Territories received financing by grants and loans from the federal government proportionately far beyond the financial transfers to even the poorest provinces. Costs in the North were and still are very much higher than in any province and neither Territory could survive on the basis of federal-provincial financial arrangements.

The first session of the Council after I became commissioner on 15 November 1953 was just three weeks later. I had precious little time to learn my job and the main work of the session, which took place in Ottawa, was to discuss and approve the Territorial budget for 1954–5 with the fiscal year beginning 1 April 1954. The debate on the budget was a good introduction to all the problems and issues of Territorial life and administration. Frank Cunningham, the deputy commissioner, and the other officials did a splendid job of briefing the newcomer they must have looked on with some surprise. My predecessor, General Hugh Young, not only had years and rank to confer status but had also spent some time in the Territories as part of his military career. The Council members were charitable and helpful, and I got by. My first session in the Territories was six months later: in Yellowknife in June 1954. It was also the first session at which there were four elected members present, all from the Mackenzie District in the western subarctic.

It turned out that the people of Yellowknife were as interested in inspecting the new commissioner they had never seen as I was in meeting them. I arrived at the basement of the Elks Hall, where the session was to be held, well before the opening time of two o'clock. The hall had not risen above the basement: presumably the Elks' ambitions had exceeded their finances. There was already a good crowd outside, enjoying the bright sun and sparkling sky of what was still a northern spring: the ice was solid on Great Slave Lake. I spent a half hour meeting and talking with everyone there before parading into the basement, preceded by an RCMP constable in scarlet coat to give proper solemnity to the opening of that manifestation of law and government in the far north.

Sessions always began with a prayer, in emulation of larger and older parliaments and legislatures, read by the commissioner who, at that moment, was at the kitchen-chair 'throne' at the head of the table around which the nine legislators sat. The numerous public had chairs set back from the table, around the walls.

Many economies are imposed when the pomp and dignity of parliamentary process has to be carried out with limited numbers and small financial means. The commissioner, who would later be acting as head of government, was at that moment acting in the role of speaker. Once having read the prayer, he would assume the role of lieutenant governor – reading the 'speech from the throne' – before again becoming speaker to preside at the debate on the address he had just read.

I had all this dignified 'three-role' process well in mind. What I had not prepared for was the failure of my eyes to adapt quickly enough from the dazzling sunlight outside to the dimly lit basement. The text of the prayer as I looked down at it, standing erect in the twilight, was a blur. Only a few words at a time would swim into clear focus and I had, foolishly, not learnt it by heart. My measured, careful enunciation, word by word and phrase by phrase, created an impression of solemnity far beyond anything I would have dared to devise. That careful precision, dictated by my near blindness but giving the impression of thoughtful meditation, established an early reputation for solid responsibility.

It seemed well to bolster that good impression by going to the Anglican Church the following Sunday. I was not familiar with the service and I was startled at one point to hear the priest praying for the commissioner of the Northwest Territories. I appreciated his thoughtfulness but I was told afterward that there was nothing either thoughtful or personal about it: it was pure ritual. In any event, on reflection, I was not sure whether the prayer was for the commissioner or for the Territories with its future in the hands of so young and green a governor.

In my annual report for 1954–5 I referred to a change I introduced at Yellowknife modelled on the debate on the address in reply to the speech from the throne in Ottawa: 'At the first session [of 1954] an amendment to the Rules of Council permitting debate on the Commissioner's opening address introduced a new practice which proved most successful. At both sessions members took the opportunity to give their views on many matters of importance to their own constituents and to the Territories as a whole. Nine bills were passed at the first session, most of them being amendments to existing legislation. Seventeen bills were passed at the second session.'[1]

The bills debated and passed into law at each session, along with discussion of expenditures and approval of the budget annually, were the primary responsibilities of the Council. The commissioner was solely responsible under the act for policy and administration: the executive aspects of government. There was no executive council to advise him as there had been for the governors in the early stages of government in colonial Canada and in the 'old' North-West Territories after 1897. To remedy this defect, and to get the judgment of the Council members who brought a wide range of experience to the table, I introduced a new device: putting to the Council 'references for advice' on various difficult and important questions. The first reference, at the Yellowknife session, was on 'the desirability of granting liquor privileges to Eskimos.'

At that time, neither Indians nor Eskimos, as they were then called, could legally buy or consume liquor in the Territories. Both Aboriginal groups were increasingly getting it and, since they could not legally buy it, the financial benefit to bootleggers was substantial. It also became well known that there was alcohol in a variety of products, from vanilla extract to shoe polish and anti-freeze. The alcohol in many cases was not safe for human consumption and several deaths resulted. Would there be more consumption if access to liquor was legal? Would the damage be greater – or would it be less – if consumption did not to have to be furtive?

After a difficult debate, the Council recommended that the same liquor privileges should be granted to Indians and Inuit as were enjoyed by other persons. The problem was that the regulations respecting Indians came under the Indian Act. The Council and the commissioner could not change them. It turned out that the federal government thought it was not an appropriate time to make such a change. To preserve the same treatment for the two groups, we left the situation of Inuit as it was.

We were, in 1954, in the early stages of a serious liquor problem that has perplexed Territorial councils and local governments in the Yukon and in the Northwest Territories ever since.

Mr Massey, the North, and a Mace for the Council

In 1952 Vincent Massey became the first Canadian governor general of Canada. He was ideally suited for the post, he enjoyed it enormously, and he discharged his high office with every ounce of the dignity and respect for ceremony that he thought it could and should have. Along with his deep attachment to the crown, he was strongly Canadian with a great interest in every aspect of Canadian development and consciousness.

Massey saw it as part of his role to visit and to get to know all parts of the country – including the North. Air travel made it possible to go places and do things in the North that no predecessor had been able to do. Massey's northern interest also led him to entertain the Council of the Northwest Territories whenever it met in Ottawa. In so doing, he learned that the Council did not have a mace, an important symbol of 'the constitutional tradition of a legislative body under our system of government.' The Inuit cooperative at Cape Dorset, with Jim Houston as its guide and adviser, was the place to have an appropriate mace created. Massey describes the result in his memoirs:

> The mace has as its shaft a narwhal tusk; ringed around it are carvings of whalebone depicting Eskimo life; the Indians in the Arctic are represented by a band of quill-work; the white man's historic exploits in the North are commemorated by some wood from H.M.S. Fury, wrecked in 1825. The mace, like nearly all such objects in the Commonwealth, is surmounted by a crown. This was fashioned from a block of free copper found in the Arctic and given its shape with great skill by the Eskimoes, who had only a picture to work from. They ran out of copper before the task was finished. A young

> Eskimo woman said that she had inherited a copper kettle left by Lapland reindeer-herders and that she would be glad to have it used. This precious article was melted down and made possible the completion of the crown ... The Eskimoes produced the mace, possessing great beauty and romance, with no real knowledge of what it was for; but they knew that it had something to do with the Queen, and that was enough.[2]

Massey was meticulous in manners and courtesy. He arranged with the RCAF on one of its northern flights to drop another copper kettle from the air as it passed over the settlement where the donor of the kettle lived.

The governor general formally presented the mace to me as commissioner of the Northwest Territories at a ceremony at Government House attended by all members of the Council on 17 January 1956.

The Council had adopted the policy, of which Massey warmly approved, of holding one meeting each year in a different part of the Territories for a twofold purpose. One was to acquaint the members of the Council with all parts of the enormous area for which they were legislating and with the people whose interests would be affected by their decisions. The other was the counterpart: to make the Council known to the people in more and more places so that they would gain a better understanding of what it was, how it worked, and what government was all about. In 1955 the Council met in Fort Smith at the southern edge of the District of Mackenzie and in August 1956 at E-3, on the east side of the delta at the mouth of the Mackenzie where work had been under way for two years and Canada's first modern Arctic town was taking shape.

My report for 1956–7 recorded that the meeting was the first the Council had held north of the Arctic Circle. It went on to say: 'The Mace, which had been presented to the Council in January, 1956, by His Excellency the Governor General, was used for the first time at a session in the North. It was placed on display at both Yellowknife and the old town of Aklavik, as well as at East 3, and attracted widespread attention.'[3] What my report did not mention was the fix the Council found itself in when the hour arrived to resume its session in E-3 on Monday morning after the weekend when the mace had been at Aklavik – and the members of the Council too – for the gathering with the people there.

The mace was too large, in its protective case, to go into the small float planes that ferried the Council by air the thirty miles or so to Aklavik. It had gone on one of the tugs used for pushing freight barges in the watery world of the Mackenzie delta. After the highly successful reception on Sunday, it had been sent off for the return trip with plenty of time overnight to reach E-3 before the sacred hour of ten o'clock when the sessions of the Council were to resume. But when the time came, there was no mace, nor any word about it. After we had been given the mace, the rules of the Council had been revised along parliamentary lines. No business could be transacted without the sacred symbol present – either on the table for a formal session or 'below the table' for a meeting in committee. No mace, no session.

We had two fascinated observers in the small '512' where we were meeting – a standardized, 512 square foot, highly versatile wooden building that had been developed for almost any use in small settlements: house, office, schoolroom, storage shed – or Council meeting. One observer was F.R. Scott, professor of law at McGill University. The other was my old associate in the Privy Council Office, Pierre Elliott Trudeau. They had come down the Mackenzie River by barge – a slow, agreeable way of travelling in the northern summer – to see the land and the people. There was plenty of freight to be unloaded at E-3 and ample time to attend our sessions. Scott was a man of many talents: an outstanding constitutionalist and also one of Canada's best-known poets. There can be few legislatures in the world that have been poetically immortalized for any reason, least of all for doing something sensible.

Frank's poem, 'A New City: E 3,' tells about the new city 'planned across from Aklavik's mud.'

> ...
> Here we went to observe
> The first Council meeting
> North of the Arctic Circle,
> The birth of democracy
> Swaddled in ancient dress

The 'two of us,' Scott said, were looking on 'With a priest in black soutane / And the RCMP in its braid.'

> All was in doubt at the start.
> The Mace, where was the Mace?
> The massive, Massey Mace
> Weighing two hundred pounds?
> A most magnificent Mace
> Fashioned of local stuff,

151

Indian beads, and the tusk
Of a narwhal, Eskimo stone,
And copper from a Franklin kettle
Set in the crest of a Crown.
Alas, the Mace ran aground
Crossing the Delta flats
In a high-speed motor boat,
Somewhere out in the murk
Where only the musk-rat thrives.
Symbols are magic, and work
As well in idea as in fact.
The great Seal dropped in the Thames
By a fleeing Jacobite King
Hindered not Parliament,
Nor the lack of the Mace this meet.
For now an obedient voice
Carefully coached in advance
Solemnly rose to speak:
'I move that we proceed
In the absence of the Mace
As if the Mace were here.'
Carried unanimously,
The gap in the ritual
Covered by common sense.[4]

Poetic inspiration and licence are not the best source of precise history. The mace is heavy, but not two hundred pounds, which might be rather beyond even a sturdy RCMP constable to carry. A kettle from Sir John Franklin's expedition was the creation of some over-enthusiastic imagination. And I suppose a tug was just too prosaic as the vessel lost in the delta. Apart from such pedestrian details, Scott's poem accurately records the crisis and the solution.

Frank sent me a copy of the collection of his poems when it was published in 1973 inscribed: 'For Gordon Robertson the Commissioner of page 67 / whose common sense enabled government to continue despite the loss of a symbol / a lesson hopefully learned by a future PM who was present. With fond memories of the occasion. Frank Scott.'

With his interest in the North stimulated by the Council and the mace, Massey was anxious to visit it. He had another purpose: 'to let the Americans know that Canada owns the High Arctic.' Every part of Massey's interest and purpose had the enthusiastic support of the Council and my department. His biography records: 'The Department of Northern Affairs and National Resources had a vigorous minister, Jean Lesage, and a senior civil servant, Gordon Robertson, who could present the case for the development of the north vividly and compellingly. Robertson was chairman of a representative committee that charted the governor-general's tour and worked out the program. For each stop a member of the department, Graham Rowley, co-ordinated the arrangements with the local representatives.'[5]

Massey's party, with representatives of the Canadian, American, and British presses, travelled in a Trans-Canada Airlines North Star[6] and visited Resolute Bay and Frobisher Bay in the Arctic Islands and Aklavik. The 'high point,' geographically and emotionally, was the North Pole. Inuit groups were visited by dog sled over the land and on the sea ice – wherever they were. It was an accomplishment for a sixty-nine-year-old governor general and a public relations triumph for the north.

Minister, Commissioner, and Deputy Minister, 1953–1963

The Northwest Territories Act provided that the commissioner was the chief executive officer of the Territories, to administer the government under instructions from time to time given by the governor general in council or the minister of northern affairs and national resources. In fact no such instructions were ever given during my ten years as commissioner. From the time Jean Lesage and I were appointed to our respective positions in 1953, we travelled together throughout the north, agreed on policy priorities, and carried out our negotiations with the churches on education. Our daily discussions – and they took place every morning that we were both in Ottawa – drew no lines between things that were federal, like the education and health of Inuit children, and those that were territorial, like the education and health of non-Aboriginal children, as well as the many other questions that arose. The lines between the constitutional responsibilities of the Territorial and the federal governments were as complex as between the peoples themselves in the ever-increasing number of settlements in the western part of the Territories.

Costs of programs and services – schools, hospitals, teachers, nurses – did have to be allocated to one government or the other on some defensible basis, but we were determined that, to the extent possible, there should be no ethnic lines in these programs and services to divide people in the North other than those related to the Indian bands in the subarctic area and the treaties that had been entered into with them. Those were Indian only and from a different department of government. There were no Indian or Inuit reserves. The Aboriginal people lived and moved in areas where they had hunted and trapped, areas that were recognized by tradition but had no basis in legal definition.

The policy of delivering our federal and territorial services without ethnic lines was not a policy of assimilation. It was simply the only practical way to provide for the wants and needs of so small a population scattered over so vast an area. It was difficult enough, and costly enough, to make education, health care, and welfare available to children, or the sick, or the destitute where geography and resources brought them together. Division by band, language, or ethnicity would have made the tasks almost impossible and certainly divisive.

When the federal government changed hands in 1957, from Liberal to Progressive Conservative, daily morning meetings of minister and deputy minister remained the pattern, with assistant deputy ministers and other officials brought in from time to time. It was for me, in my combined role as commissioner (Territorial) and deputy minister (federal), to sort out the administrative and financial consequences of policies and decisions. It was for the minister to determine when he needed to go to the prime minister, to the cabinet, or to the Treasury Board to get approval or money. The system worked efficiently and flexibly. It bore out, in an unusually complex situation, what Mitchell Sharp says:

> To work well, the relationship between ministers and their top professional advisers should be one of mutual confidence. The mandarins cannot perform well unless they have direct and regular contact with the minister. I have worked on both ends of the team. I was granted daily interviews with my minister when I was deputy and insisted on meeting daily with my deputy ministers when I became a minister. It is a mistake on the part of a minister to interpose one of his or her political staff as a conduit for the deputy's views or his own views to the deputy.[7]

Getting to Know My Empire
The trip with Jean Lesage in the summer of 1954 had been only the merest beginning in learning about the Northwest Territories. With Council sessions in different places each year, the educational process continued, both for me and for the Council members. I used the sessional locations as springboards for trips to smaller centres and side trips from those to camps, the floe-edge, and the places where people were hunting or fishing. There were only four or five airfields and not many

airstrips in the entire Territories in the 1950s. For the most part it was a matter of using small planes on floats in summer and on skis in winter, landing on lakes, the sea, or snow-covered strips of land with varying lengths and bumps to provide variety.

It was a great advantage to have the commissioner of the RCMP, L.H. Nicholson, as a member of the Council, both because of his wide experience and good judgment and also because the RCMP detachments, each usually with two members of the force, were the sole manifestations of 'government' – federal and territorial – in hundreds of square miles. A further advantage was the RCMP plane, with experienced pilots, stationed in the North. Nicholson wanted to visit his men, just as I wanted to visit my territory. 'Nick ' was one of the finest and fairest men I have met. He was deeply interested in the native people, he travelled by every means necessary to visit the RCMP detachments, and he was worshiped by his men. He later resigned from the force, at considerable monetary cost to himself and his wife, Mary, on a question of principle.

One of my longest trips was after the session at E-3 in late August 1956. It was also through one of the least known parts of the Territories – east from the mouth of the Mackenzie River along the coast to Fury and Hecla Strait, the narrow channel between the continent and Baffin Island, then south along the west coast of Foxe Basin and Hudson Bay to Churchill. The crew of two, with four passengers, sleeping bags, luggage, emergency supplies, and a host of paraphernalia just in case the worst happened, was all that the Norseman could carry. In addition to 'Nick' and me, the other two Council members aboard were C.M. Drury, then deputy minister of national defence, and L.C. Audette, the dean of the Council and chairman of the Canadian Maritime Commission. Both gave generously of their time to the Council and the North.

When we left E-3 on 1 September there was a tang of autumn in the air, which became more like early winter as we moved east. Flying along the coast from E-3 gave me my first glimpse of a phenomenon that occurs in a few areas where ground is underlain by permafrost: a number of symmetrical hills, circular at the base and perfectly regular as seen from the air – cones with rounded tops. Their name – pingo – comes from the Inuit language, Inuktitut. It appears that, by some hydraulic miracle, each pingo has inside it a core of solid ice and its outer surface is what once was the bottom of a small lake where the pingo now is. Permafrost is general in the Arctic and widespread in the subarctic, but the precise conditions to produce pingos from the permafrost must be rare: they occur in few locations.

Our stop for the first night was at Cambridge Bay on the south coast of

Victoria Island. I was not sorry to get there. The engine of our Norseman obviously had no shock-absorbing arrangement in its attachment to the frame of the plane; there wasn't a vibration that didn't get transmitted through to shake every bone. The Beavers and Otters we had normally used in flying with Max Ward were much less wearing.

The next stop was at Gjoa Haven on the southeast corner of King William Island – a bay made famous by Roald Amundsen. It was the massive flow of sea ice from the Arctic Ocean down McClintock Channel and against the west coast of King William Island that had trapped Sir John Franklin and his expedition in 1846 with the loss of all hands. In 1903 Amundsen, in his small boat *Gjoa*, after sailing from Oslo to Baffin Island and Lancaster Sound, took the route that would have saved the Franklin expedition – down the east coast of King William Island. In October, as winter was closing in, they found a sheltered bay as their refuge for the winter and named it Gjoahaven. The name, now two words, has remained. In August 1904 they continued south, rounded the island, and joined a passage that had been explored from the west. Franklin had been nearly right about the Northwest Passage. He and his whole expedition were lost by the choice of the wrong coast: a disaster for him – a later triumph for Amundsen.

As our weather deteriorated, flying a plane on floats in that area in September began to look more and more doubtful. Knowledge of detailed Arctic climate and ice conditions was steadily growing and that very year a book was published, *Arctic Canada from the Air*, which gave the most complete information then available on conditions in different Arctic regions and seasons and was especially designed for the use of 'airmen flying in the vast and frequently monotonous expanses of the Canadian Arctic.' The authors sent me a copy in August 1957, with the inscription, 'In the hope it will prove useful on your arctic trips. Moira Dunbar and Keith Greenaway.' It was indeed useful and it would have been especially so before our trip. Chapter 1 of the book advises: 'North of the mainland freezing conditions can occur at any time during the summer, causing icing of hull or floats, and it is not uncommon for a few inches of ice to form on small lakes and inlets and remain for a day or two. Snow storms are also quite usual in summer, especially in the northern islands, where the snow may remain on the ground for a brief period.'[8]

The chapter on weather has further relevant information: 'The winter pressure pattern begins to form in autumn ... Cloud coverage usually reaches its maximum over the archipelago in September and along the north mainland coast in October, when it may average as high as 90% ... Temperatures drop rapidly over continental areas but lag in the maritime regions, where the freezing level and cloud heights often coincide to produce severe icing. The worst flying conditions of the year are in the autumn.'[9]

There was no problem at Gjoa Haven or that night at Spence Bay on Boothia peninsula. But the next day, as we flew across the Gulf of Boothia, the sea below was full of ice floes. No float plane could survive if it had to come down. I suppose it was that dismal reflection that made me aware that we were doing exactly that – slowly coming down. I decided that the pilot knew everything there was to know about the loss of altitude and the reasons for it and that the best thing I could do was to keep my mouth shut.

It was only later, after the descent had finally stopped, that the pilot explained the problem. The wings had been icing up – just as *Arctic Canada from the Air* said – and the Norseman did not have the rubber surface on the leading wing edge that could be inflated to break the ice off. It had been accumulating and he had no choice but to descend. Happily for us, the air temperature began to rise as we dropped down, the ice melted, and a probably disastrous need to plunge into that sea of ice was avoided.

Fury and Hecla Strait got its unusual name from the ships of Captain Edward Parry's second expedition. His first expedition in 1819, to explore Lancaster Sound north of Baffin Island, had been highly successful. It had reached about seven hundred miles west from the entrance to Lancaster Sound before being stopped by ice south of Melville Island in September. They made virtually no progress against the ice in the summer of 1820 and returned to Britain. As George Malcolm Thomson writes: 'The North-west Passage existed – Parry was certain of that – but he had gone looking for it in the wrong place, into seas where the ice was too thick and the cold too severe. The next explorer who looked for it should, he thought, hold closer to the mainland coast where there would be the best hope of finding openings between ice and shore.'[10]

Parry's next attempt in 1821 to find a passage was accordingly around the south of Baffin Island through Hudson Bay and Foxe Basin. His instructions were to explore every inlet on the mainland coast to see if any was a channel to the west. His good luck had, however, run out on the first expedition. After spending two summers probing the coast and two winters frozen in, the first on the west side of Hudson Bay and the second farther north near Igloolik, Parry found the strait between Baffin

Island and the mainland still jammed with ice brought down by the strong current from the north. The names of his ships that the strait now bears are a memorial to both discovery and frustration.

Igloolik, not far from the outlet of Fury and Hecla Strait, is noted for the numbers there of walrus, seals, and marine life generally which has, for some three thousand years, supported a substantial Inuit population. After a night with hospitality and shelter at the RCMP and HBC posts, our next stop was to be Repulse Bay at the bottom of Melville peninsula.

The flying was entirely dependent on a good pilot, good maps, and visibility of the land below – visual flight rules. We had the first two but snow began to fall, got heavier, and soon blotted out the shore line. When an indentation in the coast, dimly seen, raised the hope that it might be Repulse Bay, the pilot decided to turn into it to land on the open water there – Repulse Bay or not. It was not and in settling on the water of the unknown inlet, a submerged rock tore a hole in one pontoon. After a few anxious moments as the plane took a list to one side, it became clear that we would still float. The pilot thought that we could probably take off again if the snow stopped and if we could prevent further damage by holding the plane offshore against an on-shore breeze without keeping the motor running with risk to our fuel supply. The only way to be sure of that was for the party to take turns, knee deep in the icy water, to hold the plane off the rocks against the wind. It was not comfortable, but the incentive was powerful.

After a half-hour or so the snow let up enough that the pilot thought it safe to try to take off and resume the flight. Repulse Bay could not be far away. As he gained speed, he rocked the plane level and the pontoon had enough buoyancy to let us rise. The water poured out and the next inlet was indeed Repulse Bay. The Catholic mission there had some large empty food cans that could be cut and shaped to patch the pontoon when it was hoisted out of the water. The air crew and the missionaries had the strength, the skills, and the tools to produce a nearly water-tight pontoon for the rest of the trip.

I have never been entirely sure whether our stops at such tiny posts were seen by our hosts as visits or visitations. In all cases there was no accommodation except in the quarters of the RCMP constables, the HBC post manager, or, if there was one, the mission. All were small and we refused to put anyone out of his bed. Every night it was a matter of drawing lots for identifiable places to sleep, in descending order a mattress (if there was one), a couch minus mattress, cushions on the floor, a rug or carpet, or the bare floor. On the whole, despite all the problems we caused, I think they were glad to see us. A break in the isolation of an Arctic post, outside news, and conversation with new people about other places and people are compensation for a lot of disturbance in the lonely Arctic. In any event, the hospitality was invariably warm and we, on the Council, learned a lot about people, places, and problems that helped as we dealt with policies and programs for our Arctic land.

Frobisher Bay,* 1957

In 1576, when Martin Frobisher entered the bay that now bears his name and sailed into it for over a hundred and fifty miles, he thought he was on the point of solving the riddle of the Northwest Passage. It looked to be a strait, and if so, it might lead to another sea and finally to China. His hopes were raised by the Asiatic appearance of the people he encountered – black hair, broad faces, and flat noses.

The bay was of no particular importance until the Second World War when it gave access by sea to an area that could be developed for an airport as part of the Crimson Staging Route, a series of fields for aircraft to use as stopping and refuelling points in long flights between the United States and Europe. The Cold War made the airfield important as part of the air defence of North America. Frobisher Bay was just mid-way between air fields in Maine and the American base in Thule in Greenland. United States air-force detachments were there until 1963 along with the facilities to accommodate several hundred people to service planes and to guide and communicate with aircraft.

A substantial part of the Inuit population of Canada lives on the coasts of Baffin Island because of their resources in marine mammals. With the excellent airfield and buildings that could be turned to domestic uses when they were no longer needed for continental defence, Frobisher Bay was the obvious place to establish an operational centre for the eastern Arctic of the kind Inuvik was to be for the west. As a step towards that, the development of a small community for Inuit, with a school, '512' houses, and other facilities, was begun in 1955 about a mile from the airfield. In June 1957 the Council of the Northwest Territories met there – the first Council meeting in the Arctic islands.

The sessions were in the new school, accommodation was in the '512s.' In permanent use, they would be houses for Inuit changing from a

---

*Now Iqaluit, capital of the Territory of Nunavut since 1 April 1999.

hunting existence to wage employment at the base. They would also house Inuit families in our first rehabilitation centre designed to help the fight against tuberculosis. Nearly 7 per cent of the entire Inuit population of Canada was then in hospitals in the south. Progress was being made but curing the disease was only part of the problem. The other was preparing the patients for a return to a normal and useful life in the Arctic. Some patients would never be able to return to their previous activities of hunting and trapping. Others would, but only after a period of rehabilitation and training. The new community at Frobisher Bay would have facilities and staff to give the people, many of whom had been in hospital for several years, a chance to adjust to some kind of independent life again.

As our sessions proceeded it looked as though nearly all the Inuit then in the area, complete with children of all ages, were attending this new form of entertainment. The Inuit mothers, sitting on the schoolroom floor with legs straight out, nursed their babies, chatted with one another, and kept an eye on their two or three year olds who were remarkably well behaved. Inuit parents are both affectionate and permissive. Whether it was indulgent treatment or inherent qualities or both, the Inuit children seemed less aggressive and assertive than ours.

The Council of the Northwest Territories in Operation
The proceedings and operation of the Council were, as Massey thought important, based firmly on the British – and Canadian – parliamentary model. The opening day of each session began with the prayer that I blindly fumbled through in Yellowknife in 1954. It was followed by the commissioner's address. I used the address, in the normal parliamentary way, to outline the principal subjects or bills for consideration at that session. As we moved from place to place, the address also focused on things of concern to the people we were visiting. There was usually an interested audience, at least at the opening session, but the novelty generally wore off, especially if there was a language problem. With eight Territorial languages (Indian and Inuit) and a limited budget – as well as with the peregrination from place to place – we did not attempt either simultaneous interpretation or a verbatim record. English was the language of discussion. The record in the Council's 'Votes and Proceedings' was of subjects and legislation, not of debate.

The creative adaptation of parliamentary procedure was imposed by two things: the non-partisan mix of the membership and our limits in manpower and money. The mix of elected and appointed members had a precedent in the North-West Territories of the earlier days on the prairies after 1876. It could have presented strains, as it did during those earlier years that led up to the establishment of the provinces of Saskatchewan and Alberta in 1905. However, it caused no problem in the Council in my time. The main reason, I think, was that there was no pressure in those years for an increase in elected membership. The Indians and the Inuit in the North had not yet developed any real understanding of the political and parliamentary process or any desire to participate in it other than by voting in the four constituencies. The number who actually voted was small. The interest and the pressure developed as political consciousness grew and as young people emerged from our schools with a growing understanding of politics and a determination to assert themselves. Then gradually a shift to the fully elected Legistive Assembly in the Territories of today occurred.

The limitations of manpower meant that I, as commissioner, and the deputy commissioner had to play the many roles I have described in the proceedings at Yellowknife. Following my opening address came the only really formal 'speech-making' of each session: the debate on the address which gave every member a chance to talk about anything he wanted and, in the case of the elected members, anything bothering their electors. The commissioner was in the chair as speaker of the Council for that. When all had spoken, a motion to go into committee of the whole relieved me of the speakership and made it possible for me to join in the discussions. A member of the Council (different from day to day) became chairman, the mace went 'off the table,' and I took the member's seat.

From that point on, until all subjects were exhausted, there were questions and discussion about anything – fur prices, problems with trapping areas, changes needed in the Game Ordinance (a favourite of the elected members), the inadequacy of health services, problems in settlements, the need for more schools and for teachers who spoke the local languages, the need for improvement in the CBC Northern Service, welfare problems, vocational training, the importance of more wage employment. The deputy commissioner was a senior departmental official – usually the director of the Northern Administration Branch in Northern Affairs. He and I were expected to deal with everything and to answer all questions: a two-man government and public service.

The debate on the address usually took about two days. The rest of each session was on legislation and money: the budget, estimates of expenditure, and the voting of supply. The sessions grew longer as administration extended into more and more activities and places, and as expenditures grew.

At the session at Frobisher Bay, the community came en masse to see their representatives, Simonie, Akeeshu, and Sageaktuk, present a formal address to the Council. The Inuit had not, in 1957, fully learned the art of making demands of their government and legislators for specific projects or expenditures but they did not take long to grasp the possibilities. The roving Council sessions were a factor in developing political consciousness and preparing the way for full Territorial self-government.

The most important item for the Council to consider at the 1957 session was a new five-year agreement with the federal government for financing the Territorial government. Its programs and its costs were increasing much faster than revenues would or could. The estimate was that annual expenditures per year would exceed probable revenues by $564,300, and this figure was established as a base payment. With that, plus its own sources of revenue from liquor and taxes, the Territorial government was to cover all costs except capital payments on new schools. Money for those would be lent to the Territory repayable over twenty years. The only flexibility was a provision that the federal payment would vary in relation to changes in the gross national product per capita of Canada.

It was an arrangement designed for financial responsibility. The Territorial government would have to cut its coat, over the five years, within the cloth it was being given by the federal government or face the pain of increasing taxes and charges. The financial support was, as it had to be, proportionately greater than any province received under federal-provincial arrangements. Our costs were far in excess of those in the south – as were the costs of the Yukon government, for which a similar system was established.

After four years of working with a Council that was partly appointed and partly elected, I had no doubt about its desirability at that stage of political development in the North. The mix of people with experience in government, business, and administration on the one hand, and elected representatives with local knowledge and sensitivity on the other, provided a balance that helped with legislation, budgeting, and policy. No other arrangement would have been as effective for that time of transition.

At no time in any Council session during my ten years as commissioner was there an issue that divided the elected members against the appointed. The elected members championed the concerns of their electors but, with appointed members to be counted on any issue, log-rolling was not possible. The appointed members served without remuneration. Accountable expenditures for attending Council meetings were covered, but nothing more. None of them had any personal interest to advance and all had a sense of concern and responsibility for the interests of the Territories and its people. It would be difficult to find a legislature or council that operated with less self-interest or more social responsibility than the councils of the Northwest Territories from 1953 to 1963.

An Aborted Political Career

From 1953 to 1957 I had become fairly well known in the Territories. Most of the community leaders had met me or seen me in Council or other meetings discussing Territorial or local problems and trying to produce solutions. I could not always promise the project or the program they wanted but, if money and policy would permit, the administration tried. At worst, we did listen. The proof that my efforts were seen, on the whole, with a friendly eye came as the federal election of 1957 approached. The executive of the Territorial Liberal party surprised me by coming to see me in Ottawa with the proposal that I become their candidate.

As a public servant, I had no political connections and had never considered going into politics. However, as I listened, the idea began to intrigue me. I was approaching forty, and I had been in the public service for over fifteen years. If I was ever going to move to the political field it was as good a time as any. And the delegation was flatteringly confident that I would win. Representing the Northwest Territories and its people in the Parliament of Canada seemed an attractive prospect. In the end, I said that I would talk it over with my wife and give them my answer the next day.

That evening I set it all out to Bea: the pros and the cons. When I finished my exposition the silence was total. I finally asked: 'Well, what do you think?' My loving wife looked me squarely in the eye: 'I don't think a divorced man could get elected in the Northwest Territories.' There was an even deeper silence and we changed the subject.

And so my political career came to an end before it started. I have never regretted it. Nothing I could have done as a member of Parliament could have been more satisfying than influencing the development of the North, as commissioner and as deputy minister, at the time when the foundations were being laid for the changes that have come in the forty years since. And the next six years were to be with a new federal government even more interested in the North and its future than St Laurent had been in 1953.

For Bea, the main consideration was that a move to politics, with a House of Commons constituency in the Northwest Territories, would probably have meant a relocation to Yellowknife and a complete change of life for her and our children, with my almost certain disappearance from the family for most of the year, either to Ottawa for parliamentary sessions or to various parts of the nearly 40 per cent of Canada that I would be representing. Our children were young: John, born in 1948, and Kerrie born in 1952.

My old boss, Norman Robertson, had once said to me, as we both finished calling our wives about yet another dinner to be late and burned, that the senior public service should be celibate, like the Catholic priesthood. Then the necessary time could be taken for the really difficult policy problems, with no concern about a ruined dinner or an angry wife – or a guilty conscience about too little time with the children even after dinner because of files to be read before a meeting with the prime minister the next morning.

When Clifford Clark, the great deputy minister of finance from 1932, saw war approaching in 1939, he realized that the problems of ministers and senior officials were going to become crushing for many years. Holidays would become impossible. The Clark solution was a fishing club not too far from Ottawa in the Gatineau Hills where a few of the most pressed public servants could find some escape along with their families. So was born the Five Lakes Fishing Club in 1940. There were thirty members: the kind of people who got to be called 'mandarins' a few years later – O.D. Skelton, Clifford Clark, Norman Robertson, Lester Pearson, Louis Rasminsky, Dana Wilgress, Robert Bryce, James Coyne, Donald Gordon, John Deutsch. The club still exists, with the revolutionary change of admitting women members, such as Jocelyne Bourgon, the first woman clerk of the Privy Council and secretary to the cabinet.

I was invited to join in 1953 and it became as much a 'club' for wives and children as for the officials Clifford Clark had had in mind. Some policy issues were discussed, but as few as possible. It was a place for relaxation, good talk, bridge, poker at 'stag' weekends, and steadily worsening fishing for the few who took the club's name seriously.

chapter eight

The Territories under the Vision, 1958–1963

The public service was totally unprepared for a change of government in June 1957. The Liberals had been in office for twenty-two years. No other party in all that time had come close to threatening their majority, based on solid Quebec support but also with substantial strength in every other province. King had survived the conscription crisis of 1944 and won the immediate post-war election of 1945 while the man who saved Britain, Winston Churchill, was decisively defeated in an election there the same year. St Laurent had achieved a position of respect: his 'Uncle Louis' image had grown with his years in office. Diefenbaker, leading the Progressive Conservatives, was new and little known outside Saskatchewan. He had never led any party anywhere.

There was a general scramble in the eleven days between the election on 10 June and the swearing in of the new government. For deputy ministers and departments, apprehension was general. The Liberals had been a known quantity, some ministers weak, some strong, but at least familiar. No one knew anything about who might come in under Diefenbaker's banner.

When the list of the new cabinet came out it was disconcerting: Northern Affairs appeared to have got half a minister. Lieutenant Colonel Douglas Harkness of Calgary had been sworn in as minister of northern affairs and national resources and also as acting minister of agriculture. With the importance at that time of agriculture in every province and with its special importance in the west – the Prime Minister's home base – I could see us getting little ministerial time or attention. And a department without a strong minister – or with only a fraction of a minister's attention – has little chance of cabinet or Treasury Board support for programs or for funds.

Doug Harkness, when he arrived, was a breath of fresh air. A high school teacher before the war and a distinguished officer during the war, he was used to command. He assumed the loyalty of everyone under him. He was utterly frank and direct and he expected the same in return. He had none of the suspicious insecurity that made it impossible for Diefenbaker to believe that public servants who had advised and worked with his enemies, the Liberals, could be loyal to him or his government. Diefenbaker even found it difficult to believe in the loyalty of some of his own ministers, especially those like Donald Fleming and Davie Fulton who had contested the leadership of the Conservative Party against him in 1956.

Harkness's directness was revealed in discussion of many policies and programs during the early days of the new government. Banff National Park is not far from Calgary and he had been told by some constituents about grievances they held against the park administration and the department. That was no surprise. Reconciling the National Parks Act dedication of the parks 'to the people of Canada for their benefit, education and enjoyment' with the injunction in the same sentence that the parks 'shall be maintained and made use of so as to leave them unimpaired for the enjoyment of future generations' was something that Solomon would have had trouble with. The 'people of Canada' who have the right to enjoy parks are tourists. The people who supply their needs for beds, shelter, food, and equipment are businessmen. Cabins, hostels, water, sewers, and roads are needed – but the parks must, nonetheless, be 'unimpaired for ... future generations.' The arguments and disagreements between the administration and the businessmen had been many.

I do not recall what the complaint was for which I and the director of the Parks Branch were called to account a day or two after Harkness arrived in June 1957. We gave him an initial explanation and promised to look into the matter and report back. It appeared to the director and to me as though the policy was sound and the application had been reasonable. He did a memorandum to the minister which I signed and sent forward. It came back the next morning with a brief scrawl at the end: 'The more I hear of this, the more it stinks. Discuss with me.' I did. The minister listened: he was an eminently reasonable man, well used to adjudicating problems that arose in his regiment and settling them quickly, firmly, and fairly. He did not dispute our need to be governed by the Parks Act. He saw our difficulties, but he also saw the concerns of businessmen with a more sympathetic eye than ours. Where there is room for differences of judgment – where there is no precise arithmetic to provide a specific answer – the minister's view must carry and it did. He is the one who will be responsible to Parliament and country. The handling of many applications became more imaginative and a lot of park businessmen were happier.

Doug had a delightful wife, Fran, and Bea joined me in the hope that the prime minister would find someone else for agriculture. It was not to be. Diefenbaker decided that no one but Harkness among his members had the stature to command the confidence of the grain farmers, the ranchers, and the whole enormous business community that made up 'agriculture' in the west. So Harkness, against his preference, resigned the Northern Affairs portfolio and became minister of agriculture. We had him less than two months.

If I had to lose Doug Harkness, the man I would have wanted to take his place was, miraculously, the man we got: Alvin Hamilton, member of Parliament for Qu'Appelle–Moose Mountain in Saskatchewan. Alvin and I had been at the University of Saskatchewan together, both taking political science under MacGregor Dawson. Alvin was a bit older than I: he had had to take a couple years out to teach school to raise money for his university education. There were no federal grants for post-secondary education then and no student loans.

Alvin gave me a bit of a jolt the day he surged into my office in the Langevin Block. We greeted one another warmly: it was several years since we had last been together in Saskatoon. Alvin's normal enthusiasm was bubbling over just minutes after he had been sworn in. He was all set to go: 'Gordie, we are going to make a real department out of this!' Jean Lesage and I thought exactly that way in 1953 and I had been working hard at it for nearly four years. However, there were any number of things that were still far from satisfactory in the north and in the other areas for which my department was responsible and the task of the opposition, in Parliament and in the country, is to focus on what is wrong. Alvin had a good list. Moreover, neither Jean Lesage nor I had Alvin's fertile imagination. I soon found that there would be a new batch of ideas almost every morning.

I think that Alvin found me a bit of a wet blanket. It was not that a great many of his ideas were not important. He brought a new insight into the handling of permits for the exploration for oil and gas in the North that both stimulated activity and added to resource revenues. He had a better understanding of the interests and difficulties of private enterprise in that difficult and costly region, while still having a sensitive concern for social and Aboriginal problems. There were many ideas that were adopted with real advantage. My difficulty often was the limitation imposed by budget and personnel. But here Alvin's originality produced what appeared to be a solution: the glowing future of the North that Diefenbaker presented as his own idea and with the help of which he converted his parliamentary minority of 1957 into the sweeping majority with which he carried the country on 31 March 1958.

The change of government in 1957 and the arrival of new ministers of northern affairs did not involve any change in the policies and programs that were my responsibility as commissioner of the Northwest Territories. Doug Harkness did not have enough time to become familiar with them because during his whole period with us he was also acting minister of agriculture – a far more important and sensitive area politically for the new government. Alvin Hamilton's greatest interest was in resource development which he rightly saw as fundamental if the North was to grow and to prosper as he hoped and believed it could. Control and administration of northern resources was federal, not Territorial. We discussed the Territorial priorities for education, health, and employment. He had questions and suggestions but no disagreement with the programs that were under way.

For the Territorial government the main impact of the change and of 'the Vision' was not in its own financing: that was established under the five-year financial agreement and was not altered. It was the spill-over from the federal resources programs – new 'roads to resources' that would not have been built except for Alvin's policy and that made communities accessible by road from the south which had not been before – such as Yellowknife; and more employment for local people; more economic activity generally. The new atmosphere also gave a greater sense of confidence, but the hard facts of the North had not changed and they had an awkward tendency to assert themselves.

Yellowknife, 1958: The Caribou Crisis

The elected members of the Council had indicated a wish to use its peripatetic sessions as a way to become acquainted with one place they had not experienced: Ottawa in the summer. The practice, for administrative convenience, had been to hold budget sessions in Ottawa in December or January. That put the summer sessions in the North, when daylight was long and travel relatively easy. The pattern was broken in 1958 and one experience of a stifling Ottawa in July was enough for our northern members. We were never again asked to hold a summer session there.

The session on the budget for 1958–9, as well as for other things, was held in Yellowknife from 14 to 21 January. It was the occasion for changes in the deputy commissioner and the legal adviser to the Council, both people who, like me, were federal civil servants with additional Territorial roles.

Since before I became commissioner, the deputy commissioner had been Frank Cunningham, director of the Northern Administration and Lands Branch of the Department of Northern Affairs. Cunningham was not imaginative, and frequently less than tactful in dealing with the elected members of the Council, but his knowledge of the administrative details and financial background in every area of activity was encyclopedic. He had been a loyal help to me in my first years. He had retired in April 1957 and Wilf Brown, formerly commissioner of the Yukon Territory, took his place at the session in Yellowknife.

Another change was in the Council's legal adviser, who was also legal adviser to my department. William Nason was one of the old hands. His knowledge of all the ordinances of the NWT that had been passed, amended, or repealed in all the years from 1875 was as total as Cunningham's was about administration and finance. His parting contribution to the Territories was the first consolidation of the ordinances, as revised and currently in effect: the Revised Statutes of the Northwest Territories. A complete revision and consolidation of laws after a long period without one is a great help to lawyers but equally valuable to administrators, for the law suddenly becomes accessible instead of being a mystery that can be unravelled only if you know where to look. Nason's place was taken by E.R. Olson from the federal Department of Justice.

A Financial Agreement Ordinance was passed authorizing the commissioner to enter into the five-year financial agreement with the federal government that had been discussed at Frobisher Bay. Apart from that, the most important legislation related to a crisis that threatened a large proportion of the Indian and nearly all the Inuit population of the Territories and of Arctic Quebec: the decline of the caribou population. Caribou were the one absolute essential for both Indians and Inuit. They provided the clothing and much of the food of both groups. Without caribou, life for most of them could not go on.

A decline in the number of caribou on the east side of Hudson Bay – Arctic Quebec – had been reported as early as 1916. The persistent problem there was the main reason for the decision in the early 1950s, before Jean Lesage and I had come on the scene, to find locations to which some of the Inuit might move with better prospects for hunting and trapping. The name 'the hungry coast' had been well earned over many years. The condition was now emerging elsewhere.

On the west side of the Bay the inland Inuit – the 'Caribou Eskimos' – were still, in the 1950s, largely unchanged in their total reliance on caribou for virtually everything: winter clothing, hides for tents when snow houses could not be built, covers on beds for warmth in all seasons, and nearly all their food. In much of the area the caribou 'did not come' in the mid-1950s and the consequences for the isolated people were devastating.

Action to determine the extent and the cause of the caribou decline had been taken jointly by the government of the Northwest Territories and those of the three neighbouring provinces – Manitoba, Saskatchewan, and Alberta – where their northern Indians were also hard hit. The Canadian Wildlife Service, which was in my department, undertook field studies to try to determine what had gone wrong. In spite of predator control, education on conservation, and increased use of other foods, the situation had continued to deteriorate.

In 1948–9 the continental caribou herds between the Mackenzie River and Hudson Bay had been estimated at 660,000 animals. In 1955 the number was estimated to be only 300,000. In 1958 the Wildlife Service advised that there were not more than 200,000. The basic trouble appeared to have been unusually low calf crops in seven of the previous eight years: the most likely cause was cold weather in the period immediately after calving when the young are extremely vulnerable and likely to die if they become too chilled. The size of the crops had varied, but generally they had been no greater than 10 per cent of the total animals, except in 1952. In 1958 I reported to the Council:

> Natural mortality inevitably takes a toll, which probably varies between 5 and 10 percent of the herd each year. If natural mortality reaches 10 percent of the total, then there is no room for any human utilization of caribou whatever if the herds are not to be depleted. If natural mortality should be as low as 5 percent, then 10,000 or so could be taken annually. In view of all the unknown factors, a compromise, although a risky one, might be to suggest that human utilization should not exceed 7,500 animals annually in the light of the present calf crops. Humans throughout the Territories and northern parts of the provinces normally take many, many times this figure. In 1949 one authority estimated the take at 100,000 per year and in 1954 and 1955 another put it at 65,000 and 73,000 respectively.

Poor hunting and shooting practices, causing caribou to be lost and wasted through crippling, have alone probably exceeded what the necessary human kill should have been in recent years.

So serious is the situation that attempts to get the co-operation of hunters under the existing legislation no longer appear to be adequate. The Technical and Administrative Committees recommend that all the governments concerned introduce legislation for a four-fold purpose: to prohibit the killing of female caribou for the months of January to July inclusive; to prohibit the killing of caribou calves at any time and of yearlings prior to the first of August of each year; to prohibit the feeding of caribou meat to dogs or other domestic animals; and to prohibit the use of .22 calibre rifles in the hunting of caribou.

I said that no ordinance to make legal provisions for controls would be introduced at that session because the problems of limitation were of such importance to the native people and their situations were so different from one part of the Territory to another. I wanted to have the views of the elected members of the Council before having a law drafted. We could not impose new restrictions without enough notice to the people concerned – and adequate opportunity for them to get food of other kinds.

The scope of the problem meant that the eleven 'numbered' Indian treaties also had to be considered. All of them stated that the Indians 'shall have the right to pursue their vocations of hunting' throughout whatever tract of land was surrendered under each treaty, 'subject to such regulations as from time to time may be made by the government.'

It was a relief, in my address, to be able to turn to something more cheerful – a start at employment of Inuit in jobs other than in government services. About seventy Inuit were employed by an imaginative company in a nickel mine that had opened at Rankin Inlet on the west coast of Hudson Bay. The company provided medical services, on-the-job training, and flexible hours to give time off for hunting by their Inuit employees. They worked out an over-staffing plan to make flexibility of work hours possible without too much added cost.

A school was going to be built at the settlement in the summer of 1958, and a teacher would be there in the autumn. A northern service officer would be posted there to help with problems of adjustment in the transition of a hunting people to regular schedules, wage employment, permanent housing, and the use of new and unusual foods. Transition was something that affected everyone; men, women, and children.

The Human Crisis in a Great Lone Land

Shortly after my report to the Council at Yellowknife in January 1958, the consequences of the decline in the caribou population began to be felt still more cruelly in the area west of Hudson Bay. A major factor in that dreadful winter was that the area, in an even truer sense than the prairies of 1870, was a 'great lone land' with tiny groups of nomadic Inuit and very few RCMP posts to provide any contact by or with government.

It is difficult for anyone who has not had direct experience to comprehend the vastness of the area, the scattered and isolated nature of the tiny population, and the difficulties in communication at that time. Some 600 Inuit inhabited an area of more than 100,000 square miles: a population density of about one for every 166 square miles. Throughout that area, only slightly less than half the land area of Manitoba, there were no more than ten RCMP and Northern Service officers and probably fewer than 100 whites in all, scattered among half a dozen settlements. The Inuit did not live in or near the settlements but wherever they had to be in order to pursue their precarious way of life: in tiny groups of one, two, or half a dozen families in no fixed place.

There were no telegraphs to tell what was going on; the Inuit families had no radio transmitters to inform anyone whether they had food or not. Even if transmitters had been provided, the people could not have carried receivers and batteries with them in their constant movements. There was no one nearby to turn to at short notice. The nearest settlement might be 150 or 200 miles away, and the only way of getting there would be by dogs that might be too weak to travel when a situation became desperate.

More than twenty-five Inuit deaths that year were the result, directly or indirectly, of the caribou crisis at three locations west of Hudson Bay. There was great hardship short of starvation in several other places. It was the federal government, primarily the Department of Northern Affairs and the RCMP, that had to do what could be done to provide assistance but the problem was enormous and the resources were few. As I said to the Council: 'Virtually all the Eskimos, in their native way of life, lead an existence that is precarious because of its dependence on a very few types of animal for food and clothing. No group, however, is exposed to as great hazards as those who depend on the caribou as do the inland Eskimos. These people have always lived close to the brink of disaster and the failure of the caribou migrations to pass by is frequently sufficient to push them over its edge.'

With an eye on future winters, emergency caches of food were being established. Patrols by the RCMP and NSOs would be increased and coordinated. There could be no guarantees, however, for people moving about to hunt, with no one knowing where they might be at any given time.

There were five field parties of the Wildlife Service following the caribou through the calving period, which was critical, and then through the entire seasonal migration. In concluding my report, I said that while the scientific studies, predator control, and the restrictions on hunting were steps in the right direction, it would be optimistic to expect that the caribou population would rebound in the near future. The long-term solution had to be in reducing dependence on the caribou and providing alternative means of livelihood.

The caribou crisis was only the most dramatic demonstration of the broader problem: the impossibility for a growing Aboriginal population in the Northwest Territories – and in Arctic Quebec – to continue to be as dependent on hunting and trapping as both the Indians and the Inuit had traditionally been and still were in 1958. It brought home with dreadful force the need to have more schools for more children so that they could have some choice about their adult lives.

Education, however, was not enough. To make a choice of occupation possible in their Arctic homeland would require inventive use of renewable Arctic resources other than game as well as development of minerals in an area where costs would inevitably be high. The provision of new economic opportunity was the most difficult problem of all.

Education for a Different Future
In September 1958 the territorial education system took a new step in equipping young people for future careers with the opening of a new high and vocational school at Yellowknife and a hostel for young people coming from all parts of the Territories to attend it.

We had decided on a policy of evoking the history of the North by naming schools, hostels, and other prominent buildings after people who played leading roles in northern exploration and development. One of the most perilous expeditions had been led by Sir John Franklin in 1819; they went across the barrens on foot from near Yellowknife on Great Slave Lake to the mouth of the Coppermine River on the Arctic Coast. From there they explored the coast to the east for five hundred miles to see if they could discover a waterway leading to the Atlantic. As autumn closed in and food ran low, they had to turn back with no answer. Almost certainly all would have died on the return trip if it had

173

not been for the chief of the Yellowknife Indians, Akaitcho. The new school was named after Sir John Franklin and the hostel after Akaitcho. Courses were developed for a wide range of vocations.

In 1958 there were forty-eight government-operated schools containing 140 classrooms serving the Northwest Territories and the Inuit population of northern Quebec.

Under the agreements with the Catholic and Anglican churches, the last of the residential church schools in the Territories – at Chesterfield Inlet – would be taken over in 1959. It would be replaced by a government school and a hostel for eighty Inuit children. Other residential schools had been taken over at Aklavik, Fort Smith, Fort Simpson, and Fort McPherson. To replace them, the new government schools were to serve both children resident in the community and others whose families 'lived on the land' or in settlements too small for schools. Those children would be housed in new hostels, which had been completed at Fort Smith and Fort McPherson and were under construction at Fort Simpson and Inuvik. At the latter, the new operational centre for the western Arctic, each hostel – one operated by the Catholic Church and one by the Anglican – would be for 150 pupils, most of whom would be Inuit. All pupils regardless of race would attend the same school. There would be separation on a religious basis in the junior grades only.

The figures for 1958 and 1959 showed that the number of Inuit children in school had nearly doubled in a single year – from 604 to 1,189. For all children, the range and the quality of education were significantly improved since the church schools, by their own admission, had not had the financial or the professional resources to provide a satisfactory standard of education. A curriculum was being developed to meet the special problems of northern children, many of whom were making a cultural and linguistic leap at the same time as they took on the new experience of education.

In later years – but not when the school and education program was launched – there was criticism of the administration for bringing native children to our large hostels to attend school. The children were away from their families for much of the year and, it was claimed, lost contact with their own cultures. Experience showed that there was only limited truth in that. The native cultures were not lost, but certainly new experiences and values changed traditional attitudes. That would probably have happened even without the hostel experience.

The problem was that the only alternative to hostels for nearly all the Inuit children, and for many of the Indians, would have been to postpone their education for several years at best and, in the most difficult situations, to cause children to miss education altogether. There were in the 1950s almost no year-round Inuit settlements. There could be few day schools until there were, and so long as the culture of 'life on the land' prevailed, families had to be moving about to follow the game on which they depended.

The reality that both the administration and native parents had to face was that, for a number of years – and how many could not be foreseen – the choice was between education with many children living in hostels, or no education for those children at all. Failure to educate during childhood years would mean a lifetime with no source of livelihood other than hunting and trapping, and the risks for that dependence were apparent in the tragedies of the winter of 1957–8. It was a risk that could not be taken.

The Queen Who Didn't Come

After a year of troubles, the people of the Northwest Territories got a lift from the news that the Queen would visit them on her tour of Canada. No reigning monarch had ever visited the Territories and the young, glamorous Queen Elizabeth II was utterly special. Her coronation, just a few years before, had had a fairy-tale quality about it. There was great excitement that she really was coming to the Territories. The visit was to be to Yellowknife on 20 July 1959. The date was perfect: school was out, days were long, flying was good. Groups of children were to be brought from all parts of the Territories and housed at government expense in the new hostel and the hotels of the town.

I even managed to persuade my wife, who detests flying, that she had to be in Yellowknife for the event. The commissioner's wife was the official hostess for a state visit: not to be there would be an unforgivable offence. Unfortunately, Murphy's law held good: everything that could go wrong on our trip did. Our reservations from Edmonton had been lost and the plane was fully booked when we turned up. When that was solved, it developed, in mid-flight, that the plane-load exceeded the legal weight limit. A forced landing at Fort McMurray, with three people bribed to get off along with their luggage and some freight, solved that after a long haggle. One of the two motors went dead over Great Slave Lake. The plane lost altitude, wheeled around, and made it back to Fort Smith. Another plane had to be flown in from Edmonton to replace it. Fortunately, we had a day to lose and still get to Yellowknife on time. Bea was scornful of my pre-trip assurance that the Edmonton-to-Yellowknife flight was the milk run on which nothing ever went wrong.

The twentieth of July was not a glorious, sunny day such as the north in summer can provide, but it was not raining and the temperature was mild. The crowd at the airfield to greet the Queen and the Duke of Edinburgh was enormous by NWT standards. They were mostly children, panting for the fairy queen to arrive.

The Queen was coming from Whitehorse in the Yukon. Communications were poor: all we learned as we waited was that she would be a bit late. That added to the excitement when the great four-motored RCAF plane did finally come in. The impatience could scarcely be contained when, after careful taxiing into position, the stairs were put in place, the red carpet rolled to their foot, and the door of the plane at last opened. Would she be wearing her crown? What colour would her gown be? What would she say? Finally someone did emerge – a man of medium height in a grey suit. No gown. No crown. No queen.

Nowhere else in Canada could the disappointment have been as great as at Yellowknife. No duke in a suit of any colour could do or say anything that could compensate. Queen Elizabeth, we were told, had become indisposed at Whitehorse and had to go directly to Edmonton. It later emerged that she was pregnant and some 'indisposition' led to medical advice against the strain of the trip to Yellowknife, the events there, and then the onward trip to Edmonton.

The Duke did his best. We all went to the gymnasium of the Sir John Franklin school for speeches, presentations, a walk-about by him to talk to the children – but the magic had gone. The Duke, with a good show of interest, received gifts for the Queen from representatives of the different Indian tribes, the schoolchildren from far places, and, most interestingly, an Inuit group. An artist among the latter had carved his own Queen out of the soapstone used for the sculptures that were beginning to get national and international recognition.

The sculptor had a magazine photograph of the Queen at her coronation to tell him what she looked like and what she wore – and there she was, about eighteen inches high, with a crown, a sceptre, and features that indeed were those of the Queen. It was beautifully done. The only thing the picture had not disclosed, because the Queen's gown was so long, was what she wore on her feet. When the carving was lifted out of its beautiful box so it could be admired by the Duke from every angle, the sculptor's solution was revealed: the Queen was barefoot. Her feet and every one of her ten toes were beautifully carved.

Chesterfield Inlet, 1959: Hope for Economic Development

My opening address to the Council at Chesterfield Inlet on 27 July, just a week after the disappointment at Yellowknife, politely alleged that the visit of the Duke of Edinburgh was 'highly appreciated' but my expression of Territorial regret at the Queen's absence was more honest. However, there was something cheerful to report with regard to a submission I had made nearly four years before to the Royal Commission on Canada's Economic Prospects, chaired by Walter Gordon.

I had, on behalf of the Territorial government, urged the building of a railway some four hundred miles from the end of steel in northern Alberta to Pine Point on the south shore of Great Slave Lake. The main argument, prepared by C.H. Herbert, the head of our small economic division, was that such a railway would stimulate economic development in the Territories by reducing costs of transportation for the most important Territorial natural resources – 'minerals – metals and oil.' The nub of it was simple: 'The greatest obstacle to the present development of the mineral resources of the Northwest Territories is the high cost of operation. This cost derives from a number of factors, some of them being the direct result of climate. The most important element, however, is a whole set of high costs due, directly and indirectly, to problems of transportation. These costs can all be brought down substantially. Nothing else will have so great an effect in stimulating economic development.'[1]

What made the argument realistic was the probability that the lead-zinc deposits at Pine Point could be brought into production if a railway was built. The administration had made a study of the costs of a railway as compared with an improved highway. 'The conclusion was that, for a volume of traffic in excess of around 75,000 to 100,000 tons a year, it would be more economic to build a railway rather than to make the necessary extension and improvements of the existing highway. Since a traffic of something between 200,000 and 250,000 tons a year is expected at an early stage, including all freight inward and outward, the figures indicate that a railway would be more economic.'[2]

The advantages would not be limited to the mine at Pine Point. 'A railhead on Great Slave Lake would have other advantages. At the present time all-year round transportation to the lake is provided by the Mackenzie Highway, and the freight rate from Edmonton to Hay River is approximately $50 a ton. The rate from Edmonton to the lake by rail would, on the basis of present representative rates, be about $32 a ton. The head of navigation would then be placed on the lake and would be some 500 miles further down the river system than it now is.'[3]

Diefenbaker's enormous majority in the general election of March 1958 and his 'vision of the North' could not have been more timely. The speech from the throne opening the following session of Parliament announced that the railway to Great Slave Lake was to be built. That led to a dispute among competing local interests in northern Alberta about the route it should take. The contest was sufficiently ferocious that resort was had to the traditional Canadian solution – a royal commission. I told the Council at Chesterfield Inlet, with more hope than conviction, that 'a report is expected later this summer.'

Cooperatives for New Opportunities

At the Council session of January 1959, a new Co-operative Associations Ordinance had been passed. Six months later I informed the Council that the first Inuit cooperatives were being established – one at Port Burwell, on an island in Hudson Strait just north of the Quebec-Labrador boundary, and the other at Cape Dorset, also on an island, this one near the southwest corner of Baffin Island. Both were going to be 'producers' cooperatives' of which the members would be Inuit. The Inuit at Port Burwell would engage in fishing for Arctic char to be sold, fresh-frozen, to top quality restaurants, initially in Montreal. Market surveys indicated that the prospects were good if quality could be maintained at a reasonable price. The co-op at Cape Dorset would be based on the Inuit sculptures, prints, and handicrafts that were already attracting the interest of the art world.

Edith Iglauer, an author living in New York City, became fascinated with the Inuit, travelled widely in the Canadian Arctic, and visited the cooperative originally intended for Port Burwell but relocated to the mainland on the George River in Arctic Quebec. (The boundaries of Quebec stop at the high-water line on the coast of Hudson Bay and Hudson Strait. All the islands offshore were part of the Northwest Territories and are now part of Nunavut.) She says:

> In the winter of 1959 a small group of Eskimos who made their home around the George River in Arctic Quebec and were almost all on relief met with federal government officials in a tent while their land, rivers and bay were covered with snow and ice, and formed the George River Eskimo Coöperative. It was the first Inuit coöperative in Canada.
>
> One of the officials, Donald Snowden, whose job was to solve the puzzle of unemployment among the Canadian Eskimos, or Inuit as they now prefer to be called, gave the George River Inuit ten dollars from his own pocket to pay the required fee to register with the Quebec government. They had no money at all and before they could get a government loan to

start their coöperative it had to be registered in the province where they were living.[4]

The cooperative at Cape Dorset became much better known. Led by James Houston, our NSO there, it produced the sculptures and later the prints that brought Inuit women into art production. The 'Enchanted Owl,' designed by Kenojuak, a tiny woman living in Cape Dorset, was later reproduced on a Canadian postage stamp, drawing attention everywhere to the Inuit artistic talent, so original and so different.

The cooperative program grew out of the realization that its philosophy would fit with the traditional Inuit way of living and sharing. It would be more natural and comprehensible than any plan involving the establishment of companies based on individual enterprise. In the initial stages the cooperatives would need technical advice, market research, and loans to get going. After that, it was hoped that they could operate without direct financial assistance.

The cooperative idea had been developed in the Industrial Division of the department whose chief, Snowden, was a man of unusual imagination and energy. Paul Godt was head of the Cooperative Development Section and responsible for development in the Ungava area. James Houston had a perfect combination of talents for Cape Dorset. He was an artist himself, he loved the North and the Inuit, he spoke Inuktitut, and he had the imagination to see how the unique artistry of the Inuit could be developed to appeal to attitudes and art markets in the south. The combination of Houston's capacities and enthusiasm and the remarkable creativity of the Cape Dorset people brought success for the co-op and for the community beyond anything that had been hoped.

While the prime purpose of the cooperatives was economic, they were also seen as a means of introducing the Inuit to the problems of planning, working, and organizing in ways that were new to them. As the cooperative movement spread, it proved to be the incubator from which political leaders emerged throughout the Territories.

Edith Iglauer's report of 1962 continues:

The novel idea of setting up a coöperative business in the Arctic wilderness that the proud but desperate George River Eskimos agreed to give a try took root and grew, until now there are fifty-two active Arctic coöperatives, forty-one of them in the Northwest Territories, eleven of them, including one that is run by Cree Indians, in northern Quebec, with assets of fourteen million dollars and annual sales of twenty-three million. They are the largest single employer of Inuit in Canada. Every year about six-and-a-half million dollars go out to coöperative members in wages, salaries, for goods produced – including the works of art cherished all over the world – and other payments.[5]

Resolute Bay, 1960: The Farthest North

There were several reasons for holding a session of the Council at Resolute Bay on Cornwallis Island as we did the following year. One – like climbing Mount Everest for the first time – was because there had never, anywhere, been a legislature meeting so far north. We were, while there, just short of seventy-five degrees north latitude: closer to Norway and the USSR than to Ottawa. It gave a reality to the polar and intercontinental facts of Canada's North that conventional maps do not reveal. The session also had a symbolic value. It was an aspect of effective occupation and administration in Canada's most northerly islands.

When Captain Parry penetrated to Cornwallis Island and beyond in the course of his remarkable expedition in 1819 that came so close to getting through the Northwest Passage, there were no Inuit there. However, archaeological investigations later showed that Inuit of the Dorset culture had lived there more than a thousand years before and were succeeded by a later culture – the Thule people. The fact that the area had been so long lived in was one of the factors, along with present-day demonstration of the abundance of game, that led to the belief that Resolute Bay would be a good place for a new start for Inuit suffering from shortage of game on the east coast of Hudson Bay.

I have mentioned in Chapter 6 my first visit to those relocated people six years before – in March 1954. In 1960 they were still living in their traditional way in snow houses as part of a highly successful economy based on the resources of both sea and land. Those resources had, as forecast, proved adequate and reliable. The community was clearly going to be permanent so a school had been built and teaching had started. However, the children were on vacation in July and it was in the school that the Council met.

As at Frobisher Bay, the Inuit who were not away fishing for Arctic char or engaging in other summer activities attended our sessions – babies, children, and all. There was a language problem for most of the Council members, but mixing was easy and cordial. In the week we were there, neither I nor any member of the Council nor any of the Council staff heard a word of unhappiness over the move to Resolute Bay or any wish to move back to Port Harrison. The people were obviously healthy, active, and well clothed. Seven years after its establishment, Resolute was a flourishing settlement, completely self-reliant in the best Inuit style.

In 1959 the Council had passed a Territorial Hospital Insurance Services Ordinance. Under it an agreement had been signed with the minister of national health and welfare for the federal government to contribute its share of Territorial costs under the federal Hospital Insurance Act. The new hospital at Inuvik was to open in the autumn. Another was planned for Frobisher Bay.

Many of the residents of the Territories were in areas far from the centres of Yellowknife, Inuvik or Frobisher Bay. To bring health services closer to them, thirteen federal nursing stations had been or would be established in smaller communities.

The incidence of tuberculosis had been decreasing for several years: in 1959 only six Inuit died from the disease. However, there had not been similar progress with infant mortality. Half of the Inuit who had died the previous year were less than one year old. The underlying causes appeared to be bad housing – the traditional skin tents and snow houses – and isolation. Some progress was being made with housing, but it was so closely associated with the culture and way of life that a dramatic change over the short term was not to be expected. The hope was for a steady improvement year by year as small wooden houses could be built in settlements with employment or close to hunting and trapping areas. Cape Dorset was one such place. Wooden houses gave the infant protection and the greater year-round comfort that the Inuit wanted when it was possible.

Later in 1960 a new program for long-term, partially subsidized, low-interest loans to Inuit for the construction of approved accommodation was initiated. The plan was designed to enable Inuit to buy houses at prices they could afford. Since the buyers could not pay very much, the houses were small, with essential facilities only, but they would be a major improvement on traditional accommodation. Snow houses could continue to be used if the way of life required them or if an Inuit family preferred or chose to avoid any loan obligation and stick to the traditional style. Few did.

Fort Simpson, 1961: Division of the Northwest Territories

After three years without a session in the Mackenzie area, the Council chose Fort Simpson, where the Liard River flows into the Mackenzie, for the session of July 1961.

Unlike the Arctic, the subarctic – and especially the Mackenzie valley –

can be hot in the summer. For the duration of our meeting, Fort Simpson was around eighty degrees Fahrenheit. The heat along with the relatively good soil there explained why Fort Simpson was the only place in the Territories where the federal Department of Agriculture had an experimental station. Gardens could and did flourish and most residents of Fort Simpson, Indian, Metis, and white, had them. In most years, field crops could ripen but the number of frost-free days for grain was less reliable than several hundred miles south. Agriculture would be even more hazardous than on the prairies.

A question of interest to the Council was what had happened to the economy and the livelihood of the residents of the Territories in the previous few years as so many changes took place. It turned out to be difficult to get any sure answers since so large a part of the 'income' of the Aboriginal people continued to be 'in kind' – from the land and the sea. The caribou population had declined. The resources of the sea continued to be successfully exploited, but the Aboriginal population dependent on them was increasing. Not surprisingly, a study made by the administration found 'no way of knowing just how the standard of life that is related to the products of the land, lake and sea has changed in total.' However, the conclusion on the whole had to be negative. None of the resources was more plentiful and many had become more scarce, especially caribou.

What could be measured was cash sales at retail outlets in the Territories. Figures on these had been secured from stores and trading posts. They were encouraging. The dollar value of merchandise sales in the Arctic District had increased by almost five times since 1949: a cumulative rate of growth of more than 15 per cent a year. The rate of growth in retail sales in that period over Canada as a whole had been 6 per cent. Growth in the Mackenzie District had been less dramatic than in the Arctic, but impressive. It had amounted to more than 7 1/2 per cent a year.

The population of the Territories had increased faster than the population of Canada as a whole, about 4 per cent per year from 1951, in contrast to the rest of the country's 2.5 per cent. On the whole, prices of fur had declined and total returns had dropped in both the Arctic and the Mackenzie areas. The question was what other factors there were to explain the increase in retail sales. We had no precise figures, but our study attempted some estimates.

In the previous year, the sale of Inuit prints had brought in $63,000 net to the artists. The longer-established market for sculptures in stone, ivory, and whale bone and the growing output of fur products and other clothing had contributed substantial cash revenues to the new cooperatives. The balance of consumer incomes came from wage employment, resource-harvesting programs, such as fisheries, lumbering, and sealskin production, and, most of all, welfare payments under various federal or federal-territorial programs – especially family allowances and old age pensions.

The most interesting item at the session was a proposal that had first been raised by the member of the Council for Mackenzie Delta, Knut Lang, at the session in January 1960: that the Northwest Territories should be divided in two.

Lang was the fascinating member who had formally proposed Graham Rowley's name 'Inuvik' for our project at E-3 in his constituency. Lang read widely, ordering books by mail on the basis of reviews he read in magazines and newspapers. In his isolated trading post, he debated with the authors by notes he wrote on the page margins and in any spaces he could find in the books. His proposal rested on his own thinking about how the western part of the Territories could make the most rapid progress to self-government.

Lang had come to the conclusion that the best course to achieve that objective would be for the west to become a separate territory, since the Inuit in the eastern part had, at that time, no experience in government. It would take some years for elections to be feasible in the east with its widely scattered population.

Apart from that difference in political development, the people of the two parts of the Territory were different. The Aboriginal people of the western region were mainly Indian or Metis. Their ways of life, their cultures, and their interests were not the same as those of the Inuit of the east. Even the Inuit of the Mackenzie Delta and the islands of the western Arctic were different from those of the east. It would be difficult for one government and one Council to represent fairly and to act effectively for so mixed a population.

Dividing off the area that was ready, or nearly ready, for responsible government would follow the pattern of the 'old' North-West Territories. There the southern part of the prairies became settled, achieved self-government, and then was divided off in 1905 with provincial status as the provinces of Alberta and Saskatchewan. The northern part followed a different timetable that fitted its own circumstances. We were faced, Lang argued, with a repetition of that situation. His proposal appealed to the other members of the Council, both elected and appointed, as realistic. We thought that it would produce better and more sensitive governments for both parts of what was in many respects too large an area with too many differences of condition and interest.

In the discussion in 1960 the Council focused on what should be included in the 'western' territory. The Votes and Proceedings record: 'It was suggested that some of the islands north of the present Mackenzie District such as Banks Island, Victoria Island and King William Island should be part of any such new territory. It was also suggested that the eastern boundary might be a northward extension of the Manitoba-Saskatchewan border but there was some objection to this because such an artificial line would not have regard to actual features of the ground.'

In 1961 the Council unanimously supported Lang's proposal. The administration was asked to look into the boundary question and any other problems, including the steps that should be taken to secure the approval of the federal government.

A Prime Ministerial Visit
The last day of the 1961 session was made special by a visit from the prime minister and Mrs Diefenbaker, en route to Inuvik for its formal opening. That was the event I had used to persuade Diefenbaker to make the trip north. He really wanted to come. It was largely a matter of having something to push the trip to the top of the pile of things pressing for his time.

I, of course, used my opportunity in welcoming the Diefenbakers to encourage the prime minister's already great interest in the North. I drew as much parallel as I thought honesty would permit between the opening of the West and the opening of the North.

Sir John A. Macdonald had visited the West in July 1886 – 'seventy-five years ago this week.' It was as sparsely populated then as the North in 1961 and as little developed. Sir John's government then was in the midst of an imaginative and courageous policy of development for the West, just as Diefenbaker's was in the 1960s for the North. The Council of the Northwest Territories, 1961 version, felt as confident as did the Council, 1886 version, that the policy of development would be vindicated.

I had to throw in some cautions. Development would not follow the agricultural course of the West – mining and oil would be its core, there would be no rush of immigrants to unprepared land. Much more capital would be needed, more research, more ingenuity. I also spoke of our main Territorial policies and concerns: education, child welfare, health, housing, protection of game, and, to sustain it all, economic development. Costs in the North were enormously high and the sources of revenue limited 'but the people of the North were prepared to do their share in meeting the costs.'

The Council, I said, had looked at the future form of the Territories. We were not 'thinking now or soon of provincial status': the population was too small, development too limited, and costs too high. The Council did, however, recommend a step towards full self-government for a western Territory of Mackenzie by dividing the overly large Northwest Territories. If the prime minister agreed, after further consideration in January 1962, the Council would submit that recommendation to the federal government.

Diefenbaker felt a personal bond with the Northwest Territories. His family had moved in 1903 to the then Territories and settled not far from Saskatoon. They had been part of the frontier of that day. In 1910 he had, as a newsboy, encountered Sir Wilfrid Laurier walking outside his private railway car when the prime minister was in Saskatoon to lay the cornerstone of the new University of Saskatchewan, where later both Diefenbaker and I would study. In his address to the Council, Diefenbaker recounted those events of the turn of the century. It was clear that he saw a new chapter in Canadian history unfolding, as it had in 1905 and 1910, with him, as prime minister, helping to make true Laurier's confidence that the twentieth century would be Canada's.

The Council presented Mrs Diefenbaker with the three best white-fox skins that Knut Lang could find for a stole to remind her of the NWT. Tastes and markets had not yet been affected by the animal-rights movement and she was delighted. On his return to Ottawa, the prime minister sent a message saying that his visit to the Council 'was the outstanding feature' of his trip to the Northwest Territories.

The visit to Inuvik the following day had more of real Arctic interest but it may be that Diefenbaker was too tired to appreciate all that was new in Canada's first modern Arctic town. He had had barely time to get to Fort Simpson after concluding a strenuous session of Parliament. Its last days were tense and dramatic, ending with a defeat in the Senate for the government's legislation to remove from office the governor of the Bank of Canada, J.E. Coyne. The prime minister slept soundly on a couch in the plane in which I accompanied the Diefenbakers to Inuvik for its opening. Mrs Diefenbaker confided to me how great his burdens were and how 'whenever he wants anything we all come running.' I thought that it would not be politic to say how much it all sounded like Mackenzie King. He had expected everyone to come running too.

Inuvik was raw and unfinished, with trucks stirring up clouds of gravel and dust as they hauled lumber and other freight from the dock to building sites, but the accommodation for the prime minister and Mrs Diefenbaker in one of the new hostels for the Inuvik Federal School, completed just the year before, was luxurious by Arctic standards. They were more rested the next day and Mrs Diefenbaker, with appropriate remarks, unveiled the symbolic bronze monument to mark, not only the formal opening of the town, but also the first visit by a prime minister to Canada north of the Arctic Circle. Diefenbaker was legitimately pleased that he should be the first: it was he who had awakened Canadians to their northern destiny – whatever that might turn out to be. The return trip to Ottawa was by way of a new telecommunication site in the Yukon: another sign of the northern awakening.

The prime minister, obviously exhilarated by the whole experience, entertained his travelling companions with a sparkling display of his wit and his qualities as a raconteur. The stories were endless, the names and details were precise, and his enjoyment was exceeded only by that of his listeners. It was hard to believe on landing at a darkened Ottawa – the first darkness in several days – that we had that day flown virtually from the northwest to the southeast corner of the country. If we had gone right to the end of the diagonal at Halifax, the prime minister would undoubtedly have recounted more stories still. It was not difficult to see how he had been able to charm the Canadian electors into that tremendous majority in 1958.

Ottawa, January 1962: Financing Growth

The principal item at the winter session in 1962 was the new five-year financial agreement with the federal government. The agreement accepted that expenditures by the Territorial government would increase substantially, principally because of the Territorial share in the comprehensive programs for education, health services, and welfare. Capital costs for the construction of schools and the building of roads were mainly federal, since Aboriginal children were a federal responsibility under the constitution and the federal government had retained jurisdiction over resources in the Territories for which the new road program – 'Roads to Resources' – was largely designed. The agreement sorted out the allocation of costs more accurately than the previous one, with a heavier load on the Territorial government. Territorial revenues from liquor sales and charges to non-Aboriginals for schools and health services would rise.

Altogether, total expenditures by the Territorial government were predicted to increase from just under $5 millon in the fiscal year 1961–2 to $9,200,000 in 1966–7. There would be subsidies and grants-in-aid for specific purposes as in the provinces and federal loans to cover the Territorial share of capital costs. The remaining difference between expenditures and revenues raised in the Territories would be covered, as before, by the federal government. The annual grant would rise from $2,190,000 in 1962–3 to $2,730,000 in 1966–7.

Neither the expenditures nor the federal grants look large in relation to those of later years or of today: the scope and scale of government in the north grew enormously in the 1970s and 1980s and inflation pushed the high costs of everything in the Territories even higher. Comparison with figures before the decision by St Laurent's government in 1953 to embark on an active policy for the North is more relevant. For the fiscal year ending 31 March 1953, revenues of the Northwest Territories totalled $660,026 and expenditures were $433,762. After including unpaid accounts and various charges for reserves, the Territorial government appears to have had a surplus for the year of $177,160.

Most of the increase in the cost of northern programs after 1953 in the Northwest Territories was charged to federal departments as their direct responsibility – to the Department of Northern Affairs and National Resources for Inuit health, education, and welfare, to Citizenship and Immigration for the same services for Indians, and to other departments such as Public Works and Transport for construction and operation of their own programs. The Territorial expenditures were for programs and services, of a provincial type such as education, hospitals, municipal services and welfare for the part of the population that was not a federal responsibility, which meant for the Metis and the whites. Also Territorial was the share of construction costs for all the services that grew in relation to those programs.

Altogether, expenditures by the government of the Northwest Territories for 'provincial' programs and services for non-Aboriginal people grew from approximately $450,000 in 1952–3 to $5,000,000 in 1961–2, a factor of ten in the first ten years of the new policy. The increase was a reflection of the change in attitude and policy towards the North that the St Laurent government had decided upon and that the Diefenbaker government had carried still further. That the fundamental change was in attitude and policy rather than in funds available is made clear by the surplus of territorial revenue over expenditure in 1952–3. It was not that there were not then serious needs for schools, health services, and welfare among the Metis and some of the whites who were a territorial responsibility. The main factor almost certainly was the acceptance of a frontier standard of services that was better than it had been in years past and better than the circumstances of the Aboriginal population but bore little relation to what was considered acceptable for Canadians in the rest of Canada. That attitude had changed with the growing interest of Canadians in the North.

Cape Dorset, 1962: Cooperatives and Inuit Art

In the course of a trip to Baffin Island in 1960 with Bob Phillips, who was then assistant director (plans and policy) in the Northern Administration Branch of Northern Affairs, we had the good luck to be weatherbound in Cape Dorset for nearly a week. It was a happy accident since it forced us to spend the time necessary to become acquainted with one of the most interesting Inuit settlements in the entire Arctic.

It was early April – spring, with all its promise, in southern Canada but winter at Cape Dorset, except for the long days and bright sun. In between storms, we took trips by dog sled to the floe edge, where the Inuit were hunting seals, and had long walks with Jim Houston, well clothed against the wind and bitter cold. Apart from the three of us, the only living things in evidence were the ravens, with nests and perches high up on the hills that descend sharply into the sea around Cape Dorset. Houston said that the ravens would soon be laying eggs which would incubate and hatch, and that young would survive in spite of the cold.

Jim considered Cape Dorset to be 'the Athens of the Arctic.' It was one of relatively few places where the Inuit could find adequate resources all year round for a life that did not require nomadic movement of families to follow game across land and sea from season to season. The reason for that happy situation was the flow of currents around the corner of Baffin Island. *Arctic Canada from the Air* refers to this phenomenon: 'By December the strait [i.e., Hudson Strait] is full of pack ice, which is kept in motion all winter by currents and wind, never forming a solid sheet. The ice is usually more tightly packed along the south side of the strait than the north, and it is not uncommon to see fairly large patches of water off Cape Dorset.'[6]

With the security and stability the currents made possible, the Inuit had, Jim said, taken their culture to a higher point than was possible for the Inuit generally. Their art, especially carvings in soapstone, bone, and walrus ivory, was unusually interesting. It was that art, in the form of the small carvings that the Inuit had done for hundreds of years for their own pleasure – or to propitiate the mischievous spirits of the sea or land – that Jim had seen when he visited Cape Dorset in 1949. They could, he thought, form the basis for larger sculptures that would be authentically Inuit and also attractive to people in the South, as the very small carvings would not be. Jim spoke Inuktitut, he had a cordial relationship with the people, and he was confident that their art could be adapted to a southern market without losing its quality or originality. How right he was we have seen in the years since.

I used part of my stay at Cape Dorset to visit the school, talk to the teachers, and sit in on some classes. All the children, except a few whites, were in the elementary grades. The teachers wanted me to tell the students something about the Canada of which they were a part. I was more than ready, with the help of an interpreter. The Inuit children were bright, interested, and eager but it was not easy to make the magnitude of Canada understood – or the number of people in Montreal or To-ronto – to children whose native language had no numbers beyond twenty. 'Very, very many' or 'like the caribou when they are many' do not quite convey the difference in scale from the tiny settlement that was their world. I got a new appreciation of some of the problems the teachers had in conveying an idea of the world beyond Baffin Island.

The only 'landing' for aircraft at Cape Dorset was on the sea – on the ice in winter, on the water in the short summer. During break-up in the spring and freeze-up in the autumn there was no way to get in or out by air. When the Council was to go to Cape Dorset in July 1962, the ice was safely gone. To carry our large party, the 'bush' pilot at Frobisher Bay used a two-motored amphibian plane – to take off from the Frobisher airfield on wheels and 'land' at Cape Dorset on the boat-shaped belly of the plane with the wheels up. Aircraft maintenance was sometimes a bit casual in the North and it was a shock, when we came down on the sea, to have a plume of water squirt up from the floor of the cabin. It was obviously no surprise to the pilot. After setting down and taxiing to the shore he knew that the leak would stop as the plane tilted up on the shelving bottom. The water would come in again when he taxied out for his return to Frobisher but it would also leak out again after he took off and all would be well. That was demonstrated for us a week later when the Council session ended and we were going back to Frobisher Bay: the hole was still there. None of that meant that the plane was not safe and the pilot was not good. It is just that, in the North, there is no point in fussing about frills. It is the basics that count.

I reported to the Council on progress since 1959 when the first two Inuit-owned cooperatives had come into existence. Eight more had since been established in the Arctic part of the Territories. I went on to say:

> During the past three and one-half years, there has been a steady increase in the business done by northern cooperatives. This year, it is expected that the 10 enterprises will do business of a gross value in the neighbourhood of $800,000. Of this, about $125,000 will represent cash payment to Eskimo people, either as dividends or as payment for production. An additional $75,000 will be used to retire debt and to buy new capital equipment.
>
> Perhaps the best known Eskimo cooperative is the one here at Cape Dorset, which began in 1959 as a tourist operation. Soon after that, it expanded into Eskimo graphic art and, last year, established its own retail store. This cooperative has shown remarkable financial success.

Other Inuit cooperatives were at George River, Resolute Bay, and Grise Fiord, the last two being the locations to which the Inuit from the east coast of Hudson Bay had gone in 1953. There were three cooperatives in the central and western Arctic – Holman Island, Coppermine, and Cambridge Bay – and at several locations in the eastern Arctic. They were engaged in a variety of business operations based on commercial fishing, handicrafts, tourism, and the operation of small retail stores. At Frobisher Bay, fifteen families had established a housing cooperative to provide the member families with adequate three-bedroom housing, a project facilitated by initial financing from the Eskimo Loan Fund that had been set up in the Department of Northern Affairs.

Apart from the job opportunities and income, it was already clear that the co-ops provided new experience to people who had had no contact with either business or the operation of organized communities. I was able to report that 'in many of the places where cooperatives have been established, community leaders are beginning to emerge, first as directors of the cooperatives and then as leading members of Eskimo councils. Through their cooperatives, many Eskimo people have been introduced to the concept of free elections and the secret ballot for the first time.'

The Inuit members were, I said, with advice from our NSOs, showing a grasp of planning for the business operations they had undertaken 'For example, several cooperatives this year could have distributed dividend payments to members during the height of winter, at a time when the economic picture in some Arctic communities is at its worst. In each case, the members voted not to declare a dividend, but to plow the profits back into additional capital equipment for their cooperatives. '

That much was good, but not everything was cheering. In the Keewatin District on the west side of Hudson Bay, where the decline in the caribou had been greatest and where the mine at Rankin Inlet had provided a substantial amount of employment, the mine would cease to operate that summer. Cooperatives were being established there for handicrafts to provide alternative employment and income.

The session at Cape Dorset was a success in the mingling of Council and community. That would have been difficult but for the presence on the trip of my son John, then thirteen years old. He carried a message from me, in the syllabic writing used for the Inuktitut language in the eastern (but not the western) Arctic, to all the summer tents of the scattered community – and in the process made an impression on some of the Inuit girls that I met years later on a visit to the school in Frobisher Bay. The Inuit men, but no women, responded to my invitation to an alcohol-free reception in the Houston house for the Council. Conversation would have been better if Jim and Allie Houston had been there, but they were out of the North on leave. One or two Inuit could speak some English and interpreted. The gathering was cordial and a dance at the end of the session was inhibited neither by gender nor by language. The dance, inherited, I was told, from Scottish whalers, involved everyone the school room had space for in two circles, women in the inner one and men in the outer, revolving in opposite directions, with breaks to dance in pairs until each had danced with everyone in the other circle. It was a test for legs and wind, ending in exhaustion for the Council members. The Inuit appeared to be tireless. The dance went on long after the councillors crept off sheepishly to bed.

During the stop at Frobisher Bay the Council had time to see progress in its development as a centre for transportation, education, and economic activity in the eastern Arctic. The Northern Canada Power Commission, of which I was chairman in one of my several hats, was building an oil-fuelled power plant to be completed by the end of 1963. A new townsite near the airport was under way with a sewer and water system, a water treatment plant, a hospital, and a number of smaller structures.

The future of Frobisher Bay would be affected if the federal government implemented the Council's proposal to divide the Territories. It would be the logical place for the capital of a new Arctic Territory. The proposal had been communicated to the Inuit, who would be the largest part of the population of that new territory. The circular explaining it in

English and Inuktitut had been widely distributed and the people had been invited to submit their suggestions for an appropriate name. Over 1,000 replies had been received, most of them from Eskimos, by the time the Council met. The most popular suggestion was 'Nunassiaq,' which meant 'beautiful land' in Inuktitut. That is the name the Council of the Territories then proposed to the government. When the new Territory was established in 1999, the name was 'Nunavut' – 'our land' – presumably a reflection, thirty years later, of a determination to assert the Inuit rights as the original occupants.

The number of replies represented an even wider sampling of opinion, since some of the answers reflected the consensus of a group rather than the views of just one individual. The response was encouraging, both about the support for division of the Territories and also as an early indication of readiness to participate in political action. The support for division remained strong in the eastern Arctic during all the years until it was finally approved. It was in the west, with its complex ethnic composition, that there was uncertainty and hesitation.

Ottawa, 1963: Territorial Progress
The winter session of the Council in Ottawa in January 1963 provided many reasons to think that the sense of change felt at Frobisher Bay and Cape Dorset the preceding summer applied to the Territories as a whole.

In the west, construction of the railway to Great Slave Lake had begun and during the summer of 1962 the end of steel had been pushed north more than seventy miles. There were about three hundred and thirty more miles to reach Pine Point and Great Slave Lake. Prospecting for minerals and exploration for oil and gas were substantially up. A new tungsten mine had come into production in the Mackenzie Mountains near the Yukon boundary.

The Council's proposal for the creation of two Territories to replace the Northwest Territories had been approved by Diefenbaker's government. In my address I quoted the announcement in the speech from the throne to Parliament then in session: 'Measures will be placed before you to provide for the division of the Northwest Territories into two territories, and to provide more self-government for the residents of that area as a step toward the ultimate creation of new provinces in Canada's great north.' The last part about 'new provinces' had not been part of the Council's recommendation. It was Diefenbaker's 'vision' – or perhaps I had overdrawn the analogy with the west in my remarks at Fort Simpson. However, the important thing was that the government had accepted our proposal. In our sense of accomplishment we reckoned without the results of the federal election four months later.

According to the federal census of 1961, the total population of the Territories was 22,998 – a small figure, but an increase of 43 per cent over the 1951 total of 16,004. In the same decade the population of Canada as a whole increased by 30 per cent. I suggested to the Council some significant differences: 'Mackenzie District grew from just over 10,000 people (10,279) to almost 15,000 (14,895). Thus the population of the district increased by about 45 per cent over the 10-year period – roughly the same rate as the population of the Territories as a whole. The District of Franklin (the eastern Arctic islands) showed the greatest increase, from 3,400 to more than 5,700, giving a percentage increase of over 62 per cent. During the same period, the population of Keewatin remained virtually unchanged at about 2,300.'

The Indian population had increased by about 40 per cent, while the Inuit had increased only 15 per cent – and in the Keewatin area not at all. The zero increase in Keewatin was not surprising after the disastrous years between 1951 and 1961. About the Inuit generally I said: 'While one cannot be certain, it seems probable that the slower increase in the Eskimo population was in the years immediately after 1951. At that time health services were much less adequate than they are now and the death rate was certainly higher. From our vital statistics we know that the rate of natural increase among the Eskimos in the last few years had been very high indeed. I suspect, therefore, that the rate of increase for the Eskimo population as shown by the census is much less than the rate of increase that is actually now occurring.'

The census showed that almost half the population of the Territories was below twenty-one years of age; the median age was twenty-one years, five months. In Canada as a whole the median was over twenty-five. This meant that there would be a rapid increase in the Aboriginal population in the next ten or twenty years. It also meant rapid growth in the number of children of school age and of the number of young people who would be looking for employment when they emerged from school.

I disputed criticism of the Territorial government and Council for over-building schools and hostels. I pointed out that, in spite of having a completely new school at Inuvik, we would be using eight temporary classrooms in 1963–4. School extensions were being built at Fort MacPherson and Fort Norman in the west, at Spence Bay and Pond Inlet in the centre and east, and at other locations. Children were staying in school longer, which was what was wanted if they were to have any real chance of new opportunities to earn a living when they grew up.

The Royal Commission on Government Organization that had examined federal-government organization had looked at federal handling of Indian and Inuit problems – the Indians were, except for education in the Northwest Territories, the responsibility of the Department of Citizenship and Immigration, while the Inuit were the responsibility of Northern Affairs and National Resources. The commission had got its facts wrong. It had somehow concluded that the school system in the Territories did not 'take account of the advantages of integrating their (the Aboriginals') education with the facilities available to the general population.' In my address I pointed out that there were in fact 'no facilities at all for the "general population" as distinct from Indians and Eskimos.' I said:

> There was a time when Indian and Eskimo children attended schools – in so far as they attended schools at all – that were to some degree distinct from the schools for children of other races. I think we in this Council have been particularly proud that the condition no longer exists anywhere in the Territories; that there are no schools for Eskimos or for Indians or for 'other' and that there are simply schools for all, regardless of race. We have felt that this is an important feature in the training of the members of a population that must, in the years ahead, live and work together with no consciousness of racial differences if the development of the Territories is to redound to the advantage of all its people.

My Last Session: Inuvik, 1963

By the time the session of the Council opened at Inuvik on 8 July, a number of things had happened to upset plans and expectations. Diefenbaker's Progressive Conservative government had been defeated in the general election of 8 April and replaced by a minority Liberal government led by Lester Pearson. In May the second-largest settlement in the Northwest Territories, at Hay River, where the river of the same name flows into Great Slave Lake, had been devastated by the worst flood in its history. Fort Simpson, for the first time in its long history, had been in danger of serious flooding. And, least on the scale of consequence for the Territories but substantial for me, I had been appointed clerk of the Privy Council and secretary to the cabinet, effective 1 July – just a week before the Council session was to open. It had been arranged that I would remain commissioner to attend the session and to ease the transition for my successor, Bent Gestur Sivertz, who became the first full-time commissioner of the Northwest Territories since 1905.

The construction camp of E-3 when the Council had met there in 1956 in a '512' cabin had, by 1963, become Canada's first modern Arctic town. The Inuit Housing Cooperative was planning to build thirteen houses to be privately owned by Inuit members. The cost of a house there was very different from costs in southern Canada. To meet the added expense for private builders, the government of the Northwest Territories had established programs for second-mortgage loans and, in some circumstances, for full financing of low-cost houses.

Three of the largest structures in Inuvik were the school and the two hostels. The school population had already grown beyond our plans. I said in my address:

> The Sir Alexander Mackenzie School, which opened its doors in 1959, was designed for 625 students. Hostel accommodation was provided for 500; it was estimated that the rest of the places would be ample for the children of the residents of the town. Indeed it was suggested to me that the school would not be filled for many years.
>
> Instead the school is already overcrowded. Enrolment was close to 850 during the school year just completed, and it is quite clear that this growth will continue. How many more classrooms are needed in Inuvik will depend in part, of course, on what decisions are taken to enlarge schools in other centres, but it seems apparent that to serve the town and the present hostels, school facilities must be provided for at least 1000 children.

New figures on the natural increase in the population of the Northwest Territories indicated the scope of the education problem ahead. The Northern Health Service advised that the birth rate in the Northwest Territories was among the highest in the world. Even with infant-mortality rates that were still distressingly high among both Indians and Inuit, the rate of natural increase was thirty-four per thousand – nearly twice the general Canadian rate of eighteen at that time.

One thing that had not been settled by the time of my final session was whether the Council and the Territorial government could begin planning for a division of the Territories. The legislation based on our recommendations had not been passed by Parliament before the dissolution for the federal election and it therefore died on the order paper. The resolutions for the two bills, one to establish the Territory of Mackenzie and the other the Territory of Nunassiaq, were again on the agenda of the House of Commons, and I shared the hope of the Council that they would be passed at the first session of Parliament under the new Pearson government.

That hope was vain. The bills became casualties of the election. With the inevitability of day following night, the fact that the Progressive Conservatives had favoured division of the Territories meant that the Liberals opposed it. When Pearson's government got around to thinking about the question, resort was had to another inevitability of Canadian politics: a commission to study the question and to recommend what to do. The Carrothers commission, when it reported three years later in 1966, recommended neither for nor against division but was emphatic that division should not occur 'at this time.' Instead, it recommended that there be a review of the situation after ten years. In fact, it took nearly twenty years for agreement to be reached among the different groups in the Territories and, in what was by then called the Legislative Assembly of the Northwest Territories, that division of the Territories, as the Council had recommended, was indeed desirable.

There were thirty bills on the order paper for the 1963 session – all in one way or another a mark of the way the Territories had changed in ten years. Some of the bills reflected recommendations of the federal-provincial commissioners on uniformity of legislation and were designed to modernize and to fill in the civil law of the Northwest Territories in accordance with the best current Canadian practice in the provinces. With the development of the Territories, and the widening responsibilities of government there, Territorial legislation was dealing with all the questions provincial law dealt with – as well as with many things, such as the Game Ordinance, that were uniquely northern.

I said farewell to the Council with genuine regret. I had the sense at every session of working with colleagues who were deeply interested in finding solutions for the problems of the people and of the Territories and in developing policies that would fit the unique population and the circumstances that the future would present.

The combination of elected and appointed members was good for its day and would be good for a few more years still. It was apparent, however, that a fully elected Council should be the objective and would soon be possible. It was also apparent that the job of commissioner was becoming one that could no longer be handled on a part-time basis. I had, before the session at Inuvik, recommended to the new minister – Arthur Laing – and to prime minister Pearson that the positions of deputy minister of the department and commissioner of the NWT should no longer be combined – there was a very full-time job for each to do. So, in a sense, the time had come for me to go – and to leave the most fascinating job I would ever have.

The Northern Service, 1953–1963

The team that worked out the programs and carried out the administration of the Northwest Territories as it moved from the 'absence of mind' of 1953 to the Vision less than a decade later was very small. That was appropriate, for the population of the Territories was small: no more than the population of modest towns in the South. But the vastness of the land, the harshness of the climate, the differences in races, languages, and cultures, the special problems of education and social adaptation, along with the difficulties of travel, transport, and communication, made for complexity out of all proportion to the numbers for whom we were responsible.

There were, moreover, no precedents in Canada to provide much experience or guidance. There had been no positive policies for the health, welfare, or adaptation of the Aboriginal population as the prairies were opened up and settled. Indian administration in the northern parts of the provinces in more recent years was for small, fringe minorities that were expected to continue to live on the land. In the Northwest Territories it became increasingly clear that that was not what the future held. Life on the land could be possible, with difficulty, for most of the mature generation of that day, but it could not be for much of the younger generation and not for children still to come. The new generations had to be prepared for a different situation with new problems and other options. At the same time, it was important to preserve, as well as could be done, the Aboriginal way of life with its reliance on the resources of the land and sea as the transition took place.

In the Department of Northern Affairs and National Resources, almost entirely new staffs had to be built up to develop policies and programs and to carry them into effect in the field. In the Territories themselves, there had to be the teachers, social workers, linguists, and administrators to live in a harsh land and to make the programs real. All had to come from 'outside,' with little or no direct knowledge of the north, but with commitment, energy, and the basic skills.

The Department of National Health and Welfare developed a new Northern Health Service with nursing stations and basic health services – often very lonely for the nurses handling them – at small centres scattered along the coast and across the land. Young doctors took on the arduous task of advising and treating in and from centres like Fort Smith, Inuvik, and Iqaluit. Yellowknife was the one place with its own hospital and doctors.

The departments of Public Works and Transport had to deal with unprecedented problems of engineering to cope with permafrost which, if not properly taken into account, could destroy structures, roads, and airfields. Sewage systems and water supply posed totally different problems for Arctic communities than for those in the south.

Conventional wisdom is not inclined to credit public servants with commitment, resource, ingenuity, and a willingness to work in conditions of risk and hardship far beyond what duty would require. Yet these were the qualities that I found in the large majority of the young staff who came to work on the problems of the North and its people. Not all were competent and not all could cope with the difficulties they faced. But on the whole they were a remarkable group – teachers, doctors, nurses, engineers, clerical staff, administrators – living and working, often alone and with cold and long darkness adding to the strain.

The social and economic problems in the north today – nearly forty years later – are real and serious. But they would have been much more numerous without the efforts of the men and women who gave so much of themselves when much had to be done by very few. The modern world was going to come upon the North: the only real question was whether to try to prepare for it or to engage in a futile effort to hold it off.

So far as I personally was concerned, my position as commissioner combined, as I have said, the duties of lieutenant governor, premier, and cabinet in one undivided whole. I was also speaker of the Northwest Territories Council when it was in session and head of the administration twelve months in the year, in the Territories or, as I had to be much of the time because of my departmental job, outside it.

Since I was legally subject to the instructions of the minister of northern affairs and national resources, I had to see that he was adequately informed – before or after the fact – of problems, decisions, and programs. The commissioner did not have to persuade the deputy minister since the two were one, but I was conscious that my responsibilities as deputy were often different from what they were with my comissioner's hat on. It would not have been hard to find myself caught between the wishes of the council and those of the minister but it never happened. The four ministers I served – Jean Lesage, Douglas Harkness, Alvin Hamilton, and Walter Dinsdale – one Liberal and three Conservatives – either were or became as interested in the North and as concerned about its people as we, the officials, were. In every case, the morning meeting of minister and deputy was the rule and with that no problem was ever insoluble and no difference ever got to the point of ministerial instruction rather than agreement.

For me, during those ten years, the greatest inspiration, and reward, was the sense of being able to participate in building a new part of Canada that would be different from anything we had seen before, in which ethnic differences would not divide, and in which adaptation to a new future would take place without destroying the identities and the pride of the Aboriginal people. With all the mistakes that can now be alleged with the wisdom of hindsight, and often with little knowledge of the circumstances of the time, I am convinced that the people who carried out the mandate of St Laurent and Diefenbaker – at whatever level from minister to nurse, clerk, or teaching assistant – did as well as could reasonably be expected with the complexities we all faced.

chapter nine

The Emerging North

John Diefenbaker and his Progressive Conservative Party swept the country in 1958. With 209 seats to the Liberals' 48, they had the largest
majority in Canadian history. Only in Newfoundland did the Liberals
win more. In the west and the two Territories, the part of the country
with most interest in 'the Vision,' the Liberals carried one seat and the
Conservatives sixty-six. There was no doubt about the mandate for northern development and Alvin Hamilton was the most committed, vigorous,
and imaginative person that could have been called on to implement it.
We in the department of Northern Affairs rejoiced in the new emphasis
on the North but with a measure of apprehension. Too much would be
expected too quickly by both government and country. The difficulties
in the North were pervasive and stubborn and would not be resolved
easily no matter how much ingenuity and money were directed at them.
For the moment, such concerns were overborne by Alvin's enthusiasm
and confidence.

His greatest interest was in economic development which, in the
North, meant minerals, oil, and gas. He had ideas that none of us in the
department had ventured to consider. He rightly understood the opportunity that was presented by the new program to stir interest in the
prospects for petroleum development in the Mackenzie valley and offshore in the Arctic. The department had little expertise of its own on
techniques to promote that interest and how best to ensure a positive
balance among work obligations by permit holders, incentives for them
to develop their permit areas, and reward for the government when
development occurred. Hamilton was knowledgeable and it was he personally who handled discussions with the Canadian Petroleum Association. The Territorial oil and gas regulations were completely overhauled

for application in 1959–60. That year 207 exploratory permits for oil and gas were issued in the Northwest Territories and 120 in the Yukon covering over fifteen million acres. Applications for permits covering 146,866,282 acres in the Arctic islands had been submitted at the time of our first report on 31 March 1960. Twenty-two wells were drilled that year, compared with nine in 1958–9. Interest was real and hopes were high.

'Roads to Resources' was Hamilton's own phrase and his own idea. By making the program available in the provinces as well as in the Territories, wide support by Members of Parliament and provincial governments was assured. In the Northwest Territories, fifty-eight miles of construction on the road from Hay River to Yellowknife at last gave it road connection to Alberta – as well as reducing transportation costs for exploration and development north of Yellowknife. However, we were fated to have the needs of agriculture given priority over the interests of the North. We had lost Harkness to Agriculture after two months and we lost Hamilton after three years, when Harkness became minister of national defence in 1960.

Walter Dinsdale, who succeeded Hamilton, did not have Alvin's creative imagination or bursting energy nor did he have the authority that was Alvin's as the acknowledged creator of 'the Vision.' A final and important difference was that Alvin, from Saskatchewan and an early supporter of Diefenbaker, was much closer to 'the Chief' than Walter was. He had 'access' and could try out ideas on the prime minister informally. A blessing from the PM is a formidable lever at every stage and at all times in all governments. However, it was not simply because of those differences that the brightness of the Vision's glow gradually diminished. Three years were enough to sow doubts that northern problems were going to be easily overcome and that costs could be brought down to what mineral and oil prices would bear to support much economic activity.

However, the Vision had brought the North firmly to the attention of the Canadian public, and when another change of government occurred in 1963 there was no danger of the mockery that had led the Liberals in 1958 to ridicule the northern program as one for roads 'from igloo to igloo.' The North had status on the national agenda and the new minister, Arthur Laing, was able to get approval and funds for many improvements in administration that might have been impossible to achieve except for the new public interest provided by the Diefenbaker vision.

Self-government in the Northwest Territories

Several things came together for government in the NWT with the federal election of 1963. My appointment to succeed Robert Bryce as clerk of the Privy Council and secretary to the cabinet provided the opportunity to separate my two northern jobs and provide more specific attention for each. Ernest Côté, assistant deputy minister of northern affairs, became deputy minister, and as noted, Ben Sivertz, director of the Northern Administration Branch, became commissioner of the Northwest Territories. The intention was that he should move, and with him the entire Territorial administration, to Yellowknife. This was important as a proclamation of change: it permitted all the officials responsible for Territorial functions to be located in the Territory for the first time since 1905. Sivertz carried the relocation through vigorously and remained commissioner until it was completed in 1967. He then retired as he had planned in advance.

When the deputy commissioner, W.G. Brown, retired in 1965, his place was filled by a man new to the north but with a record in British Columbia that had recommended him to the minister, Arthur Laing. His name was Stuart Hodgson and he quickly demonstrated the capacities that led to his appointment to succeed Sivertz as commissioner in 1967. Hodgson had enormous vigour and justifiable confidence in his judgment, as well as a flair for public relations that gave him an almost heroic status. He became the leading force in developing both Territorial and local government during his twelve years as commissioner.

Parallel with these changes, the Pearson government, having deferred action on the Diefenbaker legislation to divide the Northwest Territories, appointed the commission led by A.W.R. Carrothers to make recommendations about Territorial division and also about government in the Northwest Territories. Though the report in 1966 recommended against division at that time, it concluded that, as a step towards full government, the commissioner should be assisted by an executive council selected from the members of the Legislative Council, which would be enlarged to fourteen elected and four appointed members.

In retrospect, the recommendation to defer division of the Territories was wise. The delay and the exhaustive discussion of every possible aspect has meant that the decision has now been taken by the elected representatives of both future parts of the Territories with approval of the people by referendum. Without that democratic base there might be a sense that division had been imposed, notwithstanding the fact that the recommendation of 1960–1 was sponsored by an elected Council member and approved by the Council unanimously. There is no question but that the division is better understood and more genuinely accepted than it would have been if it had gone ahead in 1963.

In 1975 the first fully elected Council since 1905 took office with fifteen members. It adopted the name 'Legislative Assembly' in 1976. In 1979 the Assembly was increased to twenty-two and in 1983 to twenty-four elected members.

The Northwest Territories is unique in Canada in having a fully self-governing democracy without political parties. The reason for this difference from all our other governments lies in the mixed and largely Aboriginal population of the Territories with, now, many organizations to represent different ethnic and linguistic groups – something that had been totally lacking during my years as commissioner. J.D. Hamilton, after describing the development of these organizations in the 1970s and the parallel changes in government, continues:

> The next development involved having a member of council become government leader – the rudimentary equivalent of a provincial premier, although, unlike the Yukon, the NWT did not propose to adopt official party politics at the territorial level. There were good reasons for this. The Yukon's population was nearly 80 percent white, while the NWT was divided into racial thirds and subdivided into tribal, regional, and cultural groups of Aboriginals. Any further fragmentation of the ethnic groups might splinter the Territories beyond any hope of governing.
>
> From the very start, therefore, it was evident that the GNWT must be built on compromise and conciliation rather than on political principle. Government by consensus, in the tradition of many North American Indian nations, seemed to be the ideal solution, and it has worked – after a fashion. By the early 1990s, however, major problems were emerging.[1]

The complications of democratic government without political parties are many and will increase as government becomes more complex. The absence of parties means that there is no leader of a clearly recognized 'largest party' to assume the responsibility of government, to appoint the ministers, and to form a disciplined cabinet with a collective responsibility for everything the government decides or does. The ministers are elected, by secret ballot, by and among the members of the Legislative Assembly. The government leader is also so elected. He is dependent on the members of his cabinet, who have helped to elect him. As a result, discipline is difficult, coherence is precarious, and undeniable responsibility is impossible. It is an arrangement that may be necessary in the western territory, but need not be in Nunavut. The advantages of the party system are real or it would not have been adopted in virtually every successful democratic state. It would be wise, after a trial period in Nunavut, to consider whether it should not be adopted there.

Four men deserve the gratitude of the people of the Northwest Territories for the development of self-government in the years after I ceased to be commissioner. Three are my successors in that office – Sivertz from 1963 to 1967, Hodgson from 1967 to 1979, and John Parker from 1979 to 1989. Sivertz knew the most about the problems of administration and was the right person to handle the shift of government to the Territories. Hodgson was the image of a vigorous, independent, on-the-ground governor to make government real to the Aboriginal people. He was also the most expensive – but money was needed for change. Parker was the disinterested, respected resident of the Territories who could preside with grace and dignity as the commissioner moved gradually to the role of lieutenant governor and the elected head of government and the cabinet took on the powers and responsibility of governing. None of them could have done the job of the others as well. The three, in a logical succession, managed a transition that was masterful and suited to the needs of each phase.

The fourth person without whose interest and vigorous support the progress would not have been possible was Jean Chrétien, minister of Indian affairs and northern development from 1968 to 1974. Indian Affairs had been moved to the department in 1965. Chrétien was very much a hands-on minister who travelled the north widely, got to know it well, and developed a real sympathy for its people and their aspirations. The result is full self-government with two Territories: a sound basis for coping with the difficult problems ahead.

The Political Future of the North
In 1977 C.M. Drury, a former minister in the Pearson and Trudeau governments and from 1954 to 1960 a member of the Council of the Northwest Territories, was appointed special representative for constitutional development in the Northwest Territories. After two years of 'consultation, mediation and study,' Drury submitted his report.

He had received three different proposals for 'dividing the NWT into two or more autonomous political units,' one from the Inuit Tapirisat of Canada (ITC) representing the Inuit, one from the Dene Nation on behalf of the Indians, and one from the Metis Association of the Northwest Territories. A fourth proposal had come from the Committee for Original Peoples Entitlement (COPE) on behalf of the Inuvialuit, the Inuit of the western Arctic, proposing a special region within the new Territory of Nunavut that was being advocated by the ITC. It would be a Western Arctic Regional Municipality – a regionally based level of government to deal with the special conditions in the ethnically mixed Mackenzie delta.

The range of submissions made clear, as Drury said in his report, the fundamental importance of the 'social, cultural and political traditions and values of native peoples in the NWT.' While there were native people in 'Southern Canada,' Drury said, the NWT was unique in that its 'native peoples still comprise the majority of the population; they are distributed into relatively homogeneous population groups, and have retained a cultural strength. This last point is eloquently demonstrated, for example, in the survival of six major native languages: Dogrib, Slavey, Loucheux, Chipewyan, Cree and Inuktitut.'[2]

On the question of division, Drury said that 'the longer-term external consequences of division have not yet been adequately considered' nor had there been enough 'testing of ... public acceptability in the NWT.' Both of these considerations were taken up by the Legislative Assembly of the NWT through the establishment in 1982 of a 'Constitutional Alliance' of members of the Assembly and representatives of the various Aboriginal organizations. The two parts of the Territories examined their respective interests: the West in the Western Constitutional Forum and the East in the Nunavut Constitutional Forum. The boundary between the two prospective territories was the most difficult issue. It was finally resolved only in 1990 by John Parker, the former commissioner, as a trusted mediator. The question of division was finally put to the people in a referendum in May 1992. It received 54 per cent approval in the Territories as a whole. Ninety per cent approved it in the East (to become Nunavut) but a majority were opposed in the West, especially among non-Aboriginals in the Yellowknife area. With the overall majority in favour, and the overwhelming majority of Inuit behind the new territory, the two governments, Territorial and federal, decided to proceed with the establishment of the Territory of Nunavut.

Conclusion of land-claim agreements was critical for the definition of the political divisions. It was clearly desirable that the Inuit land settlement should be entirely within the new territory. In December 1991 agreement on it was reached between the government of Canada and the Tungavik Federation of Nunavut for the Inuit resident in that future territory. It was approved in a referendum in November 1992. The political accord for the new territory was signed by the two governments on 30 October 1992. Under that accord, the government of the new territory was to be established in 'evolutionary stages' over the period from 1992 to 2008 with guidance from a Nunavut implementation commission to advise the governments of the Northwest Territories and Canada.

The creation of the Territory of Nunavut imposes the as yet unresolved question of whether to restructure the western part of the Northwest Territories and, if so, how. The Northwest Territories could continue, after the separation of Nunavut, just as it did after the severance of the provinces of Alberta and Saskatchewan in 1905. Adjustments would be necessary as they were then but the Territories as such could continue as a legal and constitutional entity. It is the diversity of the population, with six major Aboriginal groups plus Metis and whites, that makes the problem much more complex than in Nunavut, where the population is 80 per cent Inuit and the rest white or of mixed blood.

The two territories will cost more than one, but the difference will not be large in national terms. The benefit in both will almost certainly be substantial. In each case there will be a government closer to the people for whom it is to govern and with a less complex array of problems. In each case the Aboriginal people will have a greater opportunity to influence government in terms of their own values and interests, although in neither case will the government be 'ethnic' or 'Aboriginal.' It will be a government for all the people, just as it has been thus far in the Northwest Territories. The greatest single problem, especially for Nunavut, is the one implied by Prime Minister Brian Mulroney at the signing of the land-claim agreement at Iqaluit on 25 May 1993, when he said that 'my goal is economic self-reliance in Northern Canada.' That is going to be extremely difficult to achieve with the high level of costs that distance and climate impose on any activity and, indeed, on mere existence in the north.

In neither case will it be wise or realistic to think, as some have in the past, that the self-governing territories will be stepping-stones to provincial status. Under the Nunavut political accord signed on 30 October 1992, an increase in the cost of government and services is frankly envisaged and, the accord continues (Part 8.1), 'Canada – shall establish the financial arrangements for the Government of Nunavut.' Part 8.4 provides: 'In establishing the financial arrangements referred to in 8.1, and following consultation with the other parties hereto, Canada shall determine and fund reasonable incremental costs arising from the creation and operation of the Government of Nunavut.'

There will undoubtedly have to be a similar clause – or an implied understanding to the same effect – for the residual Northwest Territories or for a new 'western' territory if that is agreed upon. In neither case will there be any chance that in the forseeable future the costs of northern territorial government will fit under the financial arrangements adequate for provinces in the South. Northern costs are and will remain too high. It would be a mistake and contrary to both northern and national interests to make plans or to establish structures with provincial status as a target.

In 1985 I became concerned at discussion in the legislature and the press in the Northwest Territories that reflected a fairly general assumption that division into two territories would be simply a step toward provincial status, which would follow just as it had for Saskatchewan and Alberta in 1905. I was so convinced of the error of the assumption that I set out the considerations in a small book *Northern Provinces: A Mistaken Goal*, published by the Institute for Research on Public Policy.

A major difference between the federalisms of Canada and the United States is that we have developed systems of taxation and of cash transfers designed to reduce substantially the consequences of the wide differences in the wealth of the provinces and of the revenues their governments can raise by taxation. It is done partly by 'equalization,' paid under specific federal legislation and partly by other cash and tax transfers from the federal government. The provinces whose taxable capacity is above the national average get no equalization; those below do. In 1984–5 the total tax transfers to the six neediest provinces varied from 28.2 per cent to 44.2 per cent of their gross revenues, depending on the degree to which each province fell below the national average in its capacity to raise money from the major sources of revenue.

A different system of transfers for the two territories, related to their needs and capacities to tax, produced very different figures in 1984–5: 70.2 per cent of revenues for the Northwest Territories and 65.3 per cent for the Yukon from the federal government. For Nunavut, a still higher proportion of federal transfers is going to be necessary because costs there are so high and the taxable income of its residents is so low. It is probable that something over 90 per cent of Territorial expenditures will have to come from the federal government to make it possible for 'provincial-type' services of reasonable standard to be provided by the government of Nunavut.

There is no reason to believe that the economies of the Territories, the costs of living, and the levels of unemployment are likely to change significantly for a good many years. No formula for federal-provincial financing has been devised that can work for a situation so different from those of our 'southern' provinces. If the Territories were to become provinces, it would not be realistic to expect different treatment for them from that accorded to other provinces below the national average. But if the territories were treated as provinces, they simply could not finance themselves.

My warnings provoked irritated reactions in the Territories, but the assumption of provincial status as an objective appears to have diminished as the magnitude of financial problems has become more apparent.

The Significance of Nunavut
The establishment of Nunavut in 1999 received national attention as it should but little mention of what, to me, may be seen in history as its greatest importance. It is the first time that the constitutional responsibility for the government of a political division of Canada has been placed in the hands of a sector of our Aboriginal peoples as the present and undoubtedly future majority of its population. On a smaller scale, but perhaps with a similar psychological significance, it has overtones of the wise decision of 1867 to divide the 'united' Canada of the day and create a Quebec in which the majority was and would be French-speaking. Without that arrangement, neither the political peace of Canada nor the basis for the preservation of the distinctive society of Quebec would have existed.

Our history thus far in discharging the national responsibility for our Aboriginal peoples has not been outstanding. It is a problem of enormous complexity which will not be soluble by constitutional change alone or by any arrangements of a sweeping character. The mixing of populations and the differing circumstances of life in different parts of the country are too great. However, if Nunavut does succeed in producing responsible representative government, with a successful transition of its people to new ways of life and without tensions and discriminations arising from ethnic differences, it may do a great deal to allay apprehensions that now make it difficult for both Aboriginals and non-Aboriginals to work out the differing kinds of solution that will be necessary in other parts of Canada.

Nunavut, as a symbol and as a fact, may in retrospect have a significance far greater than its tiny population would suggest.

My first photograph: about one year old, 1918.

All set for a trip to the Baltic Sea: on a motorcycle not built for three, but it and we survived. Left to right: A.E. Ritchie, R.G.R., and Ross Anderson, 2 July 1939.

Our wedding, 14 August 1943. My father was in London as Canadian Agricultural Commissioner during the war. Left to right: Bea's brother Bill Lawson, the Rev. Clarke Lawson, Mrs Lawson, Bea's sister Margaret Fraser, the bride and groom, Doug Fraser, my mother and brother.

My family in Montreal to meet my sister Lucille's fiancé, Don Douglas, summer 1942. Left to right: R.G.R., my mother and father (Lydie Adelia and Gordon), Lucille, and my brother, Ronald, in front.

Ottawa, October 5, 1946

My dear Ambassador:

I have received with much pleasure the resolution
passed by the Village Council of Pentayion, Doriodos, on
August 31st last, under the terms of which the name
Mackenzie King was given to a central square in the community, and expressing the wish that a photograph of
myself should be placed in the Town Hall.

I have likewise had pleasure in reading the
very cordial terms in which the Council requested you to
transmit to me the text of the resolution.

I should be much obliged if you would kindly
convey to the President and Members of the Council my
warm appreciation of their generous and courteous thought
of me. In giving my name to a central square they do
great honour to me, and they likewise add yet another
link to the friendship between Greece and Canada which
continues to give such satisfaction to us all. On both
grounds the honour is one which I very much appreciate.

Perhaps you will also inform the Council that
I am arranging to send a photograph as they request.

Yours sincerely,

The Hon. L. R. LaFleche, P.C.,
    Ambassador of Canada,
    Athens.

A letter with the typical revisions of Mr King's stubby pencil, even for a letter about naming a village square in Greece. What is unusual is the survival of the first paragraph with only one change!

I had learned that it was costly to advance money to Mr King without getting a receipt at the moment of doing it. He never quite managed to refuse to sign.

With John, Kerrie, Bea, and Kipper in 1959 in our house in Manor Park, a community in Ottawa built immediately after the war.

Presentation of the Mace to the Council of the Northwest Territories by the governor general, Right Honourable Vincent Massey, at Government House, Ottawa, 17 January 1956.

The council of the Northwest Territories in session, Ottawa, 1958. Left to right: Ernest 'Scottie' Gall, MLA Mackenzie North; Knut Lang, MLA Mackenzie Delta; L.H. Nicholson; Louis Audette; R.G.R. (in the chair for a formal session); Robert Porritt, MLA Mackenzie South; John Goodall, MLA Mackenzie River; Hubert Jones; Wilfrid Brown, Deputy Commissioner of the NWT. Winter sessions were normally in Ottawa where the administrative staff was located until 1967.

The elected members of the Council, with the Sergeant at Arms and the Mace, January 1962. Left to right: John Goodall, Knut Lang, R.G.R., 'Scottie' Gall, Robert Porritt. There were no elected members from the central or eastern Arctic until the next Council, 1964.

ᐃᕐᐳᓂᓕ ᐊᕐᔪᑊᐸᔅᒐᐊᓐ ᐊᕐᔪᑊᐸᐃᓐᔾ ᑲᐊᒡᓯᒥ

ᐢᐳᒥᔾ ᒦᑕᒪᔾᑎ ᐊᐳᒍᓐ 2 ᒥ ᐅᓪ ᓲᑭᒍᐢ 6 ᒐ ᐊᓂᔾ 7 ᒐ ᐃᒥᓯᒥ.

ᐅᔾᐊ ᐅᕐᒦᐊᓕ ᑕᔾᐊ :

ᓲᒥᐅᓂ ᐸᔾᔾ	Siméonie and Púdlo
ᑕᒥ ᐅᔾᒦᐊᔾ	Tommy and Oodlooriak
ᐱᔾᐊᔾ ᐅᓕᔾᔾ	Pingwarktok and Oolayuk
ᐅᒻᐊᔾ ᓂᐱᐢᔾ	Oshaweetok and Neepeesha
ᐃᐳᓕ ᔾᔾᔾᔾ	Iyola and Pootoógook
ᔾᓕ ᶜᔾᔾ	Luktak and Púdlo
ᐃᐱᐊᔾ ᐊᖃᕐᒦᔾ	Eegeevudluk and Napátchie
ᐢᐱᐊᕐᒦ ᐃᐱᐊᔾᔾ	Sakkiassie and Eegeevudluk
ᔾᔾ ᕐᐳᔾᔾ	Toonoo and Sheokjuk
ᒍᐱᐊᖃᔾᒥᐊ ᐃᒍᒥᔾ	Kovianaktoliak and Ikuma
ᐱᕐᐳᓕ ᐊᕐᐳᔾ	Pitseolak and Ageok
ᐱᓕ ᐊᖃᕐᐊᔾ	Peter and Alasuak

ᐃᐸᐳᓂᓕ ᐊᕐᔪᑊᐸᔅᒐᐊᓐ ᐊᔾᓕ.

During an intermission on the first day of the Conference of First Ministers on the Constitution, 5 February 1968. Suggesting a line to take at some point in a conference was a frequent problem. The Prime Minister is quizzical, the young Minister of Justice is interested, and Paul Martin listens in as does Carl Goldenberg. Left to right (front): Pierre Trudeau, R.G.R., Prime Minister Pearson, Paul Martin; (back) Carl Goldenberg, Jean Marchand, Mitchell Sharp, and Joe Greene, all ministers in Pearson's cabinet.

In my last Constitutional Conference with Pierre Trudeau, February 1979. Front row: Allister Gillespie, P.E.T., Otto Lang. Second row: Roger Tassé, Marc Lalonde, R.G.R., Jean Chrétien with Jeanne Sauvé, later governor general, listening in. René Lévesque (Premier, Quebec) was just out of the picture on the right, lighting up one of his constant cigarettes.

Conferring an MA degree in November 1988 (but not on Graham Robinson, age nineteen months). The convocations were full of light and personal moments for students at the end of years of work. Janice Yalden, Dean of Arts, stands ready to 'hood' the happy graduand.

Christmas in Calgary with John, Kerrie, and Bob Hale, 1992.

PART FOUR

'Mike' Pearson and a Changing Canada, 1963–1968

chapter ten

Pearson and the Quiet Revolution

John Diefenbaker's victory in the election of 1957 had been very much his own: a personal more than a party triumph. The landslide win in 1958 had been equally his. The transition from that enormous majority to the minority government of 1962 and then to the defeat of his government in the House of Commons on 5 February 1963 were also mainly attributable to his own character and ineffective leadership. Diefenbaker was a loner for most of his political life, at odds with much of his own party and frequently suspicious of some of his colleagues when he became prime minister. Basil Robinson, a generally sympathetic observer who worked closely with Diefenbaker for five years, surveying the division in the cabinet over the nuclear-warhead crisis in 1963, comments: 'An individualist himself, Diefenbaker had little experience or talent for reconciling opposing viewpoints. When two strong and respected ministers, such as Green and Harkness, were going in different directions, the prime minister had no resources to resolve the conflict. He feared that if he chose between them, he would invite a resignation. That, with good reason as it turned out, he felt he could not afford.'[1]

The problem that brought down the Diefenbaker government was over continental defence policy. It had entered into commitments with the United States for weapons, especially fighter aircraft, that would be effective only if armed with nuclear warheads. The prime minister, supported by his secretary of state for external affairs, Howard Green, was deeply worried about implementing the commitment and hoped that it might be avoided. That problem and others, as well as personality tensions during the visit of President John Kennedy to Ottawa in May 1961, produced distrust between the two governments when the Cuban missile crisis was disclosed in a statement by Kennedy to the American public on 22 October 1962. Diefenbaker had not been informed in advance and resented it as American pressure for implementation of the nuclear commitment. The United States government equally resented the Canadian reluctance to act in the face of so great a threat to continental security.

Pearson, after a shaky start as leader of the opposition in 1958, had brought the Liberals up from the depths of forty-eight seats to ninety-eight in 1962. On 25 January 1963, he announced a change in policy that would have won King's admiration both as strategy and in timing.

The Liberals had shared the hope of the government that Canada would not have to equip itself with nuclear weapons. It had been part of the Liberal campaign in 1962. Now, however, the time had come, Pearson said, when the pledge for continental defence had to be implemented. 'A Liberal government would honour those pledges made by its predecessor in agreement with our allies as long as they exist, until they were changed.'[2] Unknown to Pearson, that was the position of the minister of national defence, Douglas Harkness: that the agreement had to be honoured. The split in the cabinet was revealed in a statement by Harkness on 28 January.

Diefenbaker was faced with a difficult political and ministerial problem. But there is nothing unusual about that in the life of a government or of a prime minister. Robinson comments that Diefenbaker 'had a compulsive tendency to postpone decisions' but so did King. The difference was that King, faced with a serious problem, assessed all the options, including some no one else knew were there, and devised the least damaging solution at the last available time. It was partly genius, but it was partly from observing Sir Wilfrid Laurier control and direct a cabinet, the kind of experience that Diefenbaker never had. He could not produce a solution. Harkness resigned on 4 February; the government was defeated in the House of Commons on 5 February and a new election was called on 6 February.

Robinson concludes that 'the main fault' lay with Diefenbaker and that his political collapse was 'largely self-inflicted.'[3] In a conversation with me long after the defeat of 1963, one of Diefenbaker's then colleagues – although not a sympathetic one, Richard Bell – expressed the view that Diefenbaker's paranoia and suspicion often produced in cabinet a deepening of division rather than the devising of compromise that the collective responsibility of the cabinet requires.

It was Diefenbaker's indecision that led to the Liberal promise in the election of 8 April 1963 that, if they were elected, things would be different: there would be sixty days of decision. The sense of relief in Washington was perceptible. The hopes both there and for many in Canada were high: it soon seemed too high.

Walter Gordon's Budget

Because of the defeat of Diefenbaker's government in February, with no Parliament until after the April election, there had been no budget for the fiscal year 1963–4 that had begun on 1 April. It would undoubtedly have been possible to finance for some months on interim supply until so important a matter as the first budget of the new government could have been carefully considered by the new cabinet and the equally new minister of finance. However, in the atmosphere of 'sixty days of decision,' the budget was rushed ahead by Walter Gordon on the fifty-third day. As Tom Kent says in his report on the early days of the Liberals in power, 'The honeymoon period of the Pearson government ended on its fifty-fourth day, the day after the budget of 13 June.'[4]

The initial attack on the government was over Gordon hiring three outside consultants to advise him on a document that was at that time shrouded in mystical secrecy. No clear impropriety was proven, but the injury to the new minister and to the government was great. More serious was the nearly unanimous attack of the business community on a proposed revision of the 15 per cent withholding tax on dividends paid to non-residents of Canada to introduce a new discrimination depending on the degree of Canadian ownership of a company: a 10 per cent rate for companies more than 25 per cent Canadian-owned, 20 per cent for those with less Canadian ownership. Also attacked was a proposed 30 per cent takeover tax on sales of shares in Canadian companies to non-residents.

The whole episode was a rude shock to Pearson's confidence in his minister of finance. Lou Rasminsky, who had been appointed governor of the Bank of Canada after the Coyne crisis in 1961, communicated his criticism of the new measures to Pearson, whose knowledge of financial and business matters was slight but whose confidence in Rasminsky was reinforced by the vigorous public objection to Gordon's measures. Gordon's offer to resign was rejected but neither Pearson's confidence in his most important cabinet colleague nor the close personal relationship between the two was ever restored.

The fiasco undermined the government's self-confidence and strengthened that of the opposition. While Diefenbaker had had no part in Gordon's and the government's humiliation, it made the government more vulnerable to the kind of attack in the House of Commons that he was so skilled in mounting. Robinson says of Diefenbaker that 'all along there had been the Lester Pearson factor. Pearson was an obsession. Diefenbaker held him in envious admiration.'[5] With Pearson there equally came to be a 'John Diefenbaker factor' – but it did not involve admiration. It was deep aversion tinged with dread. As Tom Kent says of Diefenbaker in his discussion of the government's birth pangs in 1963: 'He was a matador in a contest where Pearson often seemed to be his victim, hurt, slow and blundering. Diefenbaker was entirely unscrupulous; he could set aside facts or invent whatever alleged facts suited his purpose at the moment. And he was cruel, a master of innuendo with an unerring instinct for what would most hurt his opponent.'[6]

The antipathy between Pearson and Diefenbaker was not unlike that between Meighen and King in the 1920s, but King had a greater capacity to cope with his persecutor and more skill in manoeuvring the political contest to his party's advantage. For Pearson, Diefenbaker was a menace that made his performance in Parliament uncertain and his government shaky and inept. With almost any other leader of the opposition the Pearson government would have seemed and would have been more successful.

The 'sixty days' of decision ended on 20 June. Bob Bryce had stayed in his post of clerk of the Privy Council and secretary to the cabinet to help Pearson through the critical beginning. He now succeeded Kenneth Taylor as deputy minister of finance. I took his place on my return from the meeting of the Council of the Northwest Territories in early July.

The PM and Deputy Ministers

Deputy ministers are appointed by the governor general-in-council on the advice of the prime minister. This was established by a 'minute of council' – a formal action of the governor-in-council which does not have legal effect but defines a matter of importance to the government. The first minute of council clearly establishing the prime minister's power of appointment was in 1896. It was last reissued in 1935, presumably to meet some question about it – or simply because King, after his return to power that year, wanted there to be no doubt. 'Robertson, never assume anything.'

There is no way of knowing now whose advice prime ministers took about such appointments in 1896 or 1935: there was no secretary to the cabinet and the clerk of the Privy Council was genuinely clerical: preparing, recording, and issuing orders-in-council. The prime minister is not required to take anyone's advice but the person he consults today, and whose advice he normally takes, is that of the clerk-secretary as that office has developed since 1945.

I never asked Bryce why I had been appointed to succeed him. I had not sought the office, and I had no way of knowing that Bob would not be carrying on as the crucial adviser to Prime Minister Pearson just as he had been to Diefenbaker. Nor did I want a change. After ten years, the policies worked out with Jean Lesage were beginning to bear fruit in the North – change was taking hold and accelerating on every front. So I did not rejoice when Bob told me of the prime minister's decision.

Nor did my children. John and Kerrie had found it a source of prestige that their father flew around the Arctic, went to the North Pole, and had Eskimo friends. It was not easy to convince them that becoming a clerk or a secretary was a promotion. Even Bea thought that the post had overtones of 'Charlie with the wicker sleeves' bending over a clerical desk with a celluloid eye-shade.

I knew enough of 'the system' to know that Bryce must have recommended me, although I was not the most senior of deputy ministers. I was confident I had carried out the mandate St Laurent had given me in 1953, but that would not be enough. For a prime minister, the clerk is the essential official link between him and his ministers and also with their departments. He must often rely on the clerk's judgment about a host of problems that arise. Apart from a sound record and a knowledge of the public service, the fundamental qualifications for the post are good judgment, a temperament compatible with the prime minister's, and complete reliability. I had been in External Affairs with 'Mike' Pearson and he knew me; he had seen me for nearly a year as acting secretary to the cabinet during a gap in that post; and he clearly decided that I was someone he would be comfortable with. I suspect that those considerations – together with Bryce's recommendation – weighed more than my success in Northern Affairs.

In any event the appointment went well and Pearson came to rely on me a great deal. A telephone call at home on a Sunday morning, after the PM had caught up with his accumulation of papers, became a regular event. He was a most engaging man to deal with and I grew to have a deep affection for both him and his wife, Maryon. She had a sharp tongue and a caustic wit but was great fun.

The other person on whom the prime minister relied constantly was Tom Kent. After wartime work in the British intelligence service on 'the ultra secret,' which broke the ciphers used by the German armed forces and contributed greatly to the Allied victory, and several peacetime years with *The Economist* in London, Kent had come to Canada to become editor of the Winnipeg *Free Press*, the most influential paper in the West and consistent supporter of the Liberal Party. Kent's role as editor and as friendly critic of the government led to an increasingly close association with the party. With the Liberal victory of 1963, Kent, by that time the closest policy adviser of Mike Pearson, moved to the new Prime Minister's Office as 'co-ordinator of programming.' Kent became what Pickersgill had been under King – the effective head of the PMO – but with less outward clarity of seniority than Jack had had.

The PMO and the PCO

The Prime Minister's Office and the Privy Council Office are the two instruments through which the prime minister coordinates the policy decisions of his government, the legislative program to be submitted to Parliament, and the administration of departments in handling their various responsibilities. As I have described, the PMO was very small under King and his predecessors. The Privy Council Office did not exist, except as a purely clerical office for the custody and handling of orders-in-council, until Arnold Heeney used it as the base on which to establish the secretariat for the war committee of the cabinet that was so obviously valuable that Mr King was brought, reluctantly, to agree that it should carry on the same role for the cabinet when peace came.

There was no definition then or for nearly twenty years more of the respective functions of the PMO and the PCO. Both reported to and existed to help the prime minister. The PMO's role was political and personal to the prime minister. The PCO's was non-political and part of the public service. Both dealt with policy but with different viewpoints and concerns. Shared interests or any differing views between the two offices were dealt with on a personal basis, first between Jack Pickersgill and Heeney, and later between Pickersgill and Norman Robertson or Bob Bryce. Nor did any more formal structure or definition emerge during the regimes of St Laurent and Diefenbaker. It was to a large degree the pressures in the early days of the Pearson government and the obvious increase in the scope of government in the 1960s – as well as the need to impose more order and planning – that led to consideration of how the government might be made to work better.

Tom Kent has described the sports analogy that prompted Pearson, who had little interest in organization, to see the PMO as a team in which not everyone should try to play the same position and each knew what he was supposed to do. Tom and I worked together on proposals that would improve the operation of both offices and of the cabinet itself.[7] Among other changes in August 1963, one of the simplest but most effective was to make the daily meeting of the prime minister and Kent into a three-party event at 9:00 every morning, with me the third presence. The first part of each meeting was on things that were 'government' or 'policy': not political. Things that were of a party or partisan nature were kept for the end and I left the meeting. On the exclusively governmental side, I had a regular meeting each Tuesday with the prime minister to decide on the cabinet agenda for its Thursday meeting. It was, however, the daily meeting that was critical for coordination. A further step was to establish a clearer structure of cabinet committees with rules about their operation: something there had never been before.

The new system worked well and in January 1964 Pearson announced that the use of committees in the operation of the cabinet would be carried further. 'Greater use of committees is the best way to obtain, under the Prime Minister's leadership, thorough consideration of policies, co-ordination of government action, and timely decisions in a manner consistent with ministerial and Cabinet responsibility.'[8] Nine cabinet committees were established, each directed to a defined area of the total government process. Matters requiring cabinet decision were in most cases to be brought first to the appropriate standing committee. The system was a major improvement and lasted throughout Pearson's regime. Without it, the problems that plagued his two minority governments from 1963 to 1968 would have been even more difficult and damaging than they were.

A minority government is constantly exposed to a double risk. One is the mathematics of vote counts in the House of Commons that may, if not accurately calculated, defeat the government, as happened to Pearson in February 1968 and to Joe Clark in December 1979. The other is the product of that hazard: the constant calculation by parties on the opposition side of the House as to when the risk of defeat may be used to extract from the government concessions in budgets or in legislation that would not otherwise be made. It is a high-wire operation that requires constant vigilance, careful calculation, and strong nerves on both sides of the House. Diefenbaker was temperamentally better suited to it than Pearson: he revelled in it with fiendish joy; Pearson found it a purgatory of horror and humiliation. But his capacity to withstand it was testimony to the toughness that lay under his amiable, easy manner.

The Quiet Revolution in Quebec

Premier Duplessis died suddenly in the first week of September 1959, while on a visit to the Iron Ore Company of Canada's enormous mining development north of Sept Îles, Quebec. The death of his successor, Paul Sauvé, a few months later led to an election in 1960 and the victory of the Liberal Party, led by my former minister, Jean Lesage.

The removal of the heavy Duplessis hand made possible the explosion of change that came to be known as the 'Quiet Revolution.' The instrument to carry out that revolution was to be the government of Quebec – in Lesage's hands an undoubtedly federalist government but one that considered it essential, both politically and in order to accomplish its program of change, that it should have and be able to exercise all the constitutional powers that it saw as properly provincial. That view and that program were not separatist: indeed, Lesage became increasingly pressed by the steadily growing weight of views more exteme than his, both within his own party and in the opposition in Quebec.

It is difficult to conceive, after more than three decades during which the relations between the federal and provincial governments have so dominated the political life of Canada, but in 1960 and for several years more those relations were not recognized as a genuine area of policy, either by the federal government or by the provinces. No government had within it any department or branch responsible for the whole complex of those relations and for the policy issues they raised.

Lesage, more clearly than any other premier, understood that only the premier at the provincial end, and only the prime minister in Ottawa, could oversee the many specific issues and programs that fell under the jurisdiction of many ministers. An impatient man, he recognized that Pearson had many things demanding his time and attention. So he persuaded him to agree that when he, Lesage, could not get through to the PM, he would talk to Tom Kent or to me: he preferred that to the alternative of going to the responsible federal minister. He knew us, he could speak bluntly, and he knew his views would get through.

Lesage's arrangement anticipated an organizational change that took place under Pierre Trudeau a few years later. The first step in 1964 was to make the PCO specifically responsible for federal-provincial relations as a clear policy area. The second came a few years after the election of a separatist government in Quebec in 1976 and as it was moving towards the first Quebec referendum in 1980. I proposed to Trudeau, who had become prime minister in 1968, that the stakes were becoming too high to have the secretary to the cabinet try to deal with federal-provincial relations with his left hand, while he inevitably had to give top priority to the day-to-day operation of the cabinet. Trudeau agreed. I then became secretary to the cabinet for federal-provincial relations and Michael Pitfield took my job as clerk of the Privy Council and secretary to the cabinet. Events since 1976, as the 'national unity problem' has moved through its various phases, and as federal-provincial relations have become steadily more complex and contentious, have shown that the division of functions was a necessary recognition of a feature of our federalism that is going to endure regardless of how our unity problem evolves.

But to return to 1963, no one in the federal government at that time, and probably few in the government of Quebec, saw the accommodation of the ambitions of Lesage and his party as something that would require constitutional change. There is a lot of room for flexibility under our constitution. Pearson's policy was to explore all reasonable possibilities with the confidence that ways could be found to meet the needs both of the federal government and of a federalist government in Quebec, led by a premier of his own party.

The basic approach to the Quebec problem fitted within the general concept of 'co-operative federalism,' which had been developed largely between Pearson and Tom Kent well before the Liberal government came into office in 1963. Kent recalls using the slogan as early as 1961; certainly it was already well established as a guideline of policy when I became clerk of the Privy Council. However, a general concept is one thing, and establishment of the reality is another. It was especially difficult to give substance to it when ministers and departments with programs and 'turf' to defend were reluctant to see concessions of function or of funds to the provinces, and when there was no focal point to advance the application of the policy itself.

Cooperative federalism as a policy was not developed as something for the comfort of Quebec. It was to adjust the balance of our federal system to compensate for the centralization of power in federal hands that had been necessary to fight the war and to mount a post-war reconstruction program. The growing needs in the 1960s were not in areas of federal jurisdiction but in those of the provinces. As Kent puts it: 'With a rapidly growing population, with rising affluence and the advance of technogy, with the move from rural to urban living, the mounting social needs were for education and urban development, for housing and public health facilities, for roads and urban transit, for environmental protection and social security: for services that were, solely or primarily, provincial responsibilities under the constitution.'[9]

The conferences in 1963 and 1964 were for me a haunting reminder of the two with Duplessis on the constitution in 1949 and 1950. As in 1949, the first Pearson conference was in Ottawa in November 1963. It got nowhere because of lack of federal preparation on the way to put cooperative federalism into effect and, most important, how to make it financially possible for provinces to carry out the growing responsibilities that would be theirs in the years ahead.

As in 1949, the province of Quebec extended an invitation to meet again in Quebec. The second conference took place on 31 March to 2 April 1964 – once more in the green chamber of the Legislative Assembly of Quebec. The main difference was that this time the federal government was as ill prepared as six months before and it was confronted by a Quebec government friendly in politics but completely determined to exercise its constitituional responsibilities for a public pension plan, for loans to students to attend university, and in other areas of social policy. As I knew from my years of working with him, Lesage was formidable on any financial issue. His attack on the federal government for its unwillingness to provide tax room for Quebec to finance its future responsibilities was devastating. Lesage boldly outlined to the conference a new Quebec Pension Plan – clearly more attractive than the one the federal government had hoped to launch and to see accepted by all the provinces. The developing confrontation was the more frightening because it was clear that the anti-federal forces in Quebec were growing in strength. It would be fatal if even the federalists, led by the Liberal Lesage, could not find room for the new Quebec with a friendly government led by 'Mike' Pearson.

On the night of 1 April (perhaps an appropriate date in all the unhappy circumstances), Bob Bryce, Tom Kent, and I met in Bob's hotel room to see if we could not devise something to permit the conference to end on a note of hope rather than of disaster. Bryce's fertile brain produced the idea of a joint federal-provincial study of taxation and finance – a 'tax structure committee' – with a strict and urgent timetable. As Kent describes it: 'It would be a comprehensive review of the nature and extent of federal and provincial taxes in relation to the financial responsibilities that now had to be carried by the two levels of government.'[10]

The device was not enough to assuage Lesage's wrath. He did not commit Quebec to participate in the committee and he did not, as host, share Pearson's press conference after the last session on 2 April. The atmosphere was worse and the gulf between the governments of Canada and Quebec seemed greater than when Duplessis's conference of 1950 ended. The crisis was real and serious. Pearson was worried and upset but discussion was left for our return to Ottawa.

While I did a memorandum for the prime minister on the weekend, it was Tom Kent who really saved the situation. My memorandum was on the importance for national unity of ensuring that the Lesage government did not have to abandon programs that were sound and within provincial jurisdiction. Kent's was more specific: how to make it possible for the Canada Pension Plan to be brought into line with the Quebec Pension Plan so both could survive. His intricate plan had to be placed before the prime minister, approved by him as a basis for discussion with Quebec, discussed in confidence with Lesage and his advisers, reported to a committee of senior ministers in Ottawa, put in final form by officials, and approved by the two governments – all in a few days. It then had to be submitted to all premiers 'to provide the basis for discussion of a nation-wide pension plan.' This ambitious mission was accomplished and the result announced in the House of Commons on 20 April, less than three weeks after the conference in Quebec had broken up in disarray. It was a remarkable achievement.

As a demonstration of cooperative federalism, the acceptance of a Quebec Pension Plan to exist alongside a Canada Pension Plan for the rest of Canada could not have been more persuasive. The irony is that there has been so little recognition that a 'different' treatment for Quebec, when there is good reason for it, need not be something 'more' and need not be discriminatory; it can simply be 'different' for a society that in many respects has characteristics and priorities that can be accommodated without injury to other provinces if there is a will to do so. Pearson understood that fact and subscribed to it more fully and more readily than all but a few in English-speaking Canada.

The Growing National Crisis

The demand for change that constituted the Quiet Revolution in Quebec was not limited to the province or to provincial affairs. The Bloc Populaire in Quebec had for some years been advocating greater equality of treatment for French-speaking Canadians within the federal system. André Laurendeau, once the leader of the Bloc and later editor of

Le Devoir, called in the early 1960s for a national inquiry into the problem. Laurendeau was a nationalist, but not a separatist. His arguments convinced Maurice Lamontagne, later a minister in the Pearson government but in 1962 an assistant to him as leader of the opposition.

It was indicative of Pearson's imagination and openness to innovative proposals that he was persuaded by Lamontagne of the wisdom of a course that would have had no chance of being adopted without his support. In a speech on national unity in the House of Commons in December 1962, he proposed an inquiry along the lines Lamontagne had urged. The Royal Commission on Bilingualism and Biculturalism was set up on 19 July 1963. Its terms of reference called for it 'to inquire into and report upon the existing state of bilingualism and biculturalism in Canada and to recommend what steps should be taken to develop the Canadian Confederation on the basis of an equal partnership between the two founding races, taking into account the contribution made by the other ethnic groups to the cultural enrichment of Canada and the measures that should be taken to safeguard that contribution.'[11] The commission had two co-chairmen, André Laurendeau and Davidson Dunton. Formerly of Montreal, Dunton had been chairman of the Wartime Information Board during the war, and then chairman of the Canadian Broadcasting Corporation. By 1963, he was president of Carleton University.

A preliminary report was issued in February 1965. The conclusions were stark. It found that 'the state of affairs established in 1867, and never since seriously challenged, is now for the first time being rejected by the French Canadians of Quebec.' That 'state of affairs' included many aspects that were national. In the two years since its establishment, the commission had found 'the existence of a crisis which we believe to be very serious. If it should persist and gather momentum it could destroy Canada.'[12] The general conclusion of the report was the famous statement that 'Canada, without being fully conscious of the fact, is passing through the greatest crisis in its history.'[13] The only thing that has changed, thirty-five years later, is that the fact of this crisis is recognized while agreement on a solution is as remote as ever.

Pearson was not surprised by the report. 'Many thought it much too pessimistic and much too alarming. I did not. I thought it exactly right. I wanted people to be shocked, and they were.'[14] His own strong conviction had immediate importance for the public service. 'I was convinced from the beginning, as I remain convinced now, that a prime element is the recognition of the French language.'[15]

As the royal commission found, the unilingualism of the federal public service was not entirely a matter of oversight – 'it has been strongly influenced by a particular interpretation of the concept of efficiency.' Federal politicians and public servants 'accepted the prevailing orthodoxies linking unilingualism with nationality and efficiency.' The concept 'was an article of faith,' notwithstanding the 'gross inequities' it imposed on francophone public servants.[16]

This was a problem that could be attacked without legislation and without provincial agreement, and Pearson directed that it be taken in hand at once. I, as secretary to the cabinet, was to be personally responsible for seeing that a policy that was fair, defensible, and effective be developed and introduced for the public service as soon as possible. On 6 April 1966 the prime minister announced it in the House of Commons:

> The government hopes and expects that, within a reasonable period of years, a state of affairs in the public service will be reached whereby
> (a) it will be normal practice for oral or written communications within the service to be made in either official language at the option of the persons making them, in the knowledge that they will be understood by those directly concerned;
> (b) communications with the public will normally be in either official language having regard to the person being served;
> (c) the linguistic and cultural values of both English speaking and French speaking Canadians will be reflected through civil service recruitment and training; and
> (d) a climate will be created in which public servants from both language groups will work together toward common goals, using their own language and applying their respective cultural values, but each fully understanding and appreciating those of the other.[17]

I doubt if anyone at the time realized how ambitious a policy and program it was. 'Communications within the service' in French could not be made 'with the knowledge that they would be understood' in any but a few units because so few English-speaking senior officials were bilingual. There had to be an entirely new program of language training, and the public service had neither the staff nor the courses of instruction to make it possible.

Ernest Côté, my successor as deputy minister of northern affairs and national resources, was the first head of a department to get language training under way. He did it by borrowing a few teaching positions not immediately required for the expanding school program in the North-west Territories. Language teachers were found. But what were the courses to be? There were no second-language courses for adults in any of the public services of Canada. It was a commentary on Canadian neglect of the implications of two languages that Northern Affairs found the necessary courses for adults in the Department of State of the United States. I enrolled. Every morning at eight o'clock, I began a program of 'dialogues for learning,' 'dialogues for comprehension,' 'pronunciation drills,' and all the apparatus that has since been developed and that has, over thirty-five years, changed the attitude and the climate in the public service. Incomplete as the achievement still is, it would not have happened at all without Pearson's determination. It was not a policy created by Pierre Trudeau – however much he is credited or blamed for it.

The most important recommendations of the royal commission related to constitutional and legal provisions for the two languages – English and French – that had been part of the history of Canada both before and after Confederation.' 'We are recommending a new status for the official languages in Canada. We do not propose merely to paper over an unsatisfactory situation: we shall present a new concept of an officially bilingual country in which the two official languages will have new rights and better guarantees.'[18] The commission's recommendations were based on a study of four countries that had accorded full equality to their linguistic minorities – Finland, Belgium, Switzerland, and South Africa. All four had constitutional and legal provisions that 'have established a more fundamental principle of equality than has Section 133 of the BNA Act.'[19]

The final recommendations for an official-languages act and for constitutional guarantees of equality of status for English and French were not published by the commission until October 1967, just two months before Pearson announced his intention to retire as prime minister and leader of the Liberal Party. They then became the business of the new Trudeau government: the Official Languages Act in 1969 and the constitutional guarantees as part of the Charter of Rights and Freedoms in 1982.

chapter eleven

The Symbols and Structure of Canada

A Distinctive Canadian Flag

In January 1960 Pearson criticized the failure of the Diefenbaker government 'to find a solution for the problem of a distinctive national flag.'[1] It took courage to launch his own solution a year after he became prime minister in a forum that he knew would be hostile – the annual convention of the Royal Canadian Legion in Winnipeg on 17 May 1964. 'I had perhaps one or two friends on the platform on the night of my address, but not many out in front. Nevertheless, I laid it on the line: "... I believe most sincerely that it is time now for Canadians to unfurl a flag that is truly distinctive and truly national in character, as Canadian as the Maple Leaf which should be its dominant design; a flag easily identifiable as Canada's; a flag which cannot be mistaken for the emblem of any other country; a flag of the future which honours also the past; Canada's own and only Canada's."'[2] Achieving that flag produced one of the longest and most acrimonious debates in the history of our Parliament.

Pearson introduced the resolution for a distinctive Canadian flag in the House of Commons on 5 June. It had attached to it a picture of a possible design that included neither Union Jack nor Fleur de Lys. As Pearson said: 'By this time we had agreed inside the government on a design with blue borders, a white middle and three red maple leaves as on the Canadian coat-of-arms.'[3]

The opposition by Diefenbaker to the resolution for a distinctive flag was bitter. He was supported by his followers in the House in prolonging the debate, objecting to any time limit, and opposing reference of the resolution to a committee to examine the many designs that had, by this time, been submitted by Canadians from all parts of the country. A series of meetings by the prime minister and party leaders in August failed to reach agreement on sending the design problem to a committee. A second series of meetings on September finally got agreement, with a time limit of six weeks for the committee to produce a recommendation on design.

It was clear that 'Pearson's pennant' with the three maple leaves could be chosen only with a narrow, partisan majority, which the prime minister did not want. A national symbol should have a substantial majority. John Matheson, then the member of Parliament for Leeds, Ontario, was Pearson's adviser on flags and everything heraldic. It was he who found the solution.

Most of us, including the prime minister, thought that red, white, and blue were the Canadian colours since they were in the coat of arms and in the Union Jack which was part of the red ensign. But Matheson demonstrated that it was not so: red-and-white were, heraldically, the Canadian colours. The government members in the committee switched their support to the red-and-white design and it was finally recommended by a decision of 11 to 4. In the House of Commons, again no agreement could be reached on a time limit to debate. Closure was finally invoked and on 14 December, more than six months after it had been introduced, the resolution to adopt the flag was carried – 142 to 85.

Bea and I were seated not far from the Diefenbakers at the ceremony on 15 February 1965 in the rotunda of the Centre Block of the Parliament buildings when the proclamation of the new flag was read. Afterward, outside on Parliament Hill, the red ensign was lowered and the new red and white maple leaf flag was raised. Diefenbaker's emotion throughout was apparent: there were genuine tears in his eyes and down his cheeks. His opposition had not been purely partisan: the tradition associated with the old flag and the old symbols was as important for him as the new symbolism was for Pearson.

There is on the proclamation of the flag, and on every photographic copy, an oddity that I have never seen referred to. The prime minister's signature, 'L.B. Pearson,' begins with an 'L' that is twisted downward so as to be badly out of line with the rest of the signature. It arose – and could not be remedied – because the prime minister signed the proclamation as I held it on a briefcase in the RCAF plane that was carrying us to London for the funeral of Sir Winston Churchill at the end of January 1965. The plane lurched just as Pearson was starting to sign. There was no duplicate for the richly ornamented document and it had to be put before Her Majesty for her signature at lunch forty-eight hours after the

Pearsons got to London. It did not disturb him too much; King would have had a seizure and I would have had to find a new job.

In May, three months after the raising of the new flag, as Bea and I drove back through southern Ontario after a short holiday in Virginia, it was encouraging to see how many new maple leaf flags were flying. It was a jolt, however, to see a disconcerting variety of colours – everything from pale orange through a good red to a revolting purple.

At the first morning meeting after my return I told the prime minister it was a potential disaster: the new flag would be discredited if we could not ensure a consistent colour with a red of the type the House of Commons Committee had approved and the public expected. Pearson's reaction was immediate: 'This must be remedied as soon as possible! You are now chairman of a committee to get it done.' A secretary to the cabinet becomes used to that kind of instruction but never did I know less about a problem I was directed to solve.

The Red of the Flag

I began with the Department of National Defence, which flies a lot of flags and, I thought, should know something about them. I was advised that the National Research Council (NRC) was the repository of all knowledge on colours and the man to consult was Dr G. Wyszecki in the Radiation Optics Section of the Division of Applied Physics. Wyszecki advised me that 'the problem is a rather complex one.' I soon learned how right that was. It was the beginning of a full year of learning about materials, dyes, rates of fading, differences in colour perception because of associated colours (the new flag was red and white; the red ensign had had blue in it, so the same red would not look the same), and, at the end of the line, colour specification.

It turned out that, while the Radiation Optics Section knew a great deal about colours, it did not have much information on flag manufacture, the way different materials took dyes, or rates of flag wear and fading. The committee so briskly given to me by the prime minister finally consisted of scientists, military officers, NRC technicians, and people from the departments of National Defence and Defence Production. Investigation of materials, manufacturing, and dyes, along with field testing, involved visits to companies in both Canada and the United States as well as correspondence with Porter Brothers of Liverpool, England, for advice on 'bleeding' and 'fading' in flags. We learned that 'Old Glory Red,' used in the United States flag, was darker than the red the committee had approved. We also learned that, while discussion in the committee had referred to the 'same red dye' as in the red ensign, that would not look the same as the red actually approved because of the red-white contrast. And so it went.

After several months of testing, the Division of Applied Physics of the NRC reported on 8 November 1965:

1. A Canadian flag can now be proclaimed with a satisfactory balance of colour fastness and wear life.
2. A printed fabric can have quite similar fastness characteristics to a piece-dyed fabric (which was important to keep flag costs down).
3. For control of colour two 'limit shades' should be established – one light red 'the orange limit' and the other dark red 'the blue limit.'

It was not until 1 June 1966 that the Canadian Government Specification Board in the Department of Defence Production issued Specification No. 98–GP1 for the flag. Two dyes were specified to be suitable for use – Acid Red 127 and Acid Orange 47.

By the time the press became aware of the problem, we were well on the way to its solution. It had been a most fortunate trip to Virginia and a good demonstration of the way, when a prime minister takes hold of a problem, the PCO can mobilize agencies to produce a solution.

The Election of 1965

The two years of office for the Pearson government after the unsatisfactory victory of 1963 had seen substantial accomplishment after a rough start, but the 'scandals' and the turbulence of the House of Commons, with the ominous presence of Diefenbaker constantly across the aisle, had been wearing on the prime minister. He desperately wanted to escape from the precarious minority situation and in the summer of 1965 the polls showed an increase in Liberal popularity. Walter Gordon thought the time was right. A second poll appeared to confirm his optimism.

What neither the pollsters nor the Liberals foresaw was the vigour of the campaign that would be waged by John Diefenbaker. The Liberal accomplishments could not compete on the hustings with the histrionic skill with which he ridiculed and exploited all the scandals, confusions and errors, real and imagined, of the Pearson government. It was a dazzling performance by a great prosecutor. In the end the government gained just three seats and found itself still two seats short of a majority: the curse of a minority was still there after all the effort.

Pearson recounted to Tom Kent and me, at one of our morning

meetings just after the election, Mrs Pearson's reaction election night: 'Mike, it's an utter disaster! You've even won your own seat!' It was a revealing cry of despair and Pearson was ruefully admitting it. Maryon detested much of the life that went with marriage to a politician – even if he was prime minister. If he had lost his seat, that might have opened the way to escape from all the strains and frustrations that two years in office had brought. Now – still with the wretched minority – there would be at least two or three years more.

Walter Gordon felt that he was responsible for pressing Pearson to hold the election – as, along with others, he was. He resigned. The prime minister talked to some of the ministers about their future roles and to Tom and me about reconstruction of the government. Then he and Maryon left for some days of privacy and wound-licking in the Caribbean.

An official visit to Jamaica had been arranged before the election and Pearson decided to fit in a meeting before it with Tom and me on the island of St Maarten. Our landing there in the midst of a blinding tropical rain storm on a runway really too short for the government Jet-Star was as dramatic as any of the landings I had made in Arctic white-outs, and far more violent.

The management of the resort hotel to which the Pearsons had come had, very thoughtfully, put them in the best cottage – right down at the shore. Along with the luxury and the beauty, the consequence was that the over-taxed drainage system delivered the storm-flood overflow straight into the Pearson suite. When Tom and I turned up, Mrs Pearson was perched on a bed surrounded by ugly grey water and the prime minister of Canada, with feet bare and trousers rolled up, was trying to direct the water out the cottage door. It was a perfect overture for some sad and rueful discussions.

The prime minister approved a number of changes in departmental responsibilities that Tom and I had worked out. Among them was, at last, joining Indians and Inuit in the charge of the same department. North-ern Affairs and National Resources became Indian Affairs and Northern Development.

A change I much regretted was put forward by Tom: that he leave the Prime Minister's Office and become deputy minister of manpower and immigration. Tom felt that Pearson would welcome 'a quieter life' than he had had with Tom's vigour and imagination pressing for action. 'After eight years we had come to the point where it was best that our ways should part, but he would have had difficulty in initiating a fair method of bringing it about.'[4]

The prime minister returned to Ottawa on 16 December and announced his new cabinet the next day. Among the important changes was the introduction to the federal scene of the 'Three Wise Men' who would transform Quebec's presence in Otawa and, a bit later, the atmosphere of Canada itself: Jean Marchand, Pierre Trudeau, and Gérard Pelletier. It was Marchand that Pearson really wanted, but he would not come without his two colleagues. Marchand, after much persuasion by Tom and me, became minister of manpower and immigration. It is not often that a new Member of Parliament has to be persuaded to accept a portfolio but Marchand was diffident about his capacity to operate in English. It was an excellent demonstration of the language problem that the 'B and B' commission had highlighted. Trudeau became parliamentary secretary to the prime minister.

The Order of Canada

Canada had been in an awkward position about honours and awards after 1919 when the House of Commons passed a resolution requesting the sovereign to refrain from granting British honours to Canadians, except for bravery. That remained the policy until the Second World War, except from 1933 to 1935, when Prime Minister Bennett issued several lists of British honours for Canadians. King reverted to the earlier policy after 1935 except for recognizing contributions to the war effort, again with British honours and military medals. After the end of the war we became one of the few countries with no national system for recognizing distinguished public service, outstanding merit, or gallantry.

There were two men who, in turn, thought the situation unsatisfactory and, nearly twenty years apart, tried to do something about it. In his memoirs, Vincent Massey says: 'On December 20, 1949, I was asked by the Prime Minister whether the royal commission of which I was chairman would present a report to the Government on the question of honours and awards in Canada. This subject lay, of course, well outside our terms of reference, but it was clearly a matter that deserved attention, and I told the Prime Minister that I would speak to my colleagues about his request and that I was sure they would agree to meet his wishes.' No one who knew St Laurent and Massey as I did could possibly believe that that is how it happened. St Laurent never mentioned honours and awards: they were not part of his thinking. The initiative must have come from Massey, who did think a lot about them. On 9 August 1951 he presented a report to the prime minister recommending 'the institution of a new, non-titular order of merit, through which the services of Canadians could be recognized in their own country.' The level of St Laurent's anxiety to have the advice is indicated by the fact that, with six more years in office, he did nothing whatever to implement the report.

Pearson did, like Massey, believe in the importance of national recognition of merit and public service as a way to promote a sense of unity and pride of country – just like the distinctive flag. The centennial of Confederation was the time to do something and a committee was set up in the secretary of state's department to work on it, starting from Massey's report.

The first draft of the constitution of the Order proposed three grades – that of Companion, Officer, and Member. In cabinet, the idea of grades was rejected as discriminatory. The Order was approved but with a limited number of Companions only: no other levels. Subsequently, a Medal of Courage was added, to recognize bravery, and a Medal of Service. The prime minister announced the approval by the Queen of letters patent constituting the Order of Canada on 17 April 1967:

> The Constitution of the Order provides for the creation of Companions of the Order. Fifty may be appointed in this Centennial year and not more than 25 in any year thereafter, but the maximum shall never exceed 150. The Principal Companion of the Order, the Chancellor, will be the Governor-General.
>
> Nominations for the award will not be made by the Government, but directly to the Governor-General by an Advisory Council composed as follows:
>
> a) The Chief Justice of Canada (Chairman)
> b) The Clerk of the Privy Council
> c) The Under Secretary of State
> d) The Chairman of the Canada Council
> e) The President of the Royal Society of Canada
> f) The President of the Association of Universities and Colleges of Canada.
>
> Companions will be selected on the basis of merit, especially service to Canada or to humanity at large.

Pearson dealt also with the Medal of Courage and the Medal of Service.

The prime minister had bowed to objections in the cabinet to the three grades for the Order, but five years' experience showed that he (and Vincent Massey) had been right. The difference between the designation and the elegant badge of Companion and the modest Medal of Service was too great. Moreover, the capacity to give adequate recognition to different kinds and levels of service at all levels across Canada was too limited. A revised constitution in 1972 provided for the three original levels: Companion, Officer, and Member of the Order of Canada.

As the tenth anniversary of the founding of the Order approached, the governor general, Jules Léger, called a special meeting, attended by the first chancellor of the Order, Roland Michener, to assess 'the present position of the Order ... and to consider ways in which its effectiveness as the keystone of the Canadian Honours system may be increased.' Pearson would have drawn comfort from the conclusion of a long meeting in January 1977. While a number of procedural and public-information changes about the Order were thought desirable, no alteration was recommended in the constitution as revised in 1972.

On the twentieth anniversary in 1987, a further review was made after ten more years of experience. Again the conclusion was that the Order was meeting the objectives intended for it and that no revision of structure was necessary or desirable.

The aspect of the Order that has drawn most frequent criticism is the one that caused division in the cabinet in 1967. I was, as clerk of the Privy Council, a member of the advisory council for the first eight years of the Order's existence from 1967 to 1975. It is clear from experience that two levels, as from 1967 to 1972, did not work well. A single level would produce even more difficulty. As I said when my views were sought in 1986 in preparation for the third review: 'The Order with three levels has made it possible to recognize really outstanding contributions to Canada with the tightly restricted level of Companion, important contributions of national significance with the level of Officer, and a wide range of regional and local services of value to citizens, towns and communities at the level of Member. It has made it possible to escape from the dilemma that a single level would have presented and the problem of inadequate local recognition that the two-level basis did present from 1967 to 1972.'

The key to the undoubted success and reputation of the Order is the independent, non-political advisory council, chaired by the chief justice of Canada, which advises a chancellor, who is the governor general and who approves or disapproves all recommendations for the award. Both are known to be independent and beyond partisanship. The non-political structure remains as announced by Pearson in 1967.

The first Chancellor, Roland Michener, established the second principle that ensures objectivity when he made it clear to the first advisory council that, while he would not guarantee that he would approve everyone the council recommended for appointment to the Order, he would not appoint anyone the council did not recommend. Both Pearson and Massey took honours seriously and built in the protection necessary to ensure acceptance and respect.

The Centennial

Canada's hundredth birthday could not have come at a better time. The post-war reconstruction had been successfully completed, the social-security system was well advanced, the economy was strong, and there was a new sense of confidence for which the only parallel had probably been with the opening of the west after 1900 when Laurier claimed that the twentieth century would be Canada's.

Every head of government was extended an invitation to visit Canada during the summer of 1967. The response was more than had been bargained for – fifty-nine accepted. It was probably as well that there were fewer than half as many states then as there are now. As Pearson comments in his memoirs, it meant that each of the fifty-nine had to be given a dinner by the governor general and a lunch by the prime minister – or vice versa – with appropriate gifts and suitable addresses.

It gave the country a great lift, but it also made serious inroads on the time and energy of the prime minister. Our morning meetings frequently had to be interrupted by some last-minute report on the lunch for that day and on talking points for Pearson with whomever he was to entertain. On one occasion it was King Bhumibol of Thailand. Pearson's vast knowledge of foreign statesmen and countries did not include him. When a serious young foreign-service officer was ushered in for the briefing, the prime minister helped him along: 'Oh, yes. To-day it is King Bummy Ball.' The officer hesitated for a moment. 'Well, Prime Minister, in fact they pronounce the king's name "Foom-i-fon."' Pearson's face broke into the boyish smile that was one of his attractive features. 'If my name was Bummy Ball I would call it "Foom-i-fon" too!'

But he wouldn't forget. One had to learn that Pearson was often at his most serious in a jest. It was part of his great diplomatic skill. Things could be said with a laugh and a joke that might cause offence if they were plodded out seriously. He used the technique constantly in Cabinet, in federal-provincial conferences, and in personal discussion.

'Vive le Québec Libre'

The only visit in the summer of 1967 that caused real trouble was that of the president of France, General Charles de Gaulle.

Things were awkward from the beginning. Ottawa was the national capital and Canada was the host, but the French government and the Union Nationale government of Quebec, in office since the provincial election of 1 June 1966, were insistent that the visit was not to start in Ottawa: it must start in Quebec City. The general would arrive in a French cruiser and Premier Daniel Johnson would be host for the visit there and for a triumphal procession by car to Montreal. The federal presence was to be minimal until the general, on the third day, reached Ottawa.

The invitation had been extended, the president had accepted, and the federal government had no wish to spoil the event with a quarrel, but it was very much on the outside after the arrival on Sunday morning, 23 July, except for a brief visit by de Gaulle to the governor general and Mrs Michener at the Quebec Citadel.

On 24 July the procession of cars moved along the highway from Quebec through large crowds in towns and villages, with stops for the general to meet people and talk about their aspirations, which France understood and with which it sympathized. The cavalcade reached the city hall in Montreal at about 7:30 P.M. A crowd had been assembling outside for several hours: they were told that de Gaulle would appear on the balcony overlooking Jacques-Cartier Square.

My wife and I turned on the television well before de Gaulle's performance began – and a performance it was. He played on the emotions of the crowd and they responded with growing enthusiasm: he was a superb orator with great skill at crowd control. He compared the progress from Quebec to Montreal that day with 'the liberation' – clearly of Paris in 1944, when he marched up the Champs Elysées. After a crescendo of 'Vives' – of France, of Montreal, of Quebec, but not of Canada – came 'Vive le Québec – libre!' The slogan of the growing separatist movement in Quebec! It took a minute or two to absorb it all. I was about to phone the prime minister when he called me. He was shocked and angry: there would have to be a special cabinet meeting in the morning to consider how to respond.

There was great discussion and drafting of possible statements overnight as telegrams poured in from across the country. The following morning Paul Martin was anxious to try to play down the episode, although he was deeply hurt. He had thought that he had established a relationship of trust with Couve de Murville, his opposite number in France. The prime minister was too angry, as were most of his colleagues, to accept anything but a firm and clear position. Pearson had been even more shocked by the comparison with 'the liberation' than with the 'Vive le Québec libre.'

I shared all of Pearson's anger at de Gaulle's wanton interference in so critical a problem for Canada, especially when he was here, as a guest, on the occasion of our centenary. I joined with enthusiasm in the efforts to find the best way to denounce his action. After a day of discussion, adjournments and countless drafts and re-drafts, Pearson read the government's statement to a press conference. The 'liberation' was rejected: 'The people of Canada are free ... Canadians do not need to be liberated.' He made reference to the thousands of Canadians who gave their lives in two world wars in the liberation of France. The summation of it all was that the offending statements by de Gaulle were 'unacceptable to the Canadian people and its government.'

Pearson, as a diplomat, well understood that de Gaulle could not accept so sharp a rebuke and still come to Ottawa. But the decision would be his. De Gaulle decided that same night. He completed the program in Montreal, including a lunch presided over by the mayor, Jean Drapeau, who made some pointed remarks about the people of Quebec's attachment to Canada. French-speaking Canadians had learned to survive alone for over 200 years without assistance or encouragement from France. It had been proven that French Canada could survive. Drapeau looked to a renewal of French Canada so that it would better serve 'all of Canada.' Pearson telephoned Drapeau immediately after the lunch to congratulate him and to thank him. The president of France, twice rebuked, left by air that afternoon.

There have been suggestions that de Gaulle did not understand the import of what he said: that he became worked up by the enthusiasm of the crowd and went beyond what he intended. That proposition does a great disservice to de Gaulle's careful planning and to his desire to help the growing national consciousness of 'the French of Quebec,' as he thought of them and referred to them. His planning and his execution were both superb. The result was undoubtedly what he intended: to sharpen the division between separatists and federalists in Quebec and Canada. It heightened Pearson's concern about the growing crisis in national unity and raised new doubts in his mind about the possibility of meeting the problem without constitutional change.

So far as I was concerned, it increased my interest in taking advantage of a plan that had been developed to have, each year, a few senior civil servants with their families go to live in Quebec – to learn French and to gain an understanding of Quebec as a part of the reform in government policy and in the federal public service. It was to be for a year, and both Pearson and I thought that it would be symbolically important if his own deputy minister went. It seemed possible because the deputy secretary to the cabinet, Gerry Stoner, in whom Pearson had full confidence, would be a strong replacement for me in my absence.

With all the summer's pressures, Bea and I could not leave for Quebec City until two months later, in early September. It was important to be there then so Kerrie, age fifteen, could enrol in school. The plan looked entirely plausible and the results in improved French showed some cheering signs – until in December Gerry called with a message from the prime minister. He had decided that something new had to be done to demonstrate the government's determination to meet the unity crisis. He was going to propose a federal-provincial conference on constitutional reform for February 1968. He wanted me to return – not necessarily full time – to take charge of the preparations.

It was not the utter end of my Quebec experience and I did get to the point where I could carry on a conversation in a French that was not too dreadfully fractured, but the time in Quebec was too short – and I was too old. Fifty is no age to start to learn a language.

Pearson's Decision to Retire
On 14 December 1967 Pearson announced his intention to retire early in 1968. The thought of retirement had been present in both his and Maryon's minds ever since the disappointing results in 1965. On 11 November of that year, at the prime minister's request, I telephoned Jean Lesage to tell him, as a memorandum I made on 12 November records, that 'it would help the Prime Minister very considerably in determining his own course of action in the immediate future if he were to know whether Mr. Lesage was interested in succeeding him in the leadership of the federal Liberal Party ...' It was one of several possibilities the prime minister wanted to take into account, but it reflected what I know to have been his preference at that time.

Lesage told me in reply that 'he thought it was of the greatest possible importance in the interests of Canada that Mr. Pearson should remain Prime Minister for the next couple of years – at least to and through the centennial of Confederation.' He himself could not leave the Quebec scene before another provincial election was held, probably in the autumn of 1966. I asked him if he would then be 'in the market for entering the federal field' and he said he would.

For whatever reason, Lesage advanced the election to 5 June 1966. In an article in the Ottawa *Citizen* of 17 December 1980, Christopher Young said rightly that 'in the early '60s Lesage really had no rivals for the title of chief Quebec strong-man.' In the election, the Liberals won 47.2 per cent of the vote against 40.9 for the Union Nationale. However, Lesage had omitted to reform the way Duplessis had stacked the electoral cards. The rural areas were over-represented while the urban areas, especially Montreal, were under-represented. The UN won fifty-five-seats to fifty-one for the Liberals and Lesage was out of office. With the loss of that election, and with a mild heart attack for Lesage soon after, the scene changed for the choice of Pearson's successor less than two years later.

Lesage would have made an excellent prime minister. He was every bit as firm and dynamic an opponent of separatism as Pierre Trudeau. But he had been a provincial premier and it was he who began the annual interprovincial meetings of the premiers without a federal presence. He understood provincial politics in a way Trudeau never did. The subsequent history of our unity problem would have been totally different if Pearson's original plan had worked out.

Into the Can of Worms

Premier Daniel Johnson of Quebec had used the meeting of the tax-structure committee in September 1966 to raise the question of constitutional change: 'The new Québec Government is committed to the fundamental task of obtaining legal and political recognition of the French-Canadian nation; among other things, this will require a new constitution to guarantee equal collective rights in our country to English-speaking and French-speaking Canadians, as well as to give Québec all the powers needed to safeguard its own identity.'[5]

Premier Robarts had referred at the federal-provincial conference a month later to the possibility that, if the problems of 'financial redistribution' could be resolved, it might then be possible 'to concentrate on the broader and basic questions of re-shaping the Canadian federation.'[6] He did not make any specific proposal and the federal government was surprised in January 1967 when the Ontario speech from the throne announced that the government would ask the Legislative Assembly 'to approve the policy of my government to invite the leaders of all provinces and the federal government to a conference where the future course of our federal system of government will be discussed.'[7]

Pearson was not pleased with this initiative. In October 1964 it had appeared that the Fulton-Favreau formula for amendment of the constitution had been approved, only to have the Lesage government withdraw a few weeks later. The Union Nationale under Johnson would be much more demanding. Pearson writes in his memoirs: 'We had a great deal of work to do in confidence with the provinces before we came out into the open with a further constitutional conference ... A full-scale public conference between the provinces, summoned by the head of a provincial government, was a new development. The federal government was informed that it would be welcome, but we decided not to go. We considered the whole procedure to be out of order.'[8]

One of the centennial events was pure Pearsonian diplomacy. He recommended to the governor general that all the premiers be invited to Ottawa for the hundredth birthday and afterward be sworn in as privy councillors – which would attach the title 'Honourable' to them for life and not simply while they were in office. The swearing-in ceremony was at Rideau Hall and there was an informal meeting in its happy aftermath. A press release referred to the Confederation for Tomorrow Conference as an interprovincial conference (not federal-provincial) 'which would permit a free exchange of views among the provinces on a number of problems, could form a useful first step toward consideration of the working of the Canadian federal structure.'[9]

Both Pearson and his parliamentary secretary, Pierre Trudeau, had been very hesitant about getting the country involved in constitutional change until there seemed to be good prospects of success. Trudeau called it a 'panier de crabes' – a can of worms. But, can of worms or not, Pearson came to the conclusion in December 1967 that it was necessary to take action. A federal-provincial conference was to be held to discuss the issue of constitutional change.

When the conference opened on 5 February 1968, it was the first federal-provincial conference carried on radio and television. The discussions for the first time gave Canadians outside Quebec a sense of the critical nature of the problems before the country. The prime minister, in his opening statement, set the tone he wanted:

> There are times in the life of a country when the assurance of good intentions, the discharge of normal duty and acceptance of routine responsibility, are not enough. What such times demand is the exercise of courage and decision that go far beyond the needs of the moment. I believe that this is such a time for Canada. Here the road forks. If we have the resolution and the wisdom to choose now the right course and to follow it

steadfastly, I can see few limits to what we may achieve together as a people. But if we lack the courage to choose, or if we choose wrongly, we will leave to our children and our children's children a country in fragments, and we ourselves would [*sic*] have become the failures of Confederation.[10]

Pearson suggested two changes to the British North America Act, 1867: one to establish the basic principle of 'equality for the communities of people speaking our two official languages'; the other 'agreement in principle at this conference on a constitutional bill of rights for all Canadians.' Finally, he hoped for agreement on 'a comprehensive constitutional review.' An important part of that 'would be the division of powers and jurisdiction between federal and provincial governments.'[11] The prime minister concluded by saying that 'presiding over this conference is one of my last major responsibilities as Prime Minister of Canada. So it is with a full heart – but with full confidence, too – that I join you in the task of building an even freer, greater and more generous future for our beloved country.'[12]

The three days of meeting had only one period of crisis when the premier of Quebec was unwise enough to attack Pierre Trudeau, by then minister of justice. Trudeau had much the best of the argument, so much so that Pearson imposed a coffee break until tempers could cool. It was probably the first glimpse many Canadians had of the new minister and a highly favourable one – at least in English-speaking Canada.

At the end, the conference agreed:

THAT a continuing Constitutional Conference be set up, composed of the Prime Ministers and Premiers or their delegates, to supervise the process of constitutional review;

THAT a Continuing Committee of officials be set up to assist the Constitutional Conference in its task;

THAT a secretariat be formed by the federal government, after consultation with the provinces, to serve both the Constitutional Conference and the Continuing Committee of officials.[13]

The questions to be examined by the constitutional conference and the continuing committee of officials were to include:

(a) official languages;
(b) fundamental rights;
(c) distribution of powers;

(d) reform of institutions linked with federalism, including the Senate and the Supreme Court of Canada;

(e) regional disparities;

(f) amending procedure and provisional arrangements;

(g) mechanisms of federal-provincial relations.

It was also agreed that I should be chairman of the continuing committee of officials.

The prime minister had set out in the federal government's statement of policy – *Federalism for the Future* – his concept of the scope of the undertaking: 'It is the view of the Government of Canada that a comprehensive review must involve the willingness of the heads of government to meet in Federal-Provincial Conferences at relatively frequent intervals over the next two or three years to guide and control the process of review. This may seem an arduous schedule, but we must remember that it took two or three years to write the original Constitution.'[14]

And so began a task that continued, for me, until I retired from the public service in December 1979 – eleven years later – and that remains unfinished still. Neither Pearson nor I, nor any of the participants at the conference, had the slightest idea that agreement would prove so elusive. Separatism was not yet a clear threat: the Parti Québécois was not founded until October 1968, when several 'movements' merged at a convention to create the new political party, with René Lévesque – until 1967 a minister of the Liberal provincial government – as its leader. Nor had the other provinces yet become discontented with the distribution of powers or with anything else in the way our federalism was operating.

The prime minister felt that an important step had been taken. A few days after the end of the conference he gave me his copy of *Federalism for the Future* with a typically generous inscription: 'Gordon – It was a great success – an historic beginning – and for that we owe much to you. Many, many thanks. L.B. Pearson. Feb 12/68.'

Pearson as Prime Minister

The roles and tasks of the prime minister in our parliamentary system of government are many and complex: leader of his party in elections, the one responsible for the selection of the successful few to receive ministerial prizes from among the many Members of Parliament who think they deserve them, leader for the country and the party in the House of Commons on a day-to-day basis and defender against the assaults of the opposition, participant in the weekly party caucus both to listen and to lead, and chairman of the cabinet in the determination of policy and decision on problems of all magnitude. Of these tasks, the ones that caused Pearson the most difficulty were in the House of Commons and often arose, directly or indirectly, out of the disconcerting presence of John Diefenbaker. One of the most damaging episodes for Pearson and for the government was the 'Rivard affair' in the autumn of 1964.

Lucien Rivard of the Montreal underworld was wanted in the United States on a charge of drug smuggling. The counsel acting for the American government in seeking extradition to the United States had been offered a bribe of $20,000 to drop the opposition to bail for Rivard. He informed the RCMP that the offer had come from Raymond Denis, executive assistant to the minister of citizenship and immigration. The RCMP investigated and its commissioner, who at that time reported to the minister of justice, advised the minister, Guy Favreau, that there was insufficient evidence to lay any charges against Denis. Favreau, a highly respected professor of law in Montreal in civil life, personally studied the file and agreed with the RCMP assessment. The allegations of scandal began to leak and got worse with claims that Guy Rouleau, the parliamentary secretary to the prime minister, had also tried to persuade the counsel for the United States to drop the opposition to Rivard's bail. When confronted with these allegations both Denis and Rouleau resigned, but no charges were laid.

Such were the basic facts. It was a damaging affair that became critical for the prime minister and the government when Pearson, innocently, gave an incorrect answer in the House of Commons to a question by Douglas Harkness: When had he first been informed about the Rivard affair?

Harkness's question was on Tuesday, 23 November 1964. Pearson said that he thought it was two days before: the previous Sunday. In fact, Guy Favreau had told him of it on 2 September in the aircraft returning the federal delegation to Ottawa from a conference in Charlottetown. Favreau did not then go into the details. Both Pearson and Favreau were swamped, as prime ministers and ministers so often are, and weeks had gone by with no further word to Pearson. In the midst of the flag debate and other pressures he had forgotten the short conversation in the air – but he had misinformed the House of Commons. He then had to go off for political meetings in Manitoba.

The attack on Favreau now became serious. The decision not to lay charges against Denis had been his – with the advice of the legal advisers to the commissioner of the RCMP but without further advice from the legal staff of the Department of Justice. He then, so it appeared, had not even told the prime minister until two days before. The first part of the attack had no answer except Favreau's knowledge of the law and his own integrity, which was immediately put in question. On the second part, Favreau was innocent, but he could not dispute what the prime minister had told Parliament. He was defenceless until Pearson corrected the record.

The obvious thing was for the prime minister to apologize to the House and to explain his error the first time he was present – the following Monday. When he got back to Ottawa on Sunday, 29 November, Tom Kent, Jack Pickersgill, and I had an urgent meeting with him; they were especially concerned about the need to correct the record and to defend Favreau, and I was particularly anxious to have an early statement about the ethical principles that were to govern ministers and their staffs in future. There had been no such statement up to that time. I had a letter ready which went out to ministers the following day – 30 November. It has since been expanded into the conflict-of-interest and ethical guidelines that now apply at both the political and the public-service level of government.

The most urgent part – correcting the record in the House – did not happen. A commission was set up – the Dorion commission – to enquire into the 'affair.' Pearson did not put right his answer to Harkness. Instead, he wrote to Mr Justice Dorion on 14 December explaining his error and the forgotten 2 September conversation. Dorion read the letter into the record of his commission when it began its hearings on 15 December.

The episode is worth recalling only because it explains in part why the Pearson government had so much trouble with so many 'scandals' that were, in themselves, unimportant in the total perspective of the government's accomplishments. There is little doubt but that much of the vulnerability of the prime minister and of the government were the product of his uncertainty and inadequacy in the daily gladiatorial contest in the House of Commons, which he loathed, and which was made worse by the 'John Diefenbaker factor.' The only explanation of his failure to do what he knew he should do, to relieve Favreau as soon as possible from the assault on him, was that he could not bring himself to face the withering scorn and ridicule his apology would bring from his nemesis on the opposition benches.

His tactic did not escape it. So far as the opposition was concerned, Pearson had added a new offence to his misleading the House: he had failed to apologize and to correct the record at his earliest opportunity. He was in contempt as well as in error.

The only good thing that came out of the whole sad affair, apart from the statement about ethical principles in government, was the decision to have the RCMP in future report to the solicitor general, not to the minister of justice. It was clearly dangerous – even a 'conflict of interest' of a kind – to have the same minister responsible for the police function and also for the administration of justice. They had to be kept separate and have been ever since.

Guy Favreau never recovered, in reputation or in health, from the Rivard affair. He was criticized in the Dorion report and resigned as minister of justice. He died a few months later.

The other 'scandals' were much less serious but they hurt more than they should have because of the vulnerability the Rivard case had exposed and the appetite the opposition had gained from its initial success. That appetite was diminished when, in the first session of Parliament after the election of 1965, Lucien Cardin, who had replaced Guy Favreau as minister of justice, lost his temper in an exchange with the leader of the opposition who was goading him about yet another 'scandal,' this one involving a postal clerk, George Victor Spencer. His angry reference to 'the Monseignor case when he [Diefenbaker] was Prime Minister of this country' led to the unearthing of an affair between Pierre Sévigny, associate minister of national defence in the Diefenbaker government, and one Gerda Munsinger. That led to yet another judicial inquiry, this one by Mr Justice Wishart Spence of the Supreme Court, and a report that was critical of Diefenbaker's handling of a case that could have involved national security. It became clear that there was risk as well as advantage in raking over episodes in which often the judgment of weary and harrassed ministers or prime ministers could be criticized in the cold scrutiny of infallible hindsight. Yet there is no doubt that it was the Pearson government, and to a large degree Pearson himself, who suffered most in reputation.

In contrast with his worried uncertainty in parliamentary battles, Pearson was a sure leader of his cabinet with a readiness to face difficult issues that he thought important. He was decisive and unhesitating about cooperating with Lesage on the Quebec Pension Plan; he went ahead over the doubts of many of his ministers on the flag; he made a temporary tactical retreat on the Order of Canada but ended up with his original plan; and he would accept no compromise on the reaction to de Gaulle's intervention on the balcony in Montreal. He distrusted doctrinaire positions. He was a pragmatic realist. He was prepared to yield, to adjust, and always to search for a meeting of minds. His diplomatc skills were legendary. In cabinet he was unfailingly patient and considerate. He was skilful with humorous interventions that softened hard positions and made it difficult for anyone to resist agreement – precisely the reverse of Bell's comment about Diefenbaker's influence. I only once saw him take a decision 'in the face' of his colleagues.

Orders-in-council that needed cabinet, as distinct from routine committee, attention came at the end of each meeting. The prime minister had to leave early on one occasion and he left the orders for the appointment of three or four senators with Paul Martin, the senior minister, to put through when the rest of the agenda had been completed. Several ministers were less than enthusiastic about some of Pearson's choices. They would almost certainly not have objected had he been there, but Paul did not insist. He left the orders unpassed – as I reported to Pearson. Senate appointments, whatever the written constitution may say, are the prerogative of the prime minister. Pearson announced at the opening of the next cabinet meeting that the orders had, unfortunately, been overlooked at the last meeting. They were passed without a murmur.

Pearson was not without problems with his ministers: few prime ministers are. His most serious were with Walter Gordon, perhaps in part because they had been such close friends when Pearson was establishing himself as leader of the Liberal Party. Gordon's contributions to Pearson personally and to the party were great: his reward was the finance portfolio, which he much wanted, in 1963. The budget crisis shook Pearson's confidence in him and embarrassed the government, but Pearson stuck with him, although he was under great pressure to drop him or to move him to another portfolio. The real strains began after the 1965 election. It may be that Pearson should not have accepted Gordon's resignation. The error in judgment in calling the election had been as much Pearson's as his. In any case, the situation became worse, in my view, after Gordon came back into the cabinet as president of the Privy Council in 1967.

The president of the Privy Council normally has no departmental or program responsibilities unless some are specifically assigned to him. Tom Kent says that 'he [Gordon] entertained, on the basis of vague promises from Mr. Pearson, vast illusions about what he could achieve in returning to the Cabinet in 1967.' That may well be so: one of Pearson's problems with his ministers frequently arose from were federal. Federal participation was especially important because of the financial disparities among the provinces.

Hospital insurance and medicare began as provincial programs in Saskatchewan. They were items in a paper prepared by Tom Kent for the Kingston conference of 'liberally-minded' people in September 1960. The paper – 'Towards a Philosophy of Social Security' – also included the reshaping of unemployment insurance, employment training, regional development, support for post-secondary education, and national scholarships. It set out what became the social-security program of the Pearson government after 1963. The Canada Assistance Plan, agreed to in 1965 and legislated in 1966, provided a federal-provincial social-assistance program. The Guaranteed Income Supplement filled a gap in old-age security, for which the most important elements were the Canada Pension Plan, with the Quebec Pension plan in harmony after the crisis of 1964. Financial assistance for post-secondary education was worked out in a federal-provincial conference in 1966. Medicare, introduced in stages through the 1960s, has become Canada's most valued social program, almost a defining feature of what federal-provincial cooperation, with all its difficulties, can accomplish.

Many important features of the program were adopted and were accomplished during the life of Pearson's two governments from 1963 to 1968. In that accomplishment, a major factor was the skill and flexibility Pearson brought to federal-provincial diplomacy. His sensitivity about differences to be bridged, his imagination in finding and presenting ways to accommodate the essentials of sharply differing positions, the humour that often made it seem just too crass for a premier to hold out and object to a small but significant change – all were a frequent marvel in the conferences he chaired.

In spite of the constant minority situation, the scandals, the 'John Diefenbaker factor,' and his dislike of the ill-tempered and raucous daily theatre on the floor of the House of Commons, Lester Pearson achieved most of what he set out to do. It was sad that the dissolution of Parliament by the new prime minister, Pierre Trudeau, on 23 April 1968, was handled with such haste that not a word of tribute was paid to a man who had done so much for Canada. He lived little more than four years longer.

PART FIVE

Winds of Change with Pierre Trudeau, 1968–1980

chapter twelve

Pierre Trudeau and a New Style of Governing, 1968–1970

Pierre Trudeau and I had been in touch with one another at intervals, especially after he became parliamentary secretary to the prime minister in 1966. When I returned from Quebec in early January 1968, I became chairman of a task force 'to prepare an overall constitutional position for the consideration of ministers and to make immediate preparations for the conference' the prime minister had called for 5 February.[1] The task force was to report to the prime minister but to 'keep in close touch' with Trudeau as minister of justice. In fact, Pierre attended some of the task force meetings, especially for discussion of the federal proposal for a charter of rights. Our relationship, dating back to 1949, made it easy for both of us to have me, a public servant, chairing a meeting with him, a minister, participating.

I think it was in February that Pierre and I bumped into one another at the door of the Château Laurier Hotel. Trudeau was under pressure to become a candidate for the leadership of the Liberal Party. He asked if I could walk with him to the West Block, where he had to be in a few minutes for a meeting. He wanted to talk to me about what he should do. Should he run for the leadership?

I had no doubts. I told him that I thought it was highly important for the unity of Canada that there should be a French-speaking prime minister from Quebec, which there had not been since 1957. He would also bring to the constitutional issues and the operation of federalism original thinking that no other candidate could rival. Growing separatism was the most important problem before the country; he was the best person to lead opposition to it and he should run. Whether Trudeau was really in doubt, or was simply seeking reassurance about a decision he had already made, I do not know. However, in reply to a letter of good wishes I sent when he announced his decision to retire from the position of prime minister in 1984, Trudeau said: 'Although it was sixteen years ago that you talked me into attempting to gain the leadership of the Liberal Party, the memory of our conversation is still with me. You were as convincing on that occasion as you have been on countless others since then.'[2]

As we separated at the entrance to the West Block, Pierre said: 'If I run for the leadership, and if I win, I will then become prime minister. If that happens, will you be there to be my Secretary to the cabinet?' He knew enough of the whole operation of government from his experience from 1949 to 1951 and again from two years as a minister to appreciate how critical the position was and the importance of the personal relationship between prime minister and the secretary. Again I had no hesitation: 'I will be there for as long as you want me.'

And so began an association of eleven years – until the Liberal defeat in the election of 1979 – in which there was never a clash or an angry word. Trudeau was boss, of course. But on more than one occasion, when we discussed some policy or course of action, the prime minister of Canada would say: 'Well, when I worked for you, Gordon, you used to tell me ...' His memory was incredible. He always had it right, and he remembered more than I did. However, I was the boss in those days, so he had more reason to remember. I found working with Pierre a joy throughout – but I made a point of never again calling him 'Pierre' until he ceased to be prime minister. 'Mr Trudeau' was too stilted, given our relationship, so it was 'prime minister' when a handle was needed.

Mitchell Sharp has told in his memoirs how the defeat of the budget bill on 19 February 1968 had tied him down in a parliamentary crisis and led to his withdrawal from the contest for the Liberal leadership. He gave his support to Trudeau. The third ballot at the convention had three candidates: Trudeau, Robert Winters, and John Turner, with Trudeau getting more than half the total number of votes.[3]

It was not surprising that Trudeau's success mystified some of the leading Liberals who had laboured long for the party, had aspired to the leadership, and had then been left aside, resentful and hurt. As Trudeau records it, Pearson had said that the answer was simple: 'Canadians thought of Paul Martin, or even of Paul Hellyer, in the context of Mackenzie King. They thought of Pierre Trudeau as a man for this season, uncontaminated and uninhibited.'[4]

Trudeaumania: The Election of 1968

As soon as Trudeau was sworn in as prime minister along with his first cabinet, he began what became a regular practice: to have Marc Lalonde, the principal secretary to the prime minister, and me to lunch at 24 Sussex Drive, to discuss whatever questions he thought required more time than was possible in our morning meetings in his office. At the first lunch Trudeau raised the number one question: when should he call an election? That was a problem for the politicians, not for me, but I was a fascinated listener.

Trudeau had promised the Liberal convention that he would try to win a majority of seats in every region and 'put an end to the series of minority governments that had plagued Parliament since 1962.' The Liberal mandate of 1965 would normally end in eighteen months. 'Should I first establish my credentials as a prime minister and government leader during the upcoming year? Or should I, on the contrary, strike while the iron was hot, and take our chances with the electorate right away while the leadership convention, with all the publicity that surrounded it, was still in the voters' minds?'[5]

Trudeau and Lalonde chewed the options over along with the typically good alcohol-free lunch. After a lot of weighing of pros and cons, Trudeau turned to me: 'You have been around a lot of prime ministers for a long time, Gordon. Suppose you were PM, what would you do?'

I gulped but decided that, since it was a direct question and since even public servants are entitled to opinions, I would answer: 'I don't see how the situation in a few months could be better than it is right now, and it could be worse. I would go as soon as possible.'

I doubt if my opinion had much weight, if any at all, in Trudeau's decision. However, on 23 April Parliament was dissolved and the election called for 25 June. Trudeau, in his *Memoirs*, downplays the 'Trudeaumania' that became the almost incredible feature of the election. He does, however, give an intellectually aloof admission of the fact:

Almost everywhere I went, exceptional enthusiasm was apparent in the crowds that I found around me. People came in droves to rallies where I was speaking. As well as the phalanx of party members going into the meetings, the streets would be lined with masses of people of all ages and all races. I particularly remember two astonishing turnouts, one in Victoria and another in Montreal. In the British Columbia capital, a city of peaceful, respectable folk, many of them retired, I had to be lowered from a helicopter down to a part at the top of a hill that was totally surrounded by thousands of people ... In Montreal, where the nationalist intelligentsia was already trying to make me into 'the traitor of Quebec,' the huge area of Place Ville-Marie was swarming with people.[6]

Teenage girls, young women, and women generally seemed to be the most smitten by the disease. They oo-ed and ah-ed and gushed at every somersault off a board into a pool, every provocative wink, and almost every body action anywhere. My own daughter, Kerrie, intelligent, rational, but just short of sixteen, became quite ecstatic. It was all too marvellous! Trudeau was so different! So young! So dynamic! After a particularly effusive outburst her mother could take no more: 'Oh, for heaven's sake, Kerrie, Trudeau is just two years younger than your father!'

Facts were of no importance, the ecstasy bore all before it: 'Mum! He's a *generation* younger!'

Kerrie probably had no more than an average female attack of 'Trudeaumania.' The election result was 154 Liberals returned to a House of Commons of 264, with seats in every province but Prince Edward Island.

While the mania was the main factor in the sweep, events at the Saint-Jean-Baptiste parade in Montreal just the day before the election – 24 June – undoubtedly played a role, too. Trudeau, as he describes the scene, was on the platform, 'flanked by the archbishop of Montreal on my left and Daniel Johnson, the premier of Quebec, on my right.' Separatist demonstrators began an attack, throwing rocks and bottles. Nearly all the dignitaries rose and started to leave – but not Trudeau. 'I had absolutely no desire to give in to such a ridiculous display of violence. I detest violence. As a democrat, I will never accept that a small group of agitators can make someone invited by the majority take to his heels by throwing a few stones at him.'[7] The whole attack, and Trudeau's courage in the face of it, was carried on television coast to coast.

The Philosopher in Power

Trudeau says in his *Memoirs* that, 'we had been handed the reins of authority in Canada ... What were we going to do with them?' and he then answers his own question: 'First, we would review the way government itself was run.' I doubt if any minister in his entire cabinet would have put that as a priority at all. However, if there is any part of government where the views of a prime minister reign supreme (and there are many of them), the most certain is in the organization of the cabinet. Trudeau recounts:

I therefore spent the summer after the election putting in place a more rational (my obsession!), better organized system of procedure ... I began by making it clear to the ministers that the cabinet could not consider a single question without having before it a formal memorandum drawn up on the authority of the minister responsible and signed by him or her. This document had to present a clear statement of the question, as well as a run-through of all possible solutions to it, including the one favoured by the signing minister after a careful analysis of the advantages and disadvantages of all of them.[8]

As secretary to the cabinet, I had the responsibility of implementing the changes the prime minister wanted but, in doing so, to warn him of any problems I saw. I was sceptical of the idea of a minister trying to put forward 'all possible solutions' to a question. Many so-called solutions would be straw men, put in to observe the rule but really to be knocked down. It also was likely to mean that no solution, even the best, would be totally worked through if three or four had to be given equal treatment. However, I agreed completely with Trudeau's insistence that every proposal for cabinet consideration be set out in a formal memorandum. The two of us worked out the plan by which cabinet committees would be able to take decisions for the cabinet that would be final unless a minister, not on the committee, gave notice in advance of a wish that the full cabinet reopen the question involved.

In a paper for the annual meeting of the Institute of Public Administration in September 1971, I gave a survey of the way the operation of the Canadian cabinet had changed from 1940, when King ran it out of his vest pocket with no agenda, no secretary, no records, and no written decisions, through the changes brought in by Pearson in 1964 and those instituted by Trudeau. Looking specifically at the result of the changes brought in under Trudeau in 1968, I said: 'The interesting thing is that, as compared with the situation before the revisions in the system were made in 1968, Cabinet is dealing with a larger volume of business but taking only half as many cabinet meetings to do it. The number of cabinet committee meetings has more than doubled and, according to our calculations in the Privy Council Office, the number of "minister-hours" devoted to the total executive function has remained about the same as in 1966–67. The difference is in the more probing, searching and formative nature of discussion that the committees permit, with both ministers and officials present.'[9]

Trudeau says in his *Memoirs*: 'For the cabinet members, it made the practice of ministerial solidarity much easier. This is the fundamental discipline for the coherence of any government: all ministers must be responsible for all decisions made by the government of which they are a part.'[10] I think Trudeau exaggerates the advantage. In my survey in 1971 I noted: 'Ministers now, in many cases, have to give up some share of their authority and control to other ministers if the totality of policies is to be co-ordinated ... Some ministers understandably feel their new share in the policies and programs of others unequal compensation for the subtraction they suffer in their individual capacity to decide and to act. Speed of action is certainly less in the new system and ministers have less chance to appear in roles of clear and firm decision.'[11]

. There can be little doubt but that the reforms of 1968 did considerably improve the operation of the cabinet, but there was a cost, especially for strong ministers and most of all for the minister of finance. John Turner, on one occasion, exploded to me in frustration about trying to handle his complex and critical portfolio 'with twenty-three God damned ministers of Finance!' He was not alone in that kind of feeling.

Apart from the operation of the cabinet and its committees, Trudeau had a passion for what he refers to as 'certain new managerial methods, much in vogue at the time, especially among systems engineers – such as ergonomics, the use of mathematical modelling ... the efficiency of which turned out to be somewhat short-lived.'[12] He says, 'We may have gone a bit overboard at times.' He and a few acolytes certainly did. It was a passion I did not share: I never discerned any advantage in any of it. Nor can I share his confidence in 'the systematic improvements we made in the domain of public spending.' The increase in the federal deficit and the accumulation of so large a part of our present national debt is evidence enough to the contrary. I well remember the despair of Bob Bryce, then deputy minister of Finance, at a meeting of the cabinet committee on priorities and planning, where in theory all wisdom was supposed to be marshalled to see that short-term benefits were not bought at the cost of long-term trouble. The theory was fine but temptation and optimism were sometimes irresistible. When Bob's cautions and pleadings were not succeeding, his final plea, still unheard, was, 'Minister, you can do all these things. You just can't do them all at once!'

The Trudeau government did work with greater confidence and efficiency than the Pearson government. The improved cabinet operation was a major factor, but another was the majority in the House of Commons. A third was that Robert Stanfield, as leader of the opposition, was not John Diefenbaker. He did not see the House of Commons as theatre and had as firm views as Pierre Trudeau about good government and the public interest.

A final factor was the methodical and penetrating scrutiny Trudeau directed at every cabinet document that came forward. He read every page and his superb mind detected any inconsistencies or problems. He was an excellent chairman who let every minister have full opportunity to set out his proposal or his views. But it could be intimidating. He once referred to the sessions as 'post-graduate seminars,' but the professor was unusually exacting and always well informed. Assuring the latter was the duty of the PCO. I insisted that it was not our role to rival or to compete with departments but it was our role to know all the right questions about everything coming forward and to cover them in our briefing of the prime minister.

A prime minister's relations with his colleagues are always good in the sense that no minister, unless he or she is prepared to see his or her career blunted and perhaps ended, can afford to have bad relations. The prime minister's personal regard and assessment of the intellectual quality and judgment – and the value to his government – of a minister is the critical thing. A further factor can be personal history, old friendships in some cases, old rivalries in others. The most inhibiting rivalry for a minister is to have contested with the prime minister the leadership of the party: the most helpful, to have given support when the prime minister was unsure of success and in need of help. While it did not look so at the time, Mitchell Sharp was lucky to suffer the defeat of his budgetary measures in the House of Commons. By dropping out of the contest for the leadership of the Liberal Party, he was able to swing his own support to Trudeau in April 1968 when Trudeau's victory was not certain. Those happy circumstances were not irrelevant when Sharp got the portfolio he wanted – External Affairs – and Paul Martin, who had been a candidate against Trudeau, got the government leadership in the Senate and omission from the cabinet. Sharp's preferment did not, however, soften in any way Trudeau's insistence on a full review of Canadian foreign policy which tested Sharp's patience, but never his loyalty, during countless cabinet committee meetings. It was Trudeau's relations with Pearson, his predecessor and his undeclared sponsor for the party leadership, that were damaged. The review seemed often to be a critical probing of the foreign policy of the Pearson government, of which Pearson himself was the principal architect.

Trudeau's lack of gratitude to Pearson and even of appreciation for his contributions to his party and his country began to show with the handling of the dissolution of Parliament on 23 April 1968. In his *Memoirs* Pearson gives a typically humorous but rueful account of the short session, with him sitting just to the right of the most junior cabinet minister – 'the same place where I had sat when I first entered Parliament.' 'Everyone was jovial and I was wondering what I should say when, as I expected he would, the prime minister declared this was the time to recognize the incomparable services to Canada, to the world, to the interplanetary system, of his predecessor. But I was relieved of that oratorical problem. The prime minister quietly announced dissolution and the Opposition were shocked into complete silence. Of course no one could speak, since there was no Parliament to speak to.'[13]

Pearson, as so often, is apparently light-hearted, but he was deeply hurt. He resented Trudeau's failure to handle proceedings in such a way that he could have made a farewell address to the House. Knowing Robert Stanfield, I have no doubt that he was ready to reply generously to a laudatory farewell by the prime minister but he, too, had no chance.

Prime ministers have to be tough. The enormous patronage at their disposal is a chilling power to blight the hopes of many who are not chosen and to frustrate or to end the careers of colleagues who, in his judgment, do not measure up. The welfare of his government and his party has to come first. No one who knew him could doubt Trudeau's capacity to meet this requirement for his office, but there can also be room for grace and consideration, in manner if not in substance in discharging it. Trudeau was often callous and lacking in this regard.

Trudeau's history of friendship with Jean Marchand and Gérard Pelletier gave his relationship with them a warmth that existed with no other ministers. So far as I could observe, others who came close to enjoying personal friendship and who certainly shared in Trudeau's high regard were Bud Drury, Allan MacEachen, and Otto Lang. Drury was, I think, the most totally selfless minister I ever saw in any government. Trudeau understood, valued, and profited from that quality. He could pass to Drury any disagreement between ministers and departments, especially when Drury had the thankless job of president of the Treasury Board, with the confidence that his judgment would be sound and not influenced by any personal consideration.

Trudeau's confidence in Allan MacEachen on things political was equally high, especially as Trudeau knew that his own knowledge and understanding could not compare. In the case of Otto Lang, Trudeau's regard grew as Lang showed a capacity to handle complex tasks and increasingly burdensome departments from a start as minister without portfolio in July 1968. Donald Macdonald was another for whom confidence grew with his sure handling of the most difficult and critical departments. His intelligence and wit gave a special relaxed quality to their relationship.

The one minister in the cabinet who utterly baffled Trudeau's prowess in debate was Eugene Whalen, minister of agriculture. He was the exact reverse of Trudeau: illogical in argument, obscure in presentation, and almost hopeless to pin down. Trudeau knew nothing about agriculture and found it impossible to penetrate the verbal puzzles that clearly made sense to Whelan. I never saw him get angry: he seemed rather to enjoy Whelan's demonstration that human nature could not always be made to yield to intellect and logic.

The Official Languages Act, 1969

The unilingualism of the public service, the government, and the Parliament of Canada was one of the things that had most infuriated Trudeau when he came into the Privy Council Office in 1949. Had the situation changed when he came back in 1965? 'Hardly at all,' he says in his *Memoirs*. That was not an unfair judgment, although at least one word about what Pearson had declared as the new policy and objectives of his government in April 1966, and had begun to put into effect in the little time he had left, would have been only fair. Now things were really going to change. Trudeau goes on: 'Within weeks of the federal election, I formed a work group that was to draw up, following the general outlines provided by me, a text that would eventually become the Official Languages Act, and would produce a veritable revolution within the federal public service in Ottawa.'[14]

Again Trudeau is less than generous about Pearson's contribution, in this case in setting up the Royal Commission on Bilingualism and Biculturalism five years before. The commission attached great importance to language reform in the federal government's operations. The first volume of its report was entitled 'The Official Languages' and said: 'No other part of the Commission's terms of reference appears to us to be more urgent. If we wish to "develop the Canadian Confederation on the basis of an equal partnership" between the two founding peoples, bilingualism becomes essential first in the institutions shared by all Canadians.'[15] The commission went on: 'Therefore, we recommend that English and French be formally declared the official languages of the Parliament of Canada, of the federal courts, of the federal government, and of the federal administration.'[16]

Trudeau's real contribution was in giving his full authority as prime minister to the 'B and B' recommendations and in attaching the highest priority to them. So that there could be no doubt about his support, he made me chairman of the committee responsible for preparing the Official Languages Act.

When the act was ready for introduction in Parliament, the government was fortunate in its official opposition. As Trudeau says: 'In the House of Commons, the bill occasioned some serious debate, but there was none of the emotional and strident opposition to it that had characterized the debate over the Canadian flag. The majority of the Official Opposition, led by Robert Stanfield, voted with the government. Only a handful of Conservative members – twenty or so – and two or three NDPers refused their support.'[17]

The recommendations of the royal commission on the use of the two languages in government were drafted to extend to the provinces with substantial official language minorities: Quebec, Ontario, and New Brunswick. Quebec had obligations under Section 133 of the British North America Act. New Brunswick and Ontario should, the commission said, 'recognize English and French as official languages and ... accept the language régimes that such recognition entails.'[18] For the provision of services in the languages of the minority, 'we recommend that bilingual districts be established and that negotiations between the federal government and the provincial government concerned define the exact limits of each bilingual district.'[19]

It proved impossible to get the agreement of the provincial governments to establish bilingual districts. The Official Languages Act was drafted to provide for them for federal purposes, with boundaries to be established by a commission of experts on the basis of the census figures of 1961. Drawing the lines led to great dispute; a second effort based on new census figures again was controversial. It was a good proposal, but the government finally decided that establishing the districts as a matter of law would be more provocative than helpful. In the end, provincial participation in bilingual districts for government services – both federal and provincial – could not be secured. The concept was applied for federal purposes only and as a matter of policy only: the provinces were left to their own decisions. New Brunswick, under Premier Hatfield, in the end went beyond the commission's recommendations.

The Trudeau language policy was never one of creating a 'bilingual Canada' or of shoving anything down any throat, as was so often alleged, especially in the west. Far from making it necessary for anyone to learn

French (unless he or she wanted to hold one of the small minority of positions in the federal public service designated as requiring bilingual qualifications), the objective of the policy was to make it possible for more Canadians to use and to be served in their own language. However, it was very easy to misinterpret. 'French on the cornflakes boxes' became an irritant out of all proportion to the burden. The remedy Trudeau recommended was to turn the box around.

The FLQ Crisis

The idea of Canada as 'the peaceable kingdom' was so totally accepted that the kidnapping of James Cross, the British trade commissioner in Montreal, on 5 October 1970 came as a national shock. Soon after, a communiqué by the Front de Libération du Québec (FLQ) claimed credit and set out its demands – among them a ransom of $500,000 in gold, the freeing of more than twenty 'political prisoners,' and safe conduct for the captors to Cuba or Algeria in return for freeing Cross.

A morning meeting of the cabinet committee on priorities and planning found a wide range of views among ministers as to what – if anything – the federal government should do. The government had a responsibility for Cross as a diplomatic representative in Canada but law enforcement in Montreal was a municipal and provincial function. While the RCMP acted as the 'provincial' police force in eight provinces, that was not so in Quebec or Ontario. They had their own provincial police and handled their own law enforcement.

In the course of a rambling, confused meeting I passed a note to the prime minister, as I frequently did in the cabinet and in committees. I suggested three points for government policy: its first responsibility was to ensure the preservation of law and order in Quebec; its second was to do all it could, but subject to the first consideration, to secure the safe release of Cross; its third was to ensure that no concession was made that yielded any profit to blackmail. That meant no ransom, no release of prisoners in jail for criminal offences (there were and are no 'political prisoners' in Canada), and nothing else that would make kidnapping a paying proposition. At the noon break Trudeau told me he agreed. He went on to say that such a policy meant that, if I were kidnapped, he was not going to give priority to saving my life: law and order in Canada came first. I agreed.

The cabinet met in the afternoon. After a much more focused discussion with two draft announcements before the ministers, one I had prepared and one by External Affairs Minister Mitchell Sharp, his was approved and he gave it over television. Referring to the FLQ communiqué, Sharp said: 'Clearly, these are wholly unreasonable demands and their authors could not have expected them to be accepted. I need hardly say that this set of demands will not be met. I continue, however, to hope that some basis can be found for Mr. Cross's safe return. Indeed, I hope the abductors will find a way to establish communications to achieve this end.'[20] An operations centre was set up in the External Affairs side of the East Block with links to the police for information and to the PMO and PCO for the coordination of policy and action.

In the days that followed, Sharp agreed to the reading of a 'political manifesto' of the FLQ that had been one of its demands. He says in his memoirs that the prime minister was angry. 'He thought I was succumbing to the FLQ blackmail. But he did not interfere.' It was a matter of judgment whether the reading would gain anything for the FLQ, and thus be in breach of the approved policy, or not. Trudeau says in his own memoirs that he later decided Sharp had been right.

On Saturday, 10 October, the minister of labour of Quebec, Pierre Laporte, was kidnapped in broad daylight from the lawn of his house on the south shore of the St Lawrence opposite Montreal. It was an action so bold, and apparently so well planned and coordinated, that it made the total absence of any real information about the FLQ even more disturbing and ominous.

The morning after Laporte's abduction – Sunday – Julien Chouinard, later a judge of the Supreme Court of Canada but then secretary to the cabinet of Quebec, telephoned me at my home. He told me that the Quebec and Montreal police were making no progress in locating the FLQ cell that had kidnapped Cross or in finding where he was being held. A problem was that any person picked up because of known or probable connections with the FLQ had to be released by the police in forty-eight hours under provisions of the Criminal Code. It was impossible to hold suspicious people long enough for any effective probing of stories and once they were released they 'disappeared.' The police did not have the resources to keep track of them. There had to be a legal way to hold suspicious individuals longer – and the only way they could find was by having the War Measures Act invoked. I told Chouinard that I thought there was no chance whatever of that being done unless the premier, Robert Bourassa, could personally convince the prime minister of the utter necessity of so unprecedented an action. He accepted that and Premier Bourassa did then call Trudeau.

The War Measures Act could, under its terms, be invoked by proclamation of the governor general-in-council only in a 'state of war, real or apprehended, or of insurrection, real or apprehended.' The cabinet decided that only the governments directly involved, provincial and municipal, had the necessary police and other information to decide whether an 'insurrection' was in fact 'apprehended.' If they did so believe, the premier of Quebec and the mayor of Montreal would have to say so, in writing.

The night of 15–16 October was a long one for me – and for governor general Roland Michener. The letters from Premier Bourassa and Mayor Jean Drapeau were known to be on the way. They arrived shortly after 3:00 A.M. Two orders-in-council had been approved by the cabinet. The assistant clerk of the Privy Council was at Rideau Hall with them, waiting for word from me that the governor general could sign them. One was to proclaim the War Measures Act, the other established regulations under it authorizing the Quebec police to arrest and detain persons suspected of subversive activity.

With the letters in hand, I gave the clearance and at about 3:30 the governor general signed and the act came into effect. At 4:00 A.M. I held a press conference in the Centre Block to explain what had happened, why, and what the legal consequences were. The journalists took quite some convincing that a 'War Measures Act' did not require a war for its proclaiming, that there were real law-and-order problems for which there was no other solution, and that it was not an 'invasion' of provincial jurisdiction but assistance the province had asked for.

Two days later, on Saturday, 17 October, a communiqué from the 'Dieppe Cell' of the FLQ, a different cell from the one that had kidnapped Cross, said, in a rough note of handprinted letters that could not be traced or identified, that Pierre Laporte, 'minister of unemployment and assimilation,' 'had been executed at 6:18 this evening.' It continued: 'You will find the body in the trunk of a green Chevrolet in a parking lot just off St Hubert St.' It was. Laporte had been strangled.

The whole sordid thing was made more sinister by the lack, to that point, of any progress in finding Cross or his captors. I recall wondering, as another of many meetings of ministers, officials, and police groped with the uncertainty, how much the Kerensky government in the summer of 1917 had known about the Bolsheviks who were stirring trouble in Petrograd. They were a rag-tag group whose 'October revolution' was as much attributable to the mistakes of the provisional government as to their own strength and numbers.

The army provided protection to places and people in Quebec and in the national capital area that were thought to be possible targets for attack or kidnapping. All ministers of the federal and provincial governments were in that category and, as the secretary to the cabinet, so was I. The police and the military established the rules: a squad of six soldiers to provide protection for each individual twenty-four hours a day; no movement by him or her outside the 'protected place' without an armed escort. It caused a sensation when I went to the liquor store on Saturday morning and a heavily armed soldier with a machine gun moved in after me. He flatly refused – quite rightly, under his orders – to let me go in alone.

It was hard to get used to, but it seemed harmless enough until an aide to the minister of finance was accidentally shot by a machine-gun going off. As I took a walk a few days later, with my escort beside me and a machine-gun not too far from my ear, I asked him how the accident could have happened: Weren't the safety locks supposed to be kept on? 'Yes, sir, they are, But the guard was an artillery man and he didn't get the lock quite right.' That was a disturbing idea, so I asked: 'What branch are you from?' 'The artillery, sir.'

The armed forces and the guard squads remained in place until the police found and moved in on the Montreal apartment where Cross was being held on 2 December. He was unharmed. His captors got the promised safe conduct to Cuba but nothing else.

Mitchell Sharp says: 'In some respects, it was the prime minister's finest hour when he appeared on television on 16 October. "This government is not acting out of fear. It is acting to prevent fear from spreading. It is acting to maintain the rule of law without which freedom is impossible." On this point Trudeau spoke for us all.'[21] I agree with Sharp. I would go farther. I think that Trudeau's firm leadership, putting the preservation of law and order above any other consideration, was probably the most important single contribution he made to the preservation of peace and democracy in Canada during his time as prime minister. As he put in his *Memoirs*, 'the first duty of the government is to govern – which means never giving in to chaos or terror.'

Some of Trudeau's critics have found it mystifying that the man responsible for the Charter of Rights could implement and defend the course he followed in 1970. There is no inconsistency. The rights in the Charter are established by law and depend on law. If respect for law is flouted or undermined, rights cannot be preserved. The people arrested under the War Measures Act were all released in short order; their rights, and those of Canadians generally, are more surely protected today because Trudeau had the courage not to yield to terrorism. Eighty-seven per cent of respondents to a poll held in all parts of Canada, both anglophone and francophone, indicated their approval of the action of the government.

Trudeau and the World

Pierre Trudeau, whose door in his room at Harvard had proclaimed him as 'Citizen of the World,' and who, with a friend, had gone across much of Europe and Asia on foot, could not possibly limit his interest as prime minister – or his views and style – to domestic affairs. Moreover, he had somewhere developed a degree of reserve about External Affairs and the foreign-policy establishment. His wish to have his own advice was reflected in his early appointment of Ivan Head, a professor of law at the University of Alberta, and briefly in External Affairs, as foreign-policy adviser in the PMO.

In January 1969 Trudeau went to his first meeting of the Commonwealth heads of government in London. The fact that I, as secretary to the cabinet, went with him had no relation to any views he might have about External Affairs. The Commonwealth meetings were different from all other 'international' gatherings; indeed, they were not considered by the participants to be 'international' at all. The meetings with the heads of colonial governments began in 1887 as imperial conferences, where the colonies would gather together in London, usually on the occasion of jubilees or coronations, with the 'mother country,' Britain; at such conferences, enthused in their sense of being a part of so great an imperial community, the colonies would be given some insight into the foreign policy of the Empire, which was entirely in British hands, and their loyalty to the crown would be strengthened, and so it was hoped by British authorities. Not all the colonies were invited: only the largest and most important – and all white.

In the First World War the meetings became the Imperial War Cabinet. After 'Commonwealth status' was established in 1931, they became 'Commonwealth conferences' but an important aspect of their character was – and still is – that the participants were always the heads of government getting together for informal discussions made easy by a common language and a common political heritage. With that background, there is still a frankness in the sessions never experienced in 'international' conferences where dignity and protocol are important.

Mitchell Sharp had become secretary of state for external affairs after the election of 1968 and he was one of the delegation in 1969 – as he says, 'for the first and only time.' He apparently told Trudeau at the end of the meeting that 'one of us was superfluous and I knew which one.'[22]

I had tried to give Trudeau some sense in advance of the nature and atmosphere of the meetings, for I had been to several with Mackenzie King and Lester Pearson. I told him that both prime ministers had found the meetings interesting, informative, and useful. They had also found that the chance to talk informally to other men with cabinets to direct was particularly valuable. St Laurent had formed a genuine friendship with Nehru that was important for both of them and for closer relations between India and Canada.

I do not think that I persuaded Trudeau before he experienced it himself. The pictures of his famous pirouette on going in to the Queen's banquet at Buckingham Palace, featured in all the London papers, appeared to be a gesture of disdain. However, subsequent conferences made it clear that he had changed his mind. He formed close relations with the heads of several African governments. When we were in Singapore in 1970, Trudeau talked to its prime minister, Lee Kuan Yew, about politics, party organization, and handling of a cabinet with more frankness than he would have with any provincial premier in Canada. He was anxious to have the Commonwealth meeting in Ottawa in 1973. He gave it his full attention and he carried it off with his usual style.

The full review of Canadian foreign policy and of the role of Canada in NATO in 1969 produced debate in the cabinet committee on priorities and planning and also in full cabinet of a kind there had never been before. It put the departments of external affairs and defence under great strain and absorbed the time of ministers, officials, and senior military officers for weeks. The two studies were almost certainly desirable: too much of policy had been taken for granted and had continued after international circumstances had changed. It was, perhaps, not the 'philosopher in power' who drove the review, but it was certainly the sceptic.

In the spring of 1970 contacts made at the Commonwealth meeting of 1969, as well as an invitation to visit the World's Fair in Japan, led to a 'tour of the Pacific' – to New Zealand, Australia, Singapore, Malaysia, Hong Kong, and Japan. Trudeau invited me to go with him, along with my old friend A.E. (Ed) Ritchie, who was then under-secretary of state for external affairs. We did not have much to do. Canadian relations with most of the countries except Japan were scant at that time, there were no major issues to discuss, and in Japan the focus was on the Fair at Osaka, not on business in Tokyo.

The first stop on the tour, apart from overnight in Hawaii, was Wellington, New Zealand. The airfield there was too small to handle the four-motor RCAF plane that was taking the party of officials, journalists, and high commissioners in Ottawa of the Commonwealth countries we were visiting. The idea of a 'Team Canada,' with a focus on trade and consisting of representatives of provinces and business and all the apparatus of prime ministerial expeditions, had not yet emerged, but the group was large. The plane put down at a RNZAF base and we transferred, in instalments, to a smaller plane for the short flight to Wellington. Ed and I were in the first instalment with the prime minister.

I suppose that it must have been lonely at that time to be way off in the southern Pacific with only Australia nearby. Visits by heads of governments were rare. The prime minister of New Zealand, Keith Holyoake, was on the red carpet with hand out when the prime minister of Canada emerged from the plane. He took us at once into the very small terminal for a formal ceremony of welcome before the members of the government and the diplomatic corps of Wellington. The two prime ministers were on a platform, the packed audience below.

Holyoake waxed eloquent about the distinguished visitor, the greatness of Canada, and all the things New Zealand and Canada had in common. The theme carried him to an enthusiastic peroration about the features New Zealand and Canada shared – 'We have our Maoris and you, prime minister, have your French Canadians!'

There was no real gasp, just a freezing of faces and eyes – including those of Pierre Trudeau. Not a flicker of expression on his face indicated that anything doubtful had been said. His remarks in reply were courteous and did pick up the theme of things that were shared by the two countries, including the Aboriginal peoples – Maoris in New Zealand, Indians and Inuit in Canada. It was never quite clear whether Holyoake realized what he had said, but there was not the easy warmth between the two prime ministers that was so evident later in Singapore.

In Australia, Trudeau caused his host government some anxious hours by insisting on snorkel diving at the Great Barrier Reef off the coast of Queensland. It was only a few months after Prime Minister Harold Holt, an enthusiastic swimmer, had not returned from a swim: there was never any explanation – possibly a shark, possibly an undertow. The Australians were not enthusiastic about the risk of having a visiting prime minister disappear in turn, but Trudeau was not to be deterred. It was the same spirit that kept him on the platform in Montreal in 1968 against all urging and advice.

In Hong Kong a dinner had been arranged for Trudeau with a group of business leaders and their wives. All were, not surprisingly, Chinese but all spoke English with no difficulty. The meal was delicious, with dishes of Canton, Szechwan, and Mandarin cuisine, but the most memorable thing for me was the pride those businessmen, each a millionaire dozens of times over, had in the return of China to sovereignty and power after its conquest by Japan in the 1930s. The economic system was communist – anathema to them – the government was a Marxist dictatorship, but China was their country and they were proud of it. It made it easy to believe that the scheduled return of Hong Kong to China in 1997 would not be as troublesome as one might think.

In Tokyo the magnificent residence of the Canadian ambassador, so wisely bought by our first minister to Japan, Sir Herbert Marler, for a tiny fraction of its later value, was the scene of a lunch for Trudeau and some of the Japanese business leaders. They were a most impressive group. Among other things they discussed the advantage Japan had – and would have – in, quite unlike Canada, having no significant natural resources except their people and their brains. With enormous ships, built in Japan, to carry great tonnages at costs that were a trifling part of the value of sophisticated finished products, they could get the best raw materials, no matter where, at the lowest prices and produce in great quantity. It was a new idea for someone who had thought how fortunate Canada was in having all its resources!

One result of the trip for me was to come to the same conclusion as Mitchell Sharp did after going to the 1969 Commonwealth meeting in London: in a touring party with the prime minister, with an external affairs officer for advice and Ivan Head for speeches, one of us was superfluous – and I knew which one. There was no need for the secretary to the cabinet, especially with the federal-provincial discussions on the constitution becoming more active and the problems with Quebec more troublesome. I did not go on tour again.

chapter thirteen

Trudeau and the Constitution, 1968–1979

Before he became a minister in the Pearson government in 1965, Trudeau had argued against attempting a reform of the constitution: it would be a 'can of worms.' The first ten years of his life as prime minister were to show how right he had been. That does not mean that Pearson had been wrong in launching the atttempt. In the national circumstances of 1968, a prime minister concerned about the unity of the country had little choice but to make the effort. And when he became prime minister, Trudeau realized that he in turn had no choice but to implement the commitment that had been made at the conference just two months before. However, even so fearless a man might have been appalled if he had known how completely constitutional reform was to occupy his time in office. Trudeau was prime minister for two lengthy terms: from 1968 to 1979 and from 1980 to 1984. The constitution dominated both of them and even his success in the second has left a legacy of division within Quebec, and between Quebec and the rest of Canada, that will warp our politics well into the third millennium.

From the time he accepted the inevitability of pursuing the problem, Trudeau realized that if he was to succeed, it could only be with an agenda laid down by the federal government and relentlessly pressed by him personally. Nine provinces out of the ten would cheerfully have allowed the exercise to expire: there was no change they wanted sufficiently to pay the price in time and effort as difficulties emerged over many issues.

A positive federal agenda was developed and Trudeau made it the first priority of his new government. From 1968 to 1971, conferences of first ministers, continuing committees of ministers [CCMC], and a continuing committee of officials on the constitution [CCOC] became, whether they liked it or not, a cavalcade that absorbed the time and the attention of all premiers. It looked for a time as if it would achieve success at the Victoria conference of 1971. But when Victoria failed, Trudeau let the problem lie until the growing strength of the Parti Québécois in Quebec made it clear that yet another effort had to be launched. It was barely begun when the election of a separatist government in Quebec in 1976 gave a new and special urgency to the problem of national unity.

All of this was yet to be discovered when, shortly after he became prime minister but before plunging into the election campaign of 1968, Trudeau discussed constitutional strategy with Marc Lalonde and me. He then wrote to the premiers proposing what we thought would be a necessary first step: a meeting of the continuing committee of officials that had been agreed to in February 'to assist the Constitutional Conference in its task.' The prime minister proposed that it meet 'towards the end of May.'

As chairman of the committee, I, along with a strong federal delegation, had the responsibility of bringing out of the meeting a plan of operation that would advance the government's priorities in the midst of differing provincial views, including a profound distaste among all the premiers except premiers Johnson of Quebec and Robarts of Ontario at having to give time and attention to the exercise at all.

That absence of provincial interest was subject to one important qualification that Claude Morin, the senior Quebec official, understood very well. If Quebec proposed – as it was bound to do – withdrawal of the federal government from every area that was constitutionally provincial, many provinces would find it difficult to disagree, as long as federal money continued to be available for whatever cost would be involved in a province taking over the function. By using its 'spending power' under the constitution, the federal government had, in the post-war period and with provincial agreement, developed 'shared-cost programs' in several areas of provincial jurisdiction. Hospital insurance, health care, welfare, post-secondary education grants – all were of that kind. The financial capacities of the provinces differed widely. If services of national standards, common for all Canadians, were to be available, there had to be a major federal role in developing and paying for them. But it is not an attractive proposition for federal governments and parliaments to impose taxes and raise money simply to pass it over to the provinces to spend. 'Equalization,' a federal policy that emerged in 1957, did precisely that, but there were limits to federal willingness to carry the political load of taxing and get none of the political credit for providing the service.

In addition to policy areas that were affected by use of the spending power and shared-cost programs, there were many areas not clearly either federal or provincial under the distribution of legislative powers in the British North America Act of 1867. Federal legislation had often been challenged in the courts by various provinces, most often Ontario in the early years of Confederation. During Jean Lesage's 'Quiet Revolution,' many untested areas were seen by Quebec as properly provincial – culture, research, social policy, much of environment, local broadcasting, forests, parks.

Claude Morin was not at that stage a committed separatist, if indeed he was then a separatist at all. He worked for both Liberal and Union Nationale governments. The Parti Québécois had not existed until early 1968 and was not elected to office until 1976. Morin was, however, a strong Quebec nationalist. For purposes of the continuing committee and for the conference itself, the important thing was that he was a genius at contriving proposals that were politically difficult for other provinces to resist – once they had been raised.

It was clearly going to be no easy task to produce a structure for the conference that would be manageable for the premiers in the midst of all their higher priorities at home. They would have to be convinced of the value of all constitutional changes that were proposed, with implications that might not be at all obvious. But there were limits to the time they could give to the task.

For the tedious dog work and first testing of proposals, the continuing committee of officials soon learned how well – if ambiguously – it had been named. It became its task to work through all the essential preparations, to identify the problems that would emerge, to alert the first ministers, and to test possible solutions in the hope that progress might be possible in ministerial sessions. So far as the federal delegation was concerned, the problem was to see that no positions were compromised while debate proceeded on all sorts of proposals however improbable or contrary to the federal interest.

The Rough Road to the Victoria Conference
The main part of the memorandum for the cabinet was on 'priorities and strategy in general.' It said:

At least from a tactical point of view, it is probably advantageous for the federal government to give priority to the implementation of the recommendations of the Royal Commission on Bilingualism and Biculturalism, to the adoption and entrenchment of the Canadian Charter of Human Rights, to the reform of central institutions such as the Supreme Court and the Senate, and perhaps, because of the rapidly changing situation in the field of external affairs, to the question of federalism and international relations. For the review of several of those matters, – e.g. linguistic rights and human rights, – the federal government is likely to encounter stiff resistance in provinces such as British Columbia and Alberta, and only cautious interest in some other provinces such as Ontario.

On the other hand, Quebec will press, as a matter of priority, for the review of the distribution of powers with particular reference to social security – medicare, family allowances, manpower services, old age pensions – broadcasting, the curtailment of the federal spending power and of the federal power to declare that certain local works and undertaking are for the general advantage of Canada, the federal power of disallowance and reservation, the residual powers, the power of delegation and the power over marriage and divorce.[1]

The memorandum set out proposals for dealing with various items and ended:

The general organization of the Continuing Committee and the Secretariat, the establishment of sub-committees on linguistic rights and on human rights, the general discussion although not the substance of the distribution of powers and of external powers and, if the cabinet so wishes, of the Senate and the Supreme Court, will provide more than a sufficient agenda for the first meeting of the Committee of Officials. The other matters which the Constitutional Conference had agreed should be examined are the question of regional disparities, the amending procedures and provisional arrangements and the mechanisms of federal-provincial consultation. These, it is submitted, could be kept for consideration at a later stage.[2]

The magnitude of the task was all too apparent and yet there seemed no way to avoid it.

Since the 'agreement without Quebec' in 1981, the 'patriation' of the constitution and passage of the Charter of Rights over the opposition of the government of Quebec in 1982, and his furious opposition to the Meech Lake Accord in 1987, Pierre Trudeau has come to be regarded as the consistently uncompromising opponent of any change designed to meet demands from Quebec. That reputation fails to take into account the enormous efforts he made between 1968 and the defeat of the Liberal Party in 1979 – eleven years – to meet the objectives of federalist leaders in Quebec, along with his own clear objectives for a better constitution. A condition for him from the beginning was that the changes should not endanger the needs of a strong and effective government for Canada. Subject to that fundamental, virtually every possibility for change could be on the table.

Pearson's conference in February had agreed to establish a secretariat to serve the constitutional conference and whatever committees it might set up. Edgar Gallant, a fully bilingual Acadian from Prince Edward Island, who, while a federal public servant, had the confidence of all governments, had been appointed secretary in March 1968. The secretary's report on 'The Constitutional Review, 1968–1971' provides the factual record of the first three years of the Trudeau government's virtually constant effort in the constitutional file.

The full constitutional conference had seven meetings: four mostly public conferences, televised for public information, and three working sessions in camera – the only way in which hard bargaining can go forward with a frank expression of positions and any hope of mutual concession and agreement. Several committees of ministers were established at the second conference in February 1969. Some were to examine specific questions and report to the conference as a whole: official languages, fundamental rights, the judiciary, and the Senate. Others were on regional disparities among the provinces, tax structure, and the national capital region.

The policy and priorities of the federal government had been set out in two publications for the conference of February of 1968: *Federalism for the Future*, in the name of Prime Minister Pearson, and *A Canadian Charter of Human Rights*, under that of Pierre Trudeau as minister of justice. Trudeau had a more reasoned concept of objectives and policy for the constitution than anyone else, politician or public servant, in either the federal or provincial governments. These were further developed in a third publication – *The Constitution and the People of Canada* – in February 1969.

An entrenched charter of rights was the first federal priority, including language rights. The structure and powers of the Senate should be reviewed 'to enable it to play a more vital role in reflecting the federal character of our country'; provision should be made in the constitution for the Supreme Court. Other issues were suggested, even including so rash a proposition as to study, jointly with all governments, 'the form of provincial political institutions.' Legal drafts were included for consideration by the provinces 'as part of an approach to constitutional review which would involve a systematic, logical and complete examination of the Constitution.'

No province was equipped to join in anything of the kind nor was any, except Quebec, interested in so sweeping an exercise. Indeed, it was not until 1973, after the oil-supply crisis triggered by the Organization of Petroleum Exporting Countries (OPEC) and action by the federal government to give its petroleum tax priority over provincial oil royalties, that any provincial government other than that of Quebec thought it had a real interest in any constitutional change whatever. Inevitably there were differences of view about proposals put forward by Quebec or by the federal government, especially when federal financial transfers to the provinces were involved, an issue that profoundly divided the 'have' from the 'have not' provinces. The whole exercise was a very low political priority for any premier but that of Quebec, with Premier Robarts supporting it because of his initiative in 1967, based on his sense of the importance for Ontario – and for Canada – of trying to meet the discontents of Quebec that had been brought out so dramatically by the Royal Commission on Bilingualism and Biculturalism.

After two years of largely fruitless effort and growing exasperation on the part of most premiers, it became clear that the comprehensive review contemplated by Pearson and Trudeau was not feasible within the time that was politically possible. For reasons of national unity, there had to be some progress soon. It could be achieved only with a limited 'package' of change and a specific target date for agreement. The suggestion of Premier W.A.C. Bennett that the next full conference should be held in Victoria to celebrate the centennial of the entry of British Columbia into confederation provided both target and incentive. Not the least of its advantages was that one of the most reluctant participants in the exercise would suddenly become an active promoter. 'Wacky' Bennett was too good a politician to want to be the host to a conference that failed.

A further factor that favoured the 1971 target was the victory of the Liberals led by Robert Bourassa in the Quebec election of April 1970. Trudeau says in his *Memoirs*: 'Sensing a chance to break the constitutional impasse, I sent Gordon Robertson, the Clerk of the Privy Council, and Marc Lalonde, my principal secretary, to Quebec City with the instructions: "Go to Quebec, talk to Mr. Bourassa and his officials, see what this particular Quebec government wants and we'll see if we can accept it ourselves and sell it to the rest of the country."'[3]

On his side, the new premier helped the prospects for agreement by leaving Claude Morin out of his team of constitutional advisers. As Trudeau says, Marc and I 'duly met with Julien Chouinard, the secretary of the cabinet and every detail was approved by Bourassa himself. At one point Quebec proposed an amending formula that would give it a right of veto over any constitutional amendment, which was a big thing to ask of us, and a big thing to ask of the other premiers. But Bourassa said, "That's my bottom line." So we went to work, coming up with a package of proposals that met Quebec's demands at the time and yet went a long way towards meeting our federal objectives.'[4]

In fact, there was not one but a series of meetings by Lalonde and me with Chouinard and his group. The difference in atmosphere from any session that included Morin was notable. Chouinard, later a judge on the Supreme Court of Canada, was a committed federalist. His interest was in trying to achieve arrangements that would advance the capacity of Quebec to accomplish the objectives of its 'Quiet Revolution' as a part of a united Canada.

The second working session of the constitutional conference was held in September 1970 for the first ministers to discuss in private just how to handle an escape from the comprehensive review without appearing to have failed or to have closed the door on further reform. The conclusions as recorded are brief: 'First Ministers emphasized the importance of the extensive work already done, which makes for a better understanding of the varied implications of the complex issues raised; also it enables each First Minister to have a full appreciation of the views, interests and concerns of the others.'[5]

That was undoubtedly true, but all the first ministers were agreed on the need to achieve progress soon. Accordingly: 'The Conference concluded that it was important for the federal and provincial governments to continue and complete the task which they had undertaken in 1968 and to determine what changes are required to provide constitutional arrangements in Canada that are adequate for current and future needs. It was agreed, also, that this task should be completed as quickly as was practicable.'[6] The final conclusion of the session was to 'accept the invitation of the prime minister of British Columbia to meet in Victoria in June 1971.'

The third working session of February 1971 gave shape to the 'package' for action:

In accordance with the conclusions of their working session last September, the First Ministers gave priority to the questions of an amending formula and an early patriation of the Canadian Constitution. The Conference agreed that the Government of Canada and the provinces should proceed as quickly as possible to patriate the Constitution, with an appropriate amending formula applicable entirely within Canada, and with such other changes as can be agreed upon quickly. This approach would permit a substantial degree of progress to be made quickly, while work on other aspects of constitutional revision continues.[7]

With the lines of the 'package' reasonably clear, John Turner, then minister of justice, Don Thorson, his deputy minister, and I continued a tour of the provinces that had begun in January, meeting with each premier personally. The main problem was to keep the package small: several premiers had some particular provincial concern that they would like to work in while still escaping from the former 'comprehensive' plan. Turner was an excellent envoy for the task. He was a lawyer, at ease with constitutional issues, and he was also a shrewd politician with a quick capacity to understand where the political pressures were for a premier and how they might be eased by deft drafting. He had the capacity to put himself at ease with every premier regardless of political differences. He and Trudeau had enough ambitions and qualities in common that there was a degree of rivalry between them and never any intimacy. But Trudeau had full confidence in him for his delicate task.

Marc Lalonde's and my meetings with Julien Chouinard and his team gave us confidence that Premier Bourassa and his government were in full agreement with the package we were putting to the other provinces. However, there were pressures on the premier that emerged at an ad hoc meeting of ministers on 31 May to look at the draft charter for Victoria. Claude Castonguay, the minister of social affairs of Quebec, asked for 'immediate consideration of a change with respect to family allowances and manpower training through their addition to Section 94A of the BNA Act.'[8] The secretary's report continues: 'The Chairman of the ad hoc meeting, Mr. John Turner, declared that he had understood that Quebec's proposal would be limited to making certain administrative arrangements with respect to manpower training, a proposal which he had asked other provinces to consider during his bilateral discussions on the substance of the draft Charter. He had therefore been surprised when in mid-May a specific text for revising section 94A had been put forward by Quebec with more extensive proposals.'[9]

The Quebec proposals had come as a surprise after the four months of discussions. It was indeed, as Trudeau says in his *Memoirs*, 'a shocker' but the first intimation of it was two weeks before Victoria, not, as Trudeau recalls,[10] at the conference itself. I first heard of it in a telephone call from Julien Chouinard, probably about the time of the 31 May discussion. I told him that so significant a change so late in the game had to be communicated to the prime minister at once – and by Bourassa personally. I thought it would be impossible for the prime minister to accept. There was not much difference between information then, two weeks before the conference, and at Victoria itself. It was, in the end, what was to destroy the Victoria agreement.

Trudeau invited my wife and me to fly with him and his wife of just three months in the government 'Jet Star' to Victoria for the conference. The most fascinating part of the trip was to observe what must have become an increasing frustration for Margaret in being married to a man capable of the total self-discipline and concentration that Pierre Trudeau displayed on the flight.

It was no small task for him to have in contemplation the chairmanship of a conference on which the future of the country and the shape of its constitution would turn. We, in the Privy Council Office, had prepared the usual enormous briefing book for the prime minister covering every aspect of the conference that we could foresee, including the probable positions of all the premiers, how best they could be dealt with and the implications of any surprises that might emerge – including, of course, the new development in the Quebec position. Trudeau had had no time to discuss with me, as his senior official adviser, all the issues he would have to deal with and any questions about people, policies, and drafts that might emerge. That was why Bea and I were on the plane – and why Trudeau turned to the book almost the moment the plane took off from Ottawa.

The Trudeaus were dressed in the casual outfits appropriate for the spirit of the 1960s – T-shirts, jeans, bare feet, and everything casual. Pierre had the briefing book and other papers spread out on one side of a folding desk: Margaret was on the other side. It would probably have been impossible for a bride of three months not to caress with her beautiful, bare pink feet those of her beloved. Trudeau's concentration on his papers did not flag for a second: he was totally oblivious to anything but the pages he was absorbing. He had all the main issues clear in his mind for discussion by the time we landed in Winnipeg to refuel. The Trudeaus wandered through the terminal during the refuelling, recognized by some but with no mob scene. Perhaps marriage had taken the edge off Trudeaumania. When the flight resumed, Trudeau and I got back to the book. It was a working flight.

The Trudeaus, Bea, and I stayed that night in a country house outside Victoria that had been put at the prime minister's disposal by a local admirer. Breakfast the following morning was in a nearby restaurant. Margaret had left earlier that morning for an appointment in Vancouver. I suspect it was an act when Trudeau purported to be baffled by the plastic marmalade container on the plate by his toast and turned to Bea for assistance. It took quite some time and careful demonstration before the prime minister finally got access to the inadequate daub.

Premier Bennett, as host of the conference, had planned it as a great show for both the people of British Columbia and his guests from beyond the mountains. A motorcade through Victoria preceded the formal opening in the Legislative Chamber of the ornate, domed parliament building looking out on Victoria harbour. The setting was superb. At the end of the second day, the largest and newest of the BC ferries was diverted from its appointed task to take the conference for a sunset cruise and a sumptuous dinner as the premier's guests. The centennial theme was constant as was British Columbia's role in the making of Canada 'from sea to sea.' Even Premier Duplessis, for the conference of 1950 in Quebec, had not been a more hospitable host. There were other similarities. Both premiers ran their provinces as autocrats – ministers were non-entities – and both could be charmingly impervious to argument. Neither argued a point: a position was stated and any differences were allowed to roll off under a benign smile.

The fourth day of the conference was exhausting: thirteen hours of meetings, some in a committee on the Supreme Court with John Turner in the chair, others in a closed full conference with Trudeau in the chair. At closed 'working sessions' of the constitutional conference before Victoria, all officials – federal, provincial and conference secretariat – had attended as in open sessions. On 17 June, however, it was clear that very difficult discussion and bargaining were unavoidable if all the differences that still remained, especially between an angry Trudeau and a worried Bourassa, were to be resolved. The prime minister and premiers decided that the best prospects would emerge if they, the first ministers, were utterly alone except for Henry Davis, who had taken over from Edgar Gallant as secretary of the conference. Unaided even by a stenographer, he would have to keep track of the twists and turns of discussion and try to have clear, at the end, just what had been agreed – and what not. It was a nerve-racking task with no one to spell him off. The only gaps for Henry to catch up came when the first ministers felt they needed refreshment or relief.

The most difficult problem was the Quebec position on social policy – the 'shocker' that had emerged after months of discussion both bilaterally, between the federal side and Quebec, and multilaterally as we, on the federal team, carried the apparent agreement with Quebec to the other premiers. It was not surprising that they, like Trudeau, had little sympathy with a belated effort to get 'more' after an initial 'bottom line' had been accepted. The pressure on Bourassa was intense to accept the proposed amendment to Section 94A as it had been included in the draft charter before he and his cabinet had second thoughts.

In spite of his isolation, and his awareness that the agreement, with many features he and his government wanted, might utterly vanish if it was not sealed in that session, Bourassa stayed firm: he had to consult his colleagues in the cabinet before he could commit Quebec to the charter as it stood. Frustrated and exhausted, the others finally agreed to a delay of ten days. If the charter was not rejected by any party to it within that time, it would stand. Bourassa promised to call the prime minister as soon as he had his cabinet's answer.

The normal procedure after a closed 'working session' was for the prime minister to give a press conference and for the premiers to talk to their press as they wished – or as might have been agreed. With the uncertainty about the result – and with Trudeau and Bourassa in sharp disagreement – a more modest procedure seemed wise. The charter, as it stood, would be published; most of it had been discussed in open sessions in any case. The prime minister and the premiers would say whatever each thought wise. To deal with questions, officials would meet with the press and be careful not to step off the very narrow path of a virtual agreement that was a major achievement, subject to a telephone call to confirm. My recollection is that Quebec was not represented at my session with the press which began well after midnight and ended at about two in the morning. I have rarely been more tired than when it was over.

The next day we flew to Vancouver to board the large RCAF plane that could not land at Victoria airport. It was to take all those going to Ottawa. The plane had engine trouble and I got a couple of hours of much needed sleep on the grass at the edge of the field.

The Victoria Charter, 1971
'The Canadian Constitutional Charter, 1971' began with a declaration of the political rights of Canadians: the fundamental freedoms of con-

science, religion, opinion, expression, peaceful assembly, and association. For the first time in a country based on the British system, the principle of parliamentary supremacy was to be breached. No law of the Parliament of Canada or of the legislature of a province 'shall abrogate or abridge any of the fundamental freedoms herein recognized and declared.' This declaration may now seem unimpressive – almost obvious – but agreement on it came only after a good deal of debate in sessions before Victoria when the federal draft proposals on 'rights' were under discussion. It was a revolution in a parliamentary system.

With the failure of the Victoria Charter the whole discussion about a charter of rights had to be reopened when negotiations resumed in 1976. In the interim, Manitoba, Alberta, and Saskatchewan all had elected new premiers. During the new discussions, premiers Sterling Lyon from Manitoba and Allan Blakeney from Saskatchewan – one Conservative and one NDP – argued strongly and eloquently that the best and surest protection of democratic government and human rights in the world had come through the parliamentary tradition and principles. The most impressive declaration of rights was probably in the USSR where the reality was the worst. An active democracy and a free parliament were the best guarantors and put protection in the hands of elected representatives of the people. But, in the end, the declaration of rights carried once again. It is remarkable, in retrospect, how little public interest there was in the issue either in 1971 or during sessions before 1979. It was only later, with the renewal of negotiations leading to 'patriation' of the constitution in 1981–2, that the Charter of Rights began to attract the public interest that has grown enormously since.

In the Victoria charter the provision on 'Language rights' declared that 'English and French are the official languages of Canada': another first. They were to have 'the status and protection set forth in this part.' The rights included use in the debates of Parliament and in the legislatures of seven of the ten provinces: the three most western provinces were not, at that time, prepared to cope with that commitment. Other provisions about the printing of statutes, evidence in the courts, and communications with government would bind the federal government, Quebec, and different groups of other provinces as each felt it could accept the commitment. A province not immediately bound by the charter provisions could opt in later and thereafter it would continue to be bound unless and until the right was abrogated by a formal amendment of the constitution.

The provisions were less than the federal government wanted but the most that could be squeezed out of provincial governments worried by their particular political and language problems, especially in the West where in all cases some languages other than French were spoken by far more people than spoke French. The hope was that, with the constitutional declaration of the status of French, more provinces would gradually opt in to additional rights and remain locked in. Over time, a general pattern would emerge.

The Supreme Court would, for the first time, be establishd by the constitution – indeed, by twenty-one articles that, for the most part, wrestled with the problem of giving the provinces, through their attorneys general, rights to be consulted and to agree on appointments to the court. Three judges at least were to be from the Quebec bar.

On the new process of consultation, if, after ninety days, the attorney general of Canada and that of the province concerned had not agreed on an appointment, the attorney general of Canada could inform his counterpart in the province that he proposed to convene a 'nominating council,' the membership of which was specified in the charter. Again there were provisions for agreement on membership of the nominating council within six months. And finally, if, after delays that could add up to as much as three hundred and thirty days, there still was no agreement, 'the Attorney General of Canada may select the person to be appointed.' The process was cumbersome and so much possible delay was undesirable, but the problem was real. The federal government had gone as far as it could in the commitment to consult without losing the capacity, at the end, to appoint some qualified person. It was a finely balanced process, with concessions on both sides.

The revision of Section 94A of the constitution raised the issue of the belated ambitions of the Bourassa government for full provincial control over social programs. The charter added 'family, youth and occupational training allowances' to the old age pensions and disability benefits already covered by the section.[11] It provided that federal legislation 'shall not affect the operation of any law present or future of a Provincial Legislature.' That additional scope of the section was not enough, Claude Castonguay thought, to make possible the unified social policy he wanted for Quebec, with full financial compensation for the province if it opted out of a federal social program.

Part VII of the charter committed the governments to promote 'equality of opportunity and well being for all individuals in Canada' and also to the 'promotion of economic development to reduce disparities,' along with 'equalization' payments to provinces to assure 'that essential public services of reasonable quality are available to all individuals in Canada.'

Agreement on the constitutional commitment to equalization was no small triumph for the 'have not' provinces of Canada – the Atlantic provinces especially but also Quebec, Manitoba, and Saskatchewan. It was the first time that such a constitutional provision had been accepted by a federal government and by the wealthier provinces. Premier Bennett was the hardest of all to persuade. It probably would not have been possible except in the euphoria of Victoria and the centennial.

Part IX set forth the 'Victoria formula' for amendments to the constitution. There was at that time no amending formula. Amendments to our constitution were still made by the British Parliament at the request of the two Houses of the Parliament of Canada. The extent of consultation with and agreement by the provinces was undefined and would become a critical matter when Trudeau proposed to 'go it alone' in 1982. Amendments would, under the Charter, require resolutions of the Senate and House of Commons and 'of the Legislative Assemblies of at least a majority of the provinces that includes: (1) every Province that at any time before the issue of such proclamation had, according to any previous general census, a population of at least twenty-five per cent of the population of Canada [which meant Ontario and Quebec]; (2) at least two of the Altantic Provinces; (3) at least two of the Western Provinces that have, according to the then latest general census, combined populations of at least fifty per cent of the population of all the Western Provinces.'

The logic of the formula was based on the principle established at Confederation in 1867 of equality of the then three regions – Ontario, Quebec, and the Maritime provinces – in appointments to the Senate. The regional-equality principle had been extended with a fourth equal region for Senate membership – the West – in 1915. Under the charter provision, every region would have a veto on a constitutional amendment and the western region would have to include either Alberta or British Columbia to provide 50 per cent of the western population.

There was no requirement for unanimous consent of the provinces for any amendment whatever. The result, had the charter survived, would have been a constitution much more flexible and capable of adjustment to the changing needs of Canada than we now have under the Constitution Act, 1982. The so-called Vancouver formula in that act, with subsequent federal commitments following the referendum of 1995, and provincial legislation requiring referendums in Alberta and British Columbia, has produced a constitution that is now virtually unamendable.

The final part of the charter was a provision for 'Modernization of the

Constitution' with repeal of many provisions, including the federal power of reservation and disallowance of provincial statutes.

Premier Bourassa Backs Away

At the end of the exhausting 17 June session, it was by no means certain that the Victoria charter was going to fail. Quebec had not got all it wanted but Bourassa had a good deal to lose if his answer was 'No.' On 23 June the answer came: Quebec would not accept.

There was more contempt than anger in the prime minister's reaction, but the anger was great and to my mind entirely justified. The whole constitutional review had been started because of Quebec: neither the federal government nor any other province had been seeking change in 1968. He had given the review the top priority of his new government because of Quebec and had commissioned Marc Lalonde and me to determine what Bourassa's 'bottom line' was, to work on that basis, to get a deal, and to sell it to the other provinces. His minister of justice, John Turner, had seen every premier, confident that what he was persuading them to accept would meet Quebec's demands. All of that had been done over weeks and months, and then the 'bottom line' had been changed. Not only did the government of Quebec want provincial paramountcy for all areas of social policy, it was now insisting on full financial compensation to cover the cost of any program of its own if it did not accept a federal one. And any such right for Quebec would obviously not be accepted if it was not given to all provinces. As Trudeau puts it in his *Memoirs*, Ottawa 'would be raising the money through taxes but the provinces would receive it as a lump sum and distribute as they wished.' The government of Canada would cease to have direct relations with the citizens of Quebec. A government taxing Quebecers, but unable to do anything openly for them, would not long preserve national unity. Trudeau had no doubts: it was better to have no deal than that.

It is impossible to know whether Bourassa could have won a contest with nationalist critics and organizations that had mounted a furious opposition to the Victoria charter. Quebec would have gained much from it: a veto on future constitutional change (something its governments have since sought vainly to establish), provincial paramountcy over new areas of social policy – family, youth, and occupational training allowances, a constitutional guarantee of three judges out of eight from Quebec on the Supreme Court, with consultation on their appointment, and termination of the federal powers of reservation and disallowance of provincial legislation. Trudeau was convinced – and remained convinced

– that Bourassa, with his majority in the National Assembly, could have won the fight for the charter if he had had the guts to try. The other provincial governments might never again be as ready to meet Quebec's concerns as set out by Bourassa himself.

My disappointment at Bourassa's collapse was as deep as Trudeau's. I had put great effort into months of negotiations, with firm assurance that the premier was following every step and agreeing as we went along. I was angry, but I did not despise him as Trudeau did. Bourassa, a young and new premier, had underestimated the opposition he might encounter in the Quebec media and even from some colleagues. His capacity to face risk and defy his critics might have been greater if the Victoria conference had not been so recently preceded by the 'October crisis' of 1970 and the murder of his minister of labour, Pierre Laporte. The violence then, with the army called in at his request, had shaken him. But he also had strong Liberals opposed to the accord as it stood, people like Claude Castonguay and Claude Ryan, then editor of the influential *Le Devoir*.

Trudeau's disgust at the failure of the Victoria charter brought him back to his 'can of worms' attitude: for a long time there would be no federal initiative to revive the discussions that had absorbed so much of his – and the country's – time and effort.

The constitution was not entirely forgotten. A special joint committee of the Senate and the House of Commons was set up in 1972 and held hearings across the country. But the federal election of 30 October that year provided a decisive reason to leave the effort aside: the Liberals lost forty-five seats and clung to office by a margin of two seats in the House of Commons: 109 to 107 for the Progressive Conservatives led by Robert Stanfield. A minority government could not venture into so contentious a field as the constitution.

The election of July 1974 produced a majority. Premier Bourassa had been re-elected in 1973 so both governments were in a position to try once more. In April 1975, at a dinner with the premiers, Trudeau suggested a new possibility – simply to patriate the constitution with the Victoria amending formula, and no other change. Everything else could be for later discussion. The premiers indicated a willingness to have another try and to receive me for discussion on some plan to be proposed by the prime minister.

On 31 March 1976, the prime minister sent a letter to the premiers that set out a new proposal. It was not his dinner-time suggestion of April 1975 because it had become clear that Quebec, Alberta, and British

Columbia would all oppose it. The proposal in the prime minister's letter was in the form of a draft proclamation that included much of what had been agreed to at Victoria and omitted or modified things that had caused trouble there or afterward: particularly specific language provisions at the provincial level and the charter of rights. It did include the Victoria amending procedure since every other formula seemed to raise as many or more problems. It also included the Victoria provisions about the Supreme Court and the declaration of French and English as official languages, with stated rights at the federal level to which provinces could opt in as and when they wished.

There was little enthusiasm among the premiers to return to the seemingly fruitless task but they agreed. All, with their senior advisers and sometimes ministers, had meetings with me and Frank Carter, whom I had brought from Northern Affairs to the Federal-Provincial Relations Division of the Privy Council Office. Frank had developed excellent relations with the provincial officials involved in the constitutional discussions but even those were no guarantee against surprises: provincial premiers dominate their governments to a degree no federal prime minister has until, perhaps, Jean Chrétien in the 1990s.

When I started on my travels I quickly found a new array of difficulties in the West. I made my first visit to Premier Lougheed, who had not been at Victoria: his Conservative Party had come in to office just three months after that conference – 10 September 1971. We had nearly three hours alone, including a very pleasant lunch. After being exposed to his charm I could understand why he had been able to lead his party to power for the first time in the history of Alberta when all the informed opinion of the time was that he had no chance.

In the most courteous but inflexible way, he informed me about the equality of the provinces that made the Victoria amending formula impossible for his government to accept. He then went on to other defects and difficulties in the prime minister's proposals, especially about oil, gas, and resources generally. He left no doubt that we were not going to get anywhere without meeting Alberta's concerns on them. It was all done in way that left me with more problems but a new good friend. We remained so ever afterwards, no matter what policy differences emerged.

In Regina my meetings were with Allan Blakeney the new Premier and his attorney-general, Roy Romanow, in the magnificent Parliament building on the shore of the man-made Wascana Lake. My father had had his office in the building when I was a boy and I had often played there on Sunday afternoons when he was the only one, it seemed, in the place. I asked the premier whether they had ever found my cap that soared up to the molding some forty feet above the great central stairway when I threw it a bit too hard. He claimed to have no knowledge of it.

The visit to Victoria was poignant: the wounds of the defeat in 1971, after so much effort and much high hopes, still hurt. Premier Bennett was his usual smiling, cherubic, enigmatic self. Equality of the provinces was not his theme, but the 'fifth region' concept for British Columbia that he had put forward in federal-provincial discussion on other issues after Victoria was just as deadly for the amending formula he had accepted in 1971. It was quite clear at the end of my western swing that our second effort on constitutional reform was not going to be easy.

It was, for me, depressing to find in my visits to all the premiers, often with their attorneys general or other senior ministers in charge of federal-provincial relations, that the only one with any discernible understanding of and sympathy for the dissatisfactions of Quebec was Richard Hatfield in New Brunswick. It may be that his understanding was due in part to the fact that about 40 per cent of the population of his province was French-speaking Acadian. Hatfield, in his government's policies, did more to improve the status, schools, and general position of Acadians than any English-speaking premier before him. Premier William Davis in Ontario may have shared Hatfield's understanding to some extent but he felt hemmed in by a harder resistance in his party than Hatfield had in New Brunswick. In any event, it is interesting that they were the only two premiers who supported Trudeau when he decided, in frustration, to proceed unilaterally on patriation in 1981. They had a strong sense that *something* had to be done to achieve reform.

I had several sessions with Premier Bourassa as we tried to get over Victoria and find some way to bridge the gap between his position and Trudeau's. He was a courteous, agreeable, and frustrating man to deal with. There was no doubt about his being a federalist but he was both psychologically and politically averse to taking any unqualified position. As one of our discussions drew to an end after dinner in an open-air restaurant in Old Quebec, I told the premier that I had concluded that he was the francophone reincarnation of Mackenzie King. He took it as quite a compliment, which was not, in my exasperated condition, exactly what I had intended. His eternal equivocation was a serious handicap for him in English-speaking Canada. Never, I think, did he say that Canada was a wonderful country, worth saving, and he was a federalist, with no adjective or qualifier.

It looked as though we were getting somewhere until in late 1975 the

Organization of Petroleum Exporting Countries – OPEC – boosted the world price of oil and the federal government instituted the National Energy Program to deal with the new situation internally. The greatly increased price of oil meant major new revenues for Canadian oil producers and for the producing provinces – mainly Alberta. The federal government decided that the windfall profit should not go entirely to the companies or the fortunate provinces through their royalties. To produce a general financial benefit, federal taxes were given a priority over provincial royalties. For the first time, Alberta realized that it had a very real interest in the constitution. It was the beginning of a new phase of general provincial involvement. A complex problem thus became still more difficult but at least it meant that Quebec was not isolated in seeking change in the constitution.

The provincial premiers discussed the federal proposals at the annual premiers' conference in Edmonton in August 1976 and at a second session in Toronto in October. On 14 October Premier Lougheed, in his role as 'chairman' of the conference for 1976–7, wrote to the prime minister setting forth their position. 'While there was general agreement with the objective of patriation, it should not be done "without a consensus being developed on an expansion of the role of the provinces and/or jurisdiction in the following areas: culture, communications, Supreme Court of Canada, spending power, Senate representation and regional disparities."'[12]

The provincial consensus was a final blow to the hopes of getting agreement on a limited package of change.

Parliament Has a Try

Discussion in the new Federal-Provincial Relations Office (FPRO) – by that time my 'department' since I had ceased to be clerk of the Privy Council in January 1975 – and in the Department of Justice turned to the possibility of action by Parliament on its own, with no need for provincial agreement, under St Laurent's amendment to the British North America Act in 1949. That amendment, which had never been used, gave to Parliament the same power with regard to the purely 'federal' part of government in Canada as each legislature had with respect to the purely provincial part. Parliament's power by the 1949 provision consisted of 'the amendment from time to time of the Constitution of Canada, except as regards matters coming within the classes of subjects by this Act assigned exclusively to the Legislatures of the provinces,' subject only to five specific exceptions.

The exploration in the FPRO was turned over to Jean Beetz, a brilliant professor of law from Montreal. His quality was reflected in his later appointment to the Supreme Court of Canada. The result of this new approach emerged in the Constitutional Amendment Bill – commonly known as Bill C-60 – in June 1978. The plan was explained in a booklet 'to encourage public discussion of proposed changes in the Canadian Constitution, as set out in a Bill introduced in Parliament by the Government of Canada.'[13]

The bill was the 'first phase' in a process that had been described in *A Time for Action*, released by the government of Canada a few months before. Those things that could not be done by Parliament alone would be the subject of discussion with the provinces and action in a second phase. For the first phase, Bill C-60 incorporated in a single legal document the essential features of structure and convention involved in the government of Canada as they were at that date. The bill also put in statutory form changes that the federal government proposed to meet the most important problems that had emerged in nearly ten years of constitutional discussion. If the bill were passed, most elements of our central government would not be changed: they would simply be given legal expression in one place and in language that would make much of our 'unwritten constitution' clear and understandable, instead of being based on obscure conventions that had developed over time without being put into legal form. For some elements of the government of Canada, changes were, however, proposed. The whole bill fell into five categories ranging from 'Provisions that Parliament already has exclusive authority to enact' through three categories that would involve different degrees of provincial interest and participation in future legislation to, finally, category 5: 'Provisions that relate to provincial constitutions and institutions,' which were for the provinces alone or together to change.

The concept and the bill were crystallized logic and reason brought to bear on the federal centre of the constitution. No prime minister but Pierre Trudeau would have been prepared to think in such terms, much less to contemplate putting them into a bill for Parliament to enact.

When Bill C-60 was published, two sets of provisions attracted immediate attention – those relating to the governor general and those providing for a new and quite different Senate to be called 'The House of the Federation.' The parts relating to the governor general were intended to make no change but simply to state clearly the obscure facts of the role of the governor general as it had developed from 1867 to 1947 in letters patent issued by the sovereign on the advice of the government of Canada. As the explanatory note said: 'In effect, the result would be to retain the monarchy for Canada and to constitute, at the same time, a Governor General with full status and powers in his or her own right rather than merely in the capacity of a representative of the Sovereign.'[14]

In contrast, the sections on the House of the Federation would make a sweeping change in Parliament. They would abolish the Senate – an institution that had long been recognized as the one major failure in our federal system – and establish a totally new 'house' with a new name to make clear its 'federal' purpose. That was to provide a balance offsetting the House of Commons, which, through representation by population, gives enormous predominance to Ontario and Quebec. The new House of the Federation would give much greater and more effective weight to the 'outlying provinces': the Atlantic provinces and especially the West, which had, from the beginning, been grossly under-represented in the Senate.

The change in the arithmetic of representation to increase that from the West was not the most important change. The Senate, as established in 1867, had never operated effectively as an offset to the House of Commons because its members had no representative status: they got there by the patronage of the prime minister and stayed to age seventy-five – originally for life – with no responsibility to anyone. Bill C-60 would have abolished appointment and would have substituted indirect election of members of the House of Federation. Fifty per cent would be elected by the House of Commons after each federal election; fifty per cent by the legislatures of the provinces after each provincial general election. The terms for the elected senators would be until the next election – federal or provincial.

I argued in 1978, and I wrote in *A House Divided* in 1989 after my retirement, in favour of direct popular election under a form of proportional representation modelled on that in Australia. I failed to persuade the prime minister and ministers in 1978. However, I drew comfort from the conviction that, if the partial solution of indirect election were adopted, it would not long stand. It was too gimmicky: a spurious form of election with control in the hands of the heads of governments, federal and provincial. The United States Senate had begun in 1788 with election by the state legislatures but yielded in 1890 to popular pressure for direct election. I thought our halfway house would go the same way after a period of years.

It was to be expected that the proposals for the House of Federation would bring the senators out like a swarm of bees. A Senate committee was established with a speed hitherto unknown in that comfortable chamber.

As one of the explainers and defenders of the proposed legislation before the Senate committee, I found myself in sharp dispute with an old friend, Senator Eugene Forsey. He was a strong monarchist and could not be persuaded that the sections about the governor general did not involve some devious change that he would not quite detect. But Forsey's suspicions were infectious. These proposals were later dropped as not worth the fuss. Another old friend and my room-mate at the University of Saskatchewan forty years before – Professor R.W. Lederman – was, in 1978, dean of Law at Queen's University and one of the most highly regarded constitutionalists in Canada. He was invited by the committee to give his views. Bill, like Eugene, was a constitutional conservative. He did not like the new-fangled House of the Federation and he attacked the federal argument that reform of the Senate was a purely federal matter that did not affect the provincial governments and so did not require their involvement. In short, the federal proposal for action by Parliament alone was unconstitutional.

After much debate, the committee recommended that the government should make a reference to the Supreme Court on the constitutionality of the legislation. The government accepted the recommendation so far as the Senate was concerned. The Supreme Court ruled against the federal government. It was not constitutional for Parliament alone, under the powers given by the British North America Act amendment of 1949, to legislate to affect the structure and powers of the Senate. I was not too surprised to find Bill Lederman right on a point of law – he usually was.

The decision of the Supreme Court on Bill C-60 came only in 1980, after Trudeau had been defeated in the election of 1979. It did not, therefore, affect any part of the attempt at constitutional reform that he had restarted in 1976. It did, however, add to his clear sense that the federal government, in any attempt at constitutional change, was hedged around by an array of opponents – political, provincial, and judicial – all with some power that could frustrate and defeat anything a prime minister might try to do.

A New Factor: The PQ in Power
Well before the demise of Bill C-60 came another event that had a much more profound effect on the whole picture: the election to power in

Quebec on 15 November 1976 of the Parti Québécois, led by René Lévesque. As Trudeau says in his *Memoirs*: 'The election of the Parti Québécois in 1976 had a direct and immediate effect on the prospects for constitutional reform. It made negotiations both unavoidable and unlikely to succeed ... From 1976 to 1979, our strategy was to be as reasonable as possible, and to go more than halfway to meet the provincial agenda – knowing all the while that any government headed by René Lévesque might never sign.'[15]

It seemed paradoxical and puzzling that the unity problem of Canada should have become worse after eight years of effort to meet the 'greatest crisis' in our history, a crisis that had been identified by the 'B and B' commission and accepted as the first priority of both the Pearson and Trudeau governments. Eight months after the Quebec election, the federal government established *The Task Force on Canadian Unity*, better known as the Pepin-Robarts commission after the two co-chairmen, Jean-Luc Pepin and John Robarts. It was to 'enquire into questions relating to Canadian unity' and was directed, among other things to hold public hearings, to contribute to public knowledge about Canadian unity, and to 'be a source of advice to the government on unity issues.'[16]

I think Trudeau never believed that the result of the task force's work would be something he could accept as a solution to the constitutional problem. His thinking and that of Pepin were miles apart. Pepin would be much more conciliatory to nationalist attitudes in Quebec than Trudeau ever could be. In establishing the task force, he may have hoped for a miracle but I suspect he merely believed that something had to be done to respond to the PQ victory. The task force would absorb attention and emotions for several months and it would not commit the government. Whatever was good could be adopted; the rest could be ignored.

The report of the task force was the first of a series of efforts by political parties, the Canadian Bar Association, academics, and private citizens in various groups organized for the purpose to suggest how Canada might be saved. Premier Lévesque's government, in *Quebec-Canada: A New Deal*, proposed 'a new partnership between equals: sovereignty association.' The outline in it of the history of Quebec was a very different interpretation from the one English-speaking Canadians had learned in school while still dealing with the same events from the founding of Quebec 'at the beginning of the 17th century' through 'the hazards of war' that brought it under British control in 1763. In the conferences from 1864 to 1866 'the Quebec delegates and those from other provinces were pursuing very different goals.' John A. Macdonald looms large; the presence and role of the Conservative leader of Lower Canada, George-Etienne Cartier, gets no mention whatever. The opposition in 1866 to Confederation, led by Antoine-Aimé Dorion, was strong but the Quebec representation in the Legislative Assembly of Canada was divided: '27 Francophones from Québec (two of whom represented ridings where the majority was Anglophone) approved it and 22 rejected it. As for the French-speaking population, its wishes will never be known since the government refused to consult it in a referendum as Antoine-Aimé Dorion had requested.'[17] Confederation established provinces 'subject to a senior government that exercised in its own name the essential powers of a state.' The province of Quebec as created in 1867 was 'not the homeland of a nation but merely a province among others, first four, then five, then ten.'[18] The present federal regime could not be remedied: the only solution was to establish sovereignty-association between Canada and Quebec – an arrangement similar to the European Union. It was an interesting and important statement of the thinking and philosophy of most of the articulate leadership of Quebec at that time.

The Liberal Party of Quebec tackled the problem of reform in a major study by its constitutional committee. It proposed dramatic change for Canada under a new constitution. Like Bill C-60, the committee would have abolished the Senate. It would have substituted a new 'Federal Council' to be formed of 'delegations from the provinces acting on the instructions of their respective governments.' These provincial delegates would express the political policies of their governments and the length of their mandate would be determined in accordance with this principle. The constitution would provide that the provincial premiers or their representatives would be ex-officio members of their provinces' delegations' in the new Federal Council.[19]

Two months after the Quebec election, on 19 January 1977, Trudeau replied to Lougheed's letter of 1976 in a letter I drafted after much discussion with him. The proposals of the premiers as a basis for discussion were, in his view, 'either too much or too little' – too much to be a package for quick action, too little to be a genuine constitutional reform. 'The federal government is prepared to proceed by either route: action by stages, such as we have been concentrating on, or action all at once by fundamental constitutional revision.' He proposed that another effort be made for a limited package 'so that "patriation" – can be effected as soon as possible.' With that objective, it would be best not to get into the distribution of powers. He sent a new draft proclamation for further discussion – to meet many of the premiers' points of 1976 without getting into the distribution of powers.

Taking advantage of the new sense of urgency that the Quebec election – and the prospect of a Quebec referendum on 'sovereignty-association' – gave to the political scene, Trudeau got provincial agreement to a new series of meetings. Marc Lalonde was appointed minister of state for federal-provincial relations in September 1977, so he could give full time to the constitutional and national-unity problems. Paul Tellier was made responsible for assisting both Marc and me on the special Quebec problems: he and Marc formed an effective team in watching and interpreting the actions of Premier Lévesque and his new government and in devising tactics to meet them.

In the first months of 1978 teams of federal ministers and officials visited all the premiers to discuss the federal proposals, which were made public in June. A conference of first ministers followed in Ottawa on 31 October and 1 November. There appeared to be sufficient hope of some agreement that three meetings of several days each were held at Mont Sainte-Marie, Quebec, in November, in Toronto in December, and in Vancouver in January 1979. A second conference of first ministers followed in Ottawa on 6 February 1979. The pace and the pressure were exhausting – and, in the end, to no avail.

Why did the discussions fail after all the effort? One reason was the 'constitutional creep' of which both sides were guilty. While we, on the federal side, talked about a small package for quick 'patriation,' Trudeau and the federal government had not lost their ambition to achieve a bill of rights of some kind. Putting a federal 'bill' into Bill C-60, with the possibility of provincial opting-in, meant inevitably that 'rights' came back into first ministers' meetings. On the provincial side both Quebec and the west had special interests to get into any agreement. Successive 'best efforts' drafts of the package of change were prepared at the meetings in the winter 1978–9 but, inevitably, the most difficult problems were left for the prime minister and premiers. Only they could decide how much of their government's ambitions and commitments could be omitted from any agreement they each might have to defend.

For the first ministers' conference in February 1979, the draft included a limited charter of rights based on the version in Bill C-60. There was still a lot of opposition to it among the provinces – and not exclusively from Quebec. The problem created in Alberta and the west generally by the National Energy Program raised the issue of jurisdiction over non-renewable resources to the top of western priorities. Here the critical problem was to find some way of extending provincial jurisdiction to protect control by the provinces over mineral resources and revenues without encroaching on federal powers over trade and commerce. There were compromises, new drafts, and progress but no federal commitment to any agreed text.

While the 'creep' that made the package too large was a major part of the failure, a more critical factor was the federal political calendar. The Trudeau government had been elected in July 1974. It was already near the end of its fifth year in office so an election was certain in a very few months. 'Apart from conflict over particular provisions and, in particular, the provisions guaranteeing freedom of choice in the language of education, the attempt to achieve constitutional agreement in February 1979 took place too late in the parliamentary term of the fading Liberals. The largely Conservative provincial premiers were not about to hand Prime Minister Trudeau the diplomatic coup of an agreement on the terms of patriation.'[20]

Trudeau, of course, was as aware of those political facts as the premiers. He had been confident that René Lévesque 'was unlikely ever to sign anything.' However, 'The other premiers might have been interested if it had been early in my mandate and they knew that they were still saddled with me for a long time. But by then I was into my fourth year in office, with an election coming up, and the premiers were all gambling that I would be defeated and they could do better with Clark.'[21]

The Hinge of Our Federal Fate

The failure of nearly eleven years of federal-provincial effort to achieve constitutional reform was the determining factor in our subsequent twenty years of unresolved uncertainty about the future of Canada.

No prime minister could have provided more knowledgeable or determined leadership than Trudeau did. The closest approach to success had been at Victoria in 1971. A legitimate question is whether more understanding of the worries of a young and frightened Bourassa could have produced a compromise over social policy and agreement then and there. Pearson would not have been as informed a leader as Trudeau but Suez had shown his genius at achieving agreement where no one else could. He might have found a way. His posture at every federal-provincial meeting was to detect the way a bridge might be built across apparent differences: a posture and an attitude not part of Trudeau's character.

But, even if a Pearson had succeeded, agreement then might not have lasted. The forces in Quebec in favour of more change than Victoria provided were strong – and not solely in the Parti Québécois. Jean-Luc Pepin reflected them in the federal field, however firmly Trudeau rejected the recommendations of the *Task Force on Canadian Unity* and the Liberal Party of Quebec's 'beige paper.' In the West, too, success might have been ephemeral. Premier Lougheed would not long have been content with the 'Victoria formula' for constitutional amendment and the tensions over energy policy and jurisdiction would have been no different than they were after 1973.

What would have been different would have been Trudeau's sense of angry frustration at achieving no agreement whatever for all his years of trying. There might have been no 'agreement without Quebec' in 1981 and no wounds from a Charter of Rights 'imposed' without Quebec acceptance. Those were the result of a determination to act, with or without provincial, and especially Quebec, consent.

A Victoria agreement in 1971, however inadequate, would at least have been something: a significant degree of constitutional reform that would have refuted the Parti Québécois allegation that 'confederation is unreformable: separation is the only route.' Our subsequent history might have been different if Premier Bennett's benevolent hospitality had succeeded.

A Partnership with Pierre Trudeau

The eleven years of work on the constitution and the problem of national unity had put Trudeau and me into an even closer and more intensive relationship than the PM-clerk association normally involves. In all that time, and with all the possibilities there were of conflicting views on important and emotional issues, we had no significant difference. He was, of course, the leader and final decisions were his, but discussions with him – often involving Marc Lalonde – were on a completely frank and equal basis. Trudeau would have felt it a betrayal of our responsibility to him if we had not been direct and honest.

We had no differences at all in opposing the kinds of demands the Lévesque government put forward in 1976 – exclusive provincial jurisdiction on language and culture, provincial power to enter into negotiations and to conclude treaties with other countries on any matters within provincial jurisdiction, and a provincial – or, rather, a Quebec – power of 'self-determination' in the constitution. There was more room for difference on less extreme positions advanced either by Premier Bourassa or other premiers – such as the issue that wrecked the Victoria Conference. I did not differ with Trudeau's decision there. I have subsequently wondered whether I should have but I doubt if a concession would have saved the day.

After the conference of 1979 ended in failure, Trudeau and I had lunch together at 24 Sussex Drive and I asked him whether there was anything we had put on the table – or had been prepared to agree to – that he was worried about, since I thought we had gone the limit of what was possible while still protecting the necessary powers of the federal government. He said there was not. I felt the same way.

In the area of federal and provincial powers we had no differences – with the possible exception of the second thought about Victoria. Where I sensed we could differ – and where we did over Meech Lake nearly ten years later – was over matters largely of form or method or symbolism that were of real importance for the unique circumstances of Quebec. His detestation of nationalism and nationalists – rooted in years of opposition to the 'great darkness' of the Duplessis regime – led him to reject anything with any tincture of emotion about it: all must be based on absolute equality and pure reason. We would have had real difficulty if the 'distinct society' clause had emerged from a federalist government in Quebec – as it did in 1986. I saw it as a reasonable recognition of a fact that deserved constitutional expression with no significant consequence in power and little danger of the nationalist escalation that so worried him. Trudeau saw it very differently.

I set out my views on our national crisis in a way unusual for a senior public servant in a convocation address at Dalhousie University in 1977. After referring to Abraham Lincoln's Gettysburg address, I said:

If the United States was dedicated to the proposition that all 'men are created equal,' many French Canadians believe that we had, among our purposes, the proposition, probably little understood, that two linguistic communities could live together in one country with each respecting the rights, the dignity and the full existence of the other. A major part of our problem today is that, while many French Canadians understood the underlying proposition in that sense and lived up to it in Quebec, where they had the majority, few English-speaking Canadians so understood it and we did not live up to it where we had the majority. Our history for one hundred years in the provinces other than Quebec and in the national scene belied the proposition of equal co-existence – or even of co-existence – of two cultural groups.

I argued that English-speaking Canada had 'to try to see our history with the eyes of many French Canadians or we cannot hope to understand the bitterness that we see in Quebec to-day.' Modified constitutions, more delegation of powers, more flexibility in economic policy – all were 'mechanics.' Our 'root problems' were, I thought, 'problems of human dignity and of failures – some past but some present – in spiritual generosity.' The consequence was a situation in which many French Canadians would no longer call themselves that: they were 'Québécois, people of Quebec.' 'The loyalty to Canada shrivelled with the sense that Canada felt no loyalty to them, to their language or to their community. We are paying the price today for a hundred years of failure to do what a strong majority could so easily do – to treat with generosity and respect a weaker and less numerous community that shares our country.'

The address got a tremendous response. The *Globe and Mail*, in its lead editorial of 30 May 1977, called it 'an honest look at unity' and said that it 'takes the debate beyond the safe platitudes to begin real discussion of real issues.' I had, the editorial said, been blunt about the failings of 'English Canada' but no more soothing when I questioned 'the comfortable assumptions of those in Quebec who believe that the province can become a separate country and go on to enjoy a friendly partnership with the Canada that is left.' The emotions involved were too profound – 'you do not outrage such emotions and then expect to do a friendly deal.'

The address was published in substantial part in in all three Toronto papers – the *Globe and Mail*, the *Star*, and the *Telegram* – in both Vancouver papers, and in most of the papers across the country, getting as much attention in the French press of Quebec as in the rest of Canada. The Federal-Provincial Relations Office got over five thousand requests for copies of the text.

Trudeau had nothing but praise for my views and for my strong intervention in the national debate. Our working relationship in our eleven years together could not have been better.

The United States and the Canadian Crisis

The United States ambassador in the period after the Parti Québécois victory in 1976 was Tom Enders, like me, a professional public servant, about two inches taller and an avid noon-time jogger. He came to see me several times to discuss the policy and the expectations of the Canadian government about the risk of separation.

Information between countries depends on a fair exchange. Enders said that the American government was going to keep out of our crisis and do its level best to say nothing that would suggest any intervention whatever. Point number one.

Point number two was that, as far as the American government was concerned, its aim and objective and greatest interest was in having a strong Canada north of their border. Enders said that the United States had all sorts of trouble south of their border with Mexico and in Central America. And the thing that caused it the most trepidation was the thought that the Canadian federation might get into difficulty, for, lying as it does between the United States and the Soviet Union, it might create a condition of instability in that delicate and sensitive area. So the United States policy would support the unity of Canada in any way it could without being accused of intervention.

Enders's comments to me in the winter of 1977, which I passed on to the prime minister, were the clearest statement of American policy on the possible break-up of Canada until the deft but sharply pointed admonition by President Clinton to Premier Lucien Bouchard and his associates at the conference on federalism at Mont Tremblant in October 1999. There can no longer be any doubt in any separatist mind as to the attitude and interest of the United States in a 'strong and united Canada.'

chapter fourteen

Transition and Change, 1978–1980

One of the little-known roles of the clerk of the Privy Council is, on rare occasions, to advise the governor general on some problems on which he cannot turn to the prime minister. One such question came up in February 1968, when my family and I were living in Quebec City. The prime minister – Lester Pearson – was in Jamaica for a much needed rest after the constitutional conference over which he had just presided. That rest had hardly begun when he had to come back to Ottawa: the government had been defeated in the House of Commons on the third reading of the tax bill presented by Mitchell Sharp, then minister of finance.

The governor general, Roland Michener, was in residence at the Citadel – a second Government House evoking the history of the governors of New France before 1759. As soon as he learned of the government's defeat, he telephoned me to come to see him the following morning. The defeat of a government in Parliament is rare in Canada: it is one of the situations in which the governor general may have to determine the course of events and the life or death of a government. At such times, the independence, objectivity, and judgment of a governor general are of critical importance.

Michener was well aware of the King-Byng crisis of 1926 when Prime Minister King, faced by certain defeat in the House of Commons, advised the governor general, Lord Byng, to dissolve it so that an election could be held. Byng refused the advice. The circumstances at the time were complex. The Liberals had been in office with a minority government from 1921 until the election of October 1925. The Conservatives then won more seats than the Liberals: 116 to 101. The Progressives, a western protest party voicing the grievances of the West as the Reform

Party has done recently, held the balance of power. King declined to resign in October and Byng acquiesced on the understanding with King that, if he was defeated when his government met the House of Commons, he would resign. For more than six months the Progressives supported the King government until a special committee of the House disclosed serious irregularities in the Customs Department – a genuine scandal. A vote of censure of the government was moved. King did not wait to see if his government would be defeated: he advised the governor general to dissolve Parliament and hold a new election.

Byng thought that the advice was an evasion of King's undertaking to resign if defeated in the House. King argued that the government's six months of survival had created a new situation. Byng, a military man with a high sense of honour but without the subtlety and acute political sense of Mackenzie King, did not see it that way. King warned in writing that a refusal to accept a prime minister's advice would raise 'a grave constitutional question.' In his formal reply the governor general repeated his position: 'My contention is that Mr. Meighen has not been given a chance of trying to govern, or saying that he cannot do so, and that all reasonable expedients should be tried before resorting to another election.'[1]

King then resigned in protest. Arthur Meighen's government lasted less than three days and his defeat led to the election King had advised – but with a whole new issue: the refusal of a governor general to accept the advice of his prime minister. King's skilful use of the issue helped to produce a Liberal victory. King had another minority government but with much the largest party in the House and a secure position that lasted for four years.

MacGregor Dawson had argued in his introductory political-science course at the University of Saskatchewan that King was right and Byng wrong. Eugene Forsey got his PhD degree on a thesis that argued the reverse. Mr. Michener had no wish to become a possible election issue.

Michener set out the problem as he saw it. If Pearson did not get a vote in the House that declared the defeat on third reading had not been a vote of non-confidence, the prime minister would have two options: to resign or, like King, to advise dissolution and an election. I agreed. Was there anything the governor general should do in the interim? We agreed there was not: he had to wait to see what happened and, if there was not a vote of confidence, until he received the prime minister's advice. Suppose Pearson advised dissolution and an election?

I told Michener that I thought much the most defensible course would be to accept that advice. The governor general had to have a very strong reason to reject his prime minister's advice and I did not see any such reason. There were none of the special circumstances that, in 1926, led Lord Byng to believe that he – and King – had an obligation to let Meighen form a government. I did not think I had to go on to say that, as a former Progressive Conservative Member of Parliament, Michener could be suspect if he seemed to favour the opposition by refusing the advice of a Liberal prime minister. In the end, Pearson got the confidence vote and the crisis disappeared.

Six years later, in 1974, one of my closest friends, Jules Léger, became governor general. His wife, Gabrielle, known to her friends as Gaby, was as intelligent, witty, and charming as he. Jules had been under-secretary of state for external affairs and ambassador to France. He had suffered through the hostile relations with President de Gaulle after the 'Vive le Québec libre' incident of 1967, and he was fully versed in the problem of France-Quebec relations as those had grown steadily more troublesome. It seemed ideal to have as governor general a man who thought deeply about our unity problem and who, as a former journalist, wrote and spoke with facility in both languages. All looked golden – until he was felled by a severe stroke just six months after he took office. He lost all capacity either to speak or to write.

Intensive therapy slowly restored Léger's command of spoken French: the capacity to speak in English was much slower in coming. I was one of the few people outside his family with whom he was at ease during the months when every French word was a problem and almost no English word came at all. My French, after less than six months in Quebec, was hopelessly limited for conversation with a man who had spoken it so beautifully, but I was a friend, we thought alike, and Gaby left me in no doubt about the help I was at so critical a time. She was the real saviour: without her Jules could not have carried on. She discharged, as only she could, the social and public responsibilities during the months while Jules's capacity to speak slowly improved. She even read the Speech from the throne for him when he could not do it.

Should Léger have carried on? He thought he had a responsibility to disabled people not to collapse and withdraw but rather to show that physical disability could be overcome. He did, but it was a much diminished performance and virtually all his influence on the unity issue was lost.

On 7 November 1978 Trudeau had a discussion with me, Michael Pitfield, and Jim Coutts, then his principal secretary, about the succession to Léger when his term expired in 1979. The prime minister had a 'short list' of names of possible successors but was undecided. After a half-hour or so of discussion he asked Coutts and Pitfield to leave so he could have a word with me alone. I was so surprised by what developed that I made a note about it: 'When we were alone, the prime minister said that he wondered if I would be prepared to have my name added to the short list. He said that he realized that it was a "hell of a job" and he was not at all sure how my wife would react. He said that he had in mind, however, the importance of making an appointment of someone who would understand all the inwardness of the function at a time when the constitution would be undergoing change.'

I told the prime minister that I thought I should not be added to the short list. I was too close to him: it would look like favouritism in filling what was constitutionally the highest office in the country: the representative of the Queen. In the end he asked me to 'take twenty-four or forty-eight hours to consider it.'

On 9 November I told Trudeau that 'as his principal adviser on senior appointments,' I 'had come firmly to the conclusion that my name should not be included in the short list.' Trudeau was not easily put off. My note records: 'When the bells rang for the opening of the afternoon session, the prime minister asked me if my conclusion was really final: might it not be desirable to "bring in a third party" to give an opinion on the arguments I had raised? I said I thought there would be no point in it. I said I was so certain that it would be a mistake for me to be appointed that "I would not let him make that mistake." The prime minister grimaced; said all I was doing was leaving him with a problem; and said with a smile that we could "both keep it for our memoirs."'

The Role of the Clerk of the Privy Council

It would be difficult to conceive of a title less informing and more misleading than 'Clerk of the Privy Council' for the person who has for some forty years been recognized as the senior official in the federal public service. He – or she – is not a clerk in any dictionary sense and does not deal with the Privy Council, but with the cabinet, which is different.

The explanation is, as with many things in the cabinet system of government, historical – our own history, in this case, not British history. We have touched on some of this history before, but a short review is in order to put the role of the clerk in perspective over the years of its growth.

Before the Second World War there was no cabinet secretariat of any kind. The cabinet was, as now, the decision-making body of the government, responsible for all policy and all important decisions: financial, foreign policy, trade and commerce, social security, defence – the gamut of things governments dealt with. It met, as it had done since Confederation, with no agenda, no minutes, no secretary, and no formal communication of decisions to the departments that had to apply them. King liked it that way: it put the prime minister firmly in the driver's seat for every meeting and no meddlesome officials had anything to do with any part of the operation.

When war came in 1939 King realized that the problems of government and of war policy would expand the work of cabinet enormously. In the First World War the British had established a cabinet secretariat to help with the burden of governing. King, with his infinite capacity for compromise, went part way. He would have a cabinet secretary, but not in the full cabinet where the most sensitive political things were discussed. He established a war committee of the cabinet to deal with all the vast problems of war: all the critical ministers would be members of that. There would be a secretary to the cabinet for the first time – Arnold Heeney, appointed in 1940 – and he would do all the efficient secretarial things for the war committee – but he would *not* attend full cabinet meetings and there would be no secretarial nonsense like an agenda or minutes for that: only for the war committee.

But that was not the end of King's concerns and devices. It might not appear appropriate to be waging war by creating a new top-level position in the public service. Fortunately, since Confederation there had been a clerk of the Privy Council who was a real clerk: to prepare, to record, and to keep all orders-in-council passed under any act of Parliament. The new position of secretary to the cabinet was grafted on to that historic one: hence the confusing combination out of which the uninformative and misleading term 'clerk' is the part of the title that has now survived, not only in general usage but in law. An amendment to the Public Service Employment Act in 1992 gave legal confirmation to the responsibility of the clerk of the Privy Council as 'head of the public service.'

The end of the war did not mean that the role of government diminished: it increased, with post-war reconstruction and, in the 1950s and 1960s, the growth of the income-support and social-security structure of today, which brought with it a totally new importance for federal-provincial relations. Most of the social programs were in areas that were, constitutionally, provincial: most of the initiative and financial capacity was federal. In 1964 the responsibility for coordinating federal-provincial policy was placed in the Privy Council Office, which reported to the prime minister. In 1968 a special division was established headed by a deputy secretary to the cabinet.

The result of the whole process of history and post-war growth was that, by the time Pierre Trudeau became prime minister, the clerk of the Privy Council and secretary to the cabinet had a threefold role. The first was as the prime minister's deputy minister and head of the prime minister's department: the Privy Council Office. In that role there were wide functions that related to the prime minister's overall responsibility for and control of his government. Advice on the most senior appointments, both within the public service and outside it, was one. Security policy was another. But the most important part was and is pursuing on his behalf any issue or policy of government on which the prime minister should be informed or that he raises in the daily meetings that are critical for coordination of the 'government' part of the PM's operations, with the 'political' part being handled by the Prime Minister's Office.

The second role was the 'secretary to the cabinet role': to coordinate and direct everything relating to the operation of the cabinet and the various cabinet committees. The precise organization depended on the views of the prime minister of the day, with most changes coming under Pearson and Trudeau.

The third role is the junction of the political part of government with the administrative part: the public service. Communication through the clerk is essential for coherent policy and effective administration. Links with ministers are vital to assess performance of senior officials and to resolve personal problems.

It is difficult to convey the nature of that central position in parliamentary government – indeed, it has no specific or necessary dimensions. It grew from nothing in the pre-war period to a significant but not dominant role when R.B. Bryce and I were 'clerks.' Donald Savoie has found that today both the official status and the reality of power are much greater than when I ceased to hold the post in 1975. One thing that can be said with regard to the position is that the superbly humorous British television program 'Yes, Minister' is a delightful slander both of the politicians and of the 'clerk' or 'secretary' – whatever he may be called. Sir Humphrey Appleby shrewdly twists prime ministers and ministers around his finger to frustrate any plan he does not like and to achieve the ones he does.

It would spoil the program, but the truth is that a Sir Humphrey in real life would not last long in the job. Success in it depends on judgment and confidence – good judgment on the part of the clerk, and the sure confidence of, above all, the prime minister but also of ministers and heads of departments.

Almost everyone has some sense of what good judgment is and of which people have it and which do not, but it is almost impossible to define. Isaiah Berlin is one of the few who have tackled it – in relation to political judgment – and his conclusion is pragmatic, with no clear rules: 'To be rational in any sphere, to display good judgement in it, is to apply those methods which have turned out to work best in it.'[2] It is not clear whether the balance in our government today does in fact 'work best in it.' An overly great concentration of power at the centre has a price with the best ministers and the most creative and effective heads of departments. They are the very ones who do not need to stay, if they find their role too limited or frustrated by central interference.

Federal-provincial relations were not an obvious part of the role of the clerk as they grew in importance in the 1960s, although we fitted them in to the 'operations' branch of the PCO. Trudeau and I discussed the possibility of putting the responsibility somewhere else but we agreed that, at that stage, it would not be effective to have a 'minister of federal-provincial relations' and a separate department or organization. It was after the Parti Québécois came to power in November 1976 that a special need became apparent – and an obviously 'right' minister with Trudeau's total confidence was available – Marc Lalonde. He became minister of state (federal-provincial relations) in 1977. Marc's and my relationship, which had been so close for the many years since he became policy adviser to Pearson in 1967, made it unnecessary to have an arm's length division of staffs and departments. Marc was an outstanding minister in every portfolio he took on and his relationship with Trudeau was unique: the friendship Trudeau had for Pelletier and Marchand combined with the total confidence in judgment he felt for Drury.

In the autumn of 1970, during a conversation on personnel matters, I told the prime minister that I did not want to remain secretary to the cabinet for more than a year after the next election, whenever that might be: seven or eight years was enough. He told me that it was his 'strong desire' that I stay 'at least that long' to make arrangements 'for whatever government emerged thereafter.' I said I would. In December 1971 we spoke about it again and agreed that our planning would be on the basis 'of my remaining through the election plus something like twelve months.'

The minority government produced by the election in October 1972 altered those plans. The situation was precarious and Trudeau made it clear that he wanted me to stay until yet another election – which would not be long deferred – either gave him a majority or turned him out.

In January 1974 I proposed that plans be put in hand not only for my succession but also for a division of my job, which had grown enormously in, by that time, the nearly eleven years I had held it. In a memorandum of 25 January 1974, I said: 'Two things have become increasingly apparent to me in the course of recent months. One is that a variety of developments are making the operations that have to be controlled by the secretary to the cabinet so extensive that it is impossible for one person to deal with them adequately. The other is that we are moving into a period in which federal-provincial relations are going to assume a degree of complexity that they have never had in the past. In that situation, I think we must have a stronger organization to deal with them than is now available.' That was 'judgment,' and I am sure I was right.

I recommended that a new position be established of secretary to the cabinet for federal-provincial relations, at the level of senior deputy minister, reporting to the prime minister. I would be prepared to move to that position if Trudeau so wished. It was a month later, 25 February, that the prime minister found enough time for a full discussion of my proposal. My memorandum of record reads: 'After some discussion on some other points, the prime minister said he was attracted by the proposal and would particularly feel it desirable if I took it on and kept the responsibilities for senior appointments.'

The appointment of Lalonde in 1977 as minister of state for federal-provincial relations had little effect on my role and responsibilities as, by that time, secretary to the cabinet for federal-provincial relations. Technically, Marc moved from being an official – a colleague – to being my minister, my superior. In fact, it made no difference in our own relations. What it mainly did was give Marc more capacity and authority in the federal-provincial field, especially in relation to Quebec in the post-1976 atmosphere. But he kept the prime minister informed as his superior and me informed as his colleague. Of all my relationships with colleagues and ministers, the happiest and easiest was with Marc Lalonde.

The Clerk and Senior Appointments

The prime minister's concern about my retaining the responsibility of advising on senior appointments, both within the public service and in the wider range of order-in-council appointments generally – other than the obviously political ones such as appointments to the Senate – was not surprising. It is a sensitive task. Doing it effectively requires a thorough knowledge of people and of positions, which does not come quickly, together with judgment about the 'fit' of the qualifications of individuals with the requirements for a position. It also requires the confidence of the prime minister in the objectivity of the clerk together with an equally important confidence on the part of the Public Service and of the ministers whose deputy ministers and other order-in-council appointees are involved.

The role of the clerk in advising on senior appointments developed slowly and informally particularly in the years when Robert Bryce held the office under Diefenbaker and Pearson from 1957 to 1963. It was especially important when Diefenbaker was prime minister because he did not have Pearson's personal knowledge of the public service. The confidence that he developed in Bryce's objectivity and judgment was vitally important at a difficult time for the service generally. By the time I became clerk – on Bryce's advice to Pearson in 1963 – I inherited a well-established responsibility for the clerk in advising on senior appointments generally. That did not exclude, of course, advice from the principal secretary to the prime minister on appointments outside the public service where there was or could be a political aspect.

A further element in the role of the clerk of the Privy Council and secretary to the cabinet that gave it a special sensitivity was – and is – that the clerk often is a link between an overwhelmed (and overwhelming) prime minister and ministers who want their views to get to the prime minister but are rightly hesitant about pressing for enough of his time to do it personally. His principal secretary becomes the link on things political, the clerk on policy and administration, including the performance of ministers' senior officials. I learned the importance of spending a good many hours each year with all ministers individually discussing the performance of their deputy ministers and order-in-council appointees. It was not easy to judge when complaints or criticisms were the fault of the official, or of the minister, or of both in a personal relationship that did not work. If a minister's view was not to be accepted, and there were such occasions, the only sure basis for rejecting it was the reputation and judgment of the clerk.

For that array of considerations relating to the prime minister, ministers, and the public service generally, the succession to my position as clerk was important. I put forward several names and Trudeau settled on

Pierre Juneau, then Chairman of the Canadian Radio and Television Commission (CRTC). He asked me to talk to him about his possible appointment. I did so. Juneau was interested, and then he had a meeting with the prime minister; we agreed on questions of organization and all seemed to be settled for action at the right time. On 22 March 1974 I sent Juneau a letter I had cleared with the prime minister ending:

> As a final matter, the prime minister has asked me to add that he is fully conscious of the importance you stressed to him of having a thoroughly competent and suitable person to take over from you the very important work of the Chairman of the CRTC. We have also, of course, the problems that attach in the present circumstances to securing Parliamentary authority, even if only in the estimates, for the Governor in Council to make the additional appointment at the Deputy minister level. It is hard to know just when this can best be done. For these reasons, as well as because the prime minister wants to give more thought to all aspects of arrangement and timing, he is aware that the discussions are still exploratory.

The election on 8 July gave Trudeau and the Liberals a solid majority: 141 seats out of 264. When cabinet changes had been settled, the prime minister turned to execution of our plan. The only part he changed was the appointment as clerk: it was to be Michael Pitfield instead of Pierre Juneau.

Michael had been one of my 'possible names.' But my assessment on 25 January had been: '... too soon. Michael has not yet established the necessary credit and respect in the public service generally.' I also felt and said that Michael, although brilliant and with several years experience in the Privy Council Office, had not yet had enough experience in departmental administration. He had been only two years in his first post as a deputy minister.

Trudeau had agreed with my assessment, but after the election he had a change of mind. We discussed the division of functions and the prime minister set them out, exactly as I had proposed, in a letter to Pitfield two weeks after the election. I would become secretary to the cabinet for federal-provincial relations when the necessary legislation to establish the position was passed, 'reporting directly to the prime minister.' I would, the letter said,' be responsible for ... federal-provincial relations.' I would also continue to be responsible 'for the senior personnel function' and for security and intelligence. The last responsibility was for policy only: the means by which the prime minister is kept informed of policy questions in those difficult areas of security that require the involvement of the head of government.

The speech from the throne on 2 October set out the intention to introduce legislation for my new position and on 4 October the prime minister announced his intention to appoint me to that post and for Michael Pitfield to succeed me as clerk of the Privy Council and secretary to the cabinet.

It did not take long for Pitfield's appointment to become contentious. On 8 October Joe Clark asked the prime minister in the House of Commons to make a statement 'outlining the principles now to be followed in appointments to the senior public service, and in particular show whether the elevation of Mr. Michael Pitfield indicates a replacement of the merit system by the buddy system?' The press picked up the issue. The Ottawa *Journal*, in an editorial, said: 'Two things are at issue. The first is the politicization of the public service at the highest level in the most dangerous and insidious ways. Mr. Pitfield bears the mark of a Trudeau man. The clerk of the Privy Council above all public servants should have no vestiges of political loyalties about him.' 'The second issue is the impact of the appointment upon the public service. By his mistake, Mr. Trudeau has gratuitously insulted senior civil servants, though they will not dare admit it.'[3]

There can be no question but that the consequences of Pitfield's appointment were unfortunate: not least of all for him. When Clark won the election of 1979 Pitfield was a marked man and forced out of the public service. The sense of politicization of the top position in the service was damaging and seemed confirmed when Pitfield was reappointed clerk after Trudeau came back in 1980.

Donald J. Savoie, in an excellent study of the operation of the federal government today, found that, more than twenty years after the event, the appointment of Pitfield is regarded in the public service as a critical turning point in the increasing centralization that has taken place. 'Some observers believe that Trudeau's appointment of Michael Pitfield as clerk-secretary in 1975 changed the role forever.' 'The argument also is that no clerk since Pitfield has been able to revert to the old understanding of the role. If Arnold Heeney successfully resisted Mackenzie King's desire to make the secretary to the cabinet "a kind of deputy minister to the prime minister," or "the personal staff officer to the Prime Minister," secretaries to the prime minister from Pitfield to today have not been as willing to resist the desire of the prime minister to make the position "a kind of deputy minister to the prime minister."'[4]

The role of deputy minister to the prime minister existed to some degree even under Heeney and Norman Robertson. King and St Laurent did look to them for the kind of advice and assistance a deputy minister provides to his minister. Bryce and I both operated in that role as well. However, there is no doubt but that the balance shifted greatly with Pitfield. Initially it was because his limited acceptance and standing in the senior public service made him more dependent for respect and authority on Trudeau's support than Bryce or I had been. After Trudeau's return to office in 1980, another factor was added. Trudeau wanted to be relieved of a lot of the day-to-day grind of government to focus on the constitutional problem and world affairs: it would be his last chance. So Pitfield came to speak more, whether to ministers or to departments, in the name of the prime minister, which inevitably created resentment and suspicion.

The change of balance within the government is convenient for prime mnisters and has continued and grown. Savoie concludes that both Parliament and the cabinet now tend to be bypassed to a degree unknown in our government previously and unknown in other parliamentary democracies such as Britain and Australia. 'In Canada national unity concerns and the nature of federal-provincial relations tend, in a perverse fashion, to favour the centre of government in Ottawa. They dominate our policy agenda and permeate government decision making to such an extent that the centre of government is only willing to trust itself to oversee their overall management.'[5]

I think Savoie is right in his findings and that the situation is unhealthy for a federalism with differences as great as those in Canada. The Reform Party has been the voice of a digruntled and frustrated West, the constitution is not accepted as it stands even among federalist Quebeckers, and we have no effective second chamber to impose a check on a government with a seemingly perpetual majority in the House of Commons. If even the cabinet is a less important agency than in the past, it is not clear where or how our wide differences of region, culture, and language, which made a federal system essential for Canada in the first place, are taken into account in the decisions of government. And if in fact these differences are not adequately represented and reflected, our national discontents are sure to grow.

A New Government: June 1979

On 22 May 1979 Joe Clark led his Progressive Conservative Party to a precarious victory: 136 seats out of 282. The Social Credit Party, with

6 seats, could provide a majority over the Liberal-NDP opposition if it was carefully kept on side at critical moments. Overlooking that vital fact six months later made Clark's tenure of office much briefer than anyone had expected. I assumed that his government would do the obvious thing: carefully use eighteen months or two years in office to establish a record that would provide the basis for another election from which a majority would emerge. It was only Diefenbaker's skill as a campaigner in the 1965 election that had kept Pearson from succeeding in that policy in the two years after 1963. Pierre Trudeau had provided a recent example of how to do it between 1972 and 1974.

As secretary to the cabinet for federal-provincial relations I would be reporting to the new prime minister. A week or so after he took office and had settled on his cabinet, I asked for an opportunity to meet him. While the Canadian public service is professional and non-partisan, and while I had no doubt about my having observed those principles during my years in the service, I had been close to both Pearson and Trudeau in my years as secretary to the cabinet, and both were Liberals. I had served as deputy minister of northern affairs and national resources during Mr. Diefenbaker's entire time as prime minister and our relations were excellent, but that was a long time back. I realized that it would not be surprising if Clark might have some doubt about my political neutrality. I had decided that it would be best to make clear that I could retire on full pension and would be prepared to do so then or at any later time that he might wish. I did that when we met on 30 May.

Clark thanked me, but, as I recorded our conversation, 'said he hoped that I would stay on. He said he thought that it would be important for me to help him with many of the adjustments that might be involved in taking office and particularly in connection with senior appointments.' We agreed to proceed on the basis that 'either side' could terminate the arrangement and that we would 'look at the situation again in about twelve months.'

William Jarvis was appointed to the cabinet as minister of state (federal-provincial relations), as Marc Lalonde had been under Trudeau. I liked Jarvis and we got along well but I soon formed the impression that he found it difficult, having no knowledge of federal-provincial relations, to have as his adviser someone who had been steeped in its diplomacy, problems, and people for more than fifteen years. The Conservatives, when in opposition, had been critical of the Trudeau policies. I was part of those policies. Now, in office, the Clark government wanted something different but it was not as easy as it looked from the opposition benches. It was also difficult for them to believe that I could produce genuinely new and innovative alternatives to policies I had helped to develop.

There was to be a meeting of the federal-provincial continuing commitee of ministers on the constitution in the early autumn and a conference of first ministers at the end of November. I came to the conclusion over the summer that, if relations did not appear to be working more effectively in September, I would exercise my option to retire. I did so in a letter to Prime Minister Clark that I gave him at a meeting with him on 28 September. I would retire at the end of the year.

After referring to my identification 'in a personal way with former policies and former governments to a degree that could embarrass your efforts to establish your own approach in these areas [of national unity and the constitution],' I went on: 'With the Quebec referendum to be held early in 1980, there will be decisions of critical importance to be taken in the coming months with respect to strategy and to constitutional policy. I would not want my presence, as the official head of the Federal-Provincial Relations Office, with a direct responsibility in these matters, to inhibit in any way your capacity to establish and to carry out whatever new policies you think may be needed to preserve the unity of Canada and to create a better federalism for the future.' I had judged the situation correctly: Clark was relieved. He said that 'my "intuition" was right: that the new government would think it more difficult to establish new policies and new approaches and to make these publicly credible without changes in the personnel who had been handling the old policies.'

Clark and I had a second meeting at the prime minister's residence, 24 Sussex Drive, on 1 October at which we discussed possible successors for my position. I had several names to suggest, some inside and some from outside the public service who, I thought, might bring the new lines of policy advice the government was seeking. Clark also had several names. I have never learned why none of them was appointed well before the defeat in the House of Commons on 13 December rendered it impossible for Clark to appoint anyone. The whole point of my three months' notice had been to be sure that someone could be in the position before I left. If the government had survived for two more weeks there might have been an appointment before my departure but I doubt it.

While the federal-provincial side of my responsibilities had been frustrating, my role as adviser on senior personnel and appointments had been helpful to Clark: he thanked me for having 'kept him from making at least two mistakes in the handling of deputy ministers,' and he wondered whether, in his reply to my letter, he might 'announce that I would continue to be available to the government for advice in some role.' I suggested it would be best simply to deal with my retirement 'in a clear and final way.' Any possibilities after that could be left for the future.

The prime minister's formal reply of 3 October was gracious and friendly. As might have been expected, however, the press reaction was to put my departure in terms of disagreement with the new government – which, I suppose, at base it was. Many of the media found it difficult to believe that I left without any pressure whatever. Most comments were complimentary – 'the last of the mandarins,' 'when he leaves his position in December an era will end.' The Ottawa *Journal* in an editorial of 5 October was generous under a headline reading 'A model public servant.' After saying that my influence on the public service had been enormous, the editorial went on: 'What is beyond dispute is the extraordinary breadth of his knowledge of the art of public administration at the highest level. His influence was far wider than any particular post he held. His discretion, his integrity, his humane wisdom commanded respect from very different prime ministers and cabinet ministers. He gave his advice in the highest tradition of a disinterested public servant.' It was gratifying to hear this from a paper of known Conservative tradition.

As the date of my retirement at the end of December approached, I was surprised when Clark said that he would like to be host at an official reception for me and my wife before the Christmas recess of Parliament. A ministerial reception for a senior public servant after a long career was not too unusual and I did have a minister who could have been host: William Jarvis. The prime minister was, therefore, going out of his way. The reception was to be on 17 December in the Railway Committee Room of the Centre Block. I was asked to submit my list of invitees, the prime minister had his. Everything had been in hand for nearly two weeks when, on 13 December, the government was defeated in the House of Commons on the budget. Clark then had more important things to worry about than my reception: he delegated Walter Baker, the president of the Privy Council and minister of revenue, to act for him. In some light-hearted remarks in speaking at the reception, I said that I could quite understand that what my old friend Pierre Trudeau had done on 13 December was good for him and his party, noting the absence of both the prime minister and Trudeau, but I deplored his failure to consider what he was doing to me and my farewell party.

My sense of my relationship with Trudeau was the greater because that very day – 17 December – I had had lunch with him in the Grill at the Chateau Laurier. He telephoned me that morning to say that 'he would like to talk to me, as an old friend, as to what he ought to do with respect to his difficult decision': whether, in the light of the government's defeat, to reverse the decision he had announced on 21 November to retire as leader of the Liberal Party and also from politics.

I did the kind of 'pros' and 'cons' analysis I had often done for him on difficult issues with alternative courses of action. Summing it up at the end, I said that 'if I were in Pierre Trudeau's place ... I would not reverse my decision to retire.' At the end of our lunch, Trudeau expressed his appreciation and crossed the floor to an alcove on the other side where he had arranged to meet with Allan MacEachen, Jim Coutts, and Keith Davey. There he got the political 'pros' I was in no position to give: I doubt if he got many 'cons.' The next day Trudeau announced that he 'had decided that it was his duty to accept the draft of the Liberal Party' and to lead it in the election that had been called for 18 February. He would win a clear majority.

It was an unusual tribute when the governor general, Edward Schreyer, and his wife gave a dinner at Rideau Hall on 7 January 1980 to mark my retirement from the public service. There were about sixty guests from the Légers through Chief Justice Bora Laskin and his wife, Pierre Elliott Trudeau, MP (*not* then prime minister), our family, old friends like the Pickersgills, Bryces, Duntons, Robinsons, and Alvin Hamilton to my devoted secretary, Annette Walls, who had a great but unwritten role in making the Privy Council Office work for nearly twenty years. No one could have been more loyal and selfless.

It was a happy party but the following days made more stark the question of 'what now?' I was sixty-two, in excellent health, and not at all ready to 'retire.' I had focused entirely on the public service from the time I entered it nearly forty years before. I had turned down four offers of presidencies of Canadian universities because my interest in the public service and government was greater. I also turned down the vice presidency of a British Columbia utility corporation for the same reasons and because I felt I had no talent for business. It was a curiously empty feeling after a life that had been active and creative in a field where the public impression is that life is pedestrian, bureaucratic, and dull. The senior federal public service of the war-time and post-war period was, in fact, one of the most innovative, challenging, and intellectually stimulating places to work in all of Canada. It turned out that Prime Minister

Clark's failure to fill my position before his parliamentary defeat on 13 December opened the way to a solution to my problem.

The Clerk and Political Neutrality

When I decided in the autumn of 1979 to retire from the public service, Bea was not very impressed with my plans for employing my new freedom. I said that I had put so much time and effort into national unity and constitutional reform that I was going to do some thinking about the issues, write about them, and see if I could discern any way out of the morass that appeared to have got worse, rather than better, the longer we worked at it. Her only comment was that, if I expected to sell a book on a subject like that, I was in for disappointment: the country was fed up with unity, the constitution, and everything about them.

The warning did not deter me. I entered into an arrangement with the Institute for Research on Public Policy (IRPP), of which Michael Kirby was then president, to become a 'fellow in residence' for two years. I would have an office, a share of a secretary, office facilities, no remuneration, and a contract committing me to do 'something' in my area of interest over a period of two years.

On 18 February 1980, the resurrected Trudeau led his Liberal Party to victory: 147 seats in a House of 282. Joe Clark's Conservatives dropped from 136 seats to 103. In a letter of congratulation to Pierre I said that, if I could be of any help on a renewed constitutional exercise – which I was sure there would be – to let me know but my retirement, unlike his, was not reversible. I had no wish to do anything that would give the impression that my retirement had been political and was subject to cancellation with a change of government.

Not surprisingly, but still unfortunately for the non-political character of the most senior position in the public service, Michael Pitfield was promptly reappointed clerk of the Privy Council and secretary to the cabinet. Marcel Massé, a career public servant, had been appointed to that position by Clark when he had been unwilling to accept Pitfield's continuance in office. Trudeau was not comfortable with Massé for some reason I do not know. He had asked me, while Clark was prime minister, to be the 'custodian' of the cabinet documents covering his years in office rather than Massé. The custodian role had, since an agreement between St Laurent and Diefenbaker when the governments changed in 1957, been the responsibility of the clerk of the Privy Council of the day: it was only one among several reasons why the position of clerk should, above any others in the public service, be and be seen to be non-political.

The Custodian of Cabinet Documents

Canada had lived until 1957 with no problem about the custodianship of the confidential papers of cabinet and all its works when government changed. There had been a good many changes from 1867 to 1957 – but there were no cabinet documents. It was only during the war, with masses of documents for the war committee of the cabinet and for other committees of ministers, military officers, and public servants, that the problem could arise and only in 1957, when the Progressive Conservatives, led by John Diefenbaker, replaced the Liberals, led by Louis St Laurent, that it became real. Who was to be the custodian of the papers if they were to be left in the PCO files for record, for reference, and for history? They would not be left at all by an outgoing government unless there was a custodian in whom the outgoing prime minister had confidence to apply the constitutional convention about the privacy of his cabinet's confidences. The whole basis of cabinet government rests on privacy or full discussion will not be possible. The custodian had to be someone who would say a firm 'No,' and who would have enough public status to make it stick, if someone not of or acceptable to the former government wanted access to its papers.

We were fortunate in 1957 to have a clerk whose reputation was beyond question, Robert Bryce, and also two political leaders who understood the importance of the convention. As Arnold Heeney, the first clerk to hold the office after 'documents' arose, put it: 'These two men agreed that the British tradition should be followed and that the secretary to the cabinet should be accepted as the custodian of cabinet papers, responsible for determining what communication should be made thereof to succeeding administrations.'[6]

The problem is not solely about communication to 'succeeding administrations.' In February 1980 I refused, as custodian, to produce documents requested by a lawyer in Winnipeg acting for CAE Aircraft Ltd in an action against the federal government of the Trudeau period on the ground that the documents related to 'the formulation of government policy' and were protected by constitutional convention. Less than a month later I had to decide on a request from the Commission of Enquiry into Certain Activities of the RCMP (the Macdonald Commission). In that case I agreed to provide documents 'for the use of the Commission in private and *in camera* only,' again because of the convention on access. At no time was my judgment or my authority challenged by the court, the commission, or the government.

The fundamental point is the one Heeney so clearly grasped: that the effective operation of the cabinet system depends on its being served by professional, non-partisan public servants, of whom the critical one is the clerk of the Privy Council and secretary to the cabinet.

PART SIX

Trudeau's 'Power Play,' Meech Lake, and the Charlottetown Accord, 1980–1992

chapter fifteen

The Trudeau Power Play, 1980–1982

Not long after his reappointment as clerk in March 1980, Michael Pitfield came to see me in my tiny office in the IRPP. The apparent purpose was to ask whether I wanted to return to the job I had held from 1975 to 1979 of secretary to the cabinet for federal-provincial relations.

If Michael was acting on behalf of the prime minister, he should have known that I had said in my letter of congratulation that my retirement was not reversible. Whether he knew or not, it was obviously a pro forma question to which I was supposed to answer 'No' – as I did. I had known Trudeau for thirty years and had been his senior official adviser and aide on federal-provincial matters for more than ten: if he had wanted me to return he would have invited me to come to his office to talk about his plans. The messenger was part of the message: my help was no longer wanted.

It was convenient for Trudeau that Clark had not filled my federal-provincial relations position. He appointed Michael Kirby to it. Kirby and Michael Pitfield were friends and could be counted on to work well together.

While I never had – or expected – any word from Trudeau as to why he did not seek any help from me, his remarks as quoted by Stephen Clarkson and Christina McCall sound right: '"Let's just say," Trudeau explained several years later, "that in this last stage I felt one needed almost a putsch, a coup de force, and Gordon was too much of a gentleman for that. It was clearly going to be rough and Gordon Robertson wasn't the man: a mandarin, concerned with the common weal, afraid of irreparable damage to the fabric of society. So I made a different choice."'[1]

Trudeau was right in that assessment. No one who had worked with Mackenzie King, Louis St Laurent, or Lester Pearson could believe that a power play, however successful in the short term, was the way to solve a constitutional problem.

As I gradually became aware in 1980 of the 'coup de force' that was unfolding, I told Mike Kirby that I would not want to enter into any contractual arrangement to advise or to assist. So I became a bystander at first and then, in later stages, a critic and finally an opponent of some of the positions Trudeau took. It is not yet clear whether his coup has led to the 'irreparable damage' he spoke of, but great damage there undoubtedly has been in the rise of separatism and in the decline of support for federalism among the francophone majority in Quebec. Part of that can be blamed on the 'constitution of 1981' without Quebec and the destruction of the Meech Lake Accord in which Trudeau played a significant part.

The Trudeau Campaign

The campaign that Trudeau launched in 1980 and carried through to its successful conclusion in the signing by the Queen of the proclamation of the Constitution Act, 1982, on Parliament Hill on 17 April of that year resembled nothing so much as the brilliant campaigns, beginning in 1805, in which Napoleon waged war against an alliance of continental European powers, taking them on, one by one or in various coalitions and defeating them in turn by superior tactics. Trudeau's campaign was less politics than war – war by other means – and his generalship was highly successful in achieving his immediate purposes: the full patriation of the constitution with an amending procedure located entirely in Canada, a Charter of Rights, and no concession of powers to the provinces.

Napoleon's campaigns, brilliant as they were, left one major problem – the naval power of Britain that his armies could not reach or defeat: it defeated him in the end. Trudeau's campaign has in turn left a major problem: the separatist sympathies in Quebec that cannot be tackled by 'coups de force' and have yet to be defeated by traditional political means of policy and persuasion.

The Napoleonic opponents had been Austria, Prussia, and Russia, with a scattering of smaller German states – and Britain, off in the sea but active in blockade and in financing European resistance. Trudeau's opponents were the provinces – all ten at times, eight at others; the governments of Quebec, PQ and Liberal in turn; Britain for a time, torn by its mixture of constitutional obligations; and finally, the Supreme Court of Canada. The court was the closest approach to Napoleon's

Britain: the one power that could not be defeated by any coup de force. The first battle was with the separatist forces of Quebec in the referendum of 20 May 1980. Trudeau personally was a major factor in achieving the 'No' majority: 59.4 per cent to 40.4 per cent. However, his 'solemn commitment' at the Paul Sauvé Arena 'to renew the constitution,' which brought the audience to its feet in ovation, left the question later whether the voters had been misled about the nature of his commitment. Notwithstanding those doubts, there was no question but that the first battle had been won decisively.

Whatever it was that Trudeau had committed his government to, it meant that the long and weary sessions with the provinces would be renewed, with probable frustration at the end, if there was not a change on the part either of the provinces or of the federal government. A federal-provincial meeting in June reinstituted the constitutional machinery developed after 1968 and the continuing committee of ministers on the constitution (CCMC) became the vehicle for renewed consultation. Jean Chrétien, then minister of justice and minister responsible for constitutional negotiations, and Roy Romanow, attorney general of Saskatchewan, became co-chairmen, visited all the provinces, and prepared 'best-efforts' drafts on the basis of the questions that had been left unresolved at the first ministers' conference of 1979. The main thing that was different was the mood of the new Trudeau government. It was no longer a tired government nearing the shaky end of a long term in office: it was a phoenix with all the vigour of being born again. After the commitment at the Paul Sauvé arena and the victory for 'No' in the referendum, something new was going to happen: it was not at all clear just what or how.

The outcome of the summer's consultations by the CCMC was a conference of first ministers in Ottawa from 8 to 12 September 1980. The conference was a raucous disaster. For an 'outsider,' which I was, it was not clear whether it was a planned, intended, and well-executed disaster or whether there were still illusions on both the federal and provincial sides that led to it without intention. The leaked 'Kirby memorandum,' prepared just before the conference, concluded that consensus even on the agenda was not certain and that the federal government should be prepared to proceed unilaterally if no agreement with the provinces could be reached. The likelihood is that the federal government was not surprised by or sorry for the sharp clash that developed even at the governor general's dinner before the conference. It was the perfect preparation for the unilateral federal course the Kirby memorandum proposed. It was announced on 2 October that the federal government would proceed unilaterally to get action by the British government and Parliament to transfer control of the constitution to Canada.

Trudeau's Assault on Britain

The federal initiative had the support of premiers Davis of Ontario and Hatfield of New Brunswick: the former in the moderate federalist role Ontario often took and the latter reflecting his sensitive concern for balance in his English-French province. With the eight other provinces opposed, Trudeau was moving to infringe constitutional provisions that had been worked out with care at the specific request of Canada before the passage of the Statute of Westminster in 1931.

The statute put in legal form the agreement at the Imperial Conference of 1926 that the dominions should be 'independent communities' within the Commonwealth, equal in status with Britain and in no way subordinate to it. The provinces, led by Ontario, were concerned that the new status for Canada might be interpreted to mean that the federal Parliament would acquire the legal power, that only the British Parliament had up to that time, to amend our constitution: the British North America Act. After agreement at a federal-provincial conference in April 1931, and a joint address from the House of Commons and Senate of Canada, a provision was inserted in the Statute of Westminster for the specific purpose of preserving British legislative jurisdiction over the BNA Act and over its future amendment, thus protecting provincial interests.

St Laurent in 1949 had been well aware of the provincial concerns in 1931 and of the provision then made at Canadian request. If Trudeau was aware of that background he chose not to admit it. He says in his *Memoirs*: 'The eight premiers who opposed our plan did not, of course, sit idly by. First they lobbied hard in London to see if they could persuade the British Parliament to resort to its old colonial posture and second-guess the duly elected government of Canada.'[2] Almost certainly the basis of the provision of 1931 was not part of the briefing Trudeau gave to the British prime minister, Margaret Thatcher, in June 1980, 'about our constitutional position.' He says: 'She had told me that if the Parliament of Canada asked for its constitution, there was nothing her Parliament could do but accede to that request.'[3] She apparently had no awareness of any obligation to any provinces or she would certainly have raised the question.

It was not surprising in the circumstances that the provincial premiers, other than Ontario and New Brunswick, decided to take their case to court. Three provinces – Manitoba, Newfoundland, and Quebec – put questions before their courts of appeal about the legality of the federal action. The courts of Manitoba and Quebec, by divided judgments in each case, ruled that the federal course was not unconstitutional: provincial consent for the address to the British government for action by the British Parliament was not required. The court in Newfoundland was unanimously of the opposite opinion. Now only a reference to the Supreme Court of Canada could give a final answer.

The Supreme Court gave its response on 28 September 1981. Professor Joseph E. Magnet of the University of Ottawa and I had been asked by the CBC to comment on the decision as it was read by the chief justice of Canada over television. Our comments could not have been attempted in more difficult circumstances. Apparently one of the justices had tripped over a wire and disconnected the sound system at precisely the time that the chief justice began to read. We got bits and pieces of sentences but with great gaps filled by static or silence. Whatever our difficulties, the court gave a divided opinion that I referred to as a judgment of Solomon. There had been several questions put to it and its replies were, not surprisingly, divided. By a majority of seven to two, the court held that, as a matter of strict law, provincial consent was not required for the federal 'patriation' action. However, a majority of six to three ruled that, by constitutional convention, established in the handling of amendments and disagreements on amendments from 1867 to that date, there was a requirement for a 'substantial degree' of provincial consent – which the federal action, with two consenting provinces only, did not have.

I was so much in agreement with the answer about the need for provincial consent as a matter of constitutional convention that a few days later I called my old friend and former colleague, then Mr Justice Jean Beetz. He had been a member of the majority in the six-to-three group. The opinion had been so well reasoned that I was confident that only he could have written it – and I said so as I congratulated him. I had not sufficiently considered the spot I put Jean in because of the etiquette surrounding Supreme Court judgments. If the author of a judgment is not stated, no authorship is claimed or acknowledged. No man was ever more frank and honest than Jean. His embarrassment made it clear I was right: he could not deny the authorship but he should not admit it. He squirmed, but the truth was apparent.

At the dedication of the Bora Laskin Law Library at the University of Toronto in March 1991, Pierre Trudeau claimed that the justices involved in the 'convention' decision had 'blatantly manipulated the evidence before them' to arrive at that decision. The comment, with the late Chief Justice Brian Dickson who had joined in that judgment sitting a few feet away, was rude, arrogant, and wrong. No objective person, knowing the amendment record, could question the reasonableness of the majority's opinion. Trudeau's reputation for cool, clear reason was subject to qualification, as became clear with his opposition to the Meech Lake Accord.

The Agreement without Quebec

The conference of first ministers of November 1981, made necessary by the Supreme Court's decision in September, involved a strategic approach and tactical manoeuvres to rival anything that Napoleon achieved on the field of battle – indeed, the premier of Quebec, René Lévesque, may have felt at the end that that was rather where he had been.

Trudeau had a clear plan: 'I was aiming at one of two outcomes: I could either prove to the Canadian public that the Eight were being completely unreasonable and then go ahead alone, legally but perhaps unconventionally. Or I could break the solidarity among the Eight and go to London with the support of a substantial number of premiers, which I supposed would be anywhere between five and nine of them. Lévesque's goal was to keep the Gang of Eight intact to thwart me, and mine was to make a certain number of concessions that would split their ranks and bring some of the others on side.'[4]

Lévesque was badly outmanoeuvred; the provincial ranks were split and the 'Gang of Eight' was broken. A deal was worked out, basically on provincial acceptance of the Charter of Rights, but with a 'notwithstanding' clause, in exchange for federal acceptance of the Alberta amending formula but without fiscal compensation for provinces that opted out. The notwithstanding clause went some way to meet the worries of those premiers who were concerned about passing to the courts, on Charter rights, the supremacy that had been Parliament's, although the power of override under the clause would be temporary. The Alberta amending formula was based on provincial equality and is more rigid than the federally favoured Victoria formula.

The agreement was concluded on the night of 4–5 November but without the participation of Quebec – an absence that Trudeau blames on Lévesque himself: 'It was quite obvious at the time that Lévesque left himself out, first when he broke the Gang of Eight, and then when he went back to his hotel in Hull for the night. I don't know whether he and his delegation were celebrating, just sleeping on it, or regretting that they had broken the solidarity. But they obviously were not prowling the corridors or working the phones, looking to negotiate a compromise as the others were; they decided they would rather sit it out than be part of a compromise.'[5] Premier Lévesque had a totally different interpretation of what happened. He left the conference in fury – a fury still to burn itself out in Quebec.

The resolution of the Senate and House of Commons for an address to the Queen was passed in December and the Constitution Act, 1982, was proclaimed on 17 April – just over fourteen years after Prime Minister Pearson had launched the constitutional-review exercise – and just under fourteen years since Pierre Trudeau had taken it on.

While I was unhappy at the absence of the government of Quebec from the final agreement, I could not disagree with Trudeau's decision to go ahead. There was no further need to demonstrate the effort he had made to get an agreement that did include Quebec and there was no reason to believe that Premier Lévesque's government, which was dedicated to separation from Canada, would agree to any formula for change that could gain acceptance by the other governments of Canada. In fact, the search for agreement had gone back well before 1968. St Laurent had been frustrated by Duplessis in 1950; Pearson by Lesage in 1964; Pierre Trudeau by Bourassa in 1971. It could not be said that every effort had not been made during the entire post-war period to include Quebec within the reform that had, for the most part, been launched to meet Quebec discontents.

This did not mean, however, that the result of the 'agreement without Quebec' was not a deep wound which would be made worse by the failure of the Meech Lake Accord in 1990 and of the Charlottetown Accord in 1992. In both of those failures Pierre Trudeau, although not in power, would be an important factor.

chapter sixteen

Away from Government

Within a few months of my two-year appointment as a fellow-in-residence at the Institute for Research on Public Policy, Michael Kirby, the president of the Institute, had been appointed to fill my old job as secretary to the cabinet for federal-provincial relations. I then accepted an appointment to Kirby's position as president of the Institute, which left no time to embark on the book about constitutional reform I had in mind.

The institute had been founded in 1972 as an independent organization supported by the income from an endowment fund established by grants from the federal and provincial governments, together with contracts from governments and the private sector. Its mandate was to carry out specific research projects, and in this to 'act as a catalyst' for informed public debate, to 'stimulate participation by all segments of the national community' in public-policy making, and 'to find practical solutions to important policy problems.' It was an original and innovative idea but the nearly ten years of experience had revealed a number of difficulties in achieving the laudable objectives.

John Black Aird, who became lieutenant governor of Ontario in September 1980, was chairman of the board of directors when I became president. Without him and his persuasive ways of coaxing contributions out of governments, corporations, and individuals, the endowment fund would never have reached a figure that provided a secure basic revenue. Aird was succeeded as chairman by Robert Stanfield, who had come within a hair-breadth of being prime minister of Canada in 1972. During nearly four years of working with him I came to realize how unfortunate it was that Canadians never had the opportunity of seeing him as head of our national government. His wisdom, moderation, and good judgment would have made him a superb leader through difficult years. He was one of the tiny minority in the House of Commons who voted against the resolution in 1981 that implemented the 'agreement without Quebec.' In talking about this later, he said that he could not at the time see any reason why it was so urgent to 'patriate' our constitution that it was justifiable to do it over the objection of the elected government of Quebec and the overwhelming majority of the members of its National Assembly, nor had he seen any reason later. I did not agree with Stanfield in 1981 but the bitterness and division the action has provoked in all the years since have led me to believe that he may well have been right. However that may be, there could not have been a better chairman for the institute or a wiser counsellor for its president, who was inexperienced in running such an organization.

Apart from the problems of financing, which were constant, the greatest difficulty for the institute was the high-minded founding principle that it should be utterly impartial and have no policy position of its own. That may have been necessary if the institute was to have the support of all governments, whatever their differences might be. However, the principle kept the institute from studying some of the most critical and interesting national problems. Some room was provided by the insistence that all conclusions and recommendations in institute publications were 'solely those of the author and should not be attributed to the Board of directors, Council of Trustees or contributors to the Institute.' However, it was then and has since been a problem; it is much easier to get public attention and to establish relevance if an institution can have an identifiable position and a consistent and uninhibited freedom in argument. The institute was, however, an experiment in the field of public-policy research in Canada – a successful one that raised the level of discussion and analysis at a time when that was much needed.

Chancellor, Carleton University, 1980–90

On 15 December 1979 I was elected chancellor of Carleton University for the normal three-year term. I had been a member of its board of governors from 1962 to 1971 and had maintained an interest in Carleton afterward, in part because of my close friendship with Davidson Dunton who was president from 1958 to 1972 and director of its Institute of Canadian Studies until 1978. He continued as fellow in that institute until his death in 1987, when the testimony of members of the faculty and staff at a memorial service spoke eloquently of the great esteem in which he was held.

The chancellor at Carleton – and at most if not all Canadian universities – is the formal head of the university. The prestige is great, the responsibility is slight, and the power is in the hands of the president. It is a highly decorative position at convocations: the gown is gorgeous; all remarks by the president, deans, and faculty are respectfully addressed to 'Mr Chancellor,' and all degrees are awarded as if by his grace and favour. I stepped into a most distinguished succession. My three predecessors had been Dr C.J. Mackenzie, formerly president of Canada's National Research Council, Lester B. Pearson, and Dr Gerhard Herzberg, recipient of the Nobel Prize in physics. Their otherwise oppressive stature was made bearable by the fact that I, as a student, had known both Mackenzie and Herzberg as members of the faculty at the University of Saskatchewan some forty years before when I was an undergraduate, and, of course, 'Mike' Pearson was a friend as well as a former prime minister.

As chancellor, I was a member of the Board of Governors and of its executive committee and also of the Senate of the University. I worked hard at the first two but I felt I could add little to the academic knowledge and wisdom required for the latter. The convocations were great fun: meeting every graduating student as he or she knelt to be 'hooded' and trying, in about ten seconds, to say something congratulatory, encouraging, and not too inane to each proud graduand. I was re-elected for three more terms and ended up as 'chancellor emeritus' in 1990.

The North in Canada's International Relations
In June 1986 a special joint committee of the Senate and House of Commons on Canada's international relations presented a report which included a recommendation that there should be a 'northern dimension' to Canadian foreign policy. In December of that year the government said that it recognized the importance 'of developing a coherent set of policies for the Arctic, including foreign policy' but put no flesh on that thin bone of agreement. The National Capital Branch of the Canadian Institute of International Affairs established a working group to do something about it and I was asked to be chairman, so I got back, in an unofficial way, into a study of policy relating to my great love of twenty years before – the Canadian North. We reported in March 1988.

Our report covered the full range of questions, domestic and international, that the working group considered relevant for a 'coherent set of policies' for our North. The goal of a 'northern dimension' for Canadian foreign policy should, we said, be 'the achievement and maintenance of a secure and peaceful world in the Arctic, in which aboriginal inhabitants can preserve the essentials of their cultures while living in association with Canadians of other origins. Such a world requires the preservation of the physical environment, but also the encouragement of such economic development as is consistent with it and that will provide as self-supporting an economy as the costs and problems of the North make possible.'[1] There were, we said, four principal objectives involved: '(a) preservation of national security and the promotion of peaceful co-operation in the Arctic; (b) the promotion of the well-being and self-reliance of our northern aboriginal people, who are likely to constitute the predominant population of our Arctic; (c) the protection of the Arctic environment and the increase in knowledge that will contribute to it and to the handling of problems special to the Arctic; and (d) the promotion of economic development in the Arctic and of activities related thereto, consistent with the protection of the environment.'[2]

The Polar World

Canada has within its boundaries a northern territory second in size only to that of Russia. Six other countries have territories around the Arctic Ocean – the circumpolar north. These combined Arctic territories are larger than North America in size yet have a population of only some ten million people. The small population and its distribution are, directly or indirectly, largely a reflection of climate. The most benign conditions occur where oceanic influences moderate the extreme cold. As our 1988 report said, 'these anomalously warm, high-latitude conditions are found in Scandinavia, Finland, and along the arctic coast of European Russia warmed by the Gulf Stream. To a lesser degree, similar influence is felt in western Alaska, Kamchatka, and on the coast of south-western Greenland. Northern Eurasia, apart from the western region, has a continental climate that differs from that of continental Canada. This is because it does not have the equivalent "refrigerator" of Hudson Bay bringing arctic climate (and the tree-line) deep into the heart of North America.'[3]

The report of 1988 noted that the main aspects of circumpolar relations included NATO, bilateral defence arrangements like NORAD, scientific cooperation, and northern peoples' groups like the Inuit Circumpolar Conference (ICC). The ICC was an initiative of the Inuit themselves, founded at a meeting at Barrow, Alaska, in 1977, with triennial general assemblies that combine social and cultural activities with deliberations on northern policy matters. It is the first effort by the Inuit people, scattered around the polar seas, to join together to discuss problems of common interest and to develop comprehensive approaches to the governments of the countries in which they reside.

In northern Europe the four countries with territory bordering on the circumpolar sea – Iceland, Denmark, Norway, and Sweden – together with Finland – cooperate through the Nordic Council in areas of common interest, especially for their Aboriginal peoples. The council has associate status for home-rule territories such as Greenland, the Faroe Islands, and the Aaland Islands. The Sami (Lapps) of the three Scandinavian countries are represented in the Nordic Council by a delegation to speak for them as a people, not as parts of the respective countries.

When one of the circumpolar countries was the Soviet Union and the Cold War prevailed, the international Arctic atmosphere was one of tension, if not hostility. However, an address by President Mikhail Gorbachev at Murmansk in 1987 brought a new note – a proposal for a council to facilitate international cooperation in the Arctic. At the Washington summit in December 1987, President Ronald Reagan and Gorbachev discussed 'means of encouraging expanded contacts and co-operation on issues relating to the Arctic' and 'expressed support for the development of bilateral regional co-operation among the arctic countries on these matters, including coordination of scientific research and protection of the region's environment.'[4] That initiative and developments in the last ten years present a number of new questions for Canada as well as for other Arctic states.

The Arctic Council

As a positive step towards the cooperation of which the two presidents spoke, our report urged the establishment of an Arctic Basin Council for international discussion of Arctic questions.[5] It was a timely recommendation, although it took several years before the 'Arctic Council' of today emerged. It held the first meeting of its ministerial council at Iqaluit in September 1998, with ministers from the eight member countries in attendance: the United States, Russia, Canada, Finland, Sweden, Norway, Greenland, and Iceland. Five other countries with a long record of interest in the Arctic have observer status: the United Kingdom, France, Germany, Poland, and Japan. Mary Simon, an Inuk from Arctic Quebec, was appointed Canadian ambassador for circumpolar affairs and headed the secretariat for the council, initially located in Canada but moved to Washington in late 1999.

It is too soon to tell how useful the Arctic Council will be: it will largely depend on the extent to which the member countries use it. However, it is apparent that the range of questions of common interest in the Arctic is growing and will grow in future. Global warming alone, which has the greatest impact on the two polar regions, has already raised problems that are circumpolar in nature and require the kind of shared approach for which the Arctic Council is designed.

Canada as a Polar State

A basic question for future policy is to identify what Canada's interests are in the polar world and what we can best do to promote them. One area of concern was raised by the voyages of two American vessels – the *Manhattan* in 1969 and the *Polar Sea* in 1985 – through the Northwest Passage, an important part of which follows straits between islands of the Canadian Arctic archipelago. Since claims by Norway to some islands were settled in 1930, no country has challenged the sovereignty of Canada over any land area in the archipelago. The straits between the islands are another matter. The position of the United States, with its global political and security interests, is that all straits and waters of the world, however narrow and wherever they lie, are part of the open sea if they lead from one part of the high seas to another. Canada responded to the voyage of the *Manhattan* by passing the Arctic Waters Pollution Prevention Act of 1970 – a measure short of a direct challenge to the United States position but an assertion of Canadian authority over the water itself, not necessarily as sovereign of the water itself, but to protect the extreme vulnerability of the Arctic marine environment which is important for Inuit living on the resources of the sea in the area.

The solution was a satisfying demonstration of the value, at times, of the cabinet committee system, bringing ministers and officials together over complex problems. Ministers wanted a challenge to the United States 'freedom of the straits' concept in the Arctic archipelago but not a direct assertion of Canadian sovereignty: our case in law was not good enough to be sure of winning. My experience in the Law of the Sea conference of 1958 and my knowledge of the dependence of the Inuit on the resources of the sea came together with External Affairs ingenuity in devising a measure that had relevance and also legitimacy for Canada as the coastal sovereign of the water.

In 1985 Canada took a further step by drawing baselines around the outside of the Arctic archipelago and declaring the waters within them to be historically internal. Each country – Canada and the United States – considers that it has important interests at stake and is unwilling to abandon them while still wanting to avoid a confrontation. The result was an agreement to cooperate within the differences of position. The working group report of 1988 says: 'The Canada-United States Agreement on Arctic Cooperation, signed in Ottawa on 11 January 1988, contains no recognition by the United States of Canadian sovereignty over the waters of the Canadian Arctic Archipelago. It is quite specific in stating that, "Nothing in this agreement ... nor any practice thereunder affects the respective positions" of the two governments. However, the concern by Canada must be that, despite those words, procedures under the agreement may, in fact, weaken the Canadian position in international law.'

The joint committee of the Senate and House of Commons had identified in its report a number of areas it thought should be covered in 'a coherent arctic policy,' first among them being the social and economic stability of the Canadian Inuit. 'The Inuit are Canada's most important support in the Arctic, and government policy should reflect this perception. Canada should give priority to achieving an acceptable land settlement in the North and encourage efforts to find governmental structures that would support Inuit cultural autonomy within the Canadian federation.' [6]

The political accord for the establishment of the Territory of Nunavut of 1992 and the land-claims agreement of 1993 are effective responses to the structural parts of the committee recommendations. Much more difficult are the 'social and economic stability' of the Inuit to which the committee referred and, indeed, of the Aboriginal people in the North generally.

The social and economic problems of the Aboriginal people of our northern territories are substantially the same as those of many of our Aboriginal people generally: low income, high unemployment, problems of social adjustment reflected often in alcohol, domestic violence, and high rates of juvenile suicides. In one sense the problems in the North are more difficult because, with the exception of specific locations in the Yukon and in the Mackenzie-Great Slave Lake area of the Northwest Territories, the surrounding general economy is weak and the prospects of Aboriginal employment are limited – except in government. In another sense there are for some in the North still possibilities of 'life on the land,' which for the Inuit often means 'life on the sea,' to a greater degree than for Indians and Metis in the more settled parts of Canada. The essential point is, however, that we have not yet matched the efforts for a coherent foreign policy for the Arctic with the much more difficult domestic counterpart – a policy to address the social and economic problems of the Canadian Arctic.

The working group of 1988, in applauding the recommendation for a 'northern dimension' to Canadian foreign policy, said that 'its fundamental basis must be the presence in our Arctic and in our North more generally, of a self-reliant, resident population,' the permanent part of which 'may well be preponderantly Aboriginal in future.' The group found great difficulty in discerning how that 'self-reliance' was to be assured. The problem of high costs in the North limits the possibilities for development based on non-renewable resources – minerals, oil, and gas. The anti-fur campaign had by 1988 severely damaged the traditional economies of both Indians and Inuit and that injury has continued in the years since. The group recommended that 'studies be continued and pilot projects undertaken to determine possibilities for the promotion of small-scale, decentralized industries in the Arctic, to apply the skills of northern peoples to the production of goods of a nature and value that can support the high cost of air transportation for materials and marketing.'[7]

The Inuit especially have shown a remarkable skill in mechanical, design, and manipulative work and it is difficult to believe that these aptitudes could not be turned to high-value, low-weight products as effectively as are hands and skills in Thailand, Malaysia, and Vietnam where so much is produced by men and women of communities in the course of transitions not unlike the changes in lifestyle going on in our North. The cost problem might, as in almost everything northern, again be difficult. Our 1988 report warned: 'Unless new economic prospects emerge, it seems likely that Canada will have to accept the probability that a reasonable standard of living in such extreme northern areas will, for most people, involve continuing and high subsidies of various kinds.'[8] While this may not be inevitable, the need for subsidy has been accepted by implication in the high level of federal financial support that has been necessary over the last forty years for social security, income support, and administration in our far North. It may not be realistic to base policies on the assumption that, in some of the harshest and most difficult conditions on earth, resident native populations can live – on the basis of full cost recovery in a global market – in a manner that is considered acceptable for Canadians in the south.

Our Arctic territory is there, it is the second largest in the world, and Canada obviously does not intend to abandon it. Pollution from lower latitudes is carried into the Arctic by atmospheric circulation and ocean currents. These and other problems will increase and the circumpolar countries will have to join together to deal with them. We will not be in a position to assert the influence we should unless we have a healthy, self-respecting Arctic population.

We have such a population now, although it is plagued by the problems of social and economic transition. With new government structures, especially the establishment of the Territory of Nunavut on 1 April 1999, the Aboriginal people of the North will be in a better position to control their own affairs than anywhere else in Canada. It will be neither impossible nor overly costly for one of the wealthiest societies on earth to provide economic support for small, preponderantly Aboriginal populations, made up of the people best suited to life in the Canadian Arctic and subarctic.

chapter seventeen

Meech Lake: The Best Hope Lost

Before the election of September 1984, Brian Mulroney promised that, if elected, Conservatives would endeavour to bring Quebec to accept 'with honour and enthusiasm' the constitution it had rejected in 1982. The essential condition to make that possible came with the victory of the Liberal Party of Quebec, led by Robert Bourassa, in the provincial election of December 1985. In May 1986 Gil Rémillard, the minister of intergovernmental affairs in the new Liberal government, presented Quebec's conditions for acceptance of the constitution to a conference on the future of Quebec and Canada at Mont Gabriel, Quebec.

There were five requirements, Rémillard said, to make the 'constitution of 1982' acceptable, of which formal recognition of Quebec as a 'distinct society' was the first and most important. The others were strengthening Quebec's role in immigration, giving it a share in the selection of the three judges from Quebec on the Supreme Court of Canada, permitting Quebec to opt out of federal spending programs in areas of exclusive provincial jurisdiction with financial compensation, and restoration of a Quebec veto on constitutional amendments affecting Quebec's interests. The conditions were the most moderate proposals to emerge from any Quebec government since the failure of the Victoria Conference of 1971 – fifteen years before.

I was at the Mont Gabriel meeting with participants from all parts of Canada – academics, officials, journalists, and others who had been involved or interested in the constitutional discussions of the preceding years. The general reaction was one of relief: there was no prospect of getting a more favourable basis for bringing Quebec into willing acceptance of the '1982 constitution.' The fact that there was, with a federalist government in power in Quebec, no crisis and no 'knife' at anyone's 'throat' gave hope for a calm and measured discussion by governments and, perhaps, for escape from the dangerous division left by the 'agreement without Quebec.'

Subsequent discussions by Quebec representatives with the other provinces were encouraging. The Edmonton Declaration in August 1986 said: 'The premiers unanimously agreed their top constitutional priority is to embark immediately upon a federal-provincial process, using Quebec's five proposals as a basis of discussion, to bring about Quebec's full and active participation in the Canadian federation.' The provincial governments agreed to a 'Quebec round' of constitutional negotiations which led in April 1987 to an agreement at Meech Lake, north of Ottawa, by all eleven governments.

The Meech Lake Accord and Pierre Trudeau

The Meech Lake Accord was based squarely on the five 'conditions' set forth at Mont Gabriel, but with a difference. As Peter Russell put it: 'In a nutshell, they [the conditions] had been provincialized. They had been made agreeable to the provincial premiers by respecting the principle of provincial equality and, with one exception, extending to all the provinces the powers sought by Quebec.'[1] The one exception to making the five conditions apply to all provinces was, of course, the recognition of Quebec as a distinct society.

Pierre Trudeau did not wait for the accord to be put in legal language. On 27 May articles by him in French in *La Presse* of Montreal and in English in the Toronto *Star* vehemently denounced the accord. He provided no legal analysis whatever: it was a purely political and highly emotional attack, skilfully designed to excite all the suspicions that could so easily be aroused about the most inflammatory subject in Canada. The flavour was captured in the paragraphs that headed the front-page article in the *Star*: 'Former prime minister Pierre Elliott Trudeau, in one of his strongest statements since he left office, has put on paper his views on proposed changes to bring Quebec into the Constitution. He is totally opposed to the changes. He says they mean "goodbye" to the dream of one Canada. And he says acceptance of the changes would render the Canadian state "totally impotent" and leave the country "to eventually be governed by eunuchs."'

The 'real question' Trudeau said in his lead paragraph 'is whether the French Canadians living in Quebec need a provincial government with more powers than the other provinces.' It was a shrewd attack. With no demonstration of its truth, the implication that recognition of Quebec as a 'distinct society' would mean 'more powers' for Quebec than for the other provinces created immediate suspicion in English-speaking Canada and put the premiers of the other nine provinces on the defensive. 'Mr. Mulroney has not,' Trudeau said, 'quite succeeded in achieving sovereignty-association, but he has put Canada on the fast track for getting there.' The article ended with a vigorous condemnation of the prime minister and the premiers who had undermined the constitution of 1982 with which 'the federation was set to last a thousand years! Alas, only one eventuality hadn't been foreseen: that one day the government of Canada might fall into the hands of a weakling. It has now happened. And the Right Honourable Brian Mulroney, PC, MP, with the complicity of 10 provincial premiers, has already entered into history as the author of a constitutional document which – if it is accepted by the people and their legislators – will render the Canadian state totally impotent.'

I was appalled by Trudeau's denunciation. There was nothing in the agreement to justify the allegation that it would or could 'render the Canadian state totally impotent.' The agreement had no semblance of 'sovereignty-association' about it: it was based on and embodied the modest proposals by a federalist government in Quebec – one totally opposed to the objectives that Trudeau claimed would result from the agreement.

It was one thing to proceed in 1981 and 1982, as Trudeau had done, with constitutional change against the opposition of a separatist government that had no interest in reform of the federation. It led to serious and lasting problems with Quebec, but it was not unreasonable or destructive in intent. Trudeau's outburst over Meech Lake was both.

While his vituperative comments were aimed at Prime Minister Mulroney, they would, in Quebec, be even more destructive of Premier Bourassa. However much Trudeau despised him because of backing out of the Victoria Charter – and I had ample reason to know his disgust – Bourassa was the only federalist leader in Quebec politics and his party the only one committed to the preservation of Canada. Nothing, I think, in Canadian history rivals the irresponsibility Trudeau, a former prime minister, displayed in coming out of retirement to destroy the only prospect of an agreement that would bring Quebec into willing acceptance of the constitution that he himself later admitted was the calculated result of a 'coup de force.'

If anything was needed to add to the arrogance of Trudeau's attack, it was in his assertion that, but for the disastrous mistake of Meech Lake, Canada had 'the assurance of a creative equilibrium between the provinces and the central government' and 'the federation was set to last a thousand years!' That 'assurance' did not exist either then or since. Quebec did not and would not accept the 'creative equilibrium' enacted in 1982 against its wishes. Nor was Quebec alone in dissatisfaction with our federalism as it stood. The West was and would continue to be unhappy with an 'equilibrium' in which its weight in the Parliament and government of Canada could never ensure attention for its interests. It, too, sought change and had for many years.

Trudeau made no attempt in 1987 or in the three years' debate over Meech Lake to demonstrate the validity of his assertions. The legal text of the agreement – for which Trudeau did not wait before making his attack – came out five days later. It made it clear, in the 'distinct society clause,' that 'nothing in this section derogates from the powers, rights or privileges of the Parliament or Government of Canada, or of the legislatures or governments of the provinces,' which by necessity meant that the constitutional powers of Quebec were not increased.

Why did Trudeau do what he did? He is far too intelligent a man not to know that the result of his intervention would not be amendment of the agreement: it would be its destruction. It was an extension of his 'coup de force' of 1981–2 – but why, after more than five years of demonstration that the 'constitution of 1982' was not acceptable even to the federalist party in Quebec?

Bob Rae says of Trudeau: 'Pierre Trudeau's greatest strength has also been his greatest weakness. His political life centred on "one big thing," the demolition of Quebec nationalism, nothing more, nothing less. His greatest strength, because like many others his talents and invective were always put to best use in his "j'accuse" mode. His greatest weakness, because he became the prisoner of his own rhetoric, an ideologue despite himself, and curiously rigid as he tore strips off anyone who chose to disagree.'[2]

It is a perceptive assessment with which I agree, but whether the objective of Trudeau's 'demolition' in the case of Meech Lake was Quebec nationalism is less certain. In the eleven years I worked with Trudeau to achieve agreement on constitutional reform, Quebec nationalism was never seen as a strong enough force to constitute a real danger to Canada – even after the Parti Québécois came to power in 1976. It had to be opposed and defeated, and that was to be accomplished through reforms that would undermine the appeal of separatism in Quebec. It was the frustration of great effort at reform that led to

Trudeau's determination to succeed in 1981–2. The great danger to be avoided was too great a transfer of power to the provinces in the process.

I am sceptical whether Trudeau really believed that Meech Lake did involve the kind of reduction in federal power that would make the Canadian state 'totally impotent.' Even when I attacked him in the press in 1992 for 'misleading the Canadian people,' he did not attempt to justify his extreme allegations either about Meech Lake or about the Charlottetown Accord.

The real objects of attack in the assault on Meech Lake were I think two: any attempt to lay hands on his victory over the provinces, celebrated with royal blessing on national television in 1982, and Brian Mulroney, for whom he had a contempt equalled only by that he held for Robert Bourassa. Several birds could be killed with a well-aimed rock and Trudeau set out to do it with, so far as I know, no discussion or consultation with anyone else.

When the draft April text of the Meech Lake agreement came out, I was not immediately convinced that it was the 'miracle' that two good friends – Jack Pickersgill and Robert Stanfield – believed it was. I did not like the fiddling, cosmetic improvement in the Senate where appointments by the governor general-in-council would have to be made from lists submitted by each province. That would do nothing to meet one of our greatest needs: a second chamber with genuine representative authority, which only election could provide, to offset the under-representation of the west in our Parliament. I was also worried that the 'opting out' provision on shared-cost programs was too broad. It might make federal social programs difficult in future. However, on reflection, I decided that the flaws were minor compared with the great advantage of having Quebec accept the 'constitution of 1982.' As Trudeau had said, I was worried about 'irreparable damage' to the fabric of our society and I saw the looming menace of such damage if Quebec was not a willing partner in our constitution.

I think there is no doubt that Pierre Trudeau's attack on the Meech Lake Accord was an important factor – possibly the most important factor – in the opposition that developed, especially in English-speaking Canada. The accord came very close, in the end, to being approved by all eleven governments. It would almost certainly have succeeded if Trudeau had not so immediately and so brutally attacked it. The attack did not deter Premier Bourassa. For the first time in our entire history of constitutional effort from 1935, a government of Quebec put proposals to the National Assembly of Quebec for approval: the first province to do so.

A House Divided

After a strong start in 1987 and 1988, in spite of Trudeau's attack, the Meech Lake Accord got into difficulty in New Brunswick, Manitoba, and Newfoundland after elections that upset their pro-Meech governments. By 1989 concern began to be felt about the possible consequences of the time limit that was thought to apply to approval of the accord – three years from the date of the first approval which was by Quebec on 23 June 1987. I had become sceptical of the interpretation that the limit really applied and set out the argument against it in a book published by the Institute for Research on Public Policy.[3]

The accord made some changes in the constitution that could be passed under section 38 with approval by two-thirds of the provinces. Two other changes came under section 41 and required approval of all the provinces. The time limit applies to amendments made under section 38 only. My argument was twofold. The language of the resolution of approval made it clear that the amendment was being made under section 41, which was reasonable since the approval of all provinces encompassed the approval of the two-thirds in section 38. Therefore, the time limit was not applicable at all. However, if some technical interpretation insisted that the time limit did exist for the three items that came under section 38, the approval of the necessary two-thirds of the provinces had already been given. There was no need for the other one-third. In the end, a year after my book came out, it was two provinces only – Manitoba and Newfoundland – that created the crisis. If my interpretation was correct there would have been no crisis.

I had put my argument before Ronald Martland, who had been a justice of the Supreme Court from 1958 until his retirement in 1982 and who was an old friend. He agreed with me and authorized me to say so. I urged the government of Canada to refer the question to the Supreme Court in time to get a judgment before 23 June 1990. Nothing was done.

My Senate reform proposal in the book was directed at the anger of the west that its interests were getting no attention in the entire constitutional discussion. The sense of neglect was adding to the growing opposition to the accord. The west was pressing for a 'Triple E Senate' – elected, equal, and effective. I did not think that 'equality' could work for a Canada with 80 per cent of its French-speaking population in one province. A 10 per cent Senate representation for Quebec would not be acceptable, but other 'equitable' distributions might be possible which would greatly increase the west's inadequate representation. The four western provinces together have the same representation – twenty-four – as both Ontario and Quebec have, with twenty-four for each. The representation was established in 1915 when the population of the west was very small. It is still unchanged.

Canadians for a Unifying Constitution

As the prospects for the unanimous approval of the Meech Lake Accord grew steadily more doubtful in 1989, the question, for me and others who believed that its failure would be dangerous for national unity, was whether something could be done 'from the sidelines' to undo the Trudeau damage by increasing the public's understanding of the accord's real provisions and impact. Tom d'Aquino, who had had an active role through the Business Council on National Issues in helping to gain acceptance of the Canada-United States Free Trade Agreement, suggested the possibility of establishing an independent association of Canadians whose shared concern would be to promote a solution of our constitutional problem. Jake Warren, a former deputy minister of trade and commerce, high commissioner in London, and ambassador to the United States, was in favour – as was I. We began by organizing a small meeting on 7 November 1989, from which grew agreement on the project. On 18 December, letters were sent to 'a group of prominent Canadians from all parts of Canada.' The idea had a name – 'Canadians for a Unifying Constitution.' A public launching was set for 22 January 1990 with Jean-Luc Pepin, co-chairman of the Pepin-Robarts Task Force on Canadian Unity, as moderator. By that time we had developed a statement of reasons for supporting the Accord – 'A Constitutional Initiative That Deserves to Succeed' – on which I had prepared a commentary.

I argued that the Meech Lake Accord deserved to succeed because it would remove an injury that could not be left untended. 'The source of injury is the imposition of the Constitution Act, 1982, on Quebec without its consent. It was the only time in our history that a constitutional change that directly affected the constitution of a province was made without its agreement.'[4] I went on to say that, 'if the Accord fails, no alternative solution has been proposed that has any prospect of getting unanimous consent. The constitutional deadlock that would result, and the continuing uncertainty about the situation and about the future of Canada, would heighten internal tensions, damage international confidence and cast doubt on our capacity to carry on as a united country.'[5] A statement that has, unhappily, been borne out since the defeat of the accord.

My other arguments addressed the allegation that the accord created a special legal status for Quebec 'with legislative jurisdiction in excess of that of other provinces,' which was not the case. Nor did the 'distinct society clause undermine the charter.' I went through all the arguments against the accord that had been mounted in the nearly three years from the meeting at Meech Lake. After referring to the 'great achievement' of our history as a country since 1867, I concluded that: 'A fundamental ingredient in this success has been a remarkable capacity to achieve accommodations among Canadians of differing languages and cultures and especially between our two major linguistic groups.'[6] Our present generation had before it 'its own version of our recurring trauma' of division. 'Our unity and our effectiveness in a rapidly changing world may well depend on whether we, in this generation, can again find the capacity to accommodate and to agree.'[7]

The launch got good coverage in the media. One fact that attracted interest was that the signatories supporting our organization and its objectives included four former members of the Trudeau cabinet, all French-speaking, while an attack by him on the accord just the week before had also had the support of four of his former ministers, one of whom was Jean Chrétien.

On 15 March 1990 Tom, Jake, and I, as the operating nucleus of our executive committee, had a second press conference to issue a booklet entitled 'Meech Lake: Setting the Record Straight.' It was a 'question and answer' analysis of all aspects of the accord. Two of its authors, Richard Simeon, professor of political studies at Queen's University, and Peter Russell, professor of political science at the University of Toronto, were present to deal with questions. We had five thousand copies printed, a second printing of ten thousand on 3 April, and a third of five thousand on 23 April. We were in active correspondence with the prime minister, premiers, and any others who were in a position to promote agreement on the accord. I was touched to receive a letter of 7 February 1990 from Premier Bourassa in reply to one from me about our activities, with the salutation 'Dear Mr. Robertson and dear friend' – the latter three words added in his own hand after the typed salutation. By that date, just three months before the deadline, he must have felt the need of friends.

The final effort of Canadians for a Unifying Constitution was in full-page ads in the *Globe and Mail* and *La Presse* on 1 June – both made possible by supporters in business who were convinced that a continuation of the constitutional uncertainty would be damaging to the economies of both Quebec and Canada. The ads were calls on the 'Prime Minister and First Ministers' to 'find the way to keep our country whole: You hold in trust our heritage: To-morrow's promise lies in your hands.'

When all had failed, our final message of thanks on 26 June 1990, to the more than two hundred who had joined Canadians for a Unifying Constitution, deplored the failure of Manitoba and Newfoundland to accept the accord. We added: 'It will become increasingly apparent in the months and years ahead that the Accord provided better terms than will again be possible as a firm basis for national unity. It probably will not be clear for many months or even years just what constitutional options may be available for our country. It is certain that the status quo, with Quebec unwilling to accept the situation resulting from the Constitution Act, 1982, is not one of them.'

The Final Six Months of Agony

The last six months of the 'three year time limit,' ending 23 June 1990, saw the most intense struggle in our history to achieve – and to resist – a constitutional change.

Robert Stanfield and Jack Pickersgill were so convinced that defeat of the Meech Lake Accord could have serious consequences for the Atlantic region of Canada that, on 5 January 1990, they sent an open letter to Premier Clyde Wells, elected in April 1989 on an anti–Meech Lake program. After a detailed refutation of the objections he had stated in the election campaign, they ended the open letter:

> The objections of Premier Wells to the Meech Lake Accord are in no case based on the wording of the Accord.
>
> 1. Premier Wells cannot cite precise words in the Accord which would limit the federal spending power in any way that would impede the fight against regional disparity.
> 2. Premier Wells cannot cite precise words in the Accord which give any additional legislative power to Quebec.
> 3. Premier Wells has not shown us how the rejection of Meech Lake would advance Senate reform.

Stanfield and Pickersgill made no dent: the premier did not even agree to see them if they came to St John's, which they said they were willing to do. On 6 April he had the Newfoundland House of Assembly rescind the resolution of support for the accord that the defeated Peckford government had passed.

On 21 March Premier Frank McKenna, elected in October 1987 as an opponent of Meech Lake, introduced resolutions in the New Brunswick legislature for approval of the accord provided there could be a 'companion agreement' covering several points including language rights and 'assurances that Charter rights will not be infringed upon by the Accord.' With unaccustomed speed, the next day Prime Minister Mulroney announced the formation of a House of Commons committee to study the New Brunswick proposal. On 23 March the four Atlantic premiers met in Cornerbrook, Newfoundland, to discuss Premier Wells's concerns. The three Maritime premiers then met separately to begin to explore the implications for their provinces of 'a future without Quebec' – just in case.

On 17 May the special House of Commons committee on the McKenna proposals, which had been chaired by Jean Charest, in a unanimous report urged approval of the Meech Lake Accord by 23 June with several clarifications that did not involve amendment of the Accord.[8] The report also recommended 'identifying Senate reform as a priority item for the next constitutional round.'[9] On 21 May, Lucien Bouchard resigned from the Mulroney cabinet and from the Conservative Party, saying that 'the critical factor in his decision to resign was the report of the Charest Committee.'[10]

On 31 May the prime minister invited the premiers to dinner on 3 June at the Museum of Civilization in Hull. The dinner led to a week of negotiations in the Conference Centre in Ottawa ending on 9 June. The vital part of its conclusion was 'the undertaking of the three hold-out provinces to submit the Meech Lake Accord immediately for legislative or public consideration and "to use every possible effort" to achieve a decision prior to 23 June.'[11]

An important substantive commitment, if the accord had been approved, was 'to achieve an elected, more "equitable" and more effective Senate by 1 July 1995 under Meech Lake's requirements for unanimity, with the help of a commission that will begin work this summer.'[12]

The Drama of 22 June 1990
The legislature of New Brunswick unanimously approved the Meech Lake Accord on 15 June. The debate in the Manitoba legislature began on 20 June but by 22 June the accord was in trouble. It had aroused the

opposition of many Aboriginals because it did not include anything to meet their grievances, still unresolved after four conferences held between 1982 and 1987 to deal with 'constitutional matters that directly affect the Aboriginal peoples of Canada.'[13] Chief Elijah Harper, a Cree member of the legislature dramatically waving an eagle feather before the television camera, blocked a procedural motion that required unanimous consent. With that there could be no approval by Manitoba before the deadline.

Throughout the discussions from 3 June to 9, Premier Wells had been the most relentless opponent of Meech Lake. His blue eyes looked into the television camera with a stubborn innocence that gave the impression that what was at issue was not policy but fundamentals of principle and even of morality. Premiers Peterson of Ontario and McKenna of New Brunswick appeared before the Newfoundland House of Assembly on 20 June and Prime Minister Mulroney on 21 June. There was nothing to indicate that they had made any impact on the rock-like opposition Wells displayed from first to last.

Early on 22 June, Senator Lowell Murray had announced that, provided Newfoundland had ratified the accord in its free vote, the federal government would ask the Supreme Court of Canada to rule on whether the 23 June deadline – dating from Quebec's approval of the accord – could be moved to 23 September, the anniversary of the approval by Saskatchewan, the second province to approve in 1987. This would have allowed Manitoba three more months to continue its lengthy public hearing process and to ratify the accord.

The proceedings in the Newfoundland House of Assembly had been temporarily suspended on the afternoon of 22 June when my wife and I turned on the television to see what was happening. Premier Wells was being interviewed in a press 'scrum' and he was furious.

When he learned of the Manitoba procedural blockade, he had called Senator Murray: Murray's office said he would call back. Wells had 'waited, and waited, and waited' and then he had turned on the television and there was Murray 'saying to all the world, "it now all depends on Newfoundland. If Newfoundland votes for it, everything will be okay."' Wells was especially angry about Murray's proposal to go to the Supreme Court for a ruling that would put Newfoundland on the spot by shifting the start of the time limit. He went on: 'And I say to Senator Murray: if you are going to do a reference to the Supreme Court, do a full and honest reference to the Supreme Court. Listen to Gordon Robertson and ask the Supreme Court whether indeed there is a time limit.'[14] I was stunned at this last-gasp acceptance of my argument. Wells was 'dead right' I said in an explosive comment to Bea. It would have made all the difference.

A reference could have been made just as easily on an unprejudiced question about the time limit as on the biased one clearly aimed to put Newfoundland on the spot. Wells would obviously not have objected: he repeated in the House of Assembly that evening his approval of my proposal to find out if there really was a time limit at all. No other premier would have had cause to object. And if Mr Justice Martland was right, there was a fair chance that the court would have held that there was no deadline because the accord was being dealt with as one indivisible whole under section 41 of the Constitution Act, requiring the unanimous consent of the provinces, for which there is no time limit whatever.

The only possible reason for not doing the obvious thing was precisely what made Wells so furious: to create a situation in which the blame for failure would fall on him. In fact, however, a large part of the blame should rightly fall on him. He did not have to be so utterly rigid in his opposition that it deterred his followers from a change of position in a free vote. Moreover, he did not have to wait until the final day to support my suggestion for a reference to the Supreme Court.

He was still angry with the prime minister that evening: 'The Federal Government, by the prime minister's own admission, chose to gamble with the constitutional future of this country and in his words, "roll the dice," and do it in a way to manipulate the outcome.'[15] Murray's proposal was 'the final manipulation ... We're not prepared to be manipulated any longer.' He then moved adjournment of the House of Assembly. It was the end of Meech Lake.

In the Quebec National Assembly the following day – three years after it had been the first legislature to approve the accord – Premier Bourassa said: 'English Canada must clearly understand that whatever is said, whatever is done, Quebec is today and forever a distinct society, capable of insuring its own development and destiny.'[16]

We have never since 1990 been so close to an agreement that would have opened the way to negotiation on other national problems that are insoluble except by constitutional change: reform of the Senate, to meet the perennial western grievance, and the unfinished business of the Aboriginals. Nothing in the Meech Lake Accord could have done the damage to Canada that has been done by its defeat – damage that is not yet ended.

chapter eighteen

Meech Lake Dead: Where Next?

The reaction in Quebec to the defeat of Meech Lake was immediate and enduring. The federalist government of Robert Bourassa had taken a political gamble in putting forward a program as modest as the five points at Mont Gabriel. Having the National Assembly of Quebec be the first provincial legislature to approve the accord, even though, in its final form, four of the points had been generalized in a way that made them less attractive in Quebec, increased the risk but it was necessary to forestall any fear that Quebec would, in the end, draw back as it had after the Victoria conference. After the defeat, separatist support in Quebec surged from the 40 per cent area in the 1980 referendum to more than 50 per cent. Premier Bourassa declared that he would attend no more discussions on the constitution, and he did not during the next two years. That decision was probably good politics in Quebec: the fury there was real and it had to be clear that he shared it. But it was dangerous. It meant that he was absent from new discussions at formative stages and came back only when it was too late.

It did no good in an outraged Quebec to argue that seven of the nine legislatures in English-speaking Canada had approved the accord. Opposition to it had been vocal, often offensive to its federalist supporters in Quebec, and in the end it had triumphed. Francophone Quebeckers, and especially the federalists, felt that they had held out a hand to help solve the 'greatest crisis' in the history of Canada and had been rebuffed. The Bloc Québécois entered federal politics as the voice of separatism in the federal election of 1993. It carried fifty-four of the seventy-five constituencies in Quebec and became the official opposition in the House of Commons.

In the summer of 1990 two initiatives were launched to stimulate discussion and thinking about the options for Canada's constitutional development in the light of the failure of the Meech Lake Accord. The first, sponsored by the Business Council on National Issues, 'aimed at achieving a better understanding of the strengths and weaknesses of Canadian federalism as we know it now and to examine ways of making federalism work better in the future. A key part of this initiative was to assemble a group of Canada's leading authorities on constitutional reform to consider options for the country's future constitutional development.'[1]

The study, guided by Professor Ronald Watts of Queen's University with a team of political scientists, economists, lawyers, and constitutional scholars drawn from all parts of Canada, was ready for an all-day symposium on 16 January 1991. The papers, covering virtually every aspect of Canada's constitutional options, models for future development, and lessons for Canada from other federal and non-federal countries, and were published in a book 'Options for a New Canada.' The work provided the basis for the federal proposals that emerged in the Charlottetown Accord.

The other initiative grew out of concerns by a small group in the University of Ottawa at the defeat of 23 June. Among the initiators were the late Maxwell Cohen, and Gérald Beaudoin and Théodore Geraets in the faculties of law and philosophy. I was invited to join the group.

The Economist of London, looking at the Canadian scene in one of its special surveys a few months later, summed up the question neatly: 'What's a nice country like Canada doing in a mess like this? Rich, peaceful and, by the standards of almost anywhere else, enviably successful, Canada is trying to clear up a mess that looks pretty wholesome compared with that of, say, Yugoslavia or the Soviet Union. Yet, like those two countries, Canada is on the brink of a bust-up.'[2] We decided that the best thing we could do to help avoid a 'bust-up' was to establish a 'Newsletter' – to provide information about all aspects of the 'national unity problem' and whatever thinking, proposals, and activities might emerge in an effort to solve it, and to do it in both English and French. If it was to be successful in increasing understanding of our national difficulties, it would have to carry the separatist arguments as well as those from the federalist side.

The result was 'The Network,' launched in January 1991. Its statement of purpose said: 'The Network on the Constitution is dedicated to fostering informed debate on Canada's constitutional options. It has no collective position on any particular policy or option. Any opinions expressed or implied in "The Network" therefore are not those of the "Network on the Constitution."' Its first interim editor was Professor W.J. Norman, soon succeeded by Donald G. Lenihan on a permanent basis. Subscription was free on request and by the fourth issue it had a circulation of over 6,000. We established a national council for consultation and advice and were registered as a charitable institution eligible to receive tax-deductible contributions (which, I suppose, we could not have got if we were advocates for a cause – such as preserving the unity of Canada!). The University of Ottawa gave *The Network* office space. Charles Lussier, retired clerk of the Senate, and I became co-presidents. Don Lenihan, when he became permanent editor, was highly creative with a series of 'Network Analyses' that, with 'Reactions' by readers, became a debate on all the 'unity' subjects from Aboriginal self-government through the rights of women to the philosophy of federalism. It was a good, lively, well-informed vehicle for discussion among those widely scattered concerned Canadians who were groping for some solution to the crisis made worse by the defeat of Meech Lake.

In Quebec the rebuff by English-speaking Canada brought a temporary sense of unity. Premier Bourassa and Jacques Parizeau, leader of the Parti Québécois, joined together in establishing on 4 September 1990 the Bélanger-Campeau Commission to examine the political and constitutional status of Quebec. It was widely representative – elected members of the National Assembly of Quebec, representatives of municipalities, trade unions, cooperatives, business, education, and three Quebec Members of Parliament. After hearings in eleven cities and towns in Quebec, it recommended on 27 March 1991 that the National Assembly 'adopt a referendum law that would require a referendum on sovereignty as early as June 8, 1992, and no later than October 26, 1992; and establish two legislative commissions, one to examine the question of Quebec's accession to sovereignty and one to examine any offer of renewed federalism that the Government of Canada and the other provinces might bring forward.' All the provinces and both Territories either had or soon appointed committees to examine the constitutional dilemma.

At the federal level the Beaudoin-Edwards Committee was established in December 1990 to examine the amending formula and the process for achieving constitutional change. The following year, September 1991, the government set out its program for constitutional change in 'Shaping Canada's Future Together: Proposals.' These depended greatly on the work of Professor Watts's group. Parliament established the

Castonguay-Dobbie Committee to travel across Canada to get the participation of the public.

The Road to Charlottetown

The proposals by Mulroney's government were the most comprehensive put before the Canadian public in the entire history of our constitutional discussions. Until that time, following the proposals of the Bourassa government, it had been a 'Quebec round' in 1986. The round now in contemplation was different. The 1991 proposals stated: 'This is Canada's round. We must complete the process begun with the 1982 amendments to the Constitution, and prepare for the 21st century, building a framework that responds to the aspirations of all Canadians. The foundation is there. Together, we can build a better Canada.'[3]

The 'better Canada' could not avoid the problem of Quebec and recognition of 'Quebec's distinctiveness,' but, as the 'Proposals' said, this was not an unprecedented concept in our constitution. What Quebec was asking was that the constitution reflect its distinctiveness 'as the only society with a majority French language and culture in Canada.' 'The Charter of Rights and Freedoms already contains several clauses, notably section 25 on Aboriginal rights and section 27 on our multicultural heritage, which recognize the importance of specific components of Canadian society. These clauses are intended as a guide to the interpretation of the scope and limitations of the provisions of the Charter. It is anomalous that, as it stands, the Charter includes no similar clause with respect to Quebec despite the distinctiveness of its society.'[4]

The federal proposal was that the Charter, not the whole constitution as in Meech Lake, be interpreted 'in a manner consistent with the preservation and promotion of a vibrant French-speaking society in Quebec.' The constitution should entrench a right to Aboriginal self-government, subject to the Charter, with agreements to be negotiated within a period of ten years. A 'Canada clause' should 'affirm the identity and aspirations of the people of Canada' in the constitution. Aboriginal representation should be guaranteed in a reformed Senate. The reformed Senate should be directly elected from constituencies large enough to allow for proportional representation and with 'more equitable representation for the less populous provinces and territories than at present.'

Other proposals related to appointments to the Supreme Court, enhancing trade and mobility within Canada, the harmonization of economic policies of the federal and provincial governments, changes in the distribution of powers, the exercise of the federal spending power in areas of exclusive provincial jurisdicion, a 'Council of the Federation for "intergovernmental coordination and collaboration,"' and many other changes in both the constitution and specific federal legislation. The proposals would be referred to a special joint committee of the Senate and House of Commons to travel from coast to coast so 'every Canadian will have the right – and the responsibility – to participate.' This last proposal was designed to meet the criticism of the process by which the Meech Lake Accord had been produced: at a closed meeting of political leaders, eleven, all white males, with no public participation and then – the ultimate affront – the argument that it could not be changed, only approved or rejected.

The joint committee was overtaken by a decision by the government to have five conferences of a totally new, unofficial character, each in a different region, on the 'Renewal of Canada,' with each concentrating on one aspect of the 'renewal' that the federal proposals thought necessary.

I attended three of the five: one in Calgary in January 1992 on 'Institutional Reform' which largely meant Senate reform, one in Toronto in February on 'Identity, Rights and Values' which focused on Quebec and the Aboriginal peoples, and one in Vancouver later that month to attempt to pull together the findings of the five meetings. The conferences were a totally new experiment. Of the roughly two hundred who attended each one, something less than half were people with no special knowledge or connection with any organization: simply interested Canadians. They were an undoubted success in opening up views and in increasing the understanding of those who attended. It was not to be expected, however, that the very broad and general expressions of agreement that could be achieved by avoiding troublesome details were likely to be of much help to governments that could not avoid them. However, the Vancouver conference, on the basis of discussions at all five of the meetings, did recommend distinct-society recognition for Quebec; acceptance of the inherent right of Aboriginal self-government; reform of the Senate to make it elected, effective, and more representative; and a constitutional commitment to social goals. At the end of the conference, Joe Clark, minister of constitutional affairs, announced that a conference specifically on Aboriginal issues would be held on 14 March.

The flow – or flood – of concerned discussion continued: in multilateral meetings among government representatives – not including Quebec – in mid-April, in the Assembly of First Nations a week later, and in a second round of discussion among intergovernmental representatives at the end of April. On 30 May a further session, which this time included Aboriginal representatives, ended with agreement on recognition of Quebec's distinct society, the inherent Aboriginal right to self-government, and the right of provinces to opt out of new federal shared-cost programs. Clark and nine premiers, still not including Quebec, met again in June and July and on 29 July Premier Bourassa announced that Quebec would end its two-year boycott of the constitutional talks.

On 4 August Prime Minister Mulroney and all the premiers met – again in the country north of Ottawa but not at Meech Lake. The meeting was at the Prime Minister's summer residence at Harrington Lake. Aboriginal leaders protested their exclusion from the talks but on 28 August the prime minister, ten provincial premiers, two Territorial leaders, and four Aboriginal leaders met in Charlottetown.

The Charlottetown Accord
The Mulroney government has been criticized for attempting too much in the 'Canada Round.' Its proposals in 'A Future Together' were indeed ambitious – yet there was little alternative. The death of Meech Lake meant that nothing had been done to meet Bourassa's modest 'five points' of 1986. He could clearly attend no conference where they were not still on the agenda. A conference without Quebec – like the agreement of 1981 – would be the greatest of all gifts to his separatist opponents. A Canada Round without attention to the West's demand for Senate reform and its concerns over natural resources would be equally impossible. And the Aboriginal organizations, with their widespread support from Canadians more conscious about 'human rights' than ever before, would not be content to be ignored again, as they had been at Meech Lake. On the other hand, to do nothing – to attempt to defend the 'status quo' as left by the 1982 constitution – was as fruitless then as it has proven to be in all the years since.

Faced with all these difficulties, the best course, despite all its risks, was what Mulroney and his government tried: to appeal to the Canadian people to rise above their differences and to strive for a united country for 'a future together.' The Charlottetown Accord did achieve agreement by the heads of all the governments on thirteen categories of constitutional provision, a major triumph in itself.

A 'Canada Clause' stated 'fundamental characteristics' of Canada to guide the courts in interpreting the Charter of Rights. One characteristic was the right of the Aboriginal peoples to ensure the integrity of their societies: their governments would 'constitute one of three orders of government in Canada.' Another was that 'Quebec constitutes within Canada a distinct society, in relation to language, culture and its civil law tradition,' which made the definition less general than in Meech Lake. None of the 'characteristics' would 'derogate from the powers, rights or privileges of the parliament or the government of Canada or of the legislatures or governments of the provinces,' which meant that the constitutional powers of Quebec were not increased: they could not be unless federal powers were to be diminished.

An elected Senate was envisaged with sixty-two members, six from each province and one from each territory, and provisions about its powers and relations with the House of Commons. If a bill 'materially affects the French language or culture in Canada' it would require a double majority – a majority of all senators voting and also of all French-speaking senators voting.

The 'equal' Senate meant that Quebec would be reduced from just under 25 per cent of members in the Senate, as now constituted, to less than 10 per cent. To compensate for that loss of protection for the nearly 25 per cent of people in Canada who are of the French language, Quebec was guaranteed 'no fewer than 25 per cent of the total number of members in the House of Commons.'

There were provisions about labour-market training, culture, and a group of six powers which are probably now exclusive provincial powers but in which the federal government has developed programs for research, planning, or other uses of the spending power: urban affairs, recreation, housing, mining, forestry, and tourism. These were 'affirmed' to be exclusive provincial powers and a province could require the federal government to withdraw from any program. If so, the federal government would be 'required to provide reasonable compensation' for the function the province would take on.

The Supreme Court would be provided for in the constitution, instead of in federal legislation as at present, with at least three judges from Quebec. When there was a vacancy on the court, 'the government of each province or territory may submit to the Minister of Justice ... the names of at least five candidates.' An appointment, except of a Chief Justice chosen from among the judges of the court, would be 'a person whose name has been submitted ... and who is acceptable to the Queen's Privy Council for Canada.' In short, there was to be a new provincial role in appointments but also a federal right to reject any unsatisfactory nominee.

There were a variety of other provisions about matters that had been of concern to the provinces: unilateral changes by the federal government in federal-provincial programs, and compensation where a province opted out of a shared-cost program 'in an area of exclusive provincial jurisdiction.' Also, there were a few changes in the Constitution Act, 1982, to take into account the possible creation of legislative bodies and governments for the Aboriginal peoples. They made clear that the Charter of Rights would apply to any such institutions. A new section 35 in the 1982 act would provide that 'the Aboriginal peoples of Canada have the inherent right of self-government within Canada.' There were provisions, too, for the 'Social and Economic Union' of Canada. Several of these dealt with the matters covered in 'The Social Union Framework' agreed to by the federal government and the provinces, other than Quebec, seven years later – in February 1999.

Altogether, the Charlottetown Accord tackled virtually all of the most serious dissatisfactions of the people of Canada as they had emerged in the countless meetings, committees, and conferences that had taken place during the discussion of the Meech Lake Accord and in the two years since its demise.

Initially, the reception of the accord in the country was good. There appeared to be wide support for it from the media, business, union leaders, and political parties generally – except the Parti Québécois. On 10 September the House of Commons, with a vote of 233 to 12, approved legislation for a national referendum on the accord. It would be held on 26 October.

Trudeau Again the Spoiler

On 1 October at the Maison du Egg Roll in Montreal, Pierre Trudeau spoke to a monthly dinner of *Cité Libre*, a magazine founded in the 1950s by a group led by him and Gérard Pelletier for wide-ranging discussion of public affairs. But this was no ordinary meeting. As the master of ceremonies said, in addition to the two hundred people at the dinner, 'thanks to CKAC-AM and the Télémedia radio network we have something like a half-million listeners around the province tuning in to the thirty stations of the Télémedia network.'[5] In his address Trudeau was repeating and enlarging on an article – 'Trudeau Speaks Out' – in *Maclean's* magazine a few days before.[6] His style was not quite as abusive as in his denunciation of the Meech Lake Accord in 1987 but 'the doddering fools meeting in Charlottetown' were not accorded notably more respect than the 'eunuchs' at Meech Lake. What made the attack

worse in one sense than the one against Meech Lake was that it purported to be a legal analysis, which the earlier tirade did not. It got
national coverage. After much unhappy consideration, I decided that I
could not remain silent, as I had about his attack in 1987, and allow so
dishonest an 'interpretation' to go unanswered. I wrote a letter to the
Globe and Mail which appeared in the issue of 10 October 1992.

I accused the former prime minister of using 'his great intellectual
talents, not to help the people of Canada to understand the provisions of
the Charlottetown Accord, but to mislead them' and set out in detail
where his alleged 'facts' were wrong. It was a detailed challenge, item by
item.

After referring to our association, beginning in the Privy Council
Office in 1949 to 1951, and the 'delight' it had been for me 'in a reversal
of roles to work under Pierre when he became Prime Minister in 1968,' I
said that in our years together 'he would have thought it a failure in the
duty I owed him not to be frank and direct.' I went on: 'My honest
opinion is that Mr. Trudeau is misleading the people of Canada as they
try to think through the answer they must give on October 26' to the
referendum question. I continued:

> The Globe and Mail editorial deals effectively with some of Mr. Trudeau's
> misinterpretations of the provisions of the Charlottetown Accord. As it says,
> the Canada clause, which is interpretive and not substantive, does not
> 'prevail over the provisions of the Charter of Rights.' Those rights remain
> unchanged. Trudeau's allegations about loss of rights of equality by women,
> racial minorities and others in a 'hierarchy of classes of citizens' cannot
> stand up.
>
> The accord would not 'mean the end of social programs in the power of
> the provinces.' All it would mean is that such programs, in areas of exclu-
> sive provincial jurisdiction, could not be imposed on a province without its
> consent and the chance to mount its own program. Nor does the province
> get federal money on demand: it must have a program 'that is compatible
> with the national objectives.' Nor can a court compel Parliament to vote
> money for a provincial program. Only Parliament can vote funds and only
> it can decide.
>
> And what alternative would Trudeau propose? That the federal govern-
> ment could impose a program in an area of exclusive provincial jurisdic-
> tion against the wishes of the government that has the constitutional power
> in the area? We had enough of that trouble in the 1960s.
>
> Nor is it true that we will never have a common market if the accord is

approved. It is most unfortunate that the clause on the economic union is not stronger and that Section 121 of the Constitution Act, 1867, has not been strengthened. But, as Mr. Trudeau knows, you cannot compel agreement. Nothing in the accord prevents a stronger clause if agreement can be achieved. In short, we will be no better and no worse in this area than we are today.

The accord is an intricate balancing act – and in that it is an accurate reflection of Canada. There is no point in pretending that there is some theoretical perfection that ought to be achieved.

I concluded by saying that 'neither Mr. Trudeau nor any other of the critics of the Charlottetown Accord has presented an alternative. The *status quo* is not a realistic possibility.'

Trudeau wrote what purported to be a reply that appeared on 21 October. It was not worthy of him and I replied to it in turn on 24 October. He had not met my challenge to cite one single case of 'blackmail' by Quebec after having earlier demands met. New 'facts' in his letter were as spurious as in his 'Egg Roll' speech and the *Maclean's* article – and again I went into detail. So far as his frightening assertions about the effect of the 'Canada Clause' were concerned, they stemmed 'from a totally false basis of legal interpretation.' I ended my letter: 'The Canada clause is not the source of rights and it does not change the Charter clauses. Least of all does it have the worrying consequences Mr. Trudeau suggests for people who "are much lower down among the categories of the Charter." The truth is that there are no categories in the Charter. There is no "hierarchy of categories of citizens" as Mr. Trudeau alleges.'

Trudeau gave no answer. I suspect he realized that he had stretched the truth too far; that I knew the facts of the negotiations with Quebec over the years at least as well as he did and that he could not get away with more distortion. His alleged legal interpretation was a fraud, designed to frighten, not to inform. However, polls indicated that his attack had the effect he wanted. Intentions to vote 'No' went up, especially in English-speaking Canada.

Trudeau and I met the following summer at a colloquium organized by the Royal Society of Canada, of which we both are fellows, and referred to one another as 'friends' in our remarks, but clearly neither was prepared to concede anything in our difference.

Trudeau's intervention in 1992 was as intemperate and inaccurate as the one in 1987. I found it depressing that, in retirement after brilliant accomplishments as prime minister, and having observed five years of effort by governments to achieve the unanimity he knew was so difficult to achieve, he chose only to destroy. He at no time made any constructive suggestion as he could have done from his status as our leading elder statesman. For me it was the saddest chapter in my relations with four prime ministers.

A great injustice in the whole Meech Lake–Charlottetown Accord controversy is that Brian Mulroney has been so harshly criticized for his efforts to meet the serious problems in our federalism left by Trudeau's 'power play' of 1981–2 – problems still real and still unresolved – while Trudeau has escaped so lightly after destructive interventions that have made the danger to our national unity a triumph for charisma over substance.

The Referendum, 26 October 1992

There was much in the Charlottetown Accord that I did not like. I was convinced, and had argued in 'A Country Divided' in 1989, that an 'equal' Senate for Canada would be a mistake. A second chamber in a federal system is supposed to be a balancing factor: to offset the domination of the 'lower chamber,' where representation is by population, by the populous centres of Canada. Quebec was one of the populous areas; it shared control with Ontario of the House of Commons. It did not need any guarantee of membership there. The Quebec guarantee became a major target of criticism in the rest of Canada.

It was the West that needed more representation in the Senate but 'equal' provincial representation was a mistake. Quebec could not be cut down from 25 per cent to 10 per cent when it contained 80 per cent of the French-speaking population of Canada. There were 'equitable' arrangements for the Senate that would not make necessary any distortion of the 'representation by population' principle of the House of Commons.

There were several other things that I thought could be improved, but it was better that Charlottetown should succeed than that one more effort at reform should fail and throw Canada back on the 1982 constitution which was unacceptable to even the federalists of Quebec. With those views, I threw myself into the campaign for a 'Yes' vote.

In a variety of talks and interviews I argued that our constitution, after a hundred and twenty-five years, had developed serious deficiencies for the much changed Canada that was heading into the twenty-first century, especially for Quebec, the West, and the Aboriginal peoples. The amendments of 1982, while important and desirable in themselves, addressed none of those problems. There was no recognition in our constitution of a fact very important to the French-speaking people of Quebec: that it was 'different,' 'distinctive,' or whatever word might be used and that protection of the language of its majority was a problem no other province had. That reality and that concern had to be recognized or our constitution could not be the instrument of unity it ought to be.

But equally the under-representation of the West in our Parliament should be remedied – and the best way to do it was by an effective elected Senate. What Charlottetown did was not the best formula, but it was better than no change. As to the Aboriginal peoples, the 1982 amendments recognized that their 'Aboriginal and treaty rights' did exist, but four conferences had failed to make any progress in defining them or in providing how they should be accommodated in the Canada of the future. Charlottetown was a start.

The result in the referendum could not have been much worse. Of the ten provinces, only the three least populous gave a clear 'Yes' majority – Newfoundland, New Brunswick, and Prince Edward Island. Ontario produced virtually a dead heat: 49.8 per cent 'Yes,' 49.6 'No.' The Northwest Territories also voted 'Yes.' All the rest of Canada was 'No.' The total national vote was 'No' by 54.4 per cent to 44.6 per cent. Quebec went 'No' by a very similar margin – 55.4 to 42.4 per cent, but for totally different reasons.

Why was a proposal so thoroughly discussed and so well prepared rejected by such decisive margins? Professor Watts, in a lead article in a review of the 'Constitutional Debate and the Referendum,' provided an explanation that accords with the negative reactions I heard as the referendum campaign unfolded: 'In the hurly-burly of the referendum debate the larger vision embodied in the Charlottetown Consensus Report were lost in the media and partisan preoccupations with specific provisions and with concerns about the extent to which each particular group had or had not achieved all its own specific aims.' Watts added: 'In the end, the political leaders found that in trying to accommodate every group they had drafted a document that, because it required so many compromises, made more enemies than friends.'[7]

A national referendum in Canada is a very rare event: the last one had been nearly fifty years before on the issue of conscription. Prior to the referendum on the Charlottetown Accord, a careful study was mounted, as for a once-in-a-century alignment of stars or planets, with funding from the Social Sciences and Humanities Research Council of Canada and Queen's and York universities. Polls about 'intentions to vote' were carried out on a daily basis from 24 September to 25 October, the eve of the vote.

With the referendum a month away, the intentions to vote 'Yes' were much lower in Quebec (30 per cent) than in the rest-of-Canada (ROC) where they were 60 per cent. However, in five days from 1 October to 6 October, the 'Yes' share in ROC dropped twenty points with no drop whatever in Quebec. 'What accounted for the early-October collapse of the "Yes" and of at least two if its key supporting arguments? All indications point to Pierre Trudeau's speech at the Maison du Egg Roll on the night of 1 October.'[8]

Canada: Reclaiming the Middle Ground

After the failure of the Charlottetown Accord, Donald Lenihan proposed that he, Roger Tassé, and I should attempt a book on what we thought the debate had revealed about Canada and 'whether the basis for a workable federal arrangement still exists.'[9] In the work that resulted, *Reclaiming the Middle Ground*, we had no trouble about the answer – 'federalism remains not only a viable, but the best, option' for Canada. However, Canadian thinking had begun to change when the Constitution was patriated in 1982 with a 'Charter of Rights and Freedoms.'

The Charter was based on the principle of classical liberalism which stresses equality. Federalism is about the accommodation of differences within a single state. Liberalism, as interpreted by Pierre Trudeau, had no room for any differences for communities: only the individual was the possessor of rights. Yet our constitution in 1867, in its efforts to accommodate differences within the new federation, recognized differences for regions – the Maritimes, Upper Canada, and Lower Canada – and it also recognized cultural distinctions and provided rights to denominational schools for 'the Protestant or Roman Catholic minority' in Upper Canada and Lower Canada and later in Manitoba. Equality of treatment as a principle would have made those essential accommodations impossible: it was not a feature of the constitution of 1867 except for the powers of provinces and seats in the Senate for 'regions.' In our view, Trudeau defined individual rights in a way that was unduly antagonistic to the spirit of federalism: 'He insists that in a liberal society the freedom and equality of individuals must prevail over the rights of communities. We think this pan-Canadian approach misrepresents the nature of the Charter in particular and of liberal-democratic rights in general.'[10]

We argued that Trudeau's approach to equality of rights was also 'abstract and overly intellectual.' 'To say that basic rights are universal thus does not commit one to saying that they must always be applied the same way to all citizens. The logic of a basic right is shaped in part by the social, cultural and political values of the community. In a large, modern, multinational, liberal-democratic, federal state like Canada, subgroups sometimes have fundamental differences over the nature of their commitment to liberalism.'[11] Yet the Trudeau thesis was that Canada could be founded on his highly intellectual view of human beings as 'free and equal,' 'transcending the accidents of time and place.'

At the other pole from Trudeau in the debate in Quebec were the nationalists, for whom the fundamental thing that binds the citizens of a state together is their personal identification with a cultural or linguistic group. *Reclaiming the Middle Ground* argued that neither position provided a solution to our problem. Trudeau's shared commitment to liberal principles was not an adequate foundation for a complex country like Canada nor, on the other hand, was the federal commitment to diversity open-ended. 'In Canada, it is aimed at accommodating certain quite specific forms of linguistic, cultural and regional diversity that are central to Canadians' shared history. But which specific policies can federalism be invoked to justify?'[12] That was a difficult question for the Supreme Court as it came to interpret the Charter.

Our conclusion was that, in a federal state like Canada, the idea of liberal freedom and equality had to be revised to include a respect for communities as well as for individuals. Individual citizens often have multiple allegiances. It is not possible to have a single national identity and absolute equality of treatment. We argued that a community-building program for us would be derived from four sources: 'a shared commitment to liberal principles; a respect for Canadians' shared history, including a respect for those particular values, objectives and purposes that led to the founding of the country; a respect for the particular forms of sociological diversity that run through that history, with specific considerations for the Aboriginal "diversity" neglected in 1867; and a vision for the future, that is, an agenda that promotes the over-arching values and objectives toward which the community as a whole is working.'[13]

Our analysis was published in both English and French by the Institute for Research on Public Policy and was largely ignored in both Quebec and the rest of Canada. We were not alone. The efforts of many people and groups to find solutions to our problems of national unity and constitutional reform in the years after Pearson's conference of 1968 were serious and various yet none has so far succeeded.

The Quebec Referendum of 1995

It took less than two years from the defeat of the Charlottetown Accord in the referendum of 1992 for the Parti Québécois to become the government of Quebec in the election of September 1994. Jacques Parizeau was premier – an ardent separatist, bursting with confidence in independence as the future of Quebec and in himself as the person to lead the way.

I had got to know Parizeau in the 1960s. He was an economist by training: part of his post-graduate work had been at the London School of Economics, where he acquired an English accent and a British style and manner of dress that, throughout his later life, accorded curiously with his revulsion at the idea of continuing the connection of Quebec with the 'British' Canada that he found so distasteful. He was not infrequently attached to Quebec delegations, advising Premier Lesage or various of Lesage's successors. There was no Parti Québécois until 1968. Establishment of the party, and its victory in 1976 changed everything.

Claude Morin and Jacques Parizeau had been frequent colleagues on delegations – Morin usually the senior official advising the Quebec premier of the day, whether Liberal or Union Nationale, and Parizeau frequently the senior financial adviser. Morin made his politics clear in resigning from the public service of Quebec in 1972 and joining the Parti Québécois. He leaped to prominence as the architect of 'étapisme,' the 'step by step' strategy that produced victory for the Parti Québécois in 1976 after its defeat in the election of 1970. It was no surprise that he was named minister of intergovernmental affairs: no one could have been better suited to the portfolio.

Before the opening of the first federal-provincial conference at which Morin was present in his new glory as a minister, I moved around from the federal 'top' of the great horseshoe table in the Conference Centre to where Morin and Parizeau were talking in the seats behind the Quebec section. I did not relish the gloating that I was sure I would encounter but the three of us were going to be dealing with one another, no matter what. Morin and Parizeau enjoyed every word and moment of my congratulations: they were beaming, delighted with the victory, confident of the new future unfolding for Quebec, and particularly revelling in my discomfiture as one who, in their eyes, had spent his time and effort in frustrating many of their plans and proposals of the past.

Morin took particular pleasure in suggesting that I was really part of the victory: I could regard myself as one they had to thank for it! If I had just been more reasonable – and had used my influence to get the prime ministers I had advised to be more flexible – René Lévesque would not be there as premier that day. It was jocular and good humoured but Morin meant it, too – and Parizeau whooped in delight with totally British expletives not used in Canada.

My contacts with Parizeau had been more than enough to convince me that he was a deadly serious separatist, however British his style and perfect his English. There were some among the Péquistes – even at the top – who might be open to some sort of compromise: a better deal for Quebec, but still within 'something' that could carry on as 'Canada.' René Lévesque, I feel reasonably sure, was one of them. Jacques Parizeau was not one in 1994, is not one today, and will not be one at any time in the future.

Over the winter months of 1994–5 a national commission on the future of Quebec held hearings throughout the province. Its report was no great surprise. The commission considered 'unacceptable and contrary to the higher interests of Quebec the imposition of the Constitution of 1982 which has created the political dead-end into which Quebec had been plunged against its will.' The commission found that sovereignty was the only option that could respond to the aspirations of the people of Quebec. It set out a fully developed constitution for the new state to come into existence after a declaration of sovereignty.

In January 1995 McGill University held a conference 'to open Quebec's referendum year' with a preview of the issues that would arise if the vote was 'Yes.' Professor Alan Cairns of the University of British Columbia, one of the most thoughtful of our political scientists, launched the conference with an analysis of the political and legal problems of separation that had not, at that point, been faced by either side. The Parti Québécois plan presupposed another 'partner' to negotiate with a Quebec that had voted 'Yes' in a referendum and had taken the steps to separate as set out in their draft legislation. The truth, he said, was that there had been no consideration at all 'outside Quebec' of what to do or how to do it if 'Yes' won a referendum and if Quebec then wanted to negotiate. The government of Canada was not constitutionally empowered to negotiate about the separation of a province. As for the 'Rest of Canada,' it did not exist as a legal entity: 'ROC is headless,' as Cairns put it. It was not carelessness that these issues had not been dealt with: they were politically highly dangerous. But the reality was 'that both sides are approaching the referendum in a condition of ignorance.'

Apart from the legal and constitutional issues in the event of a 'Yes' vote, the legitimacy of our federal government would be undermined by the vote since it had a prime minister and other senior ministers from Quebec. Could they speak for Canada in a negotiation about separation of their own province? The other provinces could become key players and it was not at all clear that all of them would even be in favour of preserving a single 'Canada minus Quebec.' British Columbia and Alberta had many common interests and might want to go their own way.

If Canadians in general were neither intellectually nor psychologically ready for a 'Yes' vote, it was equally the case, Cairns said, that the Parti Québécois assumption of a smooth, rational glide to negotiation was unreal. Whatever might happen would be anything but smooth, it would be packed with emotion, and, most troubling of all, it would, as things stood, take place outside the realm of law: no rules, no guides, no limits. I was in complete agreement with everything Cairns said.

On 7 September 1995 Premier Parizeau introduced Bill 1 in the National Assembly of Quebec – An Act respecting the Future of Quebec. The bill authorized the National Assembly 'to proclaim the sovereignty of Quebec and to give effect to the declaration of sovereignty appearing in the Preamble.' The proclamation was to be preceded 'by a formal offer of economic and political partnership with Canada.' Section 2 of the bill provided that, on the date fixed in the proclamation of the National Assembly, the Declaration of sovereignty appearing in the Preamble shall take effect and Quebec shall become a sovereign country; it shall acquire the exclusive power to pass all its laws, levy all its taxes and conclude all its treaties.'

Everything was set in beautiful order, to go into effect when a 'Yes' answer had been given by the people of Quebec to the question in a referendum to be held on 30 October 1995: 'Do you agree that Quebec should become sovereign, after having made a formal offer to Canada for a new Economic and Political Partnership, within the scope of the Bill respecting the future of Quebec and of the agreement signed on June 12, 1995?' The reference to the agreement of 12 June – among the PQ government, the Bloc Québécois in the House of Commons, and L'Action Démocratique, a small Quebec party led by Mario Dumont – was to remind the voter that the question was being asked not only by the government of Quebec, but by a broad constellation of provincial and political forces.

No television mystery has presented as heart-stopping a drama as the unfolding of the Quebec vote on 30 October 1995. The earliest polls gave 'Yes' a lead: narrow but definite. The figures wobbled about throughout the night as the 'Yes' lead increased, then narrowed and only late in the game became a slight lead for 'No.' The final result was the closest brush with disaster the country has ever had: 50.58 per cent for 'No' and 49.42 per cent for 'Yes': a margin of 1.16 per cent.

Jacques Parizeau resigned within hours as premier of Quebec but only two or three months later did it become clear how totally he had committed himself to winning the referendum and how carefully he and his associates had laid plans to sweep Canada and Quebec beyond a point of no return. Within forty-eight hours of the 'Yes' vote, the National Assembly of Quebec would have met to adopt a motion acknowledging the legitimacy of the vote. There would have been pledges to respect the rights of anglophone, allophone, and Native minorities. Ten months before, in January 1995, he had got a promise from Jacques Chirac, then mayor of Paris and a candidate to become President of France (which he later became), that France would recognize the sovereign Quebec. The French National Assembly was to adopt a resolution congratulating Quebeckers and offering support. The French moves and support from other countries of 'la Francophonie' would, Parizeau hoped, put pressure on Washington to recognize the new state of Quebec.

Whether the Chirac promise involved formal recognition is not clear but the plan was well designed and to be implemented with blinding speed before resistance could be mounted by Ottawa. Would it have worked? There is no way of knowing but one thing became clear: that Canada could not again be so unprepared.

Recovering from an Earthquake

Never had Canadians experienced a shock to equal that of the hairbreadth that separated us from an unprecedented political and economic crisis on 31 October 1995. Premier Parizeau would have begun his action plan as soon as the 'Yes' majority was registered early that morning: he would not have waited for anything to throw doubt on the figures and it would have been impossible to stop the spreading consequences of fact and rumour in the money markets and the media that live on instant communication.

The referendum result had been quite unforeseen but Tom d'Aquino had wisely arranged for a meeting of the Business Council on National Issues for the evening of 30 October, with the intention of resuming on 31 October to assess the political and economic implications for Canada of whatever had happened. He and I had lived in close contact through the battle by 'Canadians for a Unifying Constitution' to save Meech Lake. At a special meeting of his policy committee on 18 December, attended by a number of invited guests of which I was one, it was agreed that action should be taken, apart from whatever the federal government might do, to develop a 'framework' of proposals that could hope to swing the '20 per cent soft vote' in Quebec away from the separatist side and to the federalist side where it had been in 1980. Pursuant to that decision, the Business Council sponsored two 'Confederation 2000 Conferences' aimed at helping to build a new consensus for political change': the first was on 8 and 9 March 1996, and the second on 3 and 4 May. Over one hundred Canadians from every part of the country participated. The 'ideas and recommendations' agreed on were set out in 'Today and Tomorrow: An Agenda for Action.' The consequences of the conferences have been disappointing, as with so much of the effort that went into finding a replacement for the Meech Lake agreement.

As this is written, four years after the 'earthquake' of 30 October 1995 that shook the country, there have been some initiatives by the federal government of a non-constitutional nature to improve the operation of federalism but nothing whatever concerning the constitutional recognition of Quebec as a distinct society or anything else that requires constitutional action. In November 1995 – less than a month after the referendum – the House of Commons approved a motion by the prime minister recognizing that Quebec is a distinct society within Canada but it is debatable whether the motion alone is not more offensive to Quebec than helpful. It does nothing but provide a few words of possible guidance, of no binding character, for the legislative branch of the federal government. It has no constitutional status, no permanence, and falls far short of the kind of recognition in the Meech Lake and Charlottetown Accords.

Defending the Canadian Federation
The shock of October 1995 gave sharply greater emphasis to concerns that had been occupying a number of people, of whom I was one, about many assumptions that separatists had been taking as truth and stating as fact or law. Such assumptions underlay Jacques Parizeau's action plan to follow a 'Yes' vote. He probably did believe that such a vote would have been a clear declaration of self-determination by the people of Quebec and would have had status in international law. The thesis of 'self-determination' had been widely accepted in Quebec and, as I found, when I challenged it in a debate with Claude Morin at the opening dinner of the annual meeting of the Canadian Institute of International Affairs in Montreal in 1991, my dispute of its application to Quebec as a matter of international law was badly received even by federalists attending the dinner.

One of the most effective attacks on the assumptions about sovereignty was by Patrick J. Monahan in a paper entitled 'Cooler Heads Shall Prevail.' Monahan's paper attacked the Quebec legislation on sovereignty as tabled in draft form on 6 December 1994. The legislation assumed that Quebec 'has the unilateral right to secede from Canada on terms and conditions that it alone will determine.' Monahan's commentary took direct issue with those assumptions. 'Although the existing Constitution is silent on the issue of provincial secession, a province could secede from Canada through a constitutional amendment approved by the Senate and the House of Commons and the legislatures of all ten provinces. There is no basis for a constitutional convention supporting Quebec's right to secede from Canada unilaterally.'[14] I agreed with everything in Monahan's paper. I had, indeed, begun to work on measures I thought should be taken by the government of Canada to ensure that it would be in a position to deal with a 'Yes' vote – or the threat of one – if there were to be another referendum in Quebec.

In a February 1996 memorandum, *Contingency Legislation for a Quebec Referendum,* my main argument was that it would be important to do everything possible, in the event of another referendum, to ensure that 'the rule of law should be followed' as the best means of avoiding the uncertainty and disruption that 'illegal action could bring.'[15] I pointed out that United Nations principles made it clear that Quebec would not have the right to self-determination: 'Nothing in the foregoing paragraphs shall be construed as authorizing or encouraging any action which would dismember or impair, totally or in part, the territorial integrity of sovereign and independent states conducting themselves in compliance with the principle of equal rights and self-determination of peoples ...'[16] Canada was 'a sovereign and independent state' and almost certainly Quebec did not constitute a 'people' that had 'been subject to denial of political freedom or human rights in a discriminatory manner.'[17]

Looking at the situation in Canada after a referendum, I realized that a major problem would be the one Alan Cairns had discussed: it was not at all clear who could, with legitimacy, deal with Quebec after a 'Yes' vote on separation. I had concluded that there was no effective solution to this problem *after* a 'Yes' vote, for at that point the status of the federal government would already be in doubt: action had to be taken by Parliament *before* the vote 'on a contingency basis and subject to proclamation.' 'Essentially the provisions should be to ensure that the Government of Canada continues, for all parts of Canada, unless and until action is taken by Parliament or by the Governor in Council, as required, to change any law, institution or program of the federal government.'[18] In order to be sure of the legal capacity to cope with the problems that could be foreseen, 'there would be specific authority for the Government of Canada to enter into discussions with the Government of Quebec on possible arrangements for changes in the constitution or operation of Canada that might be acceptable to Quebec and the other provinces, and thus permit Quebec to remain a part of Canada, or, alternatively, on terms and arrangements that might permit a negotiated separation of Quebec from Canada.'[19].

My argument anticipated the conclusions the Supreme Court came to on the reference a few months later: that, if a referendum in Quebec produced a clear majority in favour of secession, there would have to be negotiation. The court's judgment was about the constitutional principles underlying an 'obligation to negotiate': my memorandum was about establishing the legal basis for a government of Canada to do it. Four years after the referendum, nothing has been done to remove the uncertainty to which my memorandum of February 1996 was addressed. The clarity legislation introduced in December 1999 does not deal with that problem.

A Premiers-Led Initiative

Once the spasm of concern from the referendum of 1995 had diminished, it became clear that the 'Agenda for Action' recommended by the Confederation 2000 conferences in 1996 was not going to produce the change of attitude by the federal government that had been hoped for. In June 1997 Tom d'Aquino wrote to the prime minister on behalf of the Business Council on National Issues suggesting that Ottawa alone could not solve the problem of improving the structure and operation of the federation. The letter appealed to the prime minister to give his 'heartfelt support to any worthwhile initiative that may emerge from other levels of government.'[20] The letter prepared the way for an appeal in turn to the premiers and Territorial leaders urging them to 'launch a series of initiatives aimed at bolstering the federation.'[21]

The initiative led to what became the 'Calgary Declaration' of September 1997 as the possible basis for a process of gradual change that might, with time, diminish the unity crisis. It dealt with the Canadian celebration of diversity and tolerance within a belief that 'all citizens share equal rights and responsibilities' and 'all provinces are equal partners under the law.' It included recognition that 'the National Assembly of Quebec, as the only provincial legislature in Canada elected by a French-speaking majority, has a particular responsibility to exercise the powers that fall within its jurisdiction to preserve and promote the unique character of Quebec's society, as expressed through its language, culture, institutions and civil law tradition.'

There were commitments in the declaration by the provincial and Territorial leaders about the social union of Canada, the economic union, and resolving concerns 'within our existing constitutional structure ... wherever possible.' The initiative disproved the oft-made allegation of Premier Bouchard that English-speaking Canada was incapable of forging a consensus on the future of Canada and Quebec's role in the federation. The Calgary Declaration received legislative sanction in every province and Territory but no initiative has followed from the federal side. The best that can be said is that the declaration remains as a 'candle in the window' to Quebeckers, a declaration of faith that one day a federalist premier in Quebec would reaffirm the Quebec government's will to seek its aspirations within Canada and that a future federal government might then be prepared to resume reform where the efforts of Meech Lake and Charlottetown had left off.

With that hope of future action in mind, in August 1997 a colloquium was organized by the University of Ottawa on 'Federalism for the Future: Essential Reforms.' It was chaired by Senator Gérald-A. Beaudoin and me. Its purpose was to discuss 'areas where, for one reason or another, there are significant deficiencies in our federal system that cannot be remedied other than by constitutional reform and which are of sufficient importance that failure to change would seriously impair the future effectiveness of the Canadian federation.'[22] These areas were the division of powers, 'flexibility' in the constitution, the 'distinct society,' Senate reform, the amending procedure, and the Aboriginal peoples. There was no thought that any of those areas of change was likely to see action soon. However, it was and it remains important to ensure that the comfortable and false view does not take hold that our problems can be solved without any constitutional change.

It is not realistic to believe that the western sense of being left out of the mainstream of Confederation can be solved without an elected Senate providing the adequate and effective representation that the west has never had in our Parliament. There is no way that the reasonable desire for formal recognition by the centuries-old founding community of French-speaking Quebec can be adequately met except in our constitution, where the Aboriginal peoples and our 'multicultural heritage' have been recognized since 1982. Nor is there any way, in the end, that the rights and the place of the Aboriginal peoples can be adequately defined and recognized except through constitutional provision. The colloquium was based on the unstated proposition that Canadians are too reasonable not to find a way one day to change our constitution to reflect the strongly felt needs of major sectors of the Canadian community that are not satisfied with the constitution of 1867 as it was left in 1982.

The Reference to the Supreme Court

By order-in-council on 30 September 1996, the government of Canada referred three questions relating to the 'Secession of Quebec' to the Supreme Court. They were designed to get judicial answers at last to some of the assumptions of the government of Quebec about Quebec's right to secede from Canada. In brief, the questions were:

1. Under the constitution of Canada, can the government or legislature of Quebec effect secession from Canada unilaterally?
2. Does international law give the government or legislature the right to effect secession from Canada unilaterally? Is there a right of self-determination under international law that would give that right?
3. If there is a conflict between domestic and international law on the right to secede, which would take precedence in Canada?

The answers by the Supreme Court, handed down in August 1998, were clear and unanimous: 'No' to the first; 'No' to the second; 'No conflict' to the third.

The answers disposed conclusively of the essential assumptions on which the government of Quebec had been relying in the legislation it had passed and in the 1995 referendum. However, the answers to the three questions were not the whole story as the Supreme Court saw it.

The federal system adopted in 1867 was, the court said, the political mechanism by which diversity could be reconciled with unity. Within our federal system, 'the evolution of our constitutional arrangements has been characterized by adherence to the rule of law, respect for democratic institutions, the accommodation of minorities, insistence that governments adhere to constitutional conduct and a desire for continuity and stability.' Behind the 'written word' of the constitution were four 'fundamental constitutional principles' that were germane to the reference: federalism, democracy, constitutionalism and the rule of law, and respect for minority rights. 'No single principle can be defined in isolation from the others, nor does any one principle trump or exclude the operation of any other.'

The principle of federalism 'facilitates the pursuit of collective goals by cultural and linguistic minorities.' The principle of democracy was 'understood as a sort of baseline' under which our constitution always operated. 'Democracy accommodates cultural and group identities.' Democracy cannot exist without the rule of law, but 'equally, however, a system of government cannot survive through adherence to the rule of law alone.' Our law's claim to legitimacy rests on an appeal to moral values. 'It would be a grave mistake to equate legitimacy with the "sovereign will" or majority rule alone, to the exclusion of other constitutional values.'

The discussion brought the court to a conclusion that was at least as important as the specific answers to the three questions. 'The Constitution Act, 1982 gives expression to this principle, by conferring a right to initiate constitutional change on each participant in Confederation. In our view, the existence of this right imposes a corresponding duty on the participants in Confederation to engage in constitutional discussions in order to acknowledge and address democratic expressions of a desire for change in other provinces. This duty is inherent in the democratic principle which is a fundamental predicate of our system of governance' (para. 69).

Returning to the three questions, the court concluded that secession of a province from Canada 'must be considered, in legal terms, to require an amendment to the Constitution, which perforce requires negotiation.' A referendum has 'no direct role or legal effect in our constitutional scheme, but it 'may provide a democratic method of ascertaining the views of the electorate.' 'The referendum result, if it is to be taken as an expression of the democratic will, must be free of ambiguity both in terms of the question asked and in terms of the support it achieves.'

The clinching opinion for the guidance of governments in any future referendums there might be on secession for Quebec was fundamental: 'The federalism principle, in conjunction with the democratic principle, dictates that the clear repudiation of the existing constitutional order and the clear expression of the desire to pursue secession by the population of a province would give rise to a reciprocal obligation on all parties to the Confederation to negotiate constitutional changes to respond to that desire' (para. 88). This did not mean, the court said, that there 'would be a legal obligation on the other provinces and the federal government to accede to the secession of a province.' Nor, on the other hand, did it mean that the continued existence of 'the Canadian constitutional order' could 'remain indifferent to the clear expression of a clear majority of Quebecers that they no longer wish to remain in Canada' (para. 92).

The court was well aware that its 'answers,' plus the discussion of the implications of the principles underlying our democratic federal system, could not guarantee a solution to a continued confrontation between Quebec and 'Canada.' 'It is foreseeable that even negotiations carried out in conformity with the underlying constitutional principles could reach an impasse. We need not speculate here as to what would then transpire. Under the Constitution, secession requires that an amendment be negotiated' (para. 97). The reader is left to add: 'And if one cannot be negotiated?' The amending procedure in the Constitution Act, 1982, was established, like the act itself, without the agreement of the Quebec government of the day or of any Quebec government since. That lack of legitimacy in the eyes of many in Quebec would have been removed if the Meech Lake Accord had passed.

The court was also aware that its opinion left many questions unanswered – 'a clear majority on a clear question in favour of secession is subject only to political evaluation and properly so.' To the extent that the questions are political in nature, it is not the role of the judiciary to interpose its own views.

The conundrum for the political leaders – and for the people – of Canada was put clearly at the end. 'Accordingly, the secession of Quebec from Canada cannot be accomplished by the National Assembly, the legislature or government of Quebec unilaterally, that is to say, without principled negotiations, and be considered a lawful act. Any attempt to effect the secession of a province from Canada must be undertaken pursuant to the Constitution of Canada, or else violate the Canadian legal order. However, the continued existence and operation of the Canadian constitutional order cannot remain unaffected by the unambiguous expression of a clear majority of Quebecers that they no longer wish to remain in Canada' (para. 104).

It was an opinion of profound importance. I was readily persuaded of its soundness, as indicated by remarks I had made in Toronto the previous April when the Public Policy Forum made me one of its 'honorees' for 1998. For the solution of our problems of national unity, I said, we should be guided by the words of a wise man of two thousand years ago:

St Paul. He said that the fundamental thing is 'not the letter, but the spirit, for the letter killeth while the spirit giveth life.' The court has declared in its decision that both are essential and for both sides in any quest for secession.

After thirty years, the essentials and the dimensions of our constitutional and national-unity problems are clear. There is nothing new to be discovered except the capacity and the willingness of Canadians to find the spirit of accommodation that made our federation possible in 1867 and that has been equal to every challenge since. The federal bill on clarity clarifies the kind of question that must be asked and the kind of majority that must vote 'yes' to meet the court's test of an 'unambiguous expression of a clear majority of Quebecers that they no longer wish to remain in Canada.' What our government has not yet clarified is the other side of the question: what Canadians are prepared to offer the people of Quebec in order to accommodate their legitimate concerns.

Epilogue

I was fortunate in the prime ministers I worked with over a period of nearly forty years. All four were highly intelligent, committed to the welfare of Canada, and effective political leaders. Each brought his own style to the office and each dominated his cabinet as a successful prime minister must. Only King was difficult to work with – or 'for' in his case – although all had cause to be at times. The problems and pressures of the office have ample rewards in prestige and power but even strong nerves can become frayed. Old age and diminished energy were factors in King's crankiness but it is clear that he was difficult from the first. His conviction that the Lord was guiding him, and that, as he himself said, he always knew what to do but not always why, made life difficult for both his ministers and his staff. Some woman was spared a life of trial when he never could find one that measured up to his ideal – his mother.

St Laurent could not have been more different: invariably clear, logical, and direct. Trudeau was just as clear and logical when he wanted to be but there were times when he preferred to be obscure and provocative. Often it was to test a plan or proposal – either his own or someone else's – and he was formidable in discussion, whether he really believed his thesis of the moment or not. It was a constant challenge and endlessly stimulating to work with him.

Pearson was the closest to St Laurent in predictability. (I have difficulty not saying 'Mr' in speaking of St Laurent: he commanded such respect and almost reverence from all who knew him.) What stood at times between Pearson and the crystal clarity of St Laurent was that Pearson's intellectual processes were often more intuitive than logical. His intuition did not leap with the confident certainty of King's to a spiritually approved decision and there was often a period when he groped for the

375

reasons why – or whether – his intuition was sound. He might be obscure in dealing with a problem or a proposal, not in order to be mischievous like Trudeau, but because he had not quite sorted out in his own mind all the relevant considerations. He also shrank from hurting people with a direct negative or with too probing a rejoinder to a proposition of doubtful merit – or even to something quite impossible like Walter Gordon becoming president of the Privy Council in 1967 with the expectation that he would then take over the prime minister's only department and source of professional advice. Pearson might conceivably have agreed to it if I had not reacted with immediate horror. Not infrequently, two ministers offering different advice both got the impression that the prime minister had agreed with them – and at least one, if not both, was likely to learn later it was not so. It gave the impression he was devious, which he was not. But he could be disingenuous. His appearance of simple, cheerful frankness cloaked a complex man. At times the appearance was used to keep alternatives open without pressing any course to a definite decision at that moment. It was superb for diplomacy but it could cause problems for colleagues who were looking for clear guidance.

It was Pearson's decency and sensitivity that rendered him defenceless before the lethal barbs of Diefenbaker in the House of Commons. He had to cope with the strongest and most relentless leader of the official opposition – and, indeed, opposition in general – in my years in Ottawa – and did it without ever having the security of a majority. His two governments were almost certainly the most consistently creative and productive we have seen with the possible exception of St Laurent's first government – but he had a majority, which Pearson never did. His intuitions about the flag, the recognition of linguistic equality as essential for Canadian unity, and the need to get into the 'can of worms' of constitutional reform were all correct. So was the logic of his decision to have his government accept the Quebec pension plan in order to achieve the Canada Pension Plan – but here his decision was aided, as it so often was on social policy, by the vigour of Tom Kent's argument. Medicare was another product of that fruitful combination but in each case the decision was Pearson's. He could be firmly decisive but his mind was never closed, just in case he had overlooked or underestimated some point.

The two prime ministers who were in one respect most alike – and who would most resent the proposition – were Mackenzie King and Pierre Trudeau. Each assumed office for the first time with a sense of uncertainty about how to handle his new power. In King's case, when he became Liberal leader in August 1919, the uncertainty was because of his minority in the House of Commons, the divided state of the Liberal Party after its split over conscription in the First World War, and his own absence from active politics for eight years because of his personal defeats in 1911 and 1917. It was a difficult situation for a new leader. Trudeau's initial uncertainty was because he had been a politician for only three years. He was almost a newcomer, lacking the ministerial experience of a large part of his cabinet. But each had confidence in his own capacity to lead and each took a firm grip on the government.

It was fascinating for me to observe, in King's case from reading and observing, in Trudeau's case from 'being there at the creation,' how each moved to complete dominance over his cabinet and ultimately to a total confidence in the rightness of his own decisions. With King, the demonstrated fact that the Lord was guiding together with the growing myth in both party and public that he could make no political mistake provided the foundation. With Trudeau, it was his formidable intellect, his superb debating skills, and his utter faith in logic and reason, especially his own. And for both it was, in the end, the lengthening years of diet on the royal jelly of the status and power of prime minister. He is not first among equals: as Donald Savoie has rightly said, he has no equal. The prime minister chooses each panting hopeful to become a member of his cabinet and all it requires to end that happy condition is the prime minister's own decision and his advice to the governor general: the advice will be accepted. One of Trudeau's favourite philosophers, Lord Acton, said that all power corrupts and Trudeau demonstrated it as much as Mackenzie King.

Apart from the initial uncertainty, Trudeau began as prime minister with a shyness that is hard to believe of the leader who would later contemplate and then carry out a 'coup de force' against the provinces or who would so obviously mislead the voters of Quebec in his address at the Paul Sauvé arena in May 1980 during the referendum campaign and then charge them with 'misunderstanding' what he had said. They should have known that he did not mean what he obviously intended them to think he meant.

His shyness emerged when, shortly after becoming prime minister, Trudeau was reluctant to call on Mrs Norman Robertson to express his sympathy on the death of the man who had, as secretary to the cabinet, brought him into the public service and who had probably been the greatest public servant in our history. I pressed him. He would not go, he said, unless I would go with him. I agreed, I did go, and I had to carry nearly all the conversation. He was also agreeably amazed at the daily briefing he got: the Privy Council Office provided him, every morning, he said, with the answers to questions he had not thought existed. The shyness did not long survive, although Trudeau did remain appreciative of the advice and help he got: King never was, even in his earliest years as prime minister. His first secretary, Fred McGregor, with all his loyalty and devotion to King, makes that clear in his *Fall and Rise of Mackenzie King.* He was driven to distraction at the end and even King realized that McGregor could stand it no longer, although he himself almost certainly would not understand why, or, if he did, would not admit it even to himself.

While Trudeau would have scoffed at the hypocrisy of King's certainty about the moral rightness of whatever he decided to do, his confidence about the wisdom of whatever course he decided upon would come close to King's in the end. I found it understandable that, after eleven years of frustration in his efforts to achieve constitutional change, he should have been determined to get results when he came back to power in 1980. But there was something approaching King's belief in God's unerring hand in Trudeau's being as sure as he was that what he had succeeded in imposing in the constitution of 1982 ('good to last for a thousand years') was so right that it was heresy or cowardice for some 'eunuch' to want to alter it with the modest changes agreed on by the elected heads of all the governments of Canada at Meech Lake in 1987. Indeed, one of their sins was to have achieved agreement at all when he – and 'we' – had failed at Victoria in 1971.

Trudeau was philosophically and temperamentally less suited than Pearson – or King or St Laurent – to the federal system of government with its constant need for agreement and compromise. He wanted decision, clarity, and a strong federal government. Pearson would have had no difficulty with the Meech Lake Accord's recognition of Quebec as a distinct society. He would have seen it, not as the first step towards separation that Trudeau claimed it to be, but as the kind of self-recognition the larger community of Canada had needed when he launched the search for a distinctive flag. That was important for Canada in 1964, and recognition of Quebec as 'distinct' was even more important for the French-speaking community there in 1987. Pearson did defend things he thought essential for the federal government but he was much less rigid than Trudeau. The consequences of a successful Meech Lake for the constitution and the country, under the worst of interpretations, could not have been as damaging to Canadian unity as its rejection has been.

Of the four prime ministers, Pearson and Trudeau were the most fun to work with. Pearson's sense of humour could never be suppressed, even at the darkest moments of Walter Gordon's failed first budget or John Diefenbaker's infuriating blockade of progress on the flag. Trudeau, too, had a lively wit and a capacity to perceive the ridiculous even in policy dilemmas of grave consequence. There was a lot of laughter in our morning meetings and a great sense that the PM, Marc Lalonde, and I were on the same wave length. It was a warm and friendly relationship.

A comparison of Pearson and Trudeau was inevitable for me as I sat behind each in turn as the prime minister's principal adviser at conferences of first ministers on federal-provincial relations and constitutional reform. Each wanted the same seating arrangement. I was to sit directly behind him so he could turn to me for advice, or I could pass him a note, at any critical point. Beside the prime minister at the table were the one or two ministers most concerned from time to time with any particular part of the agenda. Other ministers and officials were in the seats behind. The PM and I were the only ones certain to be there, in the two central seats, from beginning to end.

Pearson was a superb chairman and his diplomatic talents were in constant play. He listened carefully to the comments or argument of every premier, intent on when, where, and how he could bridge some difference and help produce an agreement he could accept. His use of humour was frequent and brilliantly effective. Pierre Trudeau was an equally skilled but very different chairman. He listened as acutely and intervened as effectively, but compromise was not usually his objective. He listened to detect some weakness in a premier's argument and could be devastating in exploiting it. He won more debating points than Pearson but agreement sometimes escaped him where Pearson might have got it.

Pearson would, under no circumstances, have adopted the 'power play' strategy of 1980. He probably would not have got an acceptable agreement in 1981 with René Lévesque as premier of Quebec, but the idea of going ahead without the agreement of Quebec would have been unthinkable to him. There would have been no 'patriation' of the constitution at that time. But he might well have got agreement ten years before at Victoria in 1971 with Robert Bourassa at the head of a federalist Quebec government. The agreement might have involved acceptance of the paramountcy for the provinces – not for Quebec alone – that Bourassa and Castonguay were seeking in areas of social policy. That seemed unacceptable to Trudeau – and to me in 1971 – but the result might not have been very different from the one that emerged in the agreement on the social union in 1998 where new federal initiatives in areas of provincial jurisdiction will require the approval of seven provinces with two-thirds of the population of Canada. Where does paramountcy lie there? Our history would have been very different – perhaps no Parti Québécois government in 1976, no referendum in 1980, no Meech Lake.

The four leaders all saw the unity of Canada as the most important single issue with which they had to deal, but it is only in the case of the most brilliant, Pierre Trudeau, that one must wonder whether, in the end, his net contribution to our unity balance sheet will not be seen as negative. His positive contributions were great – in the courageous handling of the FLQ crisis of 1970, in his relentless search for agreement on constitutional reform over eleven years from 1968 to 1979, in the Charter of Rights – but as this is being written in 2000 it is not at all clear that his irresponsible interventions after retirement to block the agreements Mulroney had achieved may not be more determining of our future than his positive contributions during all his time in office.

Our Future Problems

The Canadian political community of today is not working well and has not been for several years. That was also true of the two Canadas in the 1830s and led to the Rebellions of 1837. Initial prescriptions for cure by Lord Durham for responsible government and for merging the two colonies – in a vain hope to absorb 'the French' in a larger union – did not succeed in solving the problems of that day. It took nearly thirty years of difficulties to bring our political leaders to attempt a new solution, the Confederation of 1867. Without imaginative and effective leadership – and some pressure from Britain – it would not have happened.

Our political leaders of today, having been witness to the disastrous consequences for Mulroney and his government of the attempts at constitutional reform at Meech Lake and Charlottetown, are understandably reluctant to contemplate any new effort to achieve constitutional change. They are also acutely aware of the aversion or the apathy that Canadians generally feel about any return to a task that seems to deepen rather than to resolve our national divisions. Yet there is no prospect of a government in Quebec accepting the constitution as it stands with the imposed changes of 1982. Nor are we likely to see a West satisfied with its inadequate place in our federal system without change that cannot be achieved except in the constitution. In short, whatever else is done, Canada will not work well until at least those two problems are tackled.

Prime Minister Chrétien's role in the constitutional events from 1980 to 1992 make it difficult for him and his government to propose another attempt at so hazardous a task. It would require great courage, but courage is a quality he has shown in abundance and no government of Canada is likely to be in a more secure political position to make the effort. It might well be the most important page he could write in the history of his time as prime minister, a page worthy for the twenty-first century of the forecast Sir Wilfrid Laurier made for Canada in the twentieth.

I have spent many years and much effort in advising, writing, and speaking about the problems of our federation and especially about the unresolved issues that hold danger for our future unity. In contemplating what might best be done at this stage, I have wondered what the four prime ministers I worked with would do.

Trudeau would clearly be in accord with the avoidance of any constitutional change: the Chrétien government's policy so far has been to rely on the results of Trudeau's policy of 1981–2. But what of the other three? Each would obviously be deterred by the defeats of the initiatives at Meech Lake and Charlottetown and each would learn from them some of the things not to do another time. But from my experience I do not believe that any of the other three would be prepared to have the country run the risk of attempting no constitutional reform in the face of the obviously great discontent of two major sectors of our union: Quebec and the West. In each case the dissatisfactions arise from defects that cannot be remedied by administrative arrangements or by policy adjustments. Chrétien's 'one step at a time' approach will not do it.

Mackenzie King, the most like Chrétien in his invariable instinct to avoid risk, would have one higher priority: the vital need to prevent a cleavage of the country along the fault line of our linguistic difference. He suffered personal defeat and years in the political wilderness rather than separate from Laurier over his rejection of conscription in 1917. King's decison then was intensely unpopular in English-speaking Canada and in his own constituency but he was convinced that it would be disastrous for the country if the Liberal Party supported a policy that was so totally unacceptable to Quebec. Unity was his constant concern and would, I feel confident, prevail over caution today.

With St Laurent and Pearson, I think that there can be little doubt. St Laurent was ingenious in marrying political skill with constitutional invention to meet and frustrate Premier Duplessis's divisive tactics in 1949–50. He would use that skill and the same quiet determination today to counter Bouchard's devious and charismatic leadership. In Pearson's case there can be no doubt at all. He established the Royal Commission on Bilingualism and Biculturalism and incurred much criticism for 'stirring up a problem' most English-speaking Canadians of the day deplored and hoped would go away. He also disregarded the warnings of Pierre Trudeau in opening the 'can of worms' of the constitution in 1968. He knew that his initiative for a Canadian flag would bring opposition and he went to the heart of it in the Canadian Legion convention to say why it was needed. He would not be deterred from attempting yet again to achieve a solution or, at least, by his clear commitment to do so, to attract the critical 'swing vote' in Quebec: the unhappy 10 or 20 per cent who are not content with our federation as it stands but who want a reason to vote 'No' in another referendum if it happens.

So if three of the four would probably commit themselves to constitutional change if elected to office, what might the commitment be? All three would have analysed the failures of Meech Lake and Charlottetown and each would have decided that his government's posture should be to propose only the minimum essential change. There should be no unnecessary item, as at Charlottetown, for a voter to dislike and to vote against. Reinforcing that conclusion would be their knowledge that, even with every precaution, the procedure for amending our constitution makes it next to impossible to succeed. There obviously should be nothing requiring the unanimous consent of all provinces as there was at Meech Lake. But even the 'general procedure' under section 38 of the Constitution Act, 1982 is rigid: it requires the approval of the Senate and the House of Commons and of the legislatures of two-thirds of the provinces (seven), with at least 50 per cent of the population of all the provinces. As an additional hurdle, British Columbia and Alberta now also require referendums with majority approvals of the voters of the province. The clear conclusion for any of the three would not be difficult to discern – the proposal for reform should include *only* what is essential.

What would be judged to be those essentials? The 'Quebec round' agreed to in 1986 on the basis of proposals by Bourassa's federalist government has never been resumed since it failed with Meech Lake. The very minimum for a commitment to attract the moderate voter of Quebec would be constitutional recognition of the province's unique character.

But there would almost certainly be no chance of getting western support for action to meet Quebec's discontents without something to meet those of the West. The western equivalent of Quebec's insistence on constitutional recognition is reform that will end the domination of our Parliament and federal government by Ontario and Quebec. As the Reform Party has put it: 'The West wants in!' The only solution to this problem that has any credibility in the West is establishment of an effective, elected 'second chamber' with sufficient western representation to offset the weight of population in the centre of the country. The central importance of this provision was demonstrated at the conference held in Ottawa on 29 January 2000 to seek a 'United Alternative.' The 'Triple E' Senate became a matter of history for the new party, but two of the Es – elected and effective – received new emphasis as essentials for the West.

I suspect that St Laurent and Pearson would readily arrive at such conclusions and probably espouse them as their programs if elected. They would be the 'lamps in the window,' as was said in 1996 of the Calgary Declaration, for the dissatisfied people of Quebec and this time for the West as well.

King would probably find difficulty with something so specific and so coldly logical. He would especially worry about groups in Canada that would claim that things vital to them were being ignored. His concern for the less advantaged in society would almost certainly bring up the problems of the Aboriginal peoples. What about them? Should there not be something for them in any constitutional proposal?

After some brooding and ill-tempered grumbling about the inadequacy of the assistance he got, King would, I think, conclude that the diversity of the Aboriginal peoples – there are four great groups, the Assembly of First Nations, the non-status Indians, the Inuit, and the Metis, all of them with internal divisions and differences – presents a problem too complicated to be resolved by any simple constitutional reform. The failure of the four constitutional conferences on Aboriginal issues after 1982 would be warning enough of the danger of assuming that another conference or two would be successful.

So King, a very practical politician, might well accept something not unlike the St Laurent-Pearson plan. His conscience would draw comfort from the creation of the new Territory of Nunavut in 1999 by a Liberal government led by a prime minister – Jean Chrétien – who had spent several years as minister of Indian and northern affairs. He would see that imaginative action in the North as an extension to the Aboriginal underdog of today of the principles for which his grandfather fought in 1837.

Such specifics as these are highly speculative but what I think is *not* is that all four of the prime ministers I worked with were strong believers in the obligation of a prime minister to lead. They all knew and lived up to the conviction that nothing in history is inevitable and that leadership can make a difference. Is it too much to hope that, in spite of all that has passed, Pierre Trudeau, the statesman, could in a supreme final act of leadership bring himself to support such a proposal for one final effort to solve our critical Quebec-West dilemma? That probably would be to set hopes too high. But one should not be too sure. It would be a mistake to underestimate Trudeau's capacity to surprise and to lead.

An Example in a Troubled World

Among the 193 independent states in the world today Canada is one of the few with all the attributes for success: an established democratic federal system of government, a prosperous free-market economy, constitutional protection of human rights, friendly relations with all our neighbours, and associations with all the states essential for our trade and security.

We are among the most fortunate people on earth. Our problems are small in comparison with those of other countries newer, less developed and less prosperous, wrestling with much greater differences of race, colour, creed, and language. It will be a tragic failure if Canada does not find the means to continue to provide an example of what can be achieved by tolerance, compromise, and enlightened leadership.

Notes

Preface

1 *British North America Acts and Selected Statutes,* 1867–1948 (Ottawa: King's Printer and Controller of Stationery 1948).

Chapter 1. From the Prairies to Oxford, 1917–1938
1 Charles Taylor, *Multiculturalism and 'The Politics of Recognition': An Essay,* ed. Amy Gutman (Princeton, N.J.: Princeton University Press 1992), 32–3.
2 James H. Gray, *The Winter Years* (Toronto: Macmillan 1966), 168.
3 Michael Hayden, ed. *So Much To Do, So Little Time: The Writings of Hilda Neatby* (Vancouver: University of British Columbia Press 1983), 21.
4 Memorandum on Frank Underhill, 1966, cited in ibid., 11.

Chapter 2. From Oxford to Ottawa, 1938–1941
1 Martin Gilbert, *Churchill: A Life* (London: Mandarin Paperbacks 1991), 61.

Chapter 3. The Department of External Affairs, 1941–1945
1 J.L. Granatstein, *A Man of Influence: Norman A. Robertson and Canadian Statecraft, 1929–1968* (Ottawa: Deneau 1981), 155–6.
2 Ibid., 385.
3 John Hilliker, *Canada's Department of External Affairs,* vol. 1, *The Early Years, 1909–1946* (Montreal: McGill-Queen's University Press 1990), 243.
4 Granatstein, *Man of Influence,* 157–67, deals with the development of this problem from 1941 to 1944.
5 Doris Kearns Goodwin, *No Ordinary Time* (New York: Simon and Schuster 1994), 514.
6 Hugh L. Keenleyside, *Memoirs,* vol. 2, (Toronto: McClelland and Stewart 1982), 179.

Chapter 4. Working for Mackenzie King, 1945–1948

1 J.W. Pickersgill, *Seeing Canada Whole: A Memoir* (Toronto: Fitzhenry and Whiteside 1994), 271.

2 Ibid., 288.

3 Bruce Hutchison, *Mr Prime Minister, 1867–1964* (Toronto: Longmans 1964), 203.

4 Vincent Massey, *What's Past is Prologue: The Memoirs of the Rt. Hon. Vincent Massey* (Toronto: Macmillan 1963), 440.

5 Claude Bissell, *The Imperial Canadian: Vincent Massey in Office* (Toronto: University of Toronto Press 1986), 175.

6 Paul Martin, *A Very Public Life*, vol. 1, *Far from Home* (Ottawa: Deneau 1983), 438.

7 Ibid., 437.

8 Ibid., 438.

9 J.W. Pickersgill and D.F. Forster. ed., *The Mackenzie King Record*, vol. 4, 1947–1948 (Toronto: University of Toronto Press 1970), 5–6.

10 Ibid., 6.

11 Ibid., 392.

12 Ibid., 428.

13 Ibid., 436.

14 Pickersgill, *Seeing Canada Whole*, 250.

15 R.M. Dawson, *The Development of Dominion Status, 1900–1936* (London: Oxford University Press 1936), 40.

16 Ibid., 43.

17 Bruce Hutchison, *The Unfinished Country: To Canada with Love and Some Misgivings* (Vancouver: Douglas and McIntyre 1985), 206.

18 Isaiah Berlin, *The Sense of Reality* (London: Chatto and Windus 1996), 49.

Chapter 5. Working with Louis St Laurent, 1948–1953

1 'The Changing Role of the Privy Council Office' – Lecture to the annual meeting of the Institute of Public Administration of Canada, 8 September 1971.

2 J.L. Granatstein, *A Man of Influence: Norman A. Robertson and Canadian Statecraft, 1929–1968* (Ottawa: Deneau 1981), 251.

3 Ibid., 265–6.

4 *The Amendment of the Constitution of Canada* (Hull, Que.: Queen's Printer 1965), 19.

5 Resolution of the House of Commons, 28 January 1935.

6 *Amendment of the Constitution of Canada*, 20.

7 Ibid., 21.

8 H. Blair Neatby, *William Lyon Mackenzie King*, vol. 3, *1932–1939* (Toronto:

University of Toronto Press 1976), 162.

9 *Amendment of the Constitution of Canada*, 23.

10 J.W. Pickersgill, *My Years with Louis St Laurent: A Political Memoir* (Toronto: University of Toronto Press 1975), 113.

11 Memorandum from the prime minister to J.W. Pickersgill, 19 August 1949. Author's personal files.

12 Ibid.

13 *House of Commons Debates*, 17 October 1949, 833.

14 Letter, prime minister to E.C. Manning, 17 October 1949. Author's personal files.

15 *House of Commons Debates*, 17 October 1949, 870.

16 *Proceedings of the Constitutional Conference of Federal and Provincial Governments*, January 10–2, 1950 (Ottawa: King's Printer) 10.

17 Ibid., 16.

18 National Archives of Canada (NAC), Report of the Committee of Attorneys General, categories 4 and 5.

19 Press Release, 28 September 1950.

20 P.E. Trudeau, *Memoirs* (Toronto: McClelland and Stewart 1993), 64.

21 NAC, Record of Cabinet Decision No. 204, 14 August 1952.

22 Memorandum to the Prime Minister, 14 August 1952. Author's personal files.

23 NAC, Record of Cabinet Decision no. 211, 9 October 1952.

24 Memorandum for J.W. Pickersgill, 16 October 1952. Author's personal files.

25 Letter to Pickersgill, 9 June 1953. Author's personal files.

26 Ibid.

27 *House of Commons Debates*, 8 February 1949, 368.

28 International Court of Justice, Corfu Channel Case, 1949.

29 *House of Commons Debates*, 30 July 1956, 6702.

30 John Colville, *Footprints in Time* (London: Century Publishing 1976), 132–3.

31 Pickersgill, *My Years with Louis St Laurent*, 174–5.

32 Pickersgill and Forster, ed., *The Mackenzie King Record*, vol. 2, 1944–1945 (Toronto: University of Toronto Press 1968), 267.

33 Pickersgill, *My Years with Louis St Laurent*, 328.

Chapter 6. Canada Discovers the North, 1953–1957

1 John David Hamilton, *Arctic Revolution: Social Change in the Northwest Territories, 1935–1994* (Toronto: Dundurn Press 1994), 70.

2 *Report*, Department of Resources and Development, for the fiscal year ended 31 March 1953 (Ottawa: Queen's Printer), 84.

3 Memorandum to author, 2 October 1953.

4 *House of Commons Debates*, 8 December 1953, 698.

5 Ibid., 697.

6 Ibid., 700.

7 *House of Commons Debates*, 19 January 1954, 1237.

8 R.A.J. Phillips, *Canada's North* (Toronto: Macmillan 1967), 169.

9 Mark O. Dickerson, *Whose North?* (Vancouver: University of British Columbia Press, and Calgary: Arctic Institute of North America 1992), 38.

10 Diamond Jenness, *Eskimo Administration in Canada*, Technical Paper no. 14 (Calgary: Arctic Institute of North America, 1962), 39.

11 *Report*, Department of Resources and Development, for the fiscal year ended 31 March 1953 (Ottawa: Queen's Printer), 83.

12 Phillips, *Canada's North*, 170.

13 Hamilton, *Arctic Revolution*, 62.

14 *Report*, Department of Northern Affairs and National Resources, fiscal year 1957–8, 35.

15 Ibid., 25.

16 Ibid., 26.

17 Pickersgill, *Seeing Canada Whole*, 473.

Chapter 7. Governing the Northwest Territories, 1953–1957

1 *Report*, Department of Northern Affairs and National Resources, fiscal year 1954–5, appendix G, 100.

2 Vincent Massey, *What's Past Is Prologue: The Memoirs of the Rt. Hon. Vincent Massey* (Toronto: Macmillan 1963), 484.

3 *Report*, Department of Northern Affair and National Resources, fiscal year 1956–7, 101.

4 F.R. Scott, *The Dance Is One* (Toronto: McClelland and Stewart 1973), 67–8. Reprinted with the permission of William Toye, Literary Executor of the Estate of F.R. Scott.

5 Claude Bissell, *The Imperial Canadian: Vincent Massey in Office* (Toronto: University of Toronto Press 1986), 254–5.

6 TCA was the government-owned predecessor of Air Canada. The North Star was a Canadian-built plane memorable chiefly for the intolerable noise from its exhausts aimed straight at the passenger cabin.

7 Mitchell Sharp, *Which Reminds Me ... A Memoir* (Toronto: University of Toronto Press 1994), 82.

8 Moira Dunbar and Keith R. Greenaway, *Arctic Canada from the Air* (Ottawa: Canada Defence Research Board 1956), 17.

9 Ibid., 478–9.

10 George Malcolm Thomson, *The North-West Passage* (London: Secker and Warburg 1975), 160.

Chapter 8. The Territories under the Vision, 1958–1963

1 'Departmental Submission on the Northwest Territories: Its Economic Prospects,' presented to the Royal Commission on Canada's Economic Prospects (Edmonton, 1955), 23.
2 Ibid., 27.
3 Ibid., 25.
4 Edith Iglauer, *Inuit Journey* (Vancouver: Douglas and McIntyre 1966), ix–x.
5 Ibid., x.
6 Dunbar and Greenaway, *Arctic Canada from the Air*, 421.

Chapter 9. The Emerging North

1 John David Hamilton, *Arctic Revolution: Social Change in the Northwest Territories, 1935–1994* (Toronto: Dundurn Press 1994), 221.
2 *Constitutional Development in the Northwest Territories – Report of the Special Representative* (Hull, Que.: Canadian Government Publishing Centre 1979), 15.

Chapter 10. Pearson and the Quiet Revolution

1 H. Basil Robinson, *Diefenbaker's World: A Populist in Foreign Affairs* (Toronto: University of Toronto Press 1989), 317–18.
2 J.W. Pickersgill, *The Road Back* (Toronto: University of Toronto Press 1986), 184–5.
3 Robinson, *Diefenbaker's World*, 319.
4 Tom Kent, *A Public Purpose: An Experience of Liberal Opposition and Canadian Government* (Montreal: McGill-Queen's University Press 1988), 232.
5 Robinson, *Diefenbaker's World*, 318.
6 Kent, *A Public Purpose*, 333.
7 Ibid., 244.
8 Press Release, Office of the Prime Minister, 20 January 1964.
9 Kent, *A Public Purpose*, 267–8.
10 Ibid., 275.
11 *A Preliminary Report of the Royal Commission on Bilingualism and Biculturalism* (Ottawa: Queen's Printer 1965), 151.
12 Ibid., Preamble, 13.
13 Ibid.
14 Lester B. Pearson, *Mike: The Memoirs of the Rt. Hon. Lester B. Pearson*, vol. 3 (Toronto: University of Toronto Press 1975), 240.
15 Ibid., 236.
16 *Report of the Royal Commission on Bilingualism and Biculturalism*, Book III, (Ottawa: Queen's Printer 1969), 111.

17 Ibid., 116.
18 Ibid., Book I, 73.
19 Ibid., 83.

Chapter 11. The Symbols and Structure of Canada
1 Pearson, *Memoirs*, vol. 3, 270.
2 Ibid., 272.
3 Ibid., 273.
4 Kent, *A Public Purpose*, 392.
5 *Constitutional Review, 1968–1971* (Ottawa: Information Canada 1974), 3.
6 Ibid., 4.
7 Ibid., 4.
8 Pearson, *Memoirs*, vol. 3, 254.
9 *Constitutional Review, 1968–1971*, 5–6.
10 *Constitutional Conference Proceedings* (Ottawa: Information Canada), 5–7 February 1968, 1.
11 Ibid., 13–15.
12 Ibid., 17–19.
13 Ibid., 547.
14 *Federalism for the Future* (Ottawa: Queen's Printer 1968), 46.

Chapter 12. Pierre Trudeau and a New Style of Governing, 1968–1970
1 Letter, Prime Minister Pearson to the Hon. Pierre Elliott Trudeau, 13 December 1967. Author's personal files.
2 Letter, Prime Minister Trudeau to author, 26 March 1984.
3 Sharp, *Which Reminds Me*, 160–3.
4 P.E. Trudeau, *Memoirs* (Toronto: McClelland and Stewart 1993), 87.
5 Ibid., 97.
6 Ibid., 100.
7 Ibid., 106.
8 Ibid., 109–10.
9 Gordon Robertson, *The Changing Role of the Privy Council Office* (Ottawa: Information Canada 1971), 7–8.
10 Trudeau, *Memoirs*, 110.
11 Robertson, *Changing Role*, 14.
12 Trudeau, *Memoirs*, 113.
13 Pearson, *Memoirs*, vol. 3, 332.
14 Trudeau *Memoirs*, 123.
15 *Report of the Royal Commission on Bilingualism and Biculturalism*, Book I, 1967, 91.

16 Ibid.
17 Trudeau, *Memoirs*, 126.
18 *Report*, Book I, 97.
19 Ibid., 110.
20 Sharp, *Which Reminds Me*, 193.
21 Ibid., 197.
22 Ibid., 201.

Chapter 13. Trudeau and the Constitution, 1968–1979
1 NAC, Cabinet Document 198–68, 1 May 1968.
2 Ibid.
3 Trudeau, *Memoirs*, 230.
4 Ibid., 230.
5 *Secretary's Report*, Collation by the Canadian Intergovernmental Conference Secretarial Ottawa (1970), 347.
6 Ibid.
7 Ibid., 348.
8 Ibid., 183.
9 Ibid., 184.
10 Trudeau, *Memoirs*, 232.
11 Covered by amendments to the BNA Act, 1867, in 1951 and 1964.
12 Roy Romanow, John Whyte, and Howard Leeson, *Canada Notwithstanding: The Making of the Constitution* (Toronto: Carswell/Methuen 1984), 4.
13 The Constitutional Amendment Bill, Text and Explanatory Notes, Government of Canada, June 1978, iii.
14 Ibid., 16.
15 Trudeau, *Memoirs*, 246–7.
16 Order-in-Council P.C.1977–1910, 5 July 1977.
17 *Québec-Canada: A New Deal* (Quebec: Official Publisher Quebec 1979), 8.
18 Ibid., 9.
19 Constitutional Committee of the Quebec Liberal Party, *A New Canadian Federation* (Montreal: Quebec Liberal Party 1980), 52.
20 Romanow, Whyte, Leeson, *Canada Notwithstanding*, 237.
21 Trudeau, *Memoirs*, 249–50.

Chapter 14. Transition and Change, 1978–1980
1 R.M. Dawson, *Constitutional Issues in Canada 1900–31* (London: Oxford University Press 1933) 73.
2 Isaiah Berlin, *The Sense of Reality: Studies in Ideas and Their History* (London: Chatto and Windus, 1996), 52.

3 Ottawa *Journal*, 9 October 1974.
4 Donald J. Savoie, *Governing from the Centre* (Toronto: University of Toronto Press 1999), 112–13.
5 Ibid., 362.
6 Arnold Heeney, *The Things That Are Caesar's* (Toronto: University of Toronto Press 1972), 80.

Chapter 15. The Trudeau Power Play, 1980–1982

1 Stephen Clarkson and Christina McCall, *Trudeau and Our Times*, vol. 1, *The Magnificent Obsession* (Toronto: McClelland and Stewart 1990), 280–1.
2 Trudeau, *Memoirs*, 311.
3 Ibid., 308.
4 Ibid., 317.
5 Ibid., 326.

Chapter 16. Away from Government

1 *The North and Canada's International Relations*, report of a working group of the National Capital Branch of the Canadian Institute of International Affairs (Ottawa, March 1988), 69.
2 Ibid., 69.
3 Ibid., 10.
4 Ibid., 49.
5 Ibid., 50.
6 Report, *Independence and Internationalism* (June 1986), 128.
7 *The North and Canada's International Relations*, 56.
8 Ibid., 21

Chapter 17. Meech Lake: The Best Hope Lost

1 Peter H. Russell, *Constitutional Odyssey: Can Canadians Be a Sovereign People?* (Toronto: University of Toronto Press 1992), 136.
2 Bob Rae, *The Three Questions by Bob Rae* (Toronto: Viking Press 1998).
3 *A House Divided: Meech Lake, Senate Reform and the Canadian Union* (Ottawa: Institute for Research and Public Policy 1989), chapter 3, 15–20.
4 Gordon Robertson, *A Commentary on the 'Statement on the 1987 Constitutional Accord,'* January 1990, 1. Privately printed.
5 Ibid., 3.
6 Ibid., 15.
7 Ibid.

8 *Canada: The State of the Federation, 1990* (Kingston, Ont.: Institute of Intergovernmental Relations, Queen's University 1990), 259.
9 Ibid., 259.
10 Ibid., 260.
11 Ibid., 262.
12 Ibid.
13 The Constitution Act, 1982, s. 37(2) as amended 1983.
14 *Preliminary Transcript, General Assembly of Newfoundland,* Friday, 22 June 1990, no. 57B, column R6.
15 Ibid., column R4.
16 *Canada: State of the Federation, 1990,* 267.

Chapter 18. Meech Lake Dead: Where Next?
1 Business Council on National Issues, *Options for a New Canada* (Toronto: University of Toronto Press 1991), vii.
2 *The Economist,* 29 June 1991, Survey, 3.
3 *Shaping Canada's Future Together: Proposals* (Ottawa: Minister of Supply and Services, Canada 1991), viii.
4 Ibid., 5.
5 P.E. Trudeau, *Trudeau: 'A Mess That Deserves A Big NO'* (Toronto: Robert Davies 1992), 7.
6 *Maclean's,* 28 September 1992.
7 *Canada: The State of the Federation, 1993* (Kingston, Ont.: Institute of Intergovernmental Relations Queen's University 1993), 5.
8 Ibid., 30.
9 Donald G. Lenihan, Gordon Robertson, and Roger Tassé, *Canada: Reclaiming the Middle Ground* (Montreal: Institute for Research on Public Policy, 1994).
10 Ibid., 36.
11 Ibid., 41.
12 Ibid., 55.
13 Ibid., 57.
14 Commentary no. 65, January 1995, C.D. Howe Institute, 2.
15 Gordon Robertson, *Contingency Legislation for a Quebec Referendum* (Ottawa, 26 February 1996). Privately printed.
16 *Declaration on Principles of International Law concerning Friendly Relations and Cooperation among States,* 1970.
17 'Does Quebec Have a Right to Secede at International Law?' *Canadian Bar Review* 74 (June 1995).

18 Robertson, *Contingency Legislation.*
19 Ibid.
20 Memorandum for the Right Honourable Jean Chrétien, P.C., M.P., Prime Minister of Canada, 20 June 1997.
21 Memorandum for the Honourable Frank McKenna, Premier of New Brunswick and Chairman-Designate, Council of Premiers, for Distribution to all Premiers and Territorial Leaders, 15 July 1997.
22 Gérald-A. Beaudoin, Joseph E. Magnet, Benoît Pelletier, Gordon Robertson, and John Trent, *Federalism for the Future: Essential Reforms* (Montreal: Wilson and Lafleur 1998) ix.

Index

Index